The Global World of Indian Merchants
Traders of Sind from Bu...

In his latest book, Claude ... of Hindu merchants from th... the province of Sind. Basing h... val sources, the author chart... these communities, from the pre-colonial period through colonial conquest and up to independence, describing how they came to control trading networks throughout the world. While the book focuses on the trade of goods, money and information from Sind to such widely dispersed locations as Kobe, Panama, Bukhara and Cairo, it also throws light on the nature of trading diasporas in South Asia in their interaction with the global economy. In an epilogue, the author brings the story up to date in a discussion of the origins of the present-day diaspora of Sindhi Hindus, the most wide-ranging of all the diasporas from the Indian subcontinent.

This is a sophisticated and accessible book written by one of the most distinguished economic historians in the field. It will appeal to scholars of South Asia and of the history of diasporas, as well as to colonial historians, economic historians and to students of religion.

Claude Markovits is Director of Research at the Centre National de la Recherche Scientifique, Paris.

Cambridge Studies in Indian History and Society 6

Editorial Board
C. A. BAYLY
Vere Harmsworth Professor of Imperial and Naval History, University of Cambridge, and Fellow of St Catharine's College

RAJNARAYAN CHANDAVARKAR
Fellow of Trinity College and Lecturer in History, University of Cambridge

GORDON JOHNSON
President of Wolfson College, and Director, Centre of South Asian Studies, University of Cambridge

Cambridge Studies in Indian History and Society publishes monographs on the history and anthropology of modern India. In addition to its primary scholarly focus, the series also includes work of an interdisciplinary nature which contributes to contemporary social and cultural debates about Indian history and society. The series is thus designed to further the general development of historical and anthropological knowledge and to attract a wider readership than that concerned with India alone.

1 C. A. Bayly
 Empire and Information: Intelligence Gathering and Social Communication in India, 1780–1880
 0 521 57085 9 (hardback) 0 521 663601 (paperback)
2 Ian Copland
 The Princes of India in the Endgame of Empire, 1917–1947
 0 521 57179 0
3 Samita Sen
 Women and Labour in Late Colonial India: The Bengal Jute Industry,
 0 521 45363 1
4 Sumit Guha
 Environment and Ethnicity in India, 1200–1991
 0 521 64078 4
5 Tirthankar Roy
 Traditional Industry in the Economy of Colonial India
 0 521 65012 7

The Global World of Indian Merchants, 1750–1947

Traders of Sind from Bukhara to Panama

Claude Markovits
Centre National de la Recherche Scientifique, Paris

CAMBRIDGE UNIVERSITY PRESS

CAMBRIDGE UNIVERSITY PRESS
Cambridge, New York, Melbourne, Madrid, Cape Town, Singapore, São Paulo, Delhi

Cambridge University Press
The Edinburgh Building, Cambridge CB2 8RU, UK

Published in the United States of America by Cambridge University Press, New York

www.cambridge.org
Information on this title: www.cambridge.org/9780521622851

© Claude Markovits 2000

This publication is in copyright. Subject to statutory exception
and to the provisions of relevant collective licensing agreements,
no reproduction of any part may take place without the written
permission of Cambridge University Press.

First published 2000
This digitally printed version 2008

A catalogue record for this publication is available from the British Library

Library of Congress Cataloguing in Publication data
Markovits, Claude.
The global world of Indian merchants, 1750–1947: traders of Sind from Bukhara to Panama / Claude Markovits.
  p. cm. – (Cambridge studies in Indian History and Society; 6)
Includes bibliographical references and index.
ISBN 0 521 62285 9
1. Shikarpur (Pakistan) – Commerce – History.
2. Hyderabad (India) – Commerce – History.
3. Sindhi (South Asian people) – Commerce – History.
4. India – Commerce – History.
5. Pakistan – Commerce – History.
I. Title. II. Series.
HF3790.5.Z9 S555   2000
382'.0954918 – dc21   99-047925

ISBN 978-0-521-62285-1 hardback
ISBN 978-0-521-08940-1 paperback

To the memory of my father Paul Markovits
(1912–1993)

Contents

List of maps	*page*	viii
List of tables		ix
Acknowledgements		x
Glossary		xii

	Introduction	1
1	South Asian merchant networks	10
2	The regional context: Sind economy and society, *c.* 1750–1950	32
3	The Gate of Khorrassan: the Shikarpuri network, *c.* 1750–1947	57
4	From Kobe to Panama: the Sindworkies of Hyderabad	110
5	Patterns of circulation and business organization in two merchant networks	156
6	The business of the Sind merchants	185
7	The politics of merchant networks	212
8	Community and gender in two merchant networks	249
9	Epilogue: the Sindhi diaspora after 1947	277
	Conclusion	286

Appendices	298
Bibliography	307
Index	320

Maps

1 Sind in the colonial period *page* 33
2 The Shikarpuri network, *c.* 1900 58
3 The Sindworkie network, *c.* 1890–1940 112

Tables

3.1	Trade of the Punjab with Kabul and Bukhara, c.1860–1890	page 70
3.2	Population of Shikarpur and Sukkur 1891–1931	107
4.1	Destinations of applicants for certificates of identity in Hyderabad district 1915–1916	127
4.2	Annual emigration of skilled labour registered in Karachi 1928–1946	129
4.3	Destinations of employees of six major firms in Hyderabad	131
4.4	The population of Hyderabad 1872–1941	136
4.5	Major Sindwork firms in the 1930s according to date of foundation	140
5.1	Characteristics of partnerships in Hyderabad	162
6.1	The debt portfolio of Totomal wd Jeumal, Shikarpuri banker of Namangan	189
6.2	Reexport of silk manufactures from India to selected destinations in 1893–1894 and 1913–1914	196
6.3	The sales account of a Sindhi merchant in Port Said in 1930–1931	207
8.1	List of associations representing Sindhi merchants	258
9.1	The Sindhi worldwide diaspora	281

Acknowledgements

Many people contributed in many ways to this work. I owe particular thanks to the staff of the Oriental and India Office Collections of the British Library who dealt gracefully with my insatiable demand for documents. The Trustees of St Anthony's College, Oxford, helped considerably in awarding me a Deakin Fellowship in 1995–6 which allowed me to complete the research for this book. In Oxford, David Washbrook, Judith Brown and Nandini Gooptu, among others, contributed to the creation of an atmosphere propitious to intellectual inquiry. My colleagues of the Centre d'Etudes de l'Inde et de l'Asie du Sud in Paris did not bear me any grudge for deserting them for a while, and I thank them for it.

I am grateful to Chris Bayly and to Sanjay Subrahmanyam for the interest they showed in this project and for many pleasant moments.

Preliminary versions of some chapters of this book were presented at seminars and conferences at the University of Washington, Seattle, the Indian Institute of Management, Calcutta, the Centre for Indian Studies, St Antony's College, Oxford, the Commonwealth History Graduate Seminar at Oxford University, the Centre of South Asian Studies of the University of Cambridge, the Nehru Memorial Museum and Library, New Delhi, North Carolina State University, Raleigh, Edinburgh University, Centre d'Etudes et de Recherches Internationales, Paris, London School of Economics. I wish to thank all conveners and participants for their patience and their useful comments.

Special thanks are due to those members of the Sindhi commercial community who were kind enough to share their knowledge and their time with a stranger, and more particularly to Mr L. Khiani of Gibraltar who received me with great kindness and generous hospitality. They will probably disagree with much of what is said in this book, but I want to assure them that the spirit of scientific enquiry alone inspired my research

I wish to thank Maurice Legrand and Françoise Pirot, of the Système d'Informations Spatiales, attached to the Centre d'Etudes de l'Inde et de l'Asie du Sud, for drawing two of the maps, in spite of a very busy schedule.

Piyali, Rahul and Eva bore the brunt of the disruption caused by this project to family life. For several years I did not give them all the attention they deserved. May the final result, to which Piyali contributed enormously by her careful editing of an earlier draft, be some compensation for the many hardships endured. I shall always regret that my father did not live long enough to see the completion of this work, which is dedicated to his memory.

Glossary

ajrak   kind of quilt cover produced in Sind
Aksakal   elder (in Central Asia), head of Indian community in Russian Central Asia and Sinkiang
amban   petty Chinese official (in Sinkiang)
Amils   Hindus belonging to the superior segment of the Lohana caste in Sind, mostly employed in government service
anna   fraction of the rupee (1/16th)
badmash   bad character
bajra   indigenous millet, staple food of the lower classes in Sind
bania   generic term for Hindu traders belonging to the merchant castes
bavangami   group of fifty-four villages in Kathiawar, region of origin of Jain migrants to East Africa
bawa   Nanakpanthi priest
bhai   brother, fellow trader
Bhaiband   literally brotherhood, term used to designate the lower segment of the Lohana caste, by extension applies to Sindhi business firms
Bhatia   Hindu caste of Kutch, Kathiawar and Sind
bima   insurance
biradari   patrilineal kinship group
Bohras   community of Shia Ismaili Muslims, originating from Gujarat
chela   disciple of a Hindu holy man
Chettiars   Nattukottai Chettiars or Natukottai Nagarathars, caste of Tamilian Hindu bankers originating from Chettinad, strongly represented in Burma and Ceylon prior to 1948
Chulia   community of Tamilian Muslims, active in trade in Southeast Asia
commenda   partnership contract of medieval Italy
crore   10 million
dalal   broker
devanagari   Sanskrit script used in Sind by *banias*

dharamsala   hostel for Hindu pilgrims, also used by travelling Hindu merchants
dhow   native craft in the Persian Gulf and the Indian Ocean
firman   decree, proclamation
Ghadr Party   Revolutionary party fighting to overthrow British rule, mostly recruiting among Sikhs
guberniia of Turkestan   governorate-general of Turkestan, part of Central Asia under direct Russian administration
gumastha   a Persian term for an agent, factor or working partner
gurdwara   Sikh place of worship
hari small   cultivator, landless labourer in Sind
hatvania   small trader in Sind
Hoofd der Indiers   head of the Indians, local head of Indian community in Surabaya, in the Dutch East Indies
hundi   indigenous bill of exchange
izzat   honour, prestige
jagirdar   holder of a jagir, an assignment of state revenue derived from a specified area
Jains   followers of a religion founded by Mahavir
kafila   caravan
kala pani   'black waters', the sea, which orthodox Hindus cross only at the peril of losing caste
kangani   supervisor or headman, organizer of migration of labourers to Ceylon, Burma and Malaya
kansa   metal work of Sind
Kapol   Banias Hindu trading caste of Gujarat
kashani   rupee monetary unit of pre-colonial Sind
kashi   painting work on flower vessels, a speciality of Sind
Kayastha   North Indian Hindu caste, whose members were employed as scribes in the Mughal administration
kazi   Muslim judge or magistrate
Khalsa   Sikh order, brotherhood founded by Guru Gobind Singh in 1699
Khatri   Hindu caste of the Punjab, mostly engaged in trading
Khojas   community of Shia Muslims, divided into Ismaili and Itnaashari
kopeck   Russian copper coin
kora   rupee monetary unit of pre-colonial Sind
kothi   business firm
kran   Persian monetary unit
lakh   100,000
Lohana   principal Hindu caste of Sind, divided into Amils and Bhaibands

lungi   piece of clothing worn by men
Luwattiya   Arabic name given to Hyderabadi Khoja traders in Masqat
mamlo, mamlat   estate
Marakkayar   Muslim group from Tamilnadu, active in trade in Southeast Asia
Marwari   generic name for a cluster of Hindu and Jain castes originating from a part of Rajasthan. Marwaris constitute an important business community in India
maund   Indian measure of weight. The Surat maund was the most widespread
mazhar   Persian term for a public declaration, a kind of newsletter exchanged between merchants of different localities
Mitaksara   Code of Hindu law, applied in most of India (except Bengal)
mofussil   Anglo-Indian term for the areas outside the provincial capitals in British India
mudaraba   Arabic term for partnership contract
muhajir   Muslim refugee from India in Pakistan
mukthiyarkar   local government official in charge of revenue collection
munshi   Persian writer
murid   disiciple of a *pir*
musharaka   Arabic term for partnership contract
Nanakpanthi   follower of the Guru Nanak, non-Khalsa Sikh
nukh   fraction of caste or lineage
oblast   Russian administrative division
panchayat   Council of Five, corporate body of Hindu merchants or caste council
Parsi   Zoroastrian
picul   Chinese measure of weight (equivalent to $133.\frac{1}{3}$lb or 60.453 kg)
pie   fraction of an anna (1/12th)
pir   Muslim spiritual guide and religious preceptor, a sufi or descendant of a sufi saint
pirzadeh   descendant of pir
pongee   silk cloth woven from *tussah* silk
purdah   seclusion of women
Pushkarna   caste of Brahmins in Sind
riba   Arabic term for lending money with interest, a practice forbidden by the Koran and *sharia*
ryotwari   system of revenue collection prevalent in the Bombay Presidency under British rule, in which the cultivator pays rent directly to the state
Sahajdari   a Sikh who neither accepts baptism into the Khalsa nor observes its code of discipline

sahukar big merchant, generally Hindu
samadhi memorial, in particular of a Hindu holy man
sarai (karavansarai) halting place for travellers, where merchants often resided
Saraswat caste of Brahmins in Sind
sarraf, shroff banker and money changer, generally Hindu
Sayed Muslim holy man
shah principal, capitalist partner in a business firm
sharia Islamic law
shuddi reconversion to Hinduism of those who have embraced other faiths, a practice encouraged by the Arya Samaj
sumb monetary unit of Russian Central Asia
tabut (taziah) symbolic bier of Imams Hasan and Husain, carried during the procession of Muharram
tael Chinese silver currency unit, abolished in 1933
taluka British Indian administrative division, sub-district
taotai Chinese official
tenga monetary unit of the Emirate of Bukhara
tikhana Nanakpanthi place of worship in Sind
tilla Bukharan gold coin
tussah silk, wild silk, produced from worms fed on oak leaves
Udasi Fakir caste of non-Khalsa Sikhs
wadero big landowner in Sind, always a Muslim, often of Baluchi ancestry
wahdat-al-wujud Doctrine of the Unity of Being, a central tenet of sufism
zamindar fiscal intermediary, landowner in Colonial Sind

Introduction

Among South Asian merchants and businessmen dispersed across the world, the Sindhis are probably the most ubiquitous, if not the most conspicuous. They are found in the main tourist destinations as well as in the major business centres. In the Canary Islands, which attract tourists from all over Europe, they own hundreds of bazaars in which they sell cheap electronic goods imported from the Far East as well as souvenirs. In Nigeria, they control a fair share of the country's supermarkets and have a stake in the textile and other manufacturing industries. In Hong Kong and Singapore, in spite of the Chinese domination of business, they are actively engaged in the import–export trade. In the United Kingdom, some of the richest Asian business families, whose rise has attracted considerable attention, belong to this group. There are few countries of the world where one does not come across some traders from that community. Their origins as well as the precise nature of their activities remain, however, somewhat mysterious, and they generally adopt a low profile; the expanding literature on the South Asian diaspora generally has little to say about them. And yet their business acumen is legendary, and in India they have a well-established reputation as shrewd operators.

They are Hindu, but hail from a region which is now part of Pakistan. Although they claim an Indian identity, they do not mix much with other Indians, and seem to keep a particular distance *vis-à-vis* the more numerous and conspicuous Gujaratis, who constitute the bulk of the South Asian merchant diaspora. It is often assumed that their dispersal is the result of the Partition of 1947 which forced them to flee their homeland. Perusal of a directory of Indians abroad published in the 1930s[1] however alerted me to the fact that their worldwide spread much antedated the Partition and prompted me to start an inquiry into their story. I quickly discovered that most Sindhi businessmen trace their origins to one particular town in the province, Hyderabad (not to be

[1] S. A. Waiz (comp.), *Indians Abroad Directory*, Bombay, 1934.

confused with its better-known namesake in the Deccan), now a city of more than 1 million situated 150 km north of Karachi, which was the capital of Sind during the era of the Talpur Amirs (1783–1843). Others hail from Shikarpur, a much smaller town in Upper Sind close to the regional centre of Sukkur. Prior to Partition, these two towns were home to flourishing communities of Hindu *banias* who were actively engaged in trade and finance on a worldwide scale. The contrast between the modest size of the towns and the considerable range of their merchants appeared puzzling and worthy of attention. These merchants seem to have been possessed of a tremendous entrepreneurial drive to seek their fortunes so far away from their home towns, often in lands where no Indians had ever set foot before. Although this is a book about traders, it is not preoccupied only with dry facts and figures about sales and profits. It aims at a global understanding of such dispersed merchant communities, of their culture, their religion, as well as of the way in which their family lives were affected by their long-range travels.

The story of these two towns and their merchants has not attracted any attention from scholars. The reasons for this neglect are manyfold, the main one being that these were networks of 'Hindu' merchants in a Muslim-majority province which became part of Pakistan in 1947, leading to a mass exodus of the Hindu population towards India.

Understandably, there has been little interest in Pakistan in the history of Hindu merchants and moneylenders who are generally considered to have been exploiters of the Muslim peasantry of the province. It is worth quoting from a speech by G. M. Sayed, the Sindhi Muslim political leader, delivered to the Sind Legislative Assembly in June 1941:

During the last 40 years the Hindu has snatched away 40 per cent of land from the Mussalman and this, taken together with the enormous interest and interest over interest that the bania charges, has reduced his life to a condition of utter helplessness. He earns not for himself but for the bania. Due to the control that he wields over commerce, a bania has been able to exploit for his personal gain all the wealth which in equity and justice ought to be the possession of the poor villager. As a consequence of all this, the Mussalman has remained hopelessly poor. Due to his undisputed control over services, the bania has been able to collect an enormous sum of money through bribes and such other means, which he spends and displays by way of erecting bungalows and palaces and purchasing gorgeous and extravagantly decorated dresses. On the other hand, the poor agriculturist who toils days and night has neither a decent home to live in nor a decent cloth to cover himself, much less sufficient food to eat.[2]

Sayed's populist outpouring conveniently left in the dark the role of the Muslim landowners, the *waderos*, in the exploitation of the peasantry

---

[2] Quoted in S. Z. Lari, *A History of Sindh*, Karachi, 1994, p. 188.

Introduction 3

and the existence of a *wadero-bania* nexus in the Sind countryside. However, it echoed feelings which were widespread among the Muslims of Sind. Interestingly, Sayed does not appear to have been aware that sections of the *banias* of Sind derived their wealth not from the exploitation of the peasantry in Sind but from international trading and finance. This was true in particular of the *banias* of Hyderabad and of Shikarpur.

If their story has remained largely unknown in Pakistan, it has not fared better in India. Following Partition, Sindhi Hindus fled *en masse* to Bombay and Rajasthan, from where many then dispersed themselves across the subcontinent. They have been too busy with sheer survival and with trying to integrate within India to devote much time to a search for their historical roots. When they did, it was more in a mood of nostalgia than of historical curiosity.[3] As for the Indian academic community, it treated the history of those regions of undivided India which became part of Pakistan as 'foreign' history and showed little interest in it (with the partial exception of the history of the Punjab).

The aim of this work is not, however, primarily to rescue from oblivion a little-known and in many ways fascinating story. Its major ambition is to bring into focus the existence in the *longue durée* of a widespread circulation of merchants and commercial employees between India and many regions of the world, a phenomenon which spanned the transition between indigenous and colonial regimes. The Shikarpuri and Hyderabadi networks are only two instances, among many others, of Indian merchant networks which managed to overcome the problems created by the advent of colonial rule and to find profitable niches within a European-dominated world capitalist economy

While the study of diasporas is an expanding field in South Asian studies, little attention is being paid to the history of merchant networks. Given the rise of a so-called 'global' capitalist economy in the 1980s and 1990s, the role of widely dispersed immigrant groups in generating flows of investment and trade between different geographical areas has come more into focus. Overseas Chinese communities in particular have given rise to a vast scholarly literature. While it has focused mostly on the global reach of Chinese ethnic capital and on the links between the diaspora and the homeland, this literature has also tended to emphasize the importance of regional identities such as those of the Cantonese, the Hokkien or the Hakka, or even of local identities based on towns (such as Wenzhou in Tchekiang), in structuring communities and fostering solidarities.[4] On the other hand, recent studies of the South Asian

---
[3] A good example of this literature of nostalgia is K. R. Malkani, *The Sindh Story*, Delhi, 1984.
[4] For an overall view, see in particular L. Pan, *Sons of the Yellow Emperor: the Story of the*

diaspora[5] tend to assume the existence of one diaspora and to pay only scant attention to the role of South Asian communities in the world economy as well as to the existence of subnational identities. In his Introduction to a recent volume, P. Van der Veer, while recognizing that 'the differences are real and important and should be taken seriously', claims however not to 'want to deconstruct the South Asian diaspora to the point of dissolution'.[6]

In this work, I intend to carry this task of deconstruction to the point of dissolution, not out of any postmodernist taste for deconstructing *per se*, but because I think the unitary notion of a South Asian diaspora has been conducive to a distorted view of the historical record. Arguments for the deconstruction of such a unitary notion are many, but there is also one powerful counter-argument which cannot be dismissed off hand, namely that South Asian migrants themselves used nationalism as a resource to empower themselves and fight for their rights as human beings and as citizens. The specific 'diasporic nationalism', which played such a role, for instance, in Gandhi's emergence as a national leader in India, cannot be treated as only a product of the imagination. Nevertheless, the actual contribution of diasporic Indians to the rise of Indian nationalism is not in itself proof of the legitimacy of the unitary notion of a South Asian diaspora.

There are three major arguments against the unitary notion of diaspora. The first one is that at any given moment in history since the beginning of the nineteenth century, the majority of South Asians in the so-called diaspora were not permanent but temporary migrants, who left the subcontinent for only a limited period of time and with the avowed intention of returning there. Most of them did actually return, even if only to leave again. 'Temporary' migration accounted for 90 per cent of departures from India in the 1830–1950 period[7] and, although there are no reliable figures for the post-1950 period, it still probably accounted for the bulk of departures. This throws doubt on the legitimacy of the use of the category of 'diaspora', which involves a long-term physical separation from an imaginary or real homeland and is not

Overseas Chinese, London, 1990, and Wang Gungwu, *China and the Chinese Overseas*, Singapore, 1991.

[5] Among recent contributions, see C. Clarke, C. Peach and S. Vertovec (eds.), *South Asians Overseas: Migration and Ethnicity*, Cambridge, 1990; S. Vertovec (ed.), *Aspects of the South Asian Diaspora*, Delhi, 1991; R. Ballard (ed.), *Desh Pardesh: The South Asian Presence in Britain*, London, 1994; P. Van der Veer (ed.), *Nation and Migration: The Politics of Space in the South Asian Diaspora*, Philadelphia, 1995. See also for a review of the literature, R. K. Jain, *Indian Communities Abroad: Themes and Literature*, Delhi, 1993.

[6] P. Van der Veer, 'Introduction: the Diasporic Imagination', in Van der Veer (ed.), *Nation and Migration*, pp. 7–8.

[7] See K. Davis, *The Population of India and Pakistan*, Princeton, 1951, Table 35, p. 99.

Introduction 5

really compatible with phenomena of simple transiency or sojourning. Movements of people between South Asia and the rest of the world belong to the sphere of 'circulation' more than to the sphere of 'migration'. This is a crucial point, which has often been lost sight of.

The cursory treatment of phenomena of circulation in the scholarly literature can be attributed to the combined effect of the nature of the sources and of the ideological biases of scholars. Students of the history of the diaspora have relied almost exclusively on government archives which deal mostly with the processes of migration which were organized or regulated by the colonial state, in particular with indentured emigration to the tropical dependencies of the British Empire. These resulted in widespread settlement of Indian immigrants and the growth over time of significant clusters of populations of South Asian origin. Although settlement itself was largely involuntary, there is a tendency to reconstruct *ex post facto* these movements as aiming at settlement from the outset, a teleological view which is highly misleading. The existence of large Indian communities and the wealth of documentation available easily explain why the study of these processes dominated the field. Ideologues of a 'Greater India' saw in the existence of these overseas Indian communities grist to their mill, while sociologists had a field day trying to evaluate how social institutions such as caste, which were supposed to be uniquely Indian, adapted to a different social environment. They also devoted a lot of attention to the forms taken by Indian religions, particularly Hinduism, in a changed context.

On the other hand, movements which were not organized or at least monitored by the state and which did not give birth to significant clusters of population largely escaped their attention. The neglect of circulation also has to do with the way 'India' or 'South Asia' were constructed in the nineteenth century as a separate civilizational entity, having few links with the rest of the world. This construction, to which Orientalism and nationalism equally contributed, did not leave much place for seepage and similar phenomena. In this dominant framework of thought, South Asia was a world in itself; one was either in it or outside it, while actually millions were constantly shifting between the subcontinent and neighbouring or even faraway regions of the world. It is true that this circulation was largely limited to certain specific regions of the subcontinent, mostly coastal areas of Gujarat, Konkan, Malabar and Coromandel, parts of northwestern India as well as the Bhojpur area of northern India. That is one supplementary reason why more attention should be paid to the regional and even subregional contexts of migration from South Asia.

Deconstructing the unitary notion of one South Asian diaspora implies a methodological shift. Instead of privileging, as most existing studies do, the point of arrival of the so-called 'permanent' migrants, who actually accounted for only a small share of overall departures from the subcontinent, the research must equally focus on the point of departure, the regions and localities from where migrants left with the intention of returning, an intention which, for most of them, was translated into fact, and on the constant flow of circulation between those points. For migrants often circulated widely, and did not fix themselves in one locality for long periods. Such a shift would also give the role of gender its full place in the migration process. While there is a growing emphasis in the literature on migrant women, a point too often missed is that, even when those who left were mostly males, the women left behind were very much part of the story of migration.

I would strongly argue that region and locality were much more important in structuring migrants' identities than religion, which has been given so much prominence in the existing literature. Most authors appear to view religious categories such as Muslim, Hindu or Sikh as the most significant elements of differentiation within the diaspora. Replacing the notion of one South Asian diaspora by notions of a Hindu, a Muslim or a Sikh diaspora will however not be conducive to a better understanding. W. H. McLeod is rightly critical of the use of the notion of a Sikh diaspora[8] and the same strictures apply to notions of a Hindu and a Muslim diaspora. Migrants from Gujarat, whether they were Hindus, Muslims or Jains, had more in common with each other in their experience of migration than Gujarati Hindus had with Bhojpuri Hindus or Gujarati Muslims with Bhojpuri Muslims. But regional ethnicity *per se* was rarely the basis of identity formation among dispersed South Asians. The analysis of the origins of the migrants must move beyond the regional level to reach the subregional, microregional or even the local level, because it is at these lower levels of the polity that the identities of migrants were actually defined. Most South Asian migrants, unlike British or Irish migrants going to North America, left because they wanted to improve the situation of their family at home, not because they were hoping to make a better life elsewhere. Their aspirations centred around plots of land and real estate in their home region, better houses, better marriage prospects for their sisters. This was true of rich merchants as much as of poor agricultural workers.

[8] He writes: 'We need to be aware that when we talk about Sikh migration we are choosing to use an imprecise adjective.' See W. H. McLeod, 'The First Forty Years of Sikh Migration', in N. G. Barrier and V. A. Dusenbery (eds.), *The Sikh Diaspora: Migration and Experience Beyond the Punjab*, Delhi, 1989, p. 32. For a more recent discussion, see V. A. Dusenbery, 'A Sikh Diaspora? Contested Identities and Constructed Realities', in Van der Veer (ed.), *Nation and Migration*, pp. 17–42.

Introduction 7

Solidarities between migrants generally existed within a fairly narrow circle: people of the same village, the same town, the same immigrant ship (in the case of the indentured labourers). Ethnicity and religion were not crucial structuring factors. As to the role of caste or *biradari*, it could vary enormously from one group to another.

A third dimension in the necessary deconstruction of the unitary notion of a diaspora is a greater emphasis on occupation and class. Migrant South Asians belonged to different social classes in the subcontinent and followed different occupations, and these differences generally remained for a long period in the diaspora. Prior to 1950, there were three major streams: unskilled labourers (mostly agricultural workers), skilled and semi-skilled workers in secondary and tertiary occupations, merchants and commercial employees. Middle-class professionals, though they figured, were still a very small group. Most migrants from India were agricultural labourers who went either to neighbouring Ceylon, Burma or Malaya, the so-called *kangani* migration, or to the faraway sugar colonies of the British Empire (as well as to some French and Dutch colonies) on contracts of indenture. There was also a migration of semi-skilled or skilled workers, including secretarial staff, to various countries in the Middle East and in Asia. The world oil economy started relying on Indian labour much before the 1970s influx into the Gulf countries.[9] The widespread circulation of security personnel from India, including soldiers, policemen and watchmen, is also part of this stream. A third major stream was that of merchants and commercial employees, itself a highly differentiated group of men in which business magnates, small shopkeepers and shop assistants were equally represented.

This work seeks primarily to explore the ways in which two groups of South Asian merchants managed to carve for themselves a niche in a European-dominated world economy. In so doing, it is hoped that some light will be thrown on facts of a more general interest, such as the role of Asian merchants in the world economy, or the nature of international merchant networks. A prominent scholar in the field of merchant diasporas[10] pithily summed up the methodological problems attendant to such a study. 'The investigator', he writes, 'is faced with the problem of having to choose between an extensive, unavoidably superficial account of the whole diaspora ... or the intensive study of one

---

[9] The Asiatic Petroleum Co, the ancestor of Shell, started recruiting personnel in Malabar in the 1890s, and in the 1920s there were several thousand workers from Kerala in the oilfields of Borneo in the Dutch East Indies.

[10] A. Cohen, 'Cultural Strategies in the Organization of Trading Diasporas', in C. Meillassoux (ed.), *The Development of Indigenous Trade and Markets in West Africa*, London, 1971, p. 269.

community within the networks of communities that constitute the diaspora.' One can only concur with his conclusion that a 'combination of both approaches will be necessary'. In this work, while the dominant approach will be the general one, it will be combined with more in-depth microstudies of specific localized communities. Sight will not be lost either of the fact that these wideranging networks were very much rooted in a local reality in South Asia. It will thus be necessary to constantly keep in mind both the local level, whether in South Asia or outside the subcontinent, as the one at which the identities of merchants were defined and their social relations formed, and the global level, that of the world economy, as the one at which their activities took their full meaning. Local history will thus have to be combined with world history, while the level of 'national' history, which is largely meaningless in this case, will be ignored.

The study of the history of these two international trading networks necessitated the use of many dispersed sources. Although some merchants were interviewed, oral testimonies appeared too unreliable to be a major source. Attempts at finding family papers did not meet with success. In any case, the writing of business history as such was not the aim of this book. On the other hand, a wideranging search through official records yielded surprising results, in spite of the fact that Sind merchants never attracted much official attention. Two major sources, apparently unknown to scholars, have been the records of the British consular courts in Egypt, which supplied a wealth of material on the Hyderabadi traders known as Sindworkies who did business in that country in the late nineteenth and early twentieth centuries, and a trove of documents in the India Office Records concerning the estates of Shikarpuri merchants who died in Russian Central Asia in the same period. Many other sources, both published (such as commercial directories) and unpublished (such as histories of firms) have been used to try to reconstruct the often obscure history of these traders and of their circulation between Sind and the rest of the world. This reconstruction is necessarily partial: a lot has been lost irretrievably. My aim, however, is to produce a meaningful outline, not to fill in all the gaps in the story.

The first part of the book looks at the setting in which the two networks developed. Starting with a general view of South Asian merchants and their international trading networks with the aim of placing developments in Hyderabad and Shikarpur in a general historical perspective, it then moves to consider the regional context of Sind, focusing on aspects of the economic, social and political history of a region which has been little treated in the existing historiography. It looks more particularly at the Hindu *banias* and their role in pre-colonial

Introduction

and colonial Sind, with the aim of uncovering the factors which led some of these *banias* to seek opportunities outside their province.

The second part charts the history of the two networks between the mid-eighteenth and the mid-twentieth centuries. It looks first at the history of the Shikarpuri network, as it developed during the period of the rise of the Durrani Afghan Empire, and consolidated itself in the Central Asian khanates between 1800 and 1870. Particular attention is paid to the role played by Shikarpuri merchants in Russian Central Asia between 1880 and 1917. Other developments concern their role in Chinese Sinkiang and in southeastern Iran and, in the aftermath of the Russian Revolution in which they suffered heavy losses, their redeployment in India proper in the 1920s and 1930s. The 1933 rising in Sinkiang which led to their departure from that region is also considered. In contrast, the rise of the Sindworkie network is shown to have taken place in the context of colonial Sind in the immediate post-annexation period, while its worldwide expansion occurred between 1880 and 1930.

The third part focuses on some general characteristics of the two networks in a structural perspective. After a look at the influence of spatial dispersion on forms of business organization, through a study of partnerships and contracts between employers and salaried employees, a more systematic study of the business of the Sind merchants is presented on the basis of the limited material found in the archives. The focus then shifts to the the question of the political attitudes of the Sind merchants, of their relationship with the British and of their attempts at lobbying to defend their interests. A section is devoted to a study of their intervention in the politics of Panama. Finally, aspects of community and gender in the two networks are considered, in particular the relationship between solidarity and trust and problems of 'sexual economy'. An epilogue briefly presents some data on the worldwide Sindhi diaspora after 1947.

1   South Asian merchant networks

For many centuries, colonies of South Asian merchants were present in many ports of the Indian Ocean and of the China seas. These merchants, both Hindus and Muslims, always kept close links with the regions of South Asia where they came from. Trading networks centred on ports or even inland cities in the subcontinent spanned vast distances. The coastal areas of Gujarat and the Coromandel coast were the two regions from where most of these merchant colonies originated. From the fifteenth century onwards, Sind also contributed to this growing diaspora of South Asian merchants. During the Mughal period, some Indian merchants followed the inland routes leading to Iran and Turan, and new land-based networks developed. By the mid-eighteenth century the small town of Shikarpur in Upper Sind became the main centre of this inland diaspora. Some one hundred years later, around 1860, another inland city of Sind, Hyderabad, spawned a new international network. This chapter will therefore be concerned with defining merchant networks and delineating their functions, as well as their evolution over time, as an introductory effort meant to contextualize the study of two merchant networks from Sind. But firstly a look at the role of South Asian merchants in the world economy is needed.

South Asian merchants in the world economy

The earliest evidence of the presence of colonies of South Asian merchants outside the subcontinent comes from medieval Arab sources. They reveal that Hindu merchants were present in the port of Siraf on the Persian shore of the Gulf since at least the ninth century and that they also frequented the coasts of Oman, Socotra and Aden.[1] In the fourteenth century, Hindu merchants sailed regularly to the South China Sea, as attested by the existence of the remains of a Hindu temple

[1] A. Wink, *Al Hind: The Making of the Indo-Islamic World*, vol. I, *Early Medieval India and the expansion of Islam 7–11th centuries*, Leiden, 1990, p. 65.

in the south Chinese port of Quanzhou (Zaitun).[2] The oldest continuous Indian commercial colony is probably that in Masqat. Documents attest the presence there of a colony of Hindu merchants in the fifteenth century.[3] At the time, the Hindu merchants of Masqat appear to have been Bhatias from the town of Thatta in Lower Sind, with which Masqat had intense commercial relations. When the Portuguese entered the Indian Ocean trade, colonies of Indian merchants, especially from Gujarat, were found in all the major ports between Aden and Malacca. Gujarati merchant networks, both Hindu and Muslim, then played a dominant role in maritime trade and finance across the entire Ocean.[4] Although they suffered as a result of Portugal's attempt at controlling trade, they showed a great degree of resilience and remained active in international trade until well into the eighteenth century. The role of Surat as the major port of the entire Indian Ocean during most of the seventeenth century is well known, and the merchants of Surat had close links with the dispersed colonies of Gujarati merchants. In the late seventeenth and early eighteenth centuries, Kapol Bania merchants from Diu in Kathiawar dominated the trade of Yemen, Hadramaut and Habsh (Abyssinia).

Even with the advent of the European companies and the rise to dominance of the British on the west Indian coast, indigenous Indian merchants continued to be a force in the Indian Ocean trade. Masqat remained the seat of an important colony, although, at some point in the eighteenth century, the Bhatias of Thatta were supplanted by the Kutchi Bhatias, and by a group of Khojas from Hyderabad (Sind) locally known as Luwattiya. Other emporia in the Persian Gulf and the West Indian Ocean with large colonies of Indian merchants were Mocha[5] and Aden in Yemen, Massawa and Berberah on the African coast of the Red Sea. By the end of the eighteenth century, the East African emporium of Zanzibar also had a small but rapidly growing colony of Indian merchants. In the Persian Gulf, Bahrain has been the seat of an

---

[2] See Chen Dasheng and D. Lombard, 'Le rôle des étrangers dans le commerce maritime de Quanzhou (Zaitun) aux 13e et 14e siècles', in D. Lombard and J. Aubin (eds.), *Marchands et hommes d'affaires asiatiques dans l'Océan Indien et la Mer de Chine 13e–20e siècles*, Paris, 1988, pp. 21–9.

[3] See C. H. Allen, 'The Indian Merchant Community of Masqat', *Bulletin of the School of Oriental and African Studies*, vol. 44, 1981, p. 39.

[4] See M. Pearson, *Merchants and Rulers in Gujarat*, Berkeley, CA, 1976.

[5] According to the British traveller Valentia, there were in Mocha around 1810 some 250 resident Banyans (Hindu merchants). Quoted in R. Pankhurst, 'Indian Trade with Ethiopia, the Gulf of Aden and the Horn of Africa in the Nineteenth and Early Twentieth Centuries', *Cahiers d'Etudes Africaines*, vol. 55, 14/3, 1974, p. 455. Most of these merchants appear to have moved to Aden after the British annexation of that port in 1839.

important Indian merchant colony since the beginning of the eighteenth century,[6] while many ports like Abu Dhabi and Dubai on the Arabian shore, and Bushire and Bandar Abbas on the Persian shore, were also home to significant colonies. In the eastern part of the Indian Ocean, Indians continued to play a major role in Malacca, and colonies of Indian merchants were found also in Burma, in Thailand and in Sumatra (Banda Atjeh, in particular). These colonies of Indian merchants, never more than a few hundred strong, maintained close links with the ports of the western littoral of India, particularly Thatta in Sind, Mandvi in Kutch, and various ports in Kathiawar, as well as Surat, Broach and, from the second half of the eighteenth century onwards, Bombay. The Indian traders who resided in those ports for periods of various duration or paid occasional visits to them in the course of a trading season were generally Hindus who had left their family in their native town in India, but there were also Muslim traders from India, who often took their families with them.

Other groups of merchants, from northern India, played a similar role in relation to the land trade between India, Iran, Central Asia and Russia from the sixteenth century, and in the seventeenth century there existed colonies of Indian merchants all over Inner Asia between Lhassa in Tibet and Astrakhan on the Caspian Sea. These two merchant streams, that of the Indian Ocean and that of the Asian landmass, remained largely separate in spite of the existence of connections through Iran between maritime and land routes. This has probably more to do with the segmentation of the Indian merchant world in terms of regional groups than with any structurally determined inability to develop a pattern of integration. The evidence of this segmentation throws doubts on attempts to discover an 'Indian world economy' at work in the seventeenth century. A recent proponent of this view locates this 'world economy' in the web of ties woven between the economies of northern India and Russia, through Iran and Turan, by the so-called 'Multani' merchants.[7] The evidence he musters in support of his view is not altogether convincing. Even admitting that there was a 'Multani' 'world economy', it cannot be concluded that it was an 'Indian' world

---

[6] In a petition addressed to the viceroy, Lord Curzon, 2 November 1903, ten prominent British Indian merchants of Bahrain, Sindhi and Gujarati, wrote: 'May it be known to Your Lordship that we came up the Persian Gulf about two hundred years ago . . .'. Enclosed in Oriental and India Office Collections of the British Library, London, India Office Records (IOR), Political & Secret Department Records, Political & Secret Correspondence with India 1875–1911, Political Letters from India 1903, L/P&S/7/134.

[7] For a discussion, see S. Dale, *Indian Merchants and Eurasian Trade, 1600–1750*, Cambridge, 1994, pp. 1–13.

economy, unless one equates 'Multan' with 'India', which is a bold step. There may have been several 'Indian world economies', loosely interconnected.

Proponents of the world system approach argue that in the eighteenth century the Indian economy, or the Indian economies, became part of the new European-dominated world economy.[8] To account *inter alia* for the continued role played by Indian merchants in international trade, they come forward with the notion that India was part of the 'semi-periphery' of the world economy, that it played a role of relay and of intermediary between the centre of the world economy, Europe, and its periphery, consisting of Africa, Asia and Latin America. There is in this thesis an underlying assumption about a decline in the role of Indian merchants in the world economy, which is open to question. It is not my intention here to deny that colonialism had many negative consequences for many Indian merchants. However, an objective assessment of its overall impact is no easy task. There were wide differences in the way various merchant groups were affected: the time sequence is not without importance, as the merchant communities of west and northwest India had more time than their counterparts in the eastern and southern parts of the subcontinent to adapt themselves to the changes introduced by colonization. This may be one of the reasons why merchants from these regions which were annexed in later times were on the whole more successful under the colonial regime than the merchants of the regions which were the first to be colonized.

Between 1750 and the late nineteenth century the merchant world of India went through a complex and gradual process of redeployment, as merchants and bankers largely lost their functions, acquired in the eighteenth century, in the collection and transfer of state revenues. The change did not occur overnight. The East India Company itself remained heavily dependent on the advances of Indian bankers for the first five or six decades of its rule; it is only around 1820 that it established a treasury system which allowed it to dispense with the *hundis* of the Indian *sahukars* and *sarrafs* in providing for the financial needs of its army and administration.[9] This redeployment of Indian

---

[8] See I. Wallerstein, 'The Incorporation of the Indian Subcontinent into the Capitalist World-Economy', *Economic and Political Weekly*, vol. 21, no. 4, 25 January 1986, pp. PE 28–39.

[9] Regarding state finance in Northern India in the 1830s, C. A. Bayly writes: 'Now that the great revenue systems were established features of the landscape, Indian merchants were not needed as guarantors, and district treasury bills had begun to replace the hundi as the basic instrument of official transactions.' C. A. Bayly, *Rulers, Townsmen and Bazaars: North Indian Society in the Age of British Expansion 1770–1870*, Cambridge, 1983, p. 299.

capital was not necessarily synonymous with a decline in the role played by Indian merchants in the foreign trade of India. During the 'first colonial century' there was undoubtedly a massive fall in the share of India's foreign trade controlled by its indigenous traders, when the East India Company, and, at a later stage, British private capital, established a clear domination over many sectors and geographical areas. However, Indian merchants remained indispensable as partners of British firms, especially in the fast-expanding inter-Asian trade. In the trade with Southeast Asia, Chulia merchants, Tamilian Muslims, who had been active since the seventeenth century, took advantage of the British occupation of the island of Penang in 1786 to increase their operations, both in the tin trade as well as in various commodities imported from the coast of Coromandel.[10] It was in the opium trade, which emerged as one of the most lucrative sectors of the Indian economy after 1770, that this conjunction between British private traders and Indian merchants produced its most spectacular results.

The Malwa opium trade was actually the main source of capital accumulation for many Indian mercantile groups during the late eighteenth and early nineteenth centuries. It was a huge smuggling operation in which the main participants were, on the one hand, the 'Malwa soucars', generally Marwaris and Gujaratis, who made the advances to the cultivators (in close alliance with the authorities of some of the princely states of central India) and collected the produce, and, on the other hand, Ahmedabad and Bombay merchants, both Parsis and Gujaratis, often partly financed by European speculators of Calcutta, who arranged for the transport of the drug by caravan to various ports of the west Indian coast, including the Portuguese ports of Damao, Diu and Goa, and its shipment to the Chinese market. As will be seen later,[11] after 1820 the Malwa opium trade, in the face of attempts by the East India Company to interfere with it so as to protect its monopoly of the drug, was rerouted through Rajputana and Sind, a circuitous route which entailed the involvement of Marwari merchants from Rajputana and Hyderabadi and Shikarpuri merchants from Sind. After the First Opium War, resulting in the 'opening' of China and following the annexation of Sind to British India, this trade was reorganized. Although it was thereafter dominated by a few big British business houses such as Jardines, Indian traders, mostly Parsis,[12] continued to play an important

[10] See K. Macpherson, 'Chulias and Klings: Indigenous Trade Diasporas and European Penetration of the Indian Ocean Littoral', in G. Borsa (ed.), *Trade and Politics in the Indian Ocean*, Delhi, 1990, p. 42.
[11] See Chapter 2 below.
[12] On the role of the Parsis in the China opium trade, see D. F. Karaka, *History of the Parsis, Including their Manners, Customs, Religion and Present Position*, London, 1884, vol.

role in it, both as brokers for the Europeans and as operators on their own account.

This massive involvement of Indian traders in the opium trade has been frowned upon by nationalist authors who have labelled participants as compradores. Sight is often lost of the fact that in India most indigenous capital effected its 'primary accumulation' in operations which involved some form of partnership with British merchants. Many of the great family fortunes in Bombay have their origin in opium. In much of the literature on Indian business history, however, the foreign operations of Indian capitalists appear only as a kind of preliminary stage in a linear time sequence, a preparation to industrial investment in India. This 'teleological' reading of the history of Indian capitalism appears to be a dubious *ex post facto* rationalization. Indian businessmen responded to various kinds of opportunities on both the international and domestic markets, and, from 1920 onwards, with the adoption by the colonial government of a policy of 'discriminative protection', opportunities often appeared greater within India than in foreign trading operations. Capitalists who chose to focus on the domestic market to take advantage of that policy later liked to put some gloss on their investment decisions by painting them as being mostly inspired by patriotism, but one need not take them too much at their word.

However, foreign trade never completely lost its attraction to Indian merchants and continuous involvement by many of them, although rarely on a very spectacular scale, is worthy of more attention than it has generally received.

Even in the era of 'high imperialism', i.e. the 1858–1914 period, Indian merchants, particularly those of the west coast, continued to play a role in international trade which was not, as often stated, purely residual. While the trade between Europe and India was undoubtedly a near monopoly of the big British trading houses of Calcutta, Bombay and Madras, which generally did not operate in partnership with Indians, the trade of India with the rest of Asia, as well as with Africa, continued to be largely in the hands of Indian traders. Thus the still considerable trade between India and China, in which opium was progressively displaced by cotton yarn as China's major import from India, offered great opportunities to Bombay traders. In this particular field, Parsis increasingly gave way to Gujarati Muslims, both Khojas and Bohras. Trade with South-East Asia increased considerably in the second half of the nineteenth century, and many Indian traders, mostly from south India, but also from Gujarat, the Punjab and Sind, were

II, pp. 43–4 and J. K. Fairbank, *Trade and Diplomacy on the China Coast: The Opening of the Treaty Ports, 1842–1854*, Cambridge, MA, 1964, pp. 63–7, 155, 160, 173.

extremely active in it. The substantial trade between India and East Africa, centred till the 1890s on the emporium of Zanzibar, was largely a preserve of various groups of Gujarati capitalists, Hindus as well as Muslims. Trade with the Middle East, particularly with the Persian Gulf, remained also an important area of activity for many Indian traders from Kutch, Kathiawar, Sind, Gujarat proper and Bombay. The full extent of Indian participation in India's foreign sea trade is partly masked by the exclusion from official statistics of the data relating to the Kathiawar ports, through which a lot of the Indian Ocean and Persian Gulf *dhow* trade was carried out. Statistics concerning the foreign land trade with Afghanistan, Central Asia, Iran, Sinkiang and Tibet are even more uncertain, but it was a field which remained largely dominated by various groups of Indian traders, even if some were basically agents for British firms. In the trade with Asia and Africa, the existence of long-standing connections gave Indian merchants some kind of competitive edge over European capitalists. The latter, who were generally not familiar with the area, often needed the services of Indian middlemen as intermediaries in transactions with local producers and these middlemen were often in their turn able to entrench themselves in such a way that they maintained areas of independent operations.

After the First World War, in spite of the growing attraction of the domestic market, enhanced by 'discriminative protection', the involvement of Indian merchants in international trade also tended to increase. Groups which had operated almost exclusively within India, like the Marwaris, spotted new opportunities in the jute market, in particular, and some Marwari firms like Birla Bros became important actors on the London jute market. Bombay capitalists, looking for new sources of cotton for the mills, developed a tie with Indian middlemen in Uganda and came to control part of the cotton trade of that territory.[13] Some Indian firms, based in emporia such as Jibuti or Penang, became significant players in the world commodity markets. It exemplified a new trend, by which some Indian merchants became 'global' middlemen, using India as a resource base to raise capital and expertise, but trading in goods which were not produced in India itself. We shall see that the Sindworkies of Hyderabad were a case in point.

Lack of reliable statistical data impedes any attempt at quantifying the role played by Indian merchants in world trade, as distinct from the place of India in world trade. One indication, however, of the continuing role played by Indian merchants in the world economy is the enormous growth of the Indian commercial population settled

---

[13] See M. Mamdani, *Politics and Class Formation in Uganda*, London, 1976, pp. 86–109.

outside the subcontinent. By 1830, the entire Indian merchant diaspora of the Indian Ocean, the Persian Gulf and the Red Sea must have consisted of not more than a few thousand merchants, the largest colony being in Masqat (some 2,000 Indian merchants around 1840). To this number must be added the few thousand Indian merchants who resided in small dispersed colonies in the interior of Asia, that is in Central Asia, Iran, Afghanistan, Sinkiang, Tibet, etc. One century later, *circa* 1930, the number of Indian traders and commercial employees residing outside India was close to a quarter of a million, of whom some 60 per cent were in the three British colonies of Ceylon, Burma and Malaya.[14] During those hundred years and especially between 1880 and 1930 there was therefore a fairly massive exodus of traders from India towards the rest of the world, mostly, but not exclusively, towards territories in the British Empire. No detailed statistical record of these movements is available, because, prior to 1922, merchants and commercial employees who left India for abroad were not considered 'emigrants' in the sense of the various emigration acts and were not therefore registered. Only a broad guess can be made regarding the quantitative aspects of the migration of merchants and commercial personnel from India, prior to 1922. Even the statistics of emigration for the post-1922 period are incomplete. Some idea of the size of these movements, however, can be derived from scattered data and calculations of scholars. Thus, according to the data collected by K. S. Sandhu on migration between India and Malaya, it appears that, between 1844 and 1931, the total number of 'non-labour' migrants who reached Malaya from India was 643,000.[15] Assuming that half of these 'non-labour' migrants were commercial migrants (the rest being craftsmen, non-commercial employees and professionals), one could conclude that commercial migration between India and Malaya reached the high figure of 300,000 in less than one century. These are of course gross figures. Net commercial migration was much smaller, but the characteristic of commercial migration is precisely that it is a phenomenon of circulation rather than migration proper, rarely resulting in permanent settlement. Extrapolating on the basis of the figures for Malaya, one could estimate total commercial migration from India between 1840 and 1930 to have been in the range of 1–1.5

---

[14] Calculated by me on the basis of data provided in *Census of India, 1931*, vol. I, *India Report*, by J. H. Hutton, Delhi, 1933, Subsidiary Table IV, 'statement showing details of persons of Indian origin enumerated in various parts of the British Empire for the period 1926–31', pp. 78 ff., and various colonial censuses.

[15] K. S. Sandhu, *Indians in Malaya: Some Aspects of their Immigration and Settlement (1786–1957)*, Cambridge, 1969, Appendix 3, pp. 312–15.

million, i.e. approximately 5 per cent of total Indian migration as estimated by Kingsley Davis.[16]

Estimation of commercial migration needs to take into account that those who ended up as traders often left as labourers. It is well known that the 'dukawallas' of East Africa, who formed the backbone of the commercial economy of British East Africa from the 1910s onwards, were the leftovers and descendants of the indentured migrants, both Punjabi Sikhs and Gujarati Patidars, who built the Uganda railway in the late 1890s and early 1900s. The Jains coming from the *bavangami*, a group of fifty-four villages in the neighbourhood of Jamnagar in Kathiawar, who emerged in the twentieth century as a successful business community in Kenya, were originally agriculturists-cum-small traders who shifted to a completely urban and commercial mode of life after their migration.[17] An important distinction is therefore to be made between commercial migrants who were in commercial occupations in India before their migration, and migrants who had other occupations before migration and shifted to trade after they reached their destination. The second category is probably larger than the first one, as it includes, in particular, most of the business communities of East Africa as well as South Africa. The focus of this book however is on the first category, i.e. those who were employed in commerce before they left India. Most of these men (for it was an exclusively male migration, a fact with far-reaching implications) left with some kind of contract with a man in India who was either their employer, if they were salaried commercial employees, or their principal, if they were agents or any other kind of non-salaried employee. Rarely did capitalists themselves leave India for long periods, with the exception of some big Parsi capitalists who settled in the Chinese treaty ports after 1842, and of the occasional big trader who transferred his activities to a location outside India to be in a better position to exploit certain specific kinds of market opportunities.[18]

The interpretation of this fairly massive movement of traders from India towards many territories mostly situated within the British Empire has been dominated by the world system paradigm and it has been seen as one of the principal manifestations of the semi-peripheral status of India within the European-dominated world economy. A somewhat modified version of this paradigm has been recently proposed by Rajat

[16] Davis, *The Population of India*, p. 99.
[17] See M. Banks, 'Jain Ways of Being', in R. Ballard (ed.), *Desh Pardesh: the South Asian Presence in Britain*. London, 1994, pp. 231–50.
[18] Such as the big Tamil merchant V. M. Pillay, who migrated from India to Fiji in the early twentieth century to establish a chain of general stores in this Pacific archipelago. He is mentioned in K. A. Gillion, *Fiji's Indian Migrants*, Melbourne, 1964, p. 134.

Ray,[19] who speaks of a specific Asian bazaar economy within the European-dominated world economy. His analysis, which is articulated around a very explicit comparison between Indian and Chinese merchants, is not without its flaws. While criticizing dualistic views which posit a simple opposition between a modern European-dominated world economy and an Asian bazaar economy, he nevertheless concludes that there emerged within the world capitalist economy a specific 'subformation' which he calls the pan-Asian bazaar, and which he sees as clearly subordinated to the former, a view which also smacks of 'dualism'. Among Indian participants in this pan-Asian bazaar economy, he introduces a distinction between some, like the Nattukottai Chettiars in Southeast Asia, whom he views as largely subservient to the purposes of European imperialism, and others, like the Gujaratis in East Africa to whom he grants a greater amount of agency. The distinction is, however, fairly artificial, and the argument does not carry much conviction. It would be futile to deny agency to the Chettiar bankers in Burma and Southeast Asia: they were the ones who 'opened' Lower Burma to commercial agriculture and British banks were crucially dependent on them to reach the local peasantry. What remains to be understood is how South Asian networks were capable of adapting successfully to a trading world dominated by European capital. For this purpose, it is necessary to free oneself from dualistic models. Asian networks did not form a kind of global subformation within the European-dominated international economy of nineteenth and early twentieth-century Asia. Actually, each network found its place in the global system through a complex and prolonged process in which collaboration and conflict were intertwined themes.

Although significant colonies of Indian merchants and commercial employees were found in most parts of the world from the late nineteenth century onwards, it remains a fairly puzzling fact that they never attracted the same amount of scholarly attention as did other dispersed communities of traders, Chinese, Lebanese, Armenian or Jewish. Only two groups of Indian merchants operating outside India attracted a measure of attention: the Gujaratis in East Africa and the Nattukottai Chettiars in Burma. Both those communities have been seen as typically representative of 'middleman minorities' and the problems they faced, resulting in their final expulsion from Burma as well as Uganda, have been the focus of some studies. The reason is that the 'middleman minority' paradigm has been particularly influential in sociological studies of dispersed communities of merchants. A related approach has

[19] See R. K. Ray, 'Asian Capital in the Age of European Domination: the Rise of the Bazaar, 1800–1914', *Modern Asian Studies*, vol. 29, no. 3, 1995, pp. 449–554.

been centred on the notion of 'trade diaspora'. In the following section, I present a critique of these dominant paradigms.

Trade diasporas and middleman minorities: a critique of two paradigms

Sociological interest in dispersed merchant groups was initiated by Max Weber's work and his characterization of Jews as pariah traders. Although his views were partly challenged in the work of other sociologists like Sombart[20] or Simmel[21] who stressed the advantage the 'stranger' had in commercial transactions in terms of 'objectivity', all these early twentieth-century authors shared an exclusive preoccupation with the role of the Jews in the economy of medieval and modern Europe and tended to ignore non-European traders, even the Sephardic Jews. There was a renewal of interest in the theme on the part of sociologists from the 1960s onwards. Blalock[22] was the first to draw attention more specifically to the problem of the coincidence between minority status and middleman function. His field of empirical inquiry remained the societies of modern Europe. He emphasized scapegoating, the deliberate use by dominant landlord groups of alien minorities as intermediaries in transactions with peasants, allowing them to direct towards these minority groups the anger of the peasantry in time of crisis, as exemplified by the case of the Bogdan Khmelnitsky revolt in seventeenth-century Ukraine, when Polish landlords managed to divert the wrath of the Ukrainian peasantry towards their Jewish estate managers and thus largely to escape death and destruction. He stressed very heavily the political aspect as well as the manipulation of the masses by the elites. In her attempt in the early 1970s at generalizing Blalock's insights into a theory of middleman minorities,[23] Edna Bonacich enlarged the field of inquiry to areas outside Europe and granted the actors, both the members of the host society and those of the middleman minority, more leeway. Bonacich's two major differences with Blalock were, on the one hand, that she emphasized the importance of the sojourner mentality among the members of the minority, which led to a certain pattern of economic and political behaviour not conducive to integration with the host society, and, on the other hand, that she viewed the response of the host society as rational and not purely the

[20] W. Sombart, *The Jews and Modern Capitalism*, New Brunswick and London, 1982.
[21] G. Simmel, 'The Stranger', in K. H. Wolff (ed.), *The Sociology of Georg Simmel*, New York, 1950, pp. 402–8.
[22] H. M. Blalock, Jr., *Toward a Theory of Minority Group Relations*, New York, 1967.
[23] See E. Bonacich, 'A Theory of Middleman Minorities', *American Sociological Review*, vol. 38, October 1973, pp. 583–94.

result of elite manipulation. Her pessimistic analysis of the situation of 'middleman minorities', which led her to predict the spread of ethnic conflicts with an economic rationale, was heavily influenced by contemporary events, like the expulsion of the Uganda Asians by the Idi Amin regime. There remained a certain amount of circularity in her argument: nowhere did she make clear why some minority groups appear more successful than others at fulfilling 'middleman' functions (which are never very precisely defined), except for some cultural 'predisposition', which precisely begs the question.

In the 1970s another paradigm emerged from the side of African anthropology, that of the 'trade diaspora' of which Abner Cohen was the first proponent.[24] It was systematized in the 1980s in a well-known book by Philip Curtin,[25] who took in the whole range of human history since the rise of Mesopotamian civilizations. Curtin saw trade diasporas as historically emerging from the 'trade settlements' analysed by Polanyi when a distinction appeared between the merchants who moved and settled and those who continued to move back and forth. The latter, who might have begun with a single settlement abroad, gradually tended to set up a whole series of trade settlements in alien towns. The result was an interrelated set of commercial communities forming a trade network or a trade diaspora. Curtin's emphasis was mostly on the role of cultural brokers played by these trade diasporas. There was an implicit assumption there about 'cultures' being bonded entities clearly separated from each other. Curtin saw in trade diasporas 'one of the most widespread of all human institutions over a very long run of time', but also one which was 'limited to the long period of human history that began with invention of agriculture and ended with the coming of the industrial age'. For him, the advent of the Industrial Revolution brought in its wake the 'twilight of the trade diasporas', as the uniformization linked to the triumph of Western conceptions of capitalism rendered the function of cultural brokerage fulfilled by the trade diasporas basically superfluous.

Both the middleman minority and the trade diaspora paradigms, in spite of their different emphasis, are perfectly compatible with the world-system approach. It could plausibly be argued that, as the triumph of Western capitalism reduced all non-Western economies to peripheral or at best semi-peripheral status, the old 'trade diasporas' were being transformed into 'middleman minorities'. In a recent book, Christine Dobbin has put forward an argument of that kind on the role played by Asian merchant minorities in the making of the world-

[24] Cohen, 'Cultural Strategies in the Organization of Trading Diasporas'.
[25] P. D. Curtin, *Cross-Cultural Trade in World History*, Cambridge, 1984.

economy.[26] This work, however, distances itself from that school of interpretation. It holds that different groups of Asian merchants have maintained an independent commercial role throughout the period of European domination over Asia.

For many decades, the grand sweep of European imperialism in Asia during the 1750–1905 period (1905 being often seen as marking the beginning of an Asian revival of which victorious Japan was the torchbearer) exercised such a powerful pull on the mind of economic historians that it led them to overlook the dynamism shown by Asian commercial networks, not only at the level of the various domestic markets, but even more significantly in the arena of international trade, particularly inter-Asian trade. A 'revisionist' trend is now perceptible in the wake of the 'East Asian miracle', and a growing number of writers emphasize the long-term resilience of Asian commercial networks. They have, however, tended to focus more on Chinese than on South Asian networks.[27] It is true that the subcontinent is far from displaying the same economic dynamism as its eastern neighbours, and that the role of its diaspora is much less in evidence. A close look at the recent economic successes of such trading emporia as Singapore and Hong Kong, however, would reveal that if they owe most of their dynamism to the operation of powerful Chinese business networks, the South Asian factor is not absent. Actually there is an estimate that Indians, who account for less than 0.3 per cent of Hong Kong's population, control approximately 10 per cent of its overall foreign trade.[28] Although the empirical statistical evidence is hard to come by, and such estimates have to be taken as gross approximations, it is a fact that Indian businessmen, mostly Sindhis, played an important role in promoting Hong Kong exports to such areas as West Africa (most particularly Nigeria) and the Middle East, two regions in which Chinese networks are not known to be very active. It would seem that a sort of division of labour occurred between Chinese and Indian traders. Indians, Sindhis in particular, thus found a profitable niche and were able to take advantage of the spectacular growth in East Asian exports of manufactures to various areas of the world. This confirms the role of 'global middlemen' that South Asian merchants, as already mentioned, have

[26] C. Dobbin, *Asian Entrepreneurial Minorities: Conjoint Communities in the Making of the World-Economy, 1570–1940*, London, 1996.
[27] An exception is R. Brown, *Capital and Entrepreneurship in Southeast Asia*, London, 1994, which devotes an entire chapter to the role of Indian traders in the textile trade of Southeast Asia.
[28] Quoted in B. Sue-White, *Turbans and Traders: Hong Kong's Indian Communities*, Hong Kong, 1994.

been able to perform in the world economy for many decades in an often unnoticed way.

The often implicit assumption that there was a process of unilinear decline in the international role of Indian merchants from a peak represented by a kind of self-contained Indian world economy operating in a pristine pre-colonial world to a trough exemplified by 'middleman minorities' such as the Chettiars, does not bear close scrutiny. South Asian traders were forced by the European domination of the major channels of international trade and finance to redeploy in various ways. Not all, of course, were successful at adapting themselves to the new dispensation. Shipowners, generally Muslims, were one of the categories of merchants who found it particularly difficult to adjust to the new rules of the game. But, if there were losers in the game, there were also winners. The growth of commercial agriculture over large tracts of India offered enormous opportunities to merchant groups which had some capital and a good knowledge of the countryside. This opened one avenue of entry into foreign trade, as indigenous operators slowly moved upwards from financing of peasant cultivators to processing and ultimately exporting of commercial crops such as jute and cotton. The so-called 'Marwaris' are the best-known example of this kind of trajectory, which could be called the 'indirect' route. Other groups, less entrenched in the rural economy, managed to hold on to existing channels of trade, whether by sea or by land, and some of them were in a position to take advantage of European economic penetration of new areas in Asia or in Africa. This would be the case in particular for some of the Gujarati Muslim communities, like the Khojas and the Bohras. A third category would include groups which had no previous orientation towards foreign trade, but which were able to make use of opportunities offered by the colonial regime's outside ventures. The most conspicuous example is that of the Parsis and the role they came to play in the opium trade with China, a largely new kind of trade specifically developed by the British to deal with the problem of the drain of precious metals to China to pay for tea imports. A fourth category would include merchants who were lucky or clever enough to carve for themselves specific niches in world trade thanks to changes in flows and tastes precisely due to the increasing 'Westernization' of the world. It has to be understood that 'Westernization', far from being a purely negative phenomenon for Asian merchants, created new opportunities, in particular in the marketing of 'Oriental' goods, like carpets and different artefacts produced by Asian workshops. The development of a mass market for culturally specific goods is one of the consequences, perhaps unintended, of the growing standardization of consumer tastes the world over. In particular, it created a niche for goods which could be perceived as 'different', although their production techniques increasingly were bastardized forms of 'Western' ones.

These different categories should not be seen as mutually exclusive: they actually often overlapped. But altogether they delineate a space within which South Asian merchant networks could operate with a certain degree of independence *vis-à-vis* European capital, although not in opposition to it. To sum up, the study of the role of Indian merchants in the world economy during the period of the dominance of European capitalism is a neglected field of study, owing largely to implicit or explicit assumptions about these merchants being reduced to a 'subsidiary' role. It appears necessary to go beyond this kind of explicitly or implicitly dualistic explanation by trying firstly to restore the agency of Asian economic agents such as merchants. This must be seen as a heuristic device rather than a substantive philosophical statement. In this work we shall therefore try to approach the history of two international trading networks of South Asia by trying to reconstruct the internal logic of their operations rather than by attempting to fit them within some existing paradigm. At this stage an examination of the notion of 'merchant network' is needed.

South Asian merchant networks and their meaning

A basic argument of this book is that the notion of merchant networks centred on a micro-region or a locality provides the most appropriate category of analysis for the study of Indian merchants outside the subcontinent. Merchant networks should be distinguished from 'trade diasporas' although there are common characteristics. For Curtin, diasporas encompass networks, but while the latter are purely economic, the former include a cultural dimension. No really satisfactory definition of what constitutes a merchant network is found in the literature.[29] It is clear that purely economic definitions are insufficient. The author of one of the rare existing monograph studies of a particular trading network, the Hokkien network centred on Amoy,[30] defines 'network' as 'the fabric of interconnected activities in which the south

---

[29] For an attempt, not altogether satisfactory, see F. Braudel, *Civilization and Capitalism 15th–18th Century*, vol. II, *The Wheels of Commerce*, London, 1982, p. 149. Braudel distinguishes between 'networks' and 'circuits'. He writes: 'Any commercial network brought together a certain number of individuals or agents, whether belonging to the same firm or not, located at different points on a circuit or a group of circuits', and he sees networks as a form of merchant 'solidarity', based on trust.

[30] Ng Chin-Keong, *Trade and Society: the Amoy Network on the China Coast 1683–1735*, Singapore, 1983.

Fukienese engaged', by which he means the totality of relationships in which the merchants were implicated.[31] Adopting a more dynamic definition in terms of circulation, I would characterize a network as a structure through which goods, credit, capital and men circulate regularly across a given space which can vary enormously in terms of both size and accessibility. A network generally consists of a centre, a locality or a cluster of localities where capital is raised and where capitalists have their main place of residence, and of dispersed colonies of merchants and commercial employees which keep close links with the network centre. Between the network centre, on the one hand, and the dispersed colonies, on the other hand, goods, but also men (and sometimes women), credit and information circulate. While goods may also circulate widely outside the network (otherwise there would not be any exchange), men, credit and information circulate almost exclusively within it. Most crucial is probably the circulation of information. It is the capacity of the merchants to maintain a constant flow of information within the network that ensures its success. This means two things: first, that 'leaks' have to be avoided as much as possible to the outside world, secondly, that information must circulate smoothly within the network, both spatially and temporally, as it gets transmitted from one generation to another. Although academics are generally dismissive of the cognitive aspect of merchant activity, often deemed to consist of nothing more than the three Rs, in the long run the most successful merchant networks have been those most able to process information into a body of knowledge susceptible of continuous refinement. This body of knowledge, of a pragmatic nature, which is mostly about markets, is more or less congruent with what is often called the 'secrets of the trade'.

The question of the circulation of credit is a complex one. Practically all networks use credit from outside at some point or another. However, an essential characteristic of merchant networks is that credit circulates within the network, generally at rates which are lower than the market rate, and without collateral. This opens up the delicate question of trust. It is generally assumed that merchant networks operate largely on the basis of that immaterial and hard to define commodity that is trust. We are told that preferential rates and the absence of collateral are explained by the existence of a bond of trust between the lender and the borrower. The existence of this bond of trust is in its turn generally related to kinship, caste and community, a point which will be developed later. Regarding credit, another approach to the question would tend to emphasize the correlation between the state of development of the

[31] *Ibid.*, pp. 3–4.

'official' or 'formal' credit system, and the use of 'informal', network-based, credit systems. In other words, the less developed and accessible the 'official' banking system, the more merchants tended to borrow money from within their network.

The circulation of men, both between the network centre and the dispersed locations, and between the different locations, is the lifeblood of all networks, especially those which are far-flung. It can take several forms, and a detailed empirical analysis will be presented at a later stage. One of the major questions is that of the relationship between merchant network and kinship network. Kinship is obviously an essential ingredient of all merchant networks, but its importance can be exaggerated. Close empirical analysis reveals that business partnerships are often concluded between men who are not kin-related.

Given the importance of caste in the societies of South Asia, it is tempting to give a central role to caste in sustaining networks of South Asian merchants. In a recent work on the Nattukottai Chettiars, David Rudner has argued that caste was a crucial level of organization for this group of South Indian bankers, and he has mustered an impressive argument to support his case. According to him, it is 'the qualities of their caste organization' that enabled the Chettiars 'to take advantage of the changing colonial economy and become the chief merchant-bankers of south India and Southeast Asia'.[32] It is not sure, however, that his analysis can be generalized. In the case of the Chettiars, there was an almost complete congruence between caste and locality, in as much as all of them originated from one small region of Tamilnadu, known as Chettinad. But this kind of congruence was a rare occurrence in India. Most merchant castes were not tied to a specific locality, even if their myth of origins often referred to one. Conversely, most localities had merchants belonging to different castes or subcastes.

The literature on merchant diasporas often stresses the importance of the links created by a common religion. However, neither Hindu nor Muslim merchants represented anywhere homogenous entities. Between the strongly institutionalized religion of the Nattukottai Chettiar bankers, whose Saivaite temples served as clearing-houses, and the much more fluid religious universe of the Sind Hindu merchants, there was very little in common, in spite of the fact that the two groups could be defined as 'Hindus'. The same diversity is perceptible among Muslim merchants; between the religious practices and social institutions of the Shia merchants, both Khoja and Bohra, and those of Sunni merchants, there was also a wide gap. Even among Sunnis, Memons clearly

[32] See D. W. Rudner, *Caste and Capitalism in Colonial India: The Nattukottai Chettiars*, Berkeley, CA, 1994.

differentiated themselves from other groups. There was, however, one field in which the Hindu/Muslim difference was important. Diverging concepts of purity and impurity made it rare for Hindu merchants to take their wives out of India, while Muslim merchants generally travelled with their families, especially to Muslim lands. At this stage, a rapid discussion of the problem of the religious taboo attached for Hindus to the crossing of the *kala pani* is necessary. Little is actually known about the way that kind of taboo was conceptualized and enforced among Hindu merchant communities. There is enough evidence that Hindus have been crossing the seas without compunction for many centuries, but what is relatively obscure is the kind of ritual penances which had to be performed on their return. In some communities, such as the Gujarati Vanis of Porbandar during Gandhi's time, we know that these rituals actually took place, but for other communities we lack information. One hypothesis which seems plausible, however, is that the generalized taboo on the voyage of women represented a kind of substitution. The fact that the women of the household did not travel beyond the seas (or the mountain passes leading to Central Asia) seems to have been sufficient to ensure the continuing purity of the household.

Some analysts see a common ethnicity and a common language as more enduring bonds than a common religion. In the subcontinent, however, the frontiers between ethnic groups are often imprecise. The term 'Gujarati merchant', for instance, can apply to merchants of different regions (Kutch, Kathiawar, Gujarat proper), of different religions (Hindus, Jains, Parsis, Shia and Sunni Muslims) and does not correspond to any existing merchant 'community'. The notion of 'merchant community' is moreover fairly ambiguous, as it includes elements of ethnicity, as well as of caste and locality. A good example is that of the 'Marwari' community, on which the most authoritative source is Timberg's work.[33] As used by that author, it refers to a complex cluster of both castes (Agarwal, Maheshwari, Oswal, to name the three most important zones) and regional groups (such as Shekawatis or Bikaneris), defined by a vague common regional origin (a part of Rajasthan), but including Hindus as well as Jains. Actually the term seems to have been devised by 'indigenous' inhabitants of east India to designate all the traders from the northwest who swarmed into Bengal in the second half of the nineteenth century and it was given currency in British administrative language at the time of the 1901 and 1911 Censuses. But there is no very clear evidence that the so-called 'Marwaris' themselves felt that they belonged to one specific community. It

---

[33] See T. A. Timberg, *The Marwaris: from Traders to Industrialists*, Delhi, 1978.

seems that identification remained for a long period with caste and locality, and that an encompassing Marwari group identity developed at a fairly late stage for reasons which were largely political and had to do with changes in the structure of Bengal politics in the inter-war period.

Sociological literature on Indian merchants, which is sparse, has not put much emphasis on the importance of locality in spite of the fact that historians have noted the emergence at a fairly early stage of commercial towns endowed with specific institutions representing the various merchant groups, which they have sometimes called 'burgher cities'. C. A. Bayly has written at length on the Naupatti Sabha of eighteenth-century Benares[34] and similar institutions existed in many other towns of northern India and Gujarat, suggesting the existence of strong locally based linkages among merchants belonging to different 'castes' and 'communities'. In many cities and towns, merchants were key participants in urban politics,[35] and a kind of merchant civic culture emerged, which cut across caste and community. Cities like Surat[36] or Broach are prime examples of durable merchant-dominated urban cultures, and it is no accident if those two towns have been foci of very extended merchant networks. It would be interesting if one could produce a typology of the localities which were centres of far-flung networks. A surprising fact is that such networks often emanated from localities which were medium sized rather than large, and also from interior as much as from coastal cities. Thus if sea-ports like Bombay, Surat, Broach, Mandvi or Porbandar were the centres of several active merchant networks, interior towns such as Hoshiarpur, Campbellpore or Quetta also played a role. It would, however, be a mistake to identify merchant networks too closely with the existence of strong urban nuclei and traditions. The tiny princely state of Kutch in Gujarat is an example of a mostly rural area from where numerous far-flung merchant networks originated. Most of the many Kutchi merchants, whether Hindu (Lohana or Bhatia) or Muslim (Ismaili Khojas and Bohras as well as Sunni Memons), who traded anywhere between East Africa and the Far East, and who represented a large percentage of the overall South Asian merchant diaspora, originated from small villages in Kutch,[37] where there were in any case only very few urban agglomerations.

[34] See Bayly, *Rulers, Townsmen and Bazaars*, pp. 177–9.
[35] On the case of Bombay, see C. Dobbin, *Urban Leadership in Western India: Politics and Communities in Bombay City, 1840–1885*, Oxford, 1972.
[36] See D. Haynes, *Rhetoric and Ritual in Colonial India: the Shaping of a Public Culture in Surat City, 1852–1928*, Berkeley, CA, 1991, in particular pp. 60–8 on the role of *Mahajans* and *shetias*.
[37] See the interesting memoirs of a prominent Kutchi Khoja merchant of Singapore, R. Jumabhoy, *Multiracial Singapore*, Singapore, 1970.

These locality based far-flung networks represent an interesting case of direct linkage between the local and the global, which was not mediated in an obvious way by the 'national'.[38] These networks often existed before the advent of the colonial state, and the latter maintained towards them an attitude of studied indifference, as long as they did not interfere with powerful British interests or create political difficulties. This explains why the existence of those networks has been largely unnoticed by economic historians, who tend to reproduce even unconsciously the biases of the colonial state they often denounce. The power ascribed to colonial discourse in many recent writings to invent categories which did not exist in the social reality leads many to ignore the patent fact that the knowledge colonial administrators had of economic and social realities could be very partial. The result is that what does not figure in colonial discourse is deemed unimportant or even non-existent. As the British did not produce a coherent discourse on Indian merchant diasporas, about which they knew little and cared even less, except in very specific contexts, these diasporas have been almost obliterated from the historical record. The study of the history of those networks can throw a new light on the question of the relationship between networks, nations and empires, which is seen by many as of importance to an understanding of our present.

Merchant networks which expanded from India in the nineteenth and twentieth centuries were not migration networks in the classical sense, even if their operations sometime resulted in the establishment of a migratory stream. Men kept circulating between the network centre and the dispersed places of business. In this case, the 'migrants' cannot be studied in isolation from their home towns. This means, for instance, that the study of the (almost exclusively) male diaspora cannot be divorced from a consideration of the role of the women who stayed in the towns, for they influenced the shape of the networks in many ways. The study of the 'sexual economy' of merchant networks is an important part of their overall study. It is of particular importance in the case of the merchants of Shikarpur and Hyderabad.

These two medium-sized inland towns of Sind were home to two very different types of networks engaged in international trade and finance. Shikarpur was the centre of a financial network which developed in the

---

[38] In a short paper, Sugata Bose drew attention to the existence of direct linkages between the world economy and South Asian regional economies. See S. Bose, 'The World Economy and Regional Economies in South Asia: Some Comments on Linkages', in S. Bose (ed.), *South Asia and World Capitalism*, Delhi, 1990, pp. 357–62. I would stress here that these linkages extended even to certain localities, independently of their insertion into 'regional' economies.

second half of the eighteenth century in direct relation to the rise of the Durrani Empire, in a town of Upper Sind which was very closely linked with Kandahar. Although it suffered from the decline of the Durrani state in the first two decades of the nineteenth century and never recovered its shine of the late eighteenth century, the expertise and capital accumulated by the Shikarpuri bankers allowed them to take advantage of a new surge in Indo-Central Asian trade from the 1840s onwards to rebuild an active network based on the financing of the caravan trade and on close links with the Uzbek khanates of Central Asia. The British annexation of Sind did not modify significantly the outward orientation of the Shikarpuri bankers, as it did not lead in the short term to widely increased opportunities in Sind itself. We have there the case of a network which developed independently of the British connection and was able to maintain this relative independence until the time of the Russian Revolution. The case of the Sindwork merchants of Hyderabad is very different. Hyderabad was home to a community of bankers and merchants who had close links to the regime of the Amirs which was overthrown by the British in 1843. Faced with the extinction of their traditional role as bankers of the state and financiers of craft producers who worked mainly for the market of the court, they had to seek new outlets. They took advantage of the strengthening of commercial links between Sind and Bombay to embark upon a completely new venture, which was the sale of the local craft productions to a European clientele, first in Bombay, then in Egypt and later on a worldwide scale. Those two networks provide a study in contrast: one was land-based, the other sea-based; one was mostly financial, the other almost exclusively commercial; one was pre-colonial, the other a product of political and economic changes linked to the advent of colonialism. At the same time, they had many common features: both used 'traditional' forms of business organization and of accounting techniques, although the Sindworkies operated in the world of international maritime trade where the telegraph and the steamship had produced a real revolution in methods of business, while the Shikarpuris still relied on camels and couriers for the transport of goods and the transmission of information.

While very specific in many ways, those networks were by no means unique. Many of their most characteristic traits were found also among other groups of Indian traders who were dispersed throughout the world – Hindus, Sikhs and Muslims. I conceive this study as relevant to the study not only of South Asian merchant networks, but also of international merchant networks in general. At the same time, those two networks were very much rooted in their local context. Since little is known about the economic and social history of Sind, this work is also an attempt at opening up a little-developed field in South Asian regional studies. That is why chapter 2 will concentrate specifically on Sind.

2 The regional context: Sind economy and society, c. 1750–1950

Sind has been a neglected area in South Asian Studies, because it is a 'frontier' area, a transition zone between 'India proper' and the vast region which was often called Khorrassan, in which were included southern Afghanistan, Baluchistan and southeastern Iran. Persian cultural influences were strong, and Sind was only episodically included in the great pan-Indian empires. In the late eighteenth and early nineteenth century, under the Sindhi Kalhora and Baluchi Talpur dynasties, it evolved into an original kind of polity, a sort of tribal confederation, which was however capable of overseeing the maintenance and development of one of the largest systems of canal irrigation in Asia centred on the Lower Indus. This Sindhian state was the victim of a particularly vicious propaganda campaign in the wake of the British annexation, in 1843, aimed at presenting it as the epitome of backwardness and tyranny, which, to all appearances, it was not.[1] The fate of the Hindus of Sind was one of the themes most harped upon by Napier and his minions in their attempts at blackening the picture so as to justify the inexcusable 'piece of rascality' of which Napier himself cynically boasted.[2] The question of the role of the Hindus, and in particular, of their dominance over commercial life, both in pre-colonial and in colonial times, is therefore of great importance to the emergence of a balanced picture of the history of Sind.

Sind and its trade: an historical overview pre-1750

Sind, as the coastal region of the subcontinent closest to the Persian Gulf, has always been actively involved in maritime trade with that

[1] C. A. Bayly writes in *Imperial Meridian: the British Empire and the World 1780–1830*, London, 1989, p. 48: 'Emerging from out of the brief Afghan Empire of the Durranis, magnates from tribal backgrounds in Sindh (the Talpur emirs) had built up a viable political system by the 1790s', thus signalling a considerable shift in current historiographical views on pre-colonial Sind.

[2] For an altogether favourable account of Napier, see H. T. Lambrick, *Sir Charles Napier and Sind*, Oxford, 1952.

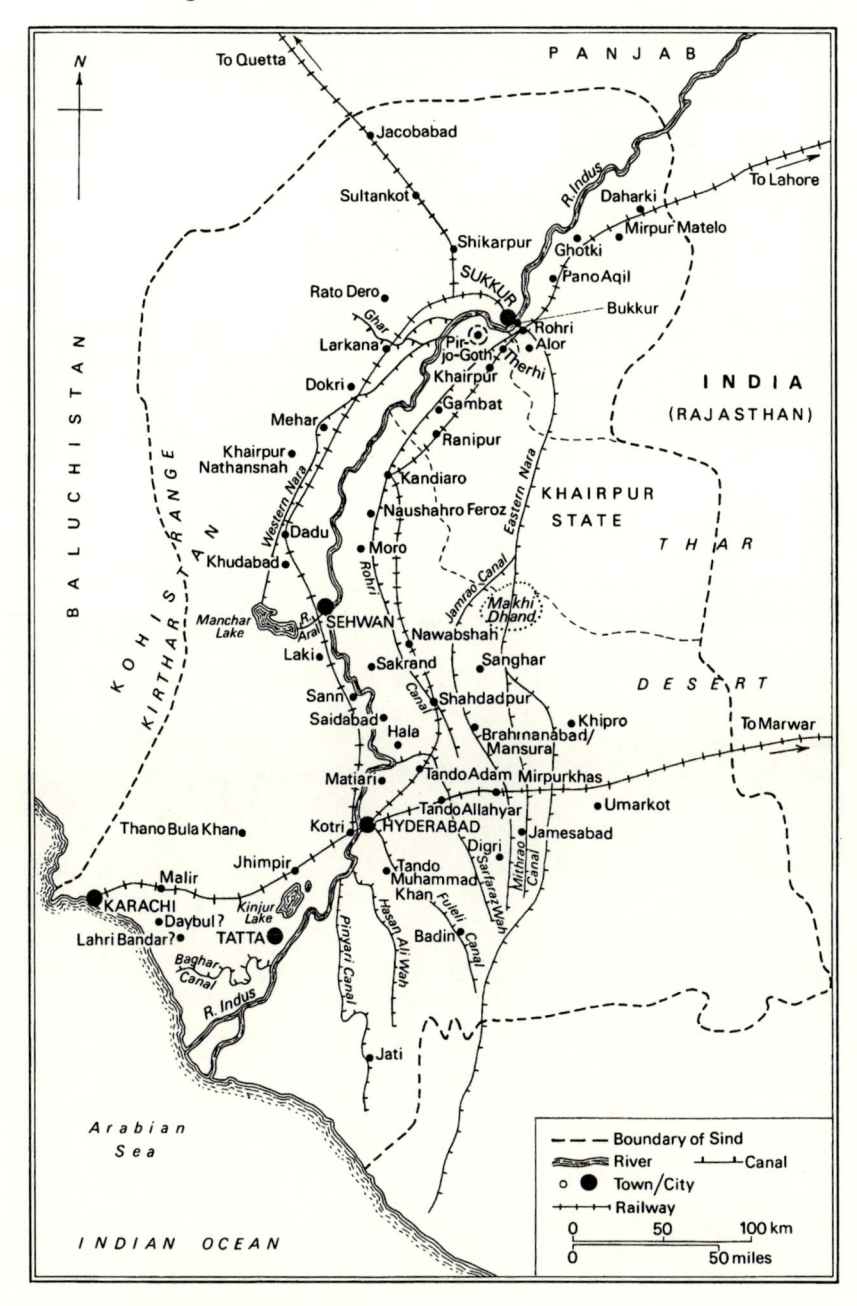

1 Sind in the colonial period
Source: Ansari, *Sufi Saints and State Power*

region of Asia. It has also played an important role as a commercial gateway between Central Asia and northern India. Thus both sea and land routes contributed to its commercial importance.[3] Without going back to the period of the Harappan culture, when trade links are known to have existed between Mohenjo-Daro and Mesopotamia, one could mention that the conquest of Sind by the Umayyads in the early eighth century AD was the culmination of contacts which were partly commercial.[4] A crucial objective of the conquering Arab armies was the port, or rather the ports, of Debal (Daybul), on one of the branches of the Indus delta, which was the main outlet of Sind. This port came into prominence in the fifth century AD, when it was in the possession of the Sassanids, and was visited for the first time by an Arab fleet in 632.[5] Its fall to the army of Muhammad bin Qasim in 711 was a decisive episode in the Arab conquest. At that time, Sind was, in the words of a recent author, 'the hinge of the Indian Ocean trade as well as the overland passway'.[6] After the conquest, Sind became part of the Muslim world, and commercial links intensified with the Persian Gulf and the Middle East, through Debal, which remained an important port till at least the twelfth century.[7] At a later stage, the twin ports of Debal were replaced by a couple of new ports, of which Thatta was the riverine emporium and Lahori Bandar the sea port. The latter was visited by Ibn Battuta in the 1330s.[8] Nothing much is known about the groups which were active in maritime trade in medieval Sind. Arab merchants played an important role, as well as unidentified 'Sindi' merchants.[9] In particular, it is not known whether Hindu *banias* were involved in that trade prior to the fifteenth century.

The first mention of *banias* of Sind occurred in Arab and Portuguese documents concerning Masqat at the end of the fifteenth century. Thatta is mentioned as 'Masqat's most important Indian trading partner', and its Hindu merchants, the Bhatias, appear to have been the main participants in the trade between Sind and Arabia.[10] They used

---

[3] See C. L. Mariwalla, *History of the Commerce of Sind (From Early Times to 1526 AD)*, Jamshoro, 1981, p. 16.

[4] See Wink, *Al Hind*, vol. I, p. 51: 'The desire to expand traffic along the Persian Gulf route was . . . the main motivation for the conquest of Sind.' The suppression of piracy in particular was a crucial objective for the Muslim conquerors.

[5] *Ibid.*, p. 181.   [6] *Ibid.*, p. 52.

[7] On Debal, see S. Q. Fatimi, 'The Twin Ports of Daybul', in H. Khuhro (ed.), *Sind Through the Centuries*, Karachi, 1981, pp. 97–105.

[8] Ibn Battuta, *Voyages*, translated from the Arabic by C. Defremery and B. R. Sanguinetti, Paris, 1854, p. 112. He calls 'Lahary' 'une belle place située sur le rivage de l'océan' and mentions that 'elle possède un grand port, où abordent des gens du Yaman, du Fars'.

[9] Wink, *Al Hind*, p. 173.

[10] Allen, 'The Indian Merchant Community of Masqat'.

Portuguese ships and many had warehouses and trading establishments at Masqat. At the time when the Portuguese took the great trading emporium of Hormuz, they reported that trade from Sind accounted for almost 10 per cent of the custom revenue of the port, and the chronicler Diego de Couto described Thatta as one of the richest cities of the Orient.[11] Thatta's prosperity was based on the one hand on its own textile production, which was of high quality, consisting of cotton cloth of different kinds, calicos and baftas, chintzes and muslins, as well as of fine silken goods,[12] and on the other, on the export of textile and other goods which came from the Punjab and northern India by caravan or river transport on the Indus. Lower Sind's incorporation into the Mughal domain at the end of the sixteenth century led to a certain fall in the prosperity of Thatta, as some of northern India's trade with the Persian Gulf was diverted to other ports in the Mughal dominions. In the 1640s there was a revival of trade as the Portuguese were supplanted by the English East India Company, but it was short lived, and in the second half of the seventeenth century the increasing silting of the main Indus channel led to a gradual abandonment of Thatta and Lahori Bandar as sea-ports. While the Mughals tried to create a new port which they called Auranga Bandar, most trade shifted to two new ports, Shahbandar and Kharrakbandar, whose prosperity however never reached that of Thatta's in its days of glory. There is some evidence that the second half of the seventeenth century, which was a period of relative decline in the maritime trade of Sind, was also the period during which the local *banias* increased their participation in trade by acquiring their own ships instead of being dependent on the ships of European traders and European companies. Alexander Hamilton, an English merchant who visited Lower Sind in 1699, reported that the trade was in the hands of Hindu merchants.[13] Although Thatta had started declining, its merchants, particularly the Bhatias, remained very active in Masqat, where they erected the first Hindu temple in the city.[14] They seem also to have extended their activities in the Gulf to new areas, such as the Bahrain islands. But the Bhatias of Thatta were not the only *banias* of Sind who were active in international trade. According to the memoirs of Seth Naomal Hotchand, a prominent nineteenth-century Karachi merchant, his ancestor Seth Bhojoomal, whose family originated from the region of Sehwan in central Sind, settled in Kharrakbandar around

[11] See S. Subrahmanyam, 'The Portuguese, Thatta and the External Trade of Sind, 1515–1635', *Revista de Cultura*, nos. 13–14, 1991, pp. 48–58.
[12] See S. P. Chablani, *Economic Conditions in Sind 1592 to 1843*, Bombay, 1951, p. 52.
[13] A. Hamilton, *A New Account of the East Indies*, London, 1744, quoted in A. Duarte, *A History of British Relations with Sind*, Karachi, 1976, p. 39.
[14] Allen, 'The Indian Merchant Community of Masqat'.

1720 and founded a powerful commercial firm which had a *gumastha* (agent) in Masqat, who in turn had agents at Bushire, Shiraz and Bahrein.[15] In the late 1720s, as Kharrakbandar declined, due to silting, Seth Bhojoomal played a major role in the creation of a new sea-port, Karachi. It is only after it was founded and endowed with rudimentary fortifications by the merchants that the Kalhora rulers of Sind took possession of it. However, they soon relinquished it to the khans of Khelat, the main rulers of Baluchistan. Pakistan's great metropolis thus started its existence as an entrepôt port for Hindu *banias*, and it was only in the late eighteenth century that the Talpur rulers of Sind started taking an interest in it.

By the mid-eighteenth century, Sind occupied a fairly important position at the crossroads of several important maritime and land routes which linked northern India with the Persian Gulf and Arabia. The prosperity of its merchants was also linked to the export of its own craft productions. In this field, Thatta, in spite of its decline as a sea-port, remained the largest centre, especially as far as textile production was concerned. Among the merchants of Sind, the Hindu *banias* were undoubtedly the dominant element, although there were also Muslim merchants. Why in a region which was under Muslim rule since at least the twelfth century, and in which the majority of the population was converted to Islam at some point between the fifteenth and the eighteenth centuries, trade and finance were largely dominated by Hindus, is a question which has often been debated, but which need not concern us here. Too little is known about the economic and social history of Sind before the eighteenth century to allow for an empirically grounded answer. The most widespread theory relates Hindu domination of finance with the so-called Koranic injunction against *riba*. However, as M. Rodinson has convincingly argued,[16] it has never prevented Muslims from engaging in moneylending. What remains true is that in most Muslim states, the functions of financier in relation to revenue collecting were generally entrusted to non-Muslims, one of the reasons being probably that they were politically more vulnerable and therefore easier to control. In Sind, those functions were entrusted to a particular

---

[15] See *A Forgotten Chapter of Indian History as Described in the Memoirs of Seth Naomal Hotchand, C. S. I. of Karachi 1804–1878*, Karachi, 1982 (1st edn, Exeter, 1915), p. 36. These memoirs, which were written in Sindhi by Seth Naomal himself, were translated into English by his grandson, Rao Bahadur Alumal Trikamdas Bhojwani, and 'edited' by Sir H. Evan M. James, who was commissioner in Sind in 1891–9, and had them privately published. This document, in spite of having been translated and 'edited', is an extraordinary and in many ways unique source on the world of the Hindu *banias* of Sind.

[16] M. Rodinson, *Islam et Capitalisme*, Paris, 1966.

section of the Hindu trading community, who were known as Amils. These men, whose rise seems to have occurred during the period of Mughal domination, played a role which was in many ways similar to the one the Kayastha played in Mughal northern India. It is striking that the rise of the *banias* to dominance in trade appears to have been largely coeval with the accession of the Amils to high functions in the revenue-collecting apparatus of the state.

Trade and society in Sind, c. 1750–1843: the role of the Hindu *banias*

The mid-eighteenth century marked a transition in the history of Sind, and one can trace back to these years the beginning of new trends. There were important political developments, which in their turn had far-reaching consequences for the structure of trading. From at least the late fifteenth to the mid-eighteenth century, the major mart in the region had been Lower Sind, with Thatta as the most prominent centre, and Karachi beginning to emerge as an alternative focus towards the end of the period. The towns of Upper Sind played a subsidiary role, being mostly transit points on the caravan routes which led from the Punjab, northern India and Central Asia to the ports of Lower Sind. Most of the direct trade between Central Asia and northern India tended to by-pass Upper Sind, as Multan, in neighbouring Punjab played the role of a major emporium and financial centre for the caravan trade.

Around the mid-eighteenth century, there started a southward shift in this system of caravan trade, which benefited Upper Sind. The reasons for it appear to have been largely political. Two separate developments converged to raise the status of Upper Sind. The first one relates to the decline in the so-called 'Multani' network, which had played a major role in financing the caravan trade between Russia, Central Asia and northern India in the seventeenth century. Stephen Dale has identified as the main causes for the decline of the Multanis the decision by the Russian state to exclude Indian merchants from internal trade, as well as the prohibition of trade between Russia and Persia.[17] Other political developments were to have even greater consequences. They were mostly the rise of what J. Gommans has recently called an 'Indo-Afghan Empire'.[18] The Pashto clan, which founded the so-called 'Durrani' Empire, had its original base in Kandahar, and was therefore particularly concerned with the trade routes between that city and northern

[17] See Dale, *Indian Merchants and Eurasian Trade*, p. 128.
[18] J. J. L. Gommans, *The Rise of the Indo-Afghan Empire, c. 1710–1780*, Leiden, 1995.

India. It happens that the shortest route between Kandahar and northern India is through Baluchistan and the Bolan Pass which links Quetta with Upper Sind and connects with the routes which cross the Thar desert to Jaisalmer and Bikaner. With the rise of the Durranis, this route, which had been relatively neglected, suddenly assumed new importance and the mart of Shikarpur on the Upper Sind side of the route received a considerable boost, at the expense of Multan. Although the exact sequence of events remains shrouded in some mystery, a point to which I shall come back later, in the second half of the eighteenth century Shikarpur emerged as the most important financial centre of the entire Durrani dominions, and its banking houses came to dominate financial transactions over a vast area comprising not only Afghanistan, but parts of Iran and Central Asia. It was also an important trade emporium, but its position in trade was not as prominent as in finance. For the first time in history, a mart in Upper Sind rivalled those of Lower Sind, and even for some time eclipsed them.

In Lower Sind, the major facts were the continued decline of Thatta, the emergence of Karachi as a significant sea-port and the rise of Hyderabad, a new urban foundation which came to play an important political and commercial role. The decline of Thatta accelerated with the increased silting of the channels leading to it and it lost its function as an emporium. At the same time, its Bhatia merchants suffered from 1785 onwards from the increasing commercial aggressiveness of their rivals, the Kutchi Bhatias, who came to dominate the trade of Masqat.[19] Thatta survived only as a centre of craft production, but it increasingly worked for a local and regional rather than an international market. The Bhatia merchants however remained a significant trading community in the Persian Gulf, and they came to play a dominant role in the pearling trade centred on Bahrein. But it was Karachi which became after 1750 the major port of Sind, and after the Talpurs took it from the khans of Khelat, they encouraged the growth of the harbour. The new port attracted merchants not only from Sind, but also from Kutch and Kathiawar, Hindus as well as Muslims, and started acquiring a cosmopolitan character which made it a rather unique city in Sind. Another town which developed rapidly was Hyderabad,[20] founded in 1769 by the Kalhoras on the site of the village of Nerunkot, along the Fuleli canal which parallels the Indus, in a fertile tract. The Kalhoras intended to make it their new capital, but it was their *murids*-turned-rivals, the Baluchi Talpurs, who actually made the move in 1782, after they had

---

[19] See Allen, 'The Indian Merchant Community of Masqat'.
[20] See A. B. Advani, 'Hyderabad: a Brief Historical Sketch', *Sindhian World*, vol. 1, no. 6, 1940, pp. 356–69.

The regional context 39

defeated the Kalhoras and razed their capital of Khudabad, near present-day Sehwan. The motivations of the Talpurs in shifting their capital are nowhere explicitly stated, but it is not far-fetched to suppose that they wished to put more distance between them and their theoretical Afghan overlords, to whom they paid tribute. The proximity of the new capital to the growing port of Karachi may also have weighed with them. Although the functions of Hyderabad were mostly military and political, the presence of the court attracted bankers, as well as traders and craftsmen, and the new town was situated astride one of the traditional caravan routes between Sind and northern India across the Thar desert, leading through Umarkot and Barmer to Jodhpur.

By the end of the eighteenth century, the trading network of Lower Sind had undergone a complete transformation in its spatial structure, as the functions traditionally associated with Thatta had been taken over by Karachi and, to a lesser extent, by Hyderabad. At the same time, Shikarpur had emerged as an important centre of trade and finance in Upper Sind, in close connection with the emergence of the Durrani Afghan Empire. Shikarpur, although mostly geared towards controlling the great trading route linking Central Asia with northern India, had some connections with Hyderabad and Karachi, but they were not very strong, and it would be a mistake to talk of late eighteenth-century Sind as an integrated hub between Central Asia, northern India and the Persian Gulf. There remained a distinction between an Upper Sind and a Lower Sind network. Shikarpur, besides, remained under direct Afghan administration till 1824, when it was occupied by the Talpurs.

A very important development in the trade of Sind in the early decades of the nineteenth century was its emergence as a major transit point for the trade in Malwa opium between Central India and China. Although it was not situated along the 'natural' route for such a trade, Sind benefited by the existence of a conflict over opium between the East India Company and Indian private capital. The story of the Malwa opium trade has never been recounted in great detail, in spite of the fact that speculation on Malwa opium was one of the major sources of capital accumulation in India between 1770 and 1870, and that various merchant groups derived large profits from their participation in it. Some data about this trade will therefore be presented here. The story need concern us here only inasmuch as it became an essential element of Sind's external economy in the 1820s and 1830s, that is, precisely during the period immediately preceding British annexation.

The existence of the 'circuitous' route via Sind for the export of Malwa opium to China came to the notice of the British authorities only at the end of 1821, but it had probably been already in existence for at least two years, from the moment the Company authorities engaged in a new policy of trying to purchase the entire Malwa crop and took measures to cut the trade route passing through British territory. The opium merchants and speculators countered the British moves by turning to a new route through the territory of the Amirs of Sind. This route, as it has been described in various official documents, started from Pali, in the territories of the maharajah of Jodhpur, where the drug was taken from the various marts in Malwa, of which the most important was Ujjain; from there it was conveyed by camel across the Thar desert to Jaisalmer, and further, via Umarkot, to the Indus valley and the port of Karachi, where it was loaded on boats which took it to Damao, a port in Portuguese India from which it was exported to Macao for the Chinese market.[21]

In February 1822, in a letter to the Supreme Government in Fort William, the Revenue Department in Bombay had, however, expressed confidence that the restrictive measures taken by the government to counteract the clandestine transit of opium through British territory and the territories of the allied native states had so forced up the cost of transit through the 'circuitous' route of Sind as to render the operation unprofitable. It added that these difficulties 'would be considerably enhanced if the route through Jeysalmer and Pallee be closed, and above all if the Ameers of Scinde could be induced to prohibit the transit of opium through the Scinde territoires, and the port of Curatchee in particular', but it made it clear that the Company Government had 'not ventured to solicit such a favour from a government whose policy and suspicion of our views are of so adverse a character'. During the following eight years, the volume of the trade fluctuated widely,[22] but all the efforts of the Company at stopping it by concluding treaties with the

---

[21] On the Malwa opium trade, see, for an overview, D. F. Owen, *British Opium Policy in China and India*, New Haven, CT, 1934, pp. 80–112, *Parliamentary Papers, House of Commons, 1831–32*, vol. VI, Appendixes to the reports of the Committee on the East India Company affairs, Appendix IV, 'Abstract of correspondence regarding Malwa opium, commencing from the Year 1818 to the Year 1828', pp. 26–59, *Royal Commission on Opium, 1894–1895*, vol. VII, *Final Report*, part II, *Historical Appendices*, London, 1895, 'Appendix B, Historical Memorandum, by R. M. Dane', pp. 28–63. For details of the route, see in particular IOR, Bengal Board of Revenue (Miscellaneous) Proceedings, Opium, Consultation 8A, 9 March 1824, enclosing letter from opium agent in Malwa to Board of Revenue, 17 February 1824, enclosing 'Memorandum respecting the export of opium to Pahlie and Demaun', and Consultation 18, 22 April 1824, from *ibid.*, enclosing information collected at Pali by a native informant.

[22] Statistics bearing on opium exports to China from Daman between 1820–1 and 1828–9 show widespread fluctuations, a peak being reached in 1827–8 with a quantity of almost 4,000 chests. See C. Pinto, *Trade and Finance in Portuguese India: a Study of the Portuguese Country Trade 1770–1840*, Delhi, 1994, Table 5.2, p. 132.

different native states in Rajputana, through which the caravans passed on their way to Sind, utterly failed.

Even after the Company abandoned its restrictive policy in 1830 and tried to control the market for Malwa opium through a system of passes aiming at favouring the Bombay route at the expense of the Damao one, the latter remained the most frequented. Opium continued to reach China via Karachi and Damao as late as 1838. According to a British report, in 1837, it was by far the largest component in the export trade of Karachi. Apart from the sheer magnitude of the trade itself, it also had the important effect of integrating Sind into a pan-Indian and international trading network linking Central India with China and the Far East. Whether closing that route was the main motivation behind the British annexation of Sind, as asserted in a recent article,[23] is not a question I shall go into. Suffice it to say that the occupation of Karachi by British troops in 1839 allowed the East India Company effectively to close the Pali–Karachi route and to redirect the Malwa opium trade through Bombay, which they had tried, unsuccessfully, to do for almost twenty years.

From the evidence of various reports, it appears that Sind *banias* were not directly involved in the trade, either as buyers of opium in Malwa or as shippers from Karachi to Damao. The principals in this large-scale smuggling operation were, on the one hand, the 'Malwa sowcars (*sahukars*)', mostly Marwari and Gujarati merchants settled in Malwa, who had close connections with the authorities of the major native states in the area, in particular Gwalior and Indore, in the territories of which the bulk of poppy cultivation took place, and, on the other hand, Parsi and Gujarati capitalists from Bombay, Ahmedabad, Surat in British territory and from the native states of Porbunder and Kutch. Some idea of the indirect benefits which could accrue from the trade to the Sind *banias* can be gathered from various sources. Their role was basically that of intermediaries in organizing the caravans and in remitting the duties to the various authorities. Although the caravans were organized at the Pali end by the Marwari merchants of the place, Burnes informs us that the Marwar camels rarely went beyond a certain point in the Thar desert. The load was therefore shifted to camels hired in Sind, a business in which the *banias* were known to have a hand. But the largest profits must have been made from the business of remitting the duties to

---

[23] See J. Y. Wong, 'British Annexation of Sind in 1843: an Economic Perspective', *Modern Asian Studies*, vol. 31, no. 2, 1997, pp. 225–44. That some correlation existed between British opium policy on the one hand and the decision to annex Sind seems indubitable, but it does not prove that the desire to close the Sind route to Malwa opium was the main motive of the annexation.

the authorities, which accounted for the bulk of the overall cost of transit between Malwa and Damao.[24] This business of remittances must have been done through *hundis*, on which the Sind *banias* are bound to have taken a commission. Though estimates of the amount of duty levied by the government of Sind vary from one source to another, and also from one year to another, there is no doubt that in some years opium revenues were a major contribution to Sind finances. In November 1830, Henry Pottinger, then the resident at Bhuj, forwarded to the authorities in Bombay a letter from the native agent in Sind in which the latter asserted that during the year 1830 540,000 Rupees had been paid to the amirs' treasury as duties on 2,400 camel loads which had passed through Sind terrritory (Rs 225 per camel load of 8 Surat maunds).[25] In March 1839, Alexander Burnes gave a detailed account of the different duties levied in Sind on opium during 1838.[26] The total amounted to 234 kora or kashani rupees (two of the currencies in use in Sind at the time) per camel load (which consisted of two picul chests) which was equivalent to 200 Company rupees. It was still lower than the price charged by the Company on one chest, which was Rs 125. Of this total, the bulk was levied in Karachi, but significant levies were also made at Mirpur, by the representatives of the local amir, a member of the Talpur ruling family who had a separate establishment from that of the Hyderabad amirs, and at Hyderabad.

A stray reference in a British report of 1848 confirms the importance of the opium trade to the Hyderabad merchants.[27] Other information in British reports suggests that the Shikarpuri merchants must also have had their finger in this pie. Lieutenant Leech, in his report on the trade between Shikarpur and Pali, does not mention opium as one of the commodities involved, but the contrast between the amount of capital

[24] See enclosure 8 B, 'Memorandum respecting the export of opium to Pahlie and Demaun', in opium agent in Malwa to Board of Revenue, Customs and Salt (Opium), 17 February 1824, Consultation no. 8 A, 9 March 1824, Bengal Board of Revenue (Miscellaneous) Proceedings, Opium, 9 March to 22 June 1824, and enclosure in *ibid.* to *ibid.*, 22 April 1824, Consultation no. 18, *ibid.*

[25] Native agent in Sind to Colonel H. Pottinger, 27 November 1830, trans. by A. Burnes, assistant resident, 20 December 1830, Bombay Revenue Proceedings, December 1830, no. 135.

[26] A. Burnes, 'On the Commerce of Hyderabad and Lower Sind', in *Reports and Papers, Political, Geographical and Commercial Submitted to Government by Sir Alexander Burnes, Lieutenant Leech, Dr Lord and Lieutenant Wood Employed on Missions in the years 1835–36–37 in Scinde, Afghanistan and Adjacent Countries*, Calcutta, 1839, p. 21.

[27] In 1848, Captain Rathbone, the magistrate of Hyderabad, answering queries regarding trade in the Hyderabad Collectorate, stated: 'The Hyderabad merchants ... had till within a year or two of the conquest a large opium trade across from Pali, which has been stopped under orders conveyed from the Supreme Government.' Enclosed in minute of Sir George Clerk, 24 April 1848. *Parliamentary Papers (House of Commons) 1854, East India (Scinde)*, p. 293.

invested by Shikarpuri merchants in the trade and the modesty of the figures of trade provided to Leech by his merchant informants leads to the inescapable conclusion that a good share of the capital must have been employed in the opium trade.[28] The complete interruption of the Malwa opium trade after 1839 certainly meant the closing of an opportunity for profit for the *banias* of Karachi, Hyderabad and Shikarpur.

British travellers in pre-annexation Sind were puzzled by the contrast which they saw between the economic domination exercised by the Hindus in Sind and their political subjection in a Muslim-dominated polity. But their view was flawed. Hindus were actually important participants in the political system of Sind, even if they had to remain in the background. The Amils, as already mentioned, were the backbone of the Talpur regime in matters of revenue collection and administration, which gave them an enormous political influence. There were Hindu *jagirdars* in Sind, although they represented only a small percentage of the total, and the Amils as well as the merchants did bear arms. It is interesting to recall that the defence of Karachi against the Talpurs in the early 1790s was organized by local *banias* acting in the name of the khan of Khelat, and that it is they who relinquished control of the city to the representative of the Talpurs.[29] The *banias*' proverbial cowardice was just a stereotype, shared by the Muslim aristocracy and British officialdom.

British attitudes to the Hindus of Sind, who were largely equated with the *banias*, oscillated between paternalistic concern for an 'oppressed race' victimized by Muslim bigotry and intolerance, and repulsion for the greed displayed by wily moneylenders against poor peasants and profligate *zamindars*. The theme of the oppression of the Hindus at the hands of the Muslims had been made popular before the British annexation by various travellers' accounts, of which the most influential was probably James Burnes'. While emphasizing that 'the revenues are for the most part in the hands of the Hindus', he described them as 'a class which possesses little favour at court, and no influence or respectability in the country, except that of wealth'.[30] He recounted an

---

[28] 'Report on the trade between Shikarpur and Marwar', *Reports and Papers, Commercial*, pp. 68–70. Leech gives the names of six Shikarpuri merchants engaged in the trade with a total capital of Rs 340,000, while he informs us that trade in the major commodities, assafoetida and saffron, is but a small share of what it was two decades earlier, one of the major reasons for the decline being the growing inroads of British goods in the markets of Rajputana.

[29] See *Memoirs of Seth Naomal Hotchand*, pp. 41–5.

[30] J. Burnes, *A Narrative of a Visit to the Court of Sinde*, Edinburgh, 1831, 2nd edn, (1st edn, Bombay, 1829), p. 76.

anecdote which attibuted to the principal mir, Murad Ali, harsh words against the Hindus.[31] In the immediate aftermath of the events of 1842–43, Napier's entourage was particularly keen on conveying the impression that British conquest had resulted for the Hindus in 'liberation' from the Muslim yoke, so as to give a 'moral' justification to an annexation which was dictated by various considerations of a largely economic nature. One of Napier's critiques, Eastwick, was, however, quick to point out, that, if the Hindus had indeed been subjected to such indignities in Talpur Sind, it was difficult to explain why they had not fled to the benevolent abode of British India, which was so close.[32]

On the other hand, it would be wrong to think that under the Talpur regime Hindu–Muslim relations were idyllic. It can be argued that in pre-colonial Sind, there was a level at which Hindus and Muslims thought of themselves as separate, and even antagonistic communities. The memoirs of Seth Naomal Hotchand include a very interesting narrative of a large-scale conflict between Hindus and Muslims which took place across the whole of Sind in 1831, twelve years before the annexation of the province by the British. Seth Naomal's father, Seth Hotchand, probably at that time the richest Hindu merchant of Sind, became involved in the dispute as he was captured by a Muslim crowd bent on obtaining his conversion. There was even a rumour at the time that he had been forcibly circumcised, which was untrue. Eventually Mir Muradali, the leading Talpur amir of Sind, had to intervene to have him freed, but the Seth was so embittered with the experience that he chose to exile himself to the dominions of the Rao of Kutch. The episode throws interesting light on the kind of underlying tension which could exist between Hindus and Muslims and at times erupted into open violence. The Talpurs were to pay dearly for their ambiguous attitude during those events, because it is clear from the narrative that the young Naomal never forgave them, and this explains at least partly the pro-British attitude he took at the time of the conquest, which contributed significantly to the British victory. But there is another very interesting passage in the same text, which throws an entirely different light on the nature of Hindu–Muslim interaction in Sind. When he had been eventually released by his captors, a shocked Seth Hotchand announced publicly that he would thence become 'a Sufi fakir'.[33] Interestingly, in a footnote, the editor, a one-time commissioner in Sind,

[31] The mir is supposed to have exclaimed, in the face of evidence of treachery by a Hindu servant: 'You do not know the Hindus of Sinde; they are all blackguards and rascals.' *Ibid.*, p. 86.
[32] F. B. Eastwick, *A Glance at Sind before Napier or Dry Leaves from Young Egypt*, Karachi, 1973, reprint (1st edn, London, 1849), pp. 214–15.
[33] *Memoirs of Seth Naomal*, p. 68.

thought prudent to censure the Seth posthumously and to add, for our benefit, that 'Probably Seth Hotchand meant that he would become a Hindu ascetic or Jogi.' However, there is no reason to think that the writer, Seth Naomal, the son of Hotchand, did not know the difference between a *sufi fakir* and a Hindu *yogi*. It is highly probable that he actually meant what he said, and there was nothing extraordinary about such a statement. As noted earlier, for many centuries, in Sind as in other parts of India, many Hindus have been *murids* of the *sufi pirs*, without becoming Muslims.

I have chosen this episode to illustrate the complexity of the relationship between Hindus and Muslims in Sind, a relationship in which conflict and hostility mingled easily with amity and a syncretic attitude to religion. The relationship between the two communities was so fluid as to make generalizations about the situation of Hindus in Sind during the Talpur regime hazardous.[34] There is no doubt that an elite section of Hindu merchants and bankers based in Karachi and Hyderabad was a crucial component of the ruling class of Talpur Sind, even if its status was not equal to that of the great *waderos*, *pirs* and *sayeds* who lorded it over the mass of the *haris* (cultivators). This elite, which had close links with the other significant element of the Hindu population, the Amils, was not devoid of political influence even if it tended to maintain a low profile. The rest of the trading population, consisting mostly of shopkeepers and rural moneylenders, occupied a kind of middling position in Sind society, well below the elites, but far above the *haris*. On such a diverse group as the Hindus of Sind, the impact of colonial rule could but be uneven and diversified. It is therefore necessary to have a closer look at Hindu society in Sind during the colonial period.

Hindu society in colonial Sind: some general traits

At some point between the fifteenth and eighteenth centuries, as Islam spread among the peasant masses of Sind, the Hindus became a minority, but numerically a sufficiently significant one to present a varied and complex picture. There is a dearth of scholarly literature about this community, which is not compensated for by an abundance of primary written sources. Prior to the British annexation, Hindus in Sind do not seem to have produced any specific literature of a non-religious character. Apart from writing devotional Nanakpanthi hymns, literate Amils and *banias* also occasionally contributed to the rich *sufi literature which developed in Sind and culminated with the work of the*

[34] See L. M. M. Thakurdas, 'Hindus and Talpurs of Sind', *Modern Review*, vol. 51, 1932, pp. 265–72.

famous Shah Abdul Latif of Bhit. Even under British rule, while literacy developed significantly, especially amongst Amils, little was produced in the way of writings about the specificities of Hindu culture and society in Sind.[35] The British themselves paid relatively little attention to the Hindus in Sind, whom they perceived as an almost 'foreign' element, and colonial scholarship, which was often of a high quality, tended to focus more on Muslim society, culture and religion. Although some basic information was collected by colonial officials and gathered in the *Gazetteers*, in particular the 1907 edition,[36] it is a measure of the poor state of advancement of Sind studies that we still have to rely to a great extent on that kind of literature to get a general idea of Hindu society in pre-Partition Sind. In post-1947 Sind, a province of Pakistan where Hindus have been reduced to the condition of a fairly insignificant minority, little attention has been paid to their role in the history of the region. In India, where the bulk of the Sindhi Hindu population emigrated after 1947, a sociological survey conducted in the 1950s among refugees from Sind resulted in the only comprehensive study of Sindhi Hindu culture and society ever produced, U. T. Thakur's *Sindhi Culture*.[37] However inadequate and flawed in many ways, this book is invaluable inasmuch as the author collected from the Sindhi refugees a lot of information on their life in pre-Partition Sind, which would otherwise be lost. On the other hand, most of the more recent literature on Sindhis in India has tended to focus on their level of integration, and to distance itself from the study of their pre-Partition roots.

The following account, pieced together from these scattered and largely inadequate materials, aims only at giving a very general picture. Hindu society in pre-1947 Sind struck all observers coming from 'India proper' as very different from 'mainstream' Hindu society, to the point of being barely recognizable. The most striking characteristic of Sindhi Hindu society was undoubtedly the absence of a proper caste system, due to the dominance of one so-called caste, the Lohana, which was more or less considered to encompass the entire Hindu society of Sind. Actually, according to the data in the different censuses, Lohanas accounted only for half of the Hindu population of Sind,[38] but statistics tell only part of the story. Non-Lohana Hindus in pre-1947 Sind included a large fringe of 'tribals', especially in the Thar and Parkar district, who were very marginal elements in Hindu society. If these

[35] See, however, B. M. Advani, *Sindh-je-Hindus-je-Tarikh* (History of Sindh Hindus) (in Sindhi), Hyderabad.
[36] *Gazetteer of the Province of Sind*, compiled by E. H. Aitken, Karachi, 1907.
[37] U. T. Thakur, *Sindhi Culture*, Bombay, 1959.
[38] Calculated from Appendix A, 'Comparative Tables showing the number and distribution of various Hindu castes (1891 to 1931) in Sind', in *ibid.*, pp. 207–33.

'tribals' are not taken into account, Lohana predominance becomes even more pronounced. Other Hindu trading castes, like the Bhatias and the Khatris, were actually very close to the Lohanas and intermarried with them. The only non-Lohana group which was socially significant in pre-Partition Sind were the Brahmins, of whom there were two castes the Saraswat and the Pushkarna, but even the Brahmins, who were numerically fairly insignificant, and were therefore not represented in most villages, did not enjoy a status which was clearly superior to that of the higher Lohana sections. In many ways, in Sind, Brahmins were a sacerdotal service caste rather than a dominant caste.

Given the quasi-homology between Sindhi Hindu society and Lohana caste, the real hierarchical distinctions were internal to the so-called Lohana caste. Hierarchical ranking among Lohanas was threefold: there was at the most general level a distinction between a higher segment known as Amil and a lower segment increasingly known as Bhaiband, but there were also distinctions internal to both Amils and Bhaibands. The Amil–Bhaiband divide was a fairly recent product of history, as a group of Lohanas in government service differentiated themselves from the bulk of their caste fellows who remained in trading occupations. In the nineteenth century, the distinction between Amils and Bhaibands had become almost equivalent to a caste distinction, except for the fact that Amils tended to take wives from the Bhaibands, but not to give them any. The two segments thus had a symbiotic, but asymmetrical relationship, which was of particular significance in Hyderabad. Not all Amils were however of the same high status. In Hyderabad, there was a distinction between Khudabadi Amils (said to have originated from that ancient capital of Sind), who were deemed to be the *crème de la crème*, and non-Khudabadi Amils, whose status was slightly less exalted. The two sections did not apparently intermarry. Outside Hyderabad, some Amil groups, like the Chandkai Amils of Larkana, were similarly endowed with a particularly high status.

Amils did not account for more than 10–15 per cent of all Lohanas, and the bulk of the caste consisted of those non-Amil elements known under different appellations, the most common in the twentieth century being that of Bhaibands. The term, which literally means 'group of brothers', is polysemic, since Sindhi family firms are also sometimes known as Bhaibands. Among Bhaibands, status seems to have been based more on occupation and wealth than on any kind of ritual purity. Thus it seems that the highest status was conferred on the owners of great *kothis*, i.e. firms which were specialized in the grain and other commodity trades, while village shopkeepers-cum-moneylenders, sometimes known as *hatvanias*, were deemed of inferior status. Shikarpuri *shroffs* and Sindwork merchants of Hyderabad, the two groups with which we are concerned here, also enjoyed high status.

Apart from the absence of a proper caste system, another specific characteristic of Hindu society in Sind was the fluidity of religious identities and affiliations. The bulk of Sindhi Hindus were Nanakpanthis, i.e. non-Khalsa or Sahajdari Sikhs, but their Nanakpanthi faith blended harmoniously with non-sectarian forms of both Saivaism and Vaisnavism, the former being apparently more prevalent in Sind. Sind was less affected than the Punjab by the Singh Sabha movement, which resulted in a growing separation between Hindus and Sikhs, and the boundary was never clearly traced there.[39] There was some uncertainty as to whether the Nanakpanthis considered themselves Sikhs or Hindus. At the time of the 1881 Census many Lohanas in the districts of Shikarpur and Hyderabad were enumerated as Sikhs, while in the 1891 Census all of them were returned as Hindus.[40] The most widespread priestly group in Sind was not the Brahmins, who were represented only in the towns, but the *bawas*, the Nanakpanthi *desservants*, who were found in every village and every street in the towns, where they managed temples-cum-*gurdwaras* generally known as *tikhanas*, which were by far the most common non-Muslim places of worship in Sind. In those *tikhanas*, images of the Hindu gods were found side by side with the Adi Granth and the image of the Guru Nanak. The religious eclecticism of the Sindhi Hindus was also demonstrated by the importance of the cult of the Indus, which focused on the mythical Hindu hero, Uderolal, also known as Jhule Lal.[41] For many centuries, 'Jhule, Jhule Lal', was the

---

[39] For an interesting although controversial analysis of this question, centred on the Punjab, see H. Oberoi, *The Construction of Religious Boundaries: Culture, Identity and Diversity in the Sikh Tradition*, Delhi, 1994. To the best of my knowledge, no study has been done of the history of Sikhism in Sind.

[40] According to the 1881 Census, there were in Sind 126,976 Sikhs (including 68,655 in Shikarpur district and 42,940 in Hyderabad district) as against 305,079 Hindus (93,341 in Shikarpur and 89,114 in Hyderabad), suggesting that the majority of Lohanas in Shikarpur district and a large minority in Hyderabad district returned themselves as Sikhs. *Census of India, 1881, Operations and Results in the Presidency of Bombay including Sind*, J. A. Baines, vol. II, Tables, Bombay, 1882, Table III, pp. 3–6. However, by the time of the 1891 Census, the situation had been totally reversed, as only 720 Sikhs were enumerated in the whole of Sind, as against 567,536 Hindus. *Census of India, 1891*, vol. VIII, *Bombay and its Feudatories*, part II, *Imperial Tables*, W. W. Drew, Bombay, 1892, Table VI, pp. 26–7. Commenting on this puzzling change, the census commissioner attributed it to the fact that in the 1891 Census 'religion' and 'sect' were distinct categories, but that only the former had been taken into account. He surmised that most of those who had previously enumerated themselves as Sikhs returned themselves in 1891 as of Hindu religion and Sikh sect, which explained that they figured under the heading 'Hindus'. *Census of India, 1891*, vol. VIII, part I, *Report*, W. W. Drew, Bombay, 1892, p. 40.

[41] On Uderolal or Lal Udero, see 'Something about Lal Udero', in Sigma (Dayaram Gidumal), *Something about Sind*, Karachi, 1882, pp. 27–31.

rallying cry of the Hindus of Sind in time of crisis, and the most articulate expression of their separate religious identity in confrontations with their Muslim compatriots.

However, the most remarkable manifestation of the eclectic character of religion in Sind was the very widespread participation of members of the two major religious communities in the worship of saints belonging to the other community. Thus there is a lot of evidence that the majority of Hindus in Sind were *murids* of the *sufi pirs*, who played such an important role in Sindhi Islam.[42] Participation of Hindu *murids* in the cult of *sufi* saints was of course fairly common in the subcontinent, but the practice was more generalized among Sindhi Hindus than in any other region of India. By becoming *murids* of powerful *pirs*, Hindus were undoubtedly aiming at benefits which were not purely spiritual, for the protection extended by the *pirs* over their *murids* could be extremely useful socially and even economically for Hindus, especially those who lived in small isolated groups among the Muslim masses. In spite of this instrumental aspect, there is no reason to doubt the sincerity of the Hindu *murids* of *sufi pirs*. The love shown by many Sindhi Hindus for the mystical poetry of Shah Abdul Latif and other *sufi* mystics is eloquent testimony to it. It is interesting to note that, in Sind, Muslims in their turn participated in the worship of the *samadhi* of Hindu saints. Widespread participation by Hindus in the Muharram festivities in Sind is mentioned by the biographer of an important Hindu religious leader.[43]

The religious eclecticism of Sindhis did not prevent conflicts between religious communities, although they were less intense than in northern India. From the 1920s onwards, politics in Sind became increasingly communalized, as Hindus tended more and more to identify with the Congress Party, while Muslims generally remained aloof from it, before

---

[42] On the role of the *sufi pirs* in Sindhi islam, see S. F. D. Ansari, *Sufi Saints and State Power: the Pirs of Sind, 1843–1947*, Cambridge, 1992, pp. 19–35. Ansari mentions, p. 20, that Suhrawardi *sufis*, who were the first to be active in Sind, acquired Hindu followers 'in part as a result of the religious tolerance engendered by their belief in the doctrine of *wahdat-al-wujud*' (Unity of Being). Although this doctrine was later attacked by the Naqshbandis, *sufis* in Sind continued to accept Hindu disciples. The most influential of the *pirs*, the Pir Pagaro Sibghatullah Shah II (1921–43) systematically tried to win the trust of local Hindus by such gestures as the organization of a *shuddhi* ceremony for a Hindu who had converted to Islam and wished to be readmitted to his original faith. Mentioned in *ibid.*, pp. 137–8.

[43] Hari P. Vaswani, in his biography of his father Sadhu T. L. Vaswani, who was the main spiritual guide of Sindhi Hindus in the twentieth century, mentions that 'Hindus in Sind participated in the Muharram, the festival of the Muslims. They considered the *tabut* to be so very holy that they brought their new-born babes to it to be blessed. They also covered the *tabut* with their kerchiefs as a mark of respect and reverence.' H. P. Vaswani, *A Saint of Modern India*, Poona, 1975, p. 4.

shifting their support to the Muslim League in the late 1930s and the 1940s.[44] There is, however, a general consensus that the final exodus of the majority of Hindus from Sind in 1947–48 was not primarily the result of a conflict within Sind between Hindus and Muslims, but much more a consequence of the overall tragedy of Partition and of the massacres in the Punjab.[45] Although there is no need to idealize the religious situation in Sind, and see it as a model of mutual tolerance, it is nevertheless true that the province was relatively free of communal tension of the kind that affected the Punjab, Bengal or the United Provinces.[46] The eclectic character of regional Hinduism, as well as the impact of *sufism* on regional Islam certainly had something to do with it.

The Sind *banias* and the political economy of colonial Sind

A view which has gained widespread currency in Sind is that the Hindu *banias* were in many ways the main beneficiaries of the socioeconomic transformations undergone by the province during the British period. Such a view needs however to be nuanced. It has its source in a growing perception by the British of the Hindus as a group of parasitical interlopers. In the second half of the nineteenth century, this trend of increasing hostility to the Hindus on the part of British writers and officials is well illustrated by Sir Richard Burton's writings. In a book published in 1851,[47] he gave an account of the Hindus of Sind which was slightly malevolent, but maintained a certain degree of objectivity. In a book written in 1877 after a lengthy visit to the province, he launched an extraordinarily virulent attack against the character of the Hindus of Sind,[48] which enormously influenced officials as well as non-

---

[44] See N. Boreham, 'Decolonisation and Provincial Muslim Politics: Sind, 1937–47', *South Asia*, new series, vol. 16, no. 1, 1993, pp. 53–72.

[45] See S. Anand, *National Integration of Sindhis*, Delhi, 1996, in particular ch. 2, 'Partition and Mass Exodus', pp. 22–60.

[46] The most significant episode of communal violence in Sind occurred in 1939 around the so-called Manzilgah agitation in Sukkur. See H. Khuhro, 'Masjid Manzilgah, 1939–40: Test Case for Hindu–Muslim Relations in Sind', *Modern Asian Studies*, vol. 32, no. 1, 1998, pp. 49–89.

[47] R. F. Burton, *Sindh and the Races that Inhabit the Valley of the Indus, with Notices of the Topography and History of the Province*, London, 1851, in particular chapter 12, 'The Hindoos of Sindh', pp. 309–37.

[48] R. F. Burton, *Sindh Revisited*, London, 1877, in particular vol. I, chapter 14, significantly entitled 'The Hindus of Sind – their Rascality and their Philoprogenitiveness', pp. 269–95, from where I extract this passage about the *banias*, pp. 283–4: 'he then takes his place in the shop, where, if you please, we shall leave him to cheat and haggle, to spoil and adulterate, and to become as speedily rich by the practice of as much conventional and commercial rascality, barely within the limits of actual felony, as he can pass off upon the world'.

officials. Since this book is not about colonial discourse, I shall not examine his views in detail. However he started a trend, and the long-term impact of such stereotypes has been important.

The anti-Hindu argument is mostly based on the claim that a large-scale transfer of land took place into the hands of Hindu *banias*. Although there is some evidence of such transfer, it is difficult to quantify it. A major problem is that little is known of the amount of land which was in Hindu hands at the time of the annexation. British officials, in Sind as elsewhere in India, were prone to exaggerating the amount of such transfers to what they perceived to be a largely parasitical class of moneylenders. They passed various pieces of legislation to try to prevent such transfers, starting with the first Sind Encumbered Estates Act of 1876, but in 1896 the then commissioner in Sind, our old acquaintance Sir Evan Jones, claimed that more than 42 per cent of arable land in the province was owned or held in beneficiary possession under mortgage by Hindus.[49] New measures were then passed which resulted in some effective curb on the level of indebtedness of the peasantry and the *zamindar*. There would thus appear to be two rather distinct phases in the agrarian history of British Sind. During the second half of the nineteenth century, the *banias* would have enormously increased their landholdings, either directly or indirectly, but the trend would have been somewhat reversed in the twentieth century.

The most detailed study of rural moneylending in Sind, by David Cheesman,[50] unfortunately limits itself to the nineteenth century and does not follow up its argument for the first half of the twentieth century. Cheesman argues that basically the *banias* were traders who used indebtedness as a mechanism to procure agricultural products. They were not interested in the earnings of moneylending, because their real profits were in the sales of agricultural products which they obtained cheap from cultivators and *zamindars* who were indebted to them. That is why they tried to avoid settlements in court and foreclosed only in the last resort. One could add that it was not very lucrative for them to become landowners, because they had problems mobilizing labour to work the land. Cheesman's analysis is very similar to that presented for the Punjab by Neeladiri Bhattacharya, who distinguishes between two groups of moneylenders, one which he calls 'usurers', mostly comprised of Pathans, who were mainly interested in extracting high interest rates

---

[49] See R. D. Choksey, *The Story of Sind (An Economic Survey), 1843–1933*, Poona, 1983, pp. 130–1.
[50] D. Cheesman, *Landlord Power and Rural Indebtedness in Colonial Sind 1865–1901*, London, 1997. See also H. Khuhro, *The Making of Modern Sind: British Policy and Social Change in the Nineteenth Century*, Karachi, 1978.

on short-term loans, and systematically resorted to the threat of violence to recover the debts, and another group, which he calls 'merchant-moneylenders' who lent at less extortionate rates and were mainly interested in appropriating the produce.[51] Although it is not sure that such a clear distinction could always actually be made 'on the ground', it appears that in Sind *banias* generally conformed to the second model, that of the 'merchant-moneylender'.

The picture Cheesman draws of nineteenth-century Sind, based on a thorough study of official archives, is rather different from that given by officials themselves. He shows that, in spite of transfer of lands to the Hindus on a significant scale, the *wadero* class maintained its hold on the countryside. British fears of a displacement of the *waderos* had no real basis in fact, and the measures taken by the government, such as the different Sind Encumbered Estates Acts, were actually of a rather cosmetic nature. They did not attack the root of the problem of indebtedness, but they gave the *waderos* the feeling that the *sarkar* cared for them, and they showed their gratitude by remaining steadfastly loyal to British rule. Structural change in Sind during the colonial period remained very limited. The *banias* undoubtedly acquired land, and generally showed themselves to be efficient managers of their estates.[52] But they remained in many ways dependent on the *waderos*, in particular in all their dealings with the agricultural labourers, the *haris*. Being a class without social prestige in comparison with the *waderos*, *pirs* and *sayeds*, *banias* could not expect any loyalty and attachment on the part of the *haris*, nor could they strike fear in their hearts. They were in the countryside basically on sufferance of the *waderos*, and the latter brought it home to them in various ways, in particular by a controlled use of violence. Murders of moneylenders were a common occurrence in the Sind countryside, probably more than in most other regions of the subcontinent, and the culprits were rarely, if ever, caught and convicted.[53] Everything suggests that these murders were generally not spontaneous acts of revenge perpetrated by aggrieved *haris* but were organized with the connivence and support of the *waderos*. In spite of their wealth, which could be considerable, *banias* were not a hegemonic class in Sind.

To explain why some of the Sind *banias* were tempted by outside ventures in the second half of the nineteenth century, ventures which are precisely the topic of this book, one could point to the high level of risk

---

[51] See N. Bhattacharya, 'Lenders and Debtors: Punjab Countryside, 1880–1940', *Studies in History*, new series, vol. 1, no. 2, 1985, pp. 305–42.
[52] See Cheesman, *Landlord Power*, p. 164.
[53] For some instances, see *ibid.*, pp. 186–8.

The regional context 53

and uncertainty which their operations in the countryside entailed. A knowledge of the trend in grain prices is also essential, since it was the main commodity in which they traded. Data on grain prices in Sind during the second half of the nineteenth century indicate a secular rise,[54] which suggests that the profit margins of the *bania* were not squeezed. But, in spite of this, it can be said with a degree of confidence that rural moneylending in Sind remained a high-risk operation, even if the rewards could also be substantial. *Banias* are often said to be gamblers, but there are limits to the level of risk they are ready to accept. They also tend to diversify their assets, or, as popular wisdom has it, not to put all their eggs in the same basket. But in Sind during the first three decades of British rule, opportunities in the non-rural sector were limited.

The British annexation of Sind led to difficulties in four major areas: state finance, currency exchange, craft production and the transit trade. As regards state finance, at the time of the annexation of Sind, the British already had a well-established treasury system, and they did not need advances from local bankers. Lending to the state was the major business of the Sind bankers, particularly of those in Hyderabad, and they were therefore forced to find new outlets. They also lost a thriving business in currency exchange, as the Company rupee was introduced as the legal tender, in place of different local currencies, and as the transit trade with neighbouring regions went through a depression. The crisis in the transit trade of Sind had multiple dimensions. The closing of the opium trade from Malwa was certainly one of the most important. But, following disorders in Khelat and Afghanistan, the hoped-for revival of Central Asian trade did not take place on the expected scale, while the Indus river did not prove to be the great waterway to the Punjab and Central Asia that ill-informed reports had led the Company to believe that it would be. Similarly, craft production entered a period of crisis as the court and the army, which were its main customers, disappeared, and the merchants who used to organize and finance production were in difficult straits. Therefore, in the aftermath of the annexation, some *banias* were looking for new avenues of investment for their capital.

During the 1843–75 period, the most enterprising elements among the Sind *banias* sought opportunities outside the province. The Shikarpuris and the Bhatias of Thatta renewed and deepened existing outside

---

[54] According to the *Gazetteer of the Province of Sind*, p. 331, the average price of *bajra*, the staple grain crop in Sind, went up from Rs 1–1–10 per maund during 1844–50 to Rs 2–7–0 in 1896–1905.

connections, while some Hyderabadi merchants established entirely new connections.

This new orientation was strengthened by other developments relating to the role of Sind in the economy of British India. While, prior to the annexation, Sind was a participant in a wide-ranging system of interregional and international trade, under British rule, its function was increasingly reduced to that of an outlet for the agricultural production of the Punjab. In the second half of the nineteenth century, the bulk of the investment the British made in Sind was in the construction of a modern harbour in Karachi and of railway lines linking the port with the Punjab.[55] The decision taken in 1847 to make Sind part of the Bombay presidency, with which it had only weak economic and cultural links, eventually proved farsighted. For it amounted to an indirect subsidy by Bombay to the Punjab.[56] Sind's transformation into the maritime outlet of the Punjab mostly benefited Karachi, more than ever its only modern sea-port, although the development of railway traffic between Punjab and Karachi energized the economies of the towns which were situated along the railway line.

At this juncture, it is necessary to investigate in some detail the reasons why the Sind *banias* were incapable of preserving their long-standing hegemony over provincial trade and finance, and why in particular they could not prevent 'outsiders' from acquiring dominant positions in Karachi, which emerged in the second half of the nineteenth century as the lynchpin of the provincial economy. Some of the reasons have to do simply with the establishment of British domination. After 1839 and even more after 1843, British firms from Bombay, with their relatively large capital resources, and their good knowledge of overseas markets, particularly in cotton, were in a position to corner the best opportunities in foreign trade in Karachi. The foundation of the Karachi Chamber of Commerce in 1860 epitomised the dominant role played by

[55] On the growth of the port of Karachi and its connections with the Punjab, see A. F. Baillie, *Kurrachee (Karachi), Past, Present and Future*, London, 1890, and I. Banga, 'Karachi and its Hinterland under Colonial Rule', in I. Banga (ed.), *Ports and their Hinterlands in India (1700–1950)*, Delhi, 1992, pp. 337–58.

[56] In the second half of the nineteenth century it was Bombay revenue which largely paid for the construction of a port which served primarily the Punjab. For Punjab finances it was a very good operation, and it explains why Punjab officials were never particularly keen to have Sind become part of their province. In 1903, when Sir Denzil Ibbetson, having been made lieutenant-governor of the Punjab, tried to have his domain (which had been diminished by the separation of the North-West Frontier Province in 1901) increased by the inclusion of Sind, Lord Curzon, whose grasp of interprovincial financial transfers was better than Ibbetson's, quashed his attempt. See P. Mahto, 'The Separation of Sind from Bombay Presidency', in M. Y. Mughul (ed.), *Studies in Sind*, Jamshoro, 1989.

these firms in the trade of Karachi.[57] But, in the wake of the annexation, other groups of traders came from British India, particularly from Bombay, and established themselves on the Karachi market. Prominent among them were Parsi contractors, who rapidly controlled the market of supplies to British troops and British civilians, a particularly lucrative branch of trade. From the commissariat, the Parsis quickly branched out into other fields, and by the late nineteenth century they were the most powerful group in the trading world of Karachi after the British.[58] Parsi firms in Karachi ceased after a while to be mere branches of Bombay firms and they became a power in their own right. Other groups of newcomers from Bombay who were active in trade in Karachi included Jewish traders as well as Gujarati *banias*. Some groups which were already active before the annexation, such as the Ismaili Khojas and the Kutchi Memons, were reinforced by an influx of immigrants from Bombay and Kutch. The increasingly close connection of the port with the Punjab and adjacent regions of northern India also attracted Punjabi and Marwari traders. It is striking that the major trading houses of Sind *banias* in Karachi, such as those of Seth Naomal Hotchand and Wissundas Khemchand, went into rapid decline after the annexation. The only group of Sind *banias* who held their own in Karachi during the second half of the nineteenth century appear to have been the Shikarpuris, who were able to carve a niche for themselves as intermediaries between the small town and village traders of Sind and the big trading houses of Karachi,[59] and also exploited their Central Asian connections to monopolize some lines of trade, such as the export of British piecegoods to southeastern Iran. But, on the whole, it can be said that in the second half of the nineteenth century the Sind *banias* lost ground in their own province, largely because other groups superseded them in the major trading centre of the province, Karachi. *Vis-à-vis* Karachi the two major groups of Sind *banias*, the Hyderabadis, on the one hand and the Shikarpuris on the other hand, adopted different strategies. While the latter sought to carve a niche there for themselves, the former tried to

---

[57] See H. Feldman, *One Hundred Years of Karachi*, Karachi, 1960.
[58] On the Parsis in Karachi, see T. R. Metcalf and S. B. Freitag, 'Karachi's Early Merchant Families: entrepreneurship and community', in D. K. Basu, *The Rise and Growth of the Colonial Port Cities in Asia*, Berkeley, CA, 1985, pp. 55–9.
[59] On the role of the Shikarpuris in Karachi, see Banga, 'Karachi and its Hinterland', pp. 357–8: 'The Shikarpuri Banias . . . migrated to Karachi to take over its grain and cotton trade as brokers which placed them in a position of dominance in the commodity export trade . . . Their firms or bhaibands played an important role in the Buyers and Shippers Chamber – an organization of firms engaged in maritime trade. They dominated the Karachi Indian Merchants Association founded in 1902 and played an important role in the Karachi Cotton Association founded in 1933.'

bypass it altogether and to develop direct links to Bombay, a strategy which proved farsighted.

So as to understand how merchants from two medium-sized towns in the interior of Sind could control far-flung networks covering, on the one hand, a vast area of Central Asia, from southeastern Persia to southwestern Sinkiang, and, on the other hand, extending to the whole world, along the maritime routes between Kobe in Japan and Panama in Central America, the following two chapters will present separately the history of the Shikarpuri and the Hyderabadi networks.

3 The Gate of Khorrassan: the Shikarpuri network, c. 1750–1947

In May 1837, Alexander Burnes, then on a 'commercial' mission to Kabul, wrote from Bahawalpur a paper 'On the Commerce of Shikarpoor and Upper Sinde', in which he gave a detailed description of the town, its trade and its merchants.[1] He wrote: 'Shikarpoor is a town of first importance to the Indus trade and it may be said, to that of Asia', laying the basis for what was to develop into a kind of myth and exercise some influence on British policymakers. Stressing the town's proximity to the Bolan Pass leading to Kandahar, he mentioned that the merchants always spoke of Shikarpoor and Dera Ghazee Khan as 'the gates of Khorrassan, by which name they here distinguish the kingdom of Cabul'. He estimated the population to be in excess of 30,000, of whom nin-tenths were Hindus, 'of the Bunya, Lohana and Bhattea (Bhatia) tribes', of whom more than half were 'Baba Nanuk Seiks' (i.e. Nanakshahis or Nanakpanthis, Sahajdari Sikhs). By Bunya, he actually meant Khatri. He did not praise the physical appearance of the town, finding the bazaar 'without elegance or beauty' and the houses 'lofty and comfortable but destitute of elegance'. What most impressed him, undoubtedly, was the extent of the network of the Shikarpuri merchants. He wrote: 'It will only be necessary to name the towns at which the Shikarpoor merchants have agents to judge of the unlimited influence which they can command.' There followed an enumeration of localities, of which the westernmost was Astrakhan and the easternmost Calcutta, where Shikarpuri merchants had their agents. It was an impressive list, and the total area covered was vast, including Masqat in Arabia, all the important towns of Afghanistan, some towns in Persia, some of the major towns of India, the three principal towns in the Uzbek khanates of Central Asia, Bukhara, Samarkand and Kokand, as well as Yarkand in Sinkiang. He added that in all these places a bill could be negotiated, and that with most of them there was a direct trade

[1] A. Burnes, 'On the Commerce of Shikarpoor and Upper Sinde', *Reports and Papers, Political, Commercial and Geographical Submitted to the Government* . . ., Bombay, 1839, Commercial, pp. 23–31.

58   Indian merchants, 1750–1947

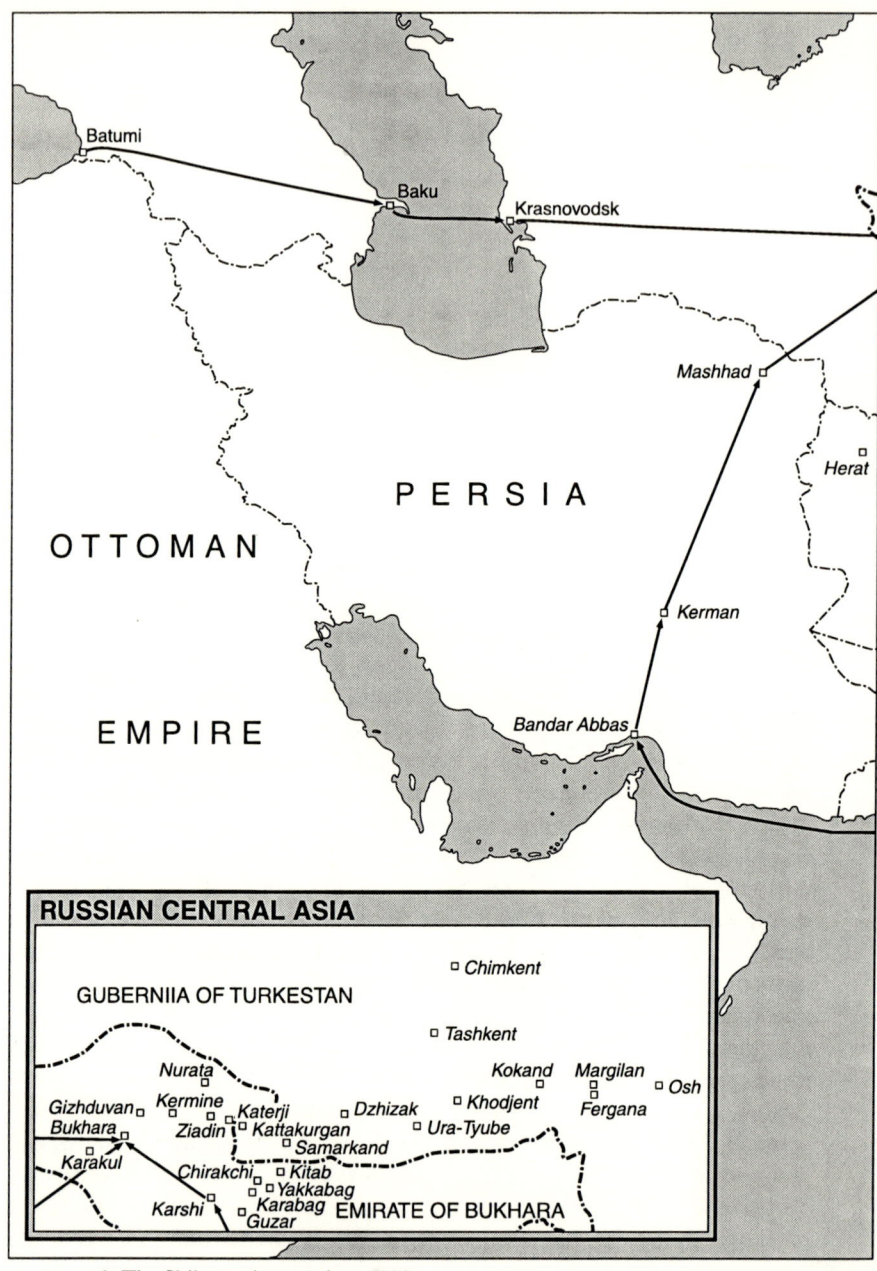

2 The Shikarpuri network, c. 1900.
Source: Base Mondiale ESRI (DWC), C. Markovits, M. Legrand and F. Pirot, 1998

The Gate of Khorrassan

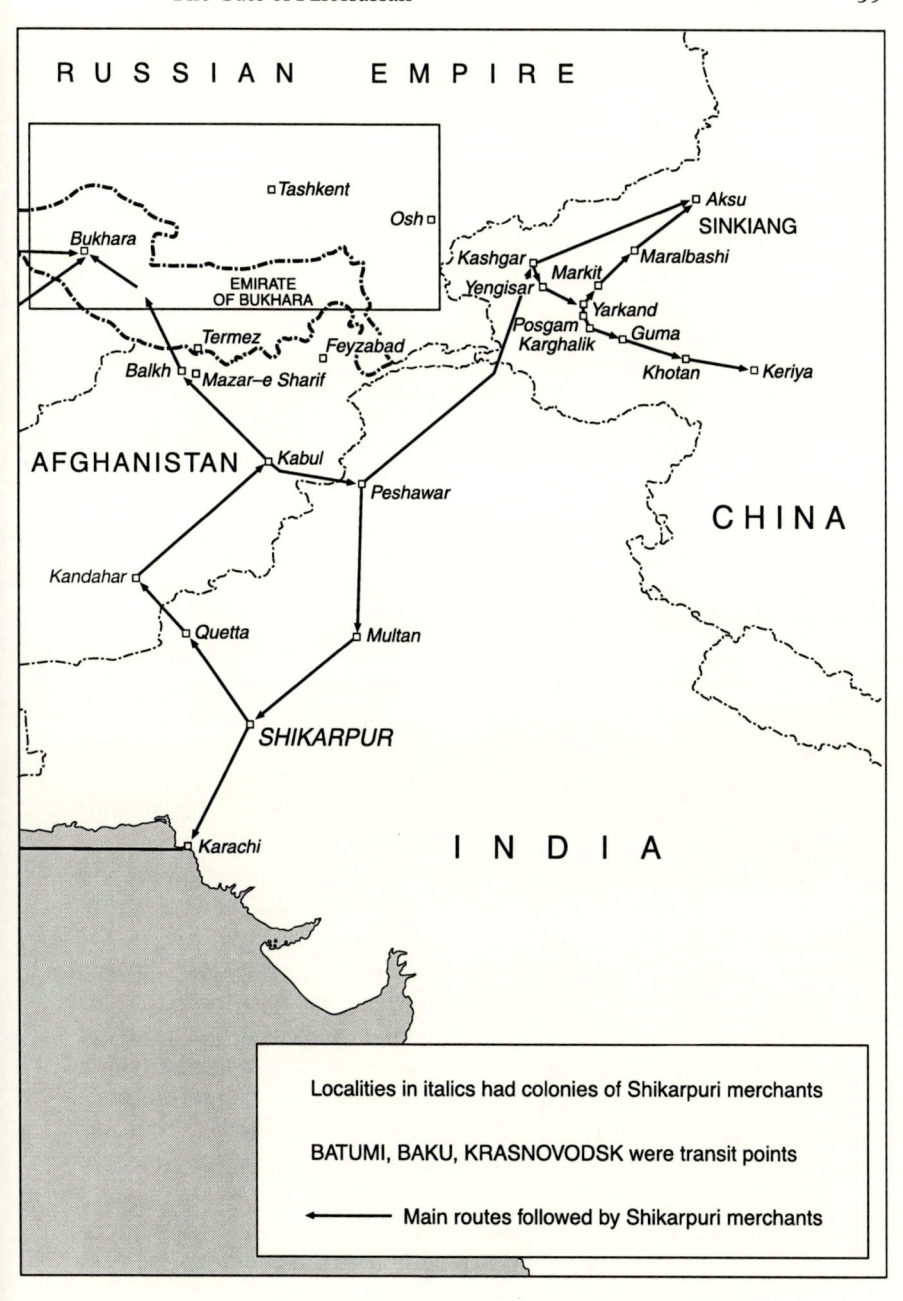

Localities in italics had colonies of Shikarpuri merchants

BATUMI, BAKU, KRASNOVODSK were transit points

⬅ Main routes followed by Shikarpuri merchants

either from Shikarpur or one of its subordinate agencies. He did not dwell at length on the geographical situation of the town and gave a very perfunctory account of its history, dating its prosperity from the year 1786, in the reign of Timur Shah.

Although there are many gaps and inadequacies in Burnes' picture of Shikarpur in the late 1830s, he was one of the first to draw attention to the existence of a Shikarpuri diaspora across Central Asia. The town was to figure prominently in British accounts of Sind at the time of its conquest and annexation during 1839–43, prior to falling into complete oblivion. The story of its rise to prominence as a financial centre for a vast region of Asia remains however riddled with uncertainties.

The origins of the Shikarpuri network

Questions remain as to the actual connection between Multan and Shikarpur, and as to the exact chronological sequence. The term 'Multani' has been in use intermittently, applied to different groups of merchants of northwest India. In the thirteenth century, the term was used by the historian Zia Barani and applied to rich merchant-bankers in Delhi, who were said to have come from Multan.[2] After having apparently fallen into disuse, it seems to have been used in the seventeenth century as a generic term to designate the North Indian merchants who traded in Central Asia and Russia, and particularly the colony of them residing in Astrakhan on the Caspian Sea.[3] Most of these merchants were Khatris, but there appear to have been amongst them also *banias* from Gujarat and Rajasthan. They operated a far-flung network extending from northern India to Russia through Iran and Central Asia. The presence of these merchants is thus attested to in Bukhara from at least the middle of the sixteenth century.[4] In the eighteenth century, following restrictions on their activities in Russia and difficulties in Iran, this network appears to have been on the decline. On the other hand, Shikarpur looms large in the commercial and financial history of the Durrani 'Empire' which established a measure of control over the caravan trade between India and Central Asia around the 1750s. The merchant-bankers of Shikarpur are generally also referred to as Khatris. Hence the existence of a widely accepted

---

[2] Zia Barani, *Tarikh-i-Firuz Shahi*, Sayid Ahmad Khan (ed.), Calcutta, 1862, pp. 305–7, quoted in I. Habib, 'Merchant Communities in Pre-colonial India', in J. Tracy (ed.), *The Rise of Merchant Empires: Long-distance Trade in the Early Modern World*, Cambridge, 1990, p. 373.

[3] According to S. Dale, the name was used in Iran and Turan in reference to all the merchants from the Punjab. Dale, *Indian Merchants and Eurasian Trade*, p. 55.

[4] A. Burton, *The Bukharans*, London, 1997, p. 5.

theory that in the second half of the eighteenth century there was a large-scale transfer of capital and men from Multan to Shikarpur. This theory is, however, based on little hard documentary evidence and has to be taken with caution. Sources relating to Multan generally date the decline of the city as a major commercial centre from the time of a short-lived Maratha invasion which took place in 1759.[5] On the other hand, there is some uncertainty as to the exact moment when Shikarpur emerged as an important centre. The version proposed by Alexander Burnes in 1837 that the prosperity of Shikarpur 'may be dated from the year 1786, in the reign of Timur Shah, who first established Hindoos in the town'[6] seems open to question as no *firman* or other document emanating from Timur Shah has come to light to support Burnes' contention. There is, however, a different version in a Pashto history published in Afghanistan.[7] That text traces the origins of the dominant role played by Hindus and Sikhs in the trade and finance of Afghanistan in the nineteenth and part of the twentieth century to an earlier phase in Afghan history when merchants from Shikarpur financed several of Ahmad Shah's military campaigns into the Punjab and northern India and in payment received part of the loot which they then put back into circulation. The Russian historian Gankovsky mentions that 'merchants and usurers from the city of Shikarpur' financed Ahmad Shah's campaigns.[8] This version probably has its ultimate source in Charles Masson's travel memoirs published in 1842.[9] If credence is given to it, it becomes more difficult to argue for too direct a correlation between Multan's decline and Shikarpur's rise. A supplementary argument

---

[5] See Dale, *Indian Merchants and Eurasian Trade*, pp. 130–1.
[6] Burnes, 'On the Commerce of Shikarpoor and Upper Sinde', p. 24.
[7] *Didgah Kotah ba Pushtunha-i-ansui-marz* (A short glance of the Pushtuns on the other side), Kabul, AH 1374, p. 11, quoted in Z. A. Gulzad, *External Influences and the Development of the Afghan State in the Nineteenth Century*, New York, 1994, p. 38, n. 28.
[8] See Yu. Gankovsky, 'The Durrani Empire', in USSR Academy of Sciences, *Afghanistan Past and Present*, Moscow, 1981, pp. 84–5.
[9] Charles Masson, *Narrative of Various Journeys in Baloochistan, Afghanistan and the Panjab, Including a Residence in these Countries from 1826 to 1838*, London, 1842, p. 355: 'To the curious in Durrani history, it may be pointed out, that from Shikarpur were supplied the funds which set on foot those successive inroads into, and invasions of the neighbouring countries, which are recorded in every page of it.' On Masson, whose real name was James Lewis, a deserter of the British Army who led the life of an adventurer before being pardoned and officially enrolled as a British spy, see G. Whitteridge, *Charles Masson of Afghanistan*, Warminster, 1985. Interestingly, Masson's views were criticized at the beginning of the twentieth century by Sir Thomas Holdich, a British general involved in border negotiations with Afghanistan, who wrote: 'whether Masson is correct in his estimate of the mischief done by the reckless supply of funds from Shikarpur to the restless nobles of Afghanistan . . . is, I think, doubtful. The want of money never stayed an Afghan raid – on the contrary it was more apt to instigate it', thus displaying a surprising ignorance of the mechanics of tribal warfare. Sir T. Holdich, *The Gates of India, Being an Historical Narrative*, London, 1910, p. 363.

pointing in the same direction is that, contrary to the version given by Stephen Dale, Multani merchants in Astrakhan remained active during the first half of the nineteenth century, and maintained a connection with the Punjab. This is corroborated in particular by evidence about two very large successions which came to the knowledge of the British authorities.[10] There was still a Multani network in Russia in the first half of the nineteenth century which was apparently distinct from the Shikarpuri network operating in the Central Asian khanates.

It is most probable then that there were Hindu *banias* in Shikarpur from the time when the town was founded in 1617 as a hunting resort (hence its name of Shikarpur) by members of the Daudputra clan which at a later stage ruled over Bahawalpur. However, the rise to prominence of the Shikarpuri *banias* coincided with the transformation of the town into the financial capital of the Durrani Empire, a transformation which was no doubt facilitated by its relative proximity to the first Durrani capital, Kandahar, with which it was linked through the Bolan Pass route, one of the routes used by the *kafilas* connecting Upper Sind and northern India with Afghanistan and Central Asia. The ranks of the Shikapuri *banias* were strengthened by a constant stream of migration from outside, judging from Burnes' account and also from the census taken by the British in 1840–41, according to which the town had a Hindu majority. It seems difficult to imagine that all the migrant *banias* hailed from Multan. A 'History of Shikarpur' compiled in 1854 by Captain F. G. Goldsmid,[11] praises the local Muslims for 'tamely (suffering) themselves to be outnumbered by an influx of Hindoos from all quarters of the compass'.[12] Judging from later ethnographical data and the evidence of onomastics, it would appear that the origins of the Shikarpuri *banias* were indeed very diverse. In a sample of merchants of Shikarpur who left estates in Central Asia in the late nineteenth and

---

[10] A large succession in Astrakhan, known to the Russian authorities as the 'succession Mojoundassoff et Rouchelaraeff', the value of which was estimated to be close to 200,000 roubles (£28,000) was traced in 1861 to a Punjabi from Jhang district. The bulk of it consisted of a sum of money paid in compensation for the destruction, during the Russo-Persian war of 1828, of fisheries which had been farmed to a partnership of two Multani merchants. See Public Despatch to India no. 101, 17 August 1861, in *Selections from Despatches Addressed to the Several Governments in India by the Secretary of State in Council between the 1 January and the 31 December 1861*, London, 1862, pp. 362–7. Another succession, the Vokatria succession, worth £5,000, was traced to a family in Multan. Public Despatch to India no. 19 of Sir Charles Wood, 17 February 1863, IOR, Public & Judicial Department Records, Public Despatches to Bengal and India 1830–79.

[11] 'Shikarpoor – An Historical Memoir, by Captain F. G. Goldsmid', in *Selections from the Records of the Bombay Government*, new series, XVII, *Memoirs on Shikarpoor: the Syuds of Roree and Bukkur: the Khyrepoor State; etc.*, Bombay, 1855, pp. 1–70.

[12] *Ibid.*, part II, p. 24.

twentieth centuries, Khatris did not account for more than 5 per cent of the total, while Lohanas represented the vast majority. Some of the Lohanas, however, had names which indicated a Marwari origin. Of the *banias* who settled in the second half of the eighteenth century, some undoubtedly hailed from Multan and other localities in the Punjab, but there were also *banias* from Iran (where, according to S. Dale, there was a very large Hindu merchant community in the seventeenth century, mostly settled in Isfahan), Afghanistan, Rajasthan, Gujarat, as well as from other localities in Sind. Shikarpur in the second half of the eighteenth century appears to have been a kind of *bania* 'melting pot', where merchants of different origins established a residence and over time developed a very specific sense of identity.

Thus Hindu merchants who lived in dispersed colonies in the Islamic lands of Central Asia who had been known as Multanis, although they did not all originate from that town in the Punjab, gradually became known as Shikarpuris. A look at different travel accounts over a period of thirty years will give an idea of the transition between a 'Multani' and a 'Shikarpuri' network. In his account of his travels of 1782–83 through Iran and the Caspian region on his way from India to Russia, George Forster, a Madras civilian, drew an interesting picture of the 'Multani' network as he saw it operate in the late eighteenth century.[13] According to him, the range of the Hindu merchants of Multan and Jaisalmer in Iran extended as far west as the town of Turshish, where he found about one hundred families engaged in the selling of English cloth which they procured through Yezd.[14] He also observed an active group of Multani merchants in Baku, where, together with Armenian merchants, they dominated local trade. He crossed the Caspian Sea to Astrakhan in a boat in the company of two Multani merchants who were going there 'on a commercial adventure',[15] a clear indication that 'Multanis' were still active in Astrakhan in the 1780s.

In an account of his travels in Baluchistan in 1810, Henry Pottinger, who was to play an important role in the British annexation of Sind, mentions both Shikarpur and Multan as the places from where the Hindu merchants he met in Bela, Khelat and other localities, originated,[16] thus suggesting a certain lack of differentiation between the two groups. The first mention of the Shikarpuris as a group completely different from the Multanis seems to occurr in a manuscript written in Persian by Mir Izzatullah in 1813, recording a visit to Central Asia in

[13] G. Forster, *A Journey from Bengal to England*, London, 1808, 3rd edn (reprint Patiala, 1970).
[14] *Ibid.*, vol. II, pp. 186–7.   [15] *Ibid.*, p. 291.
[16] H. Pottinger, *Travels in Beloochistan and Sinde*, London, 1816, pp. 19–20, 36–7, 77–8.

1812–13.[17] This Indian traveller informs us that 'Hindus of Shikarpur are to be found in considerable numbers in Bokhara; they go there merely for purposes of trade, and remain a year or two, at the end of which they return to their own country, never settling permanently in that country'.[18] There is no mention of Multanis in his account, and subsequent texts generally call 'Shikarpuris' the Hindu merchants found in Afghanistan, in Iran and across Central Asia. However the term Multani was not completely discarded, and George Nathaniel Curzon, the future viceroy, travelling in Russian Central Asia in the 1880s, reported that it was still in use.[19] In India also in the 1920s, the Shikarpuri *shroffs* were generally known as Multanis.

Although no final conclusion can be drawn as to the exact chronological sequence of the transition from a 'Multani' to a 'Shikarpuri' network, by the time the British took a close interest in the town, in the 1830s, it was clearly established as the centre of an extended merchant network encompassing most of Central Asia. The rudimentary census taken by the British after they had occupied Shikarpur and made it their forward base for the advance into Afghanistan gives interesting indications about the local *bania* population. It identified 903 'Hindoo shops', which it divided according to categories, such as grain sellers, cloth merchants, dealers in salt and sundries, etc. The merchant aristocracy of the town consisted of the two categories of 'soucars' (*sahukars*) and 'shroffs' (*sarrafs*), whose numbers are given respectively as thirty-five and sixty-six. It is actually difficult to distinguish between the two groups: *sarrafs* are usually moneychangers, dealers in bills of exchange and deposit bankers, while *sahukars* are big merchants. One finds also included in the census 'many Hindoos, who are employed in distant countries as agents from the Soucars, returning at various periods to their families, who are always left at Shikarpoor'.[20] It was among the 'Soucars' then that the richest merchants of Shikarpur were found. The names of some of them have even come down to us: Juyut Sing, Ram

---

[17] Mir Izzatullah, *Masir-i-Bukhara*, written for William Moorcroft. There are several versions of this manuscript, which was translated for the first time into English by H. H. Wilson in 1825. See M. Szuppé, 'En quête de chevaux turkmènes: le journal de voyage de Mir Izzatullah de Delhi à Boukhara en 1812–1813', *Cahiers d'Asie Centrale*, no. 1–2, 1996, pp. 91–111. A more recent, though slightly abridged translation, was published as *Travels in Central Asia by Meer Izzut Oollah in the years 1812–13. Translated by Captain Henderson*, Calcutta, 1872.

[18] *Travels in Central Asia by Meer Izzut Oollah*, pp. 64–5.

[19] G. N. Curzon, *Russia in Central Asia in 1889 and the Anglo-Russian Question*, London, 1889, p. 172.

[20] 'Miscellaneous Information Connected with the Town of Shikarpoor, by the Late Lieutenant T. Postans', in *Selections from the Bombay Records*, new series, no. XVII, Bombay, 1855, pp. 85–93.

Dass, Dwarka Dass, Chuman Dass, Duya Ram Lohana and Narayan Dass Bhatia. Of the first, Captain Goldsmid says that, 'he looks and moves the aristocratic banker and merchant every inch', while Ram Dass is described as a 'very shrewd, useful Sahookar'.[21]

When it comes, however, to analysing the exact role played by the Shikarpuris in the system of commercial exchange between northern India and Central Asia, we are again faced with the existence of enormous gaps in our information. All contemporary travellers, as well as later writers (who are few) agree that the importance of Shikarpur to Central Asian trade was more that of a financial centre than of a trading emporium. All concur to state that, as a purely trading town, it could not compete with Dera Ghazi Khan, Multan or Bahawalpur, whose productions contributed much more to the trade with Central Asia than those of the modest workshops of Shikarpur and of its fertile but small *umland*. There is also unanimous agreement on the fact that it was the Shikarpuri *shroffs*, and not those of neighbouring towns, who played the major role in organizing and financing the caravan trade from Hind to Khorrassan and Turkestan. Therefore the town's appellation as the 'Gate of Khorrassan' was no misnomer. Little is known though of the way in which the Shikarpuri *shroffs* financed the Central Asian trade, except for the ubiquity of the Shikarpuri *hundi* (bill of exchange), which various travellers reported using to avoid carrying specie on the dangerous roads of Central Asia. Alexander Burnes, probably the best-known of these travellers, informs us that, when in Kabul, the Shikarpuri bankers of the place offered to provide him with *hundis* payable at Bukhara, Astrakhan or St Macaire (Nijni-Novgorod) and that he took up their offer on Bukhara, to his complete satisfaction.[22]

But this does not tell us anything on the amount of bills negotiated or their actual currency. Writing about Bukhara, twenty years before Burnes, Mir Izzatullah remarked that 'bills of exchange are not procurable except from the Hindu merchants of Shikarpur, who are occasionally induced to grant drafts on their firms or local agents; for this accommodation they often charge from twenty to twenty-five per cent'.[23] From this text, three inferences can be drawn: (a) that the Shikarpuris

---

[21] Goldsmid, 'Shikarpoor – An Historical Memoir . . .', p. 45.
[22] Burnes was even led to draw from this experience lessons of a philosophical nature, as in the following excerpt: 'what a gratifying proof have we here of the high character of our nation, to find the bills of those who almost appeared as beggars cashed, without hesitation, in a foreign and far distant capital. Above all, how much is our wonder excited to find the ramifications of commerce extending uninterruptedly over such vast and remote regions, differing as they do from each other in language, religion, manners and laws.' A. Burnes, *Travels into Bokhara Together with a Narrative of a Voyage on the Indus*, London, 1834, 1st edn (reprint, Karachi, 1973), vol. I, pp. 169–70.
[23] *Travels in Central Asia by Meer Izzut Oollah . . .*, p. 65.

had a monopoly over *hundis* in Bukhara; (b) that these *hundis* did not circulate widely outside the Shikarpuri network; (c) that outsiders using these *hundis* had to pay a rather high commission.

There is some uncertainty as to how regularly Shikarpuri merchants travelled to Central Asia with the trading caravans. According to various sources, the caravans which carried the goods between northern India and Central Asia through Afghanistan, which was the preferred route until at least the 1880s (when the route through Iran became more popular) were manned by Afghan merchants, who were generally known as Lohanis (later called in British sources Powindahs). Lohanis and Shikarpuris obviously had a symbiotic relationship, but little is known of the way in which they worked together. It is probable that the Lohanis were financed by the Shikarpuris, but they also had capital of their own and were not therefore entirely dependent on advances from the *shroffs*. The Lohanis' main asset, apart from their command over vast flocks of camels, was their connections with the Pashto tribes whose territories the caravans had to cross on their way between the Punjab and Sind and Kabul. Their massive presence more or less ensured safe passage for the caravans, provided the duties were paid to the various tribal chieftains. However, apart from the Lohani caravans, other caravans also made the voyage, and they might have included specific Shikarpuri caravans.

The best description of the caravan trade between northern India and Central Asia is the one given by Mohan Lal, Burnes' Kashmiri assistant who accompanied him on his famous journey to Bukhara in 1832, and whose account is more reliable than his patron's.[24] He gives us a detailed account of the silk trade between Bukhara and Multan, which, he claimed, 'is generally conducted by Lohanis and Shikarpuris'.[25] He is, however, vague about the relationship between the two groups. The silk, of which there were three different varieties fetching different prices, was loaded on camels in Bukhara, each camel carrying $6\frac{1}{2}$ maunds (presumably Surat maunds). In two weeks it reached Kholum (in Afghan Turkestan) where it was transferred to ponies for the crossing of the Hindu Kush to Kabul. There some of the goods, mostly Russian textiles, were disposed of. The second leg of the journey, which appears to have been made again on camels, led the caravan to Darband, beyond the Sulaiman range, where it was divided into three: one group continued to Hindustan via Dera Ghazi Khan and Bahawalpur, one to

---

[24] Mohan Lal, *Travels in the Panjab, Afghanistan and Turkestan to Balk, Bokhara and Herat* . . ., London, 1846 (1st edn, Calcutta, 1834). On Mohan Lal, see C. A. Bayly, *Empire and Information: Intelligence Gathering and Social Communication in India, 1780–1870*, Cambridge, 1996, pp. 230–2, who calls him 'India's first modern anti-imperialist'.

[25] Mohan Lal, *Travels*, p. 393.

Multan and one to Amritsar. Details of various duties and prices are given. An interesting indication is that there was no custom of insurance or *bima* on such caravans, which could mean either that it was considered unnecessary, or more probably that the risk was so high that premiums would have pushed up costs too much.

Silk appears to have been by far the main commodity sent from Bukhara to India, where it was used for clothing and embroidery. It is not known whether Shikarpuris were involved in the financing of the craftsmen who produced silk thread and cloth. They certainly bought the silk from the Bukhara merchants through their local agents, and paid for the cost of the transport, but we do not know who were the purchasers of the silk on the Indian side. The role of the Shikarpuris thus appears to have been that of middlemen between the Bukhara merchants and north Indian merchants, a role they could perform thanks to their networks of agents in Bukhara and in the towns where the silk was bought.

Mohan Lal provides some incidental information on the network in the course of his narrative. We are thus told that there were three Shikarpuri merchants in Dera Ghazi Khan, who were connected with those of different localities, including Multan. Mohan Lal informs us that 'the Shikarpur merchants of Cabul and Kandahar, as well as the few Afghan merchants of these places, who are not as rich as the former, provide Dera Ghazi Khan with the productions and imports of the above countries'.[26]

The return cargo taken by the caravans from India to Bukhara consisted mostly of indigo. According to Mohan Lal, in 1831, 'The Lohanis and Shikarpuris sent to Khorrassan fifteen hundred loads of indigo, produced in the country of Multan and Dera, which cost them seventy-five thousand rupees'.[27] They purchased it at Rs 55 per maund and sold it at Rs 60, 'including expenses of the road', a moderate profit margin. In an interesting aside, Mohan Lal explains the advantages the Shikarpuris, as Hindu-Sikhs, had over their Lohani Muslim colleagues in the territories under Sikh rule, such as Dera. They paid a duty on the import of silk which was half that paid by the Afghans and a sales tax which was only one fourth.[28] It becomes clearer then why the two groups of merchants operated in such close cooperation: each benefited from some kind of 'discriminative protection' on one side of the mountains.

Coming to the trade of Shikarpur proper, Mohan Lal described it as carried out mostly with Kandahar and Herat, and consisting primarily

---

[26] *Ibid.*, pp. 403–4. [27] *Ibid.*, p. 404. [28] *Ibid.*, p. 405.

of silk for consumption in Shikarpur. Its value was but a fraction of that carried between Bukhara and Multan. It is clear from his account that the Shikarpuris derived much more profit from their position of intermediaries between far-flung places such as Bukhara and Bombay than from the direct trade they carried from Shikarpur.

More information on the Shikarpuri merchant diaspora is scattered in various contemporary sources, but it bears more on the social aspects than on the economics of the trade. A typical piece is the account given by Burnes of the Shikarpuri merchants he met at Kabul while he was on his way to Bukhara. While offering what was probably an exaggerated assessment of their commercial role (he wrote that 'the whole trade of Central Asia is in the hands of those people, who have houses of agency from Astracan and Meshid to Calcutta'), he described them as 'a plodding race, who take no share in any other matter than their own' and observed that 'they have a peculiar cast of countenance, with a very high nose', adding that they dressed 'very daintily'. More importantly, he noted that they never brought their families from their country, 'and are constantly passing to and from it; which keeps up a national spirit among them'. He claimed that they had 'eight great houses of agency' in Kabul and kept themselves 'quite separate from the other Hindu inhabitants' (of whom he estimated there were a total of 300 families).[29]

In British writings of the 1830s, a myth of Shikarpur was created and it is not easy for today's historian to disentangle the myth and the reality which was behind it. A particular question-mark hangs about the 'decline' of Shikarpur, noticed by some of the contemporary observers. Thus Masson, who is generally well informed if not totally reliable, is a forceful exponent of the thesis of decline. The fall of the Durrani Empire, he claims, has been accompanied by a corresponding decline at Shikarpur, both by depriving its capitalists of one great source of their gains, and by causing an uncertain and disturbed state of affairs in the surrounding countries, and he adds that many bankers of Shikarpur moved to Multan and Amritsar to take advantage of the economic resurgence of the Punjab under Ranjit Singh.[30] This is however no proof of the decline of the Shikarpuri network. If the bankers moved to the Punjab but kept their families in Shikarpur, it meant that they remitted at least part of the profits to their home town. There are many indications of the fierce loyalty that Shikarpuri *banias*, even in the most far-flung locations, kept *vis-à-vis* Shikarpur. Dispersal as such was no proof of decline; on the contrary, it meant that the network was spreading to new localities. Evidence of the decline in the volume of

[29] Burnes, *Travels*, vol. I, p. 168.   [30] Masson, *Narrative*, p. 354.

trade from Shikarpur is abundant enough, but, given the primary role of the Shikarpuris as intermediaries in commercial transactions carried out between various far-off localities, it is not strong *prima facie* evidence for a decline in the profits of its merchants. Of more direct importance is the question of whether or not there was an overall decline in the trade between northern India and Central Asia. No definitive answer to this question can be given in the absence of reliable statistics bearing on the trade. We are, however, left with a lingering impression that in the first half of the nineteenth century the caravan trade was passing through a phase of relative decline, due largely to unsettled political conditions, following the collapse of Durrani predominance after 1809. This decline was certainly not spectacular, nor was it linear, but there are indications that Shikarpuris were trying to diversify out of Central Asian trade. The most important of their new ventures seems to have been their participation in the Malwa opium trade and there is evidence of a large Shikarpuri presence in Karachi at the time of the British occupation of that port. Among the merchant communities mentioned by Hart in his survey,[31] Khatris figure as one of the largest, and it is most probable that they hailed from Shikarpur.

At the time of the annexation of the town to British India in 1843, it is therefore clear that, if the *bania* community of Shikarpur still drew its sustenance largely from its participation in Central Asian trade, it had also acquired a stake in trade with British India via Karachi. The following period saw the continuation of this dual trend. While links with Karachi and the economy of British India were consolidated, there was also a resurgence of trade with Central Asia, which led to greater involvement of Shikarpuris in the region.

Shikarpuris and Central Asian trade, c. 1843–1890

After the disastrous campaign of 1839–42 in Afghanistan, Shikarpur fell into complete oblivion. While between 1830 and 1840 it had inspired a score of writings, in the following century very few passed through it or cared to mention it. The only significant notice it got was from Sir Richard Burton in his *Sind Revisited* of 1877. Although there were occasional bursts of interest in Central Asian trade, they were not

---

[31] See 'Report on the town and port of Kurachee, accompanied by information relative to its inhabitants, trade, revenues, imports and exports, etc., by the late Captain S. V. W. Hart, submitted to Government on 28 January 1840', in *Selections from the Bombay Records*, new series, no. XVII, pp. 211–45. Hart estimated there were 1400 'Khatree Mahajuns' in Karachi.

Table 3.1. *Trade of the Punjab with Kabul and Bukhara c.1860–1890*

Year	Imports	Exports
1860–61	£286,513	£284,643
1870–71	Rs 2,388,099	Rs 1,493,698
1875–76	Rs 9,143,712	Rs 8,166,555
1890–91	Rs 2,073,790	Rs 4,598,704

Sources: Report by R. H. Davies on the Trade of Central Asia, 15 February 1862, copy in *Parliamentary Papers (House of Commons), 1864,* vol. XLII; *Note on the Trade Statistics of the Punjab for the years 1870–71, 1875–76 and 1890–91* Lahore.

sufficient to focus the attention of policymakers on what was after all just a *mofussil* town of British India.

Nor was it a particularly dynamic *mofussil* town. It grew slowly in the post-annexation period. Its population, estimated at 30,000 in 1839–40, had reached 38,107 at the time of the 1872 census, and between 1881 and 1891 it even decreased slightly.[32] This reflected a far from buoyant economy, a situation which probably contributed to a renewed exodus of Hindu *banias*.

In the second half of the nineteenth century, the dispersal of Shikarpuri *banias* across Central Asia remained unnoticed until it started creating problems of a juridico-legal nature, on which more will be said later. About this earlier episode, government archives have nothing to say, since it was not a matter of concern to the Government of India, and secondary sources are scarce. Evidence of two kinds is available. Statistics of land trade which were collected by British Indian authorities and also by Russian authorities after 1865 show that trade between India and Central Asia, which had been depressed in the 1820–50 period, tended to increase between 1850 and 1890. Table 3.1 gives some data on the trade between the Punjab and Central Asia between 1860 and 1890.

This table shows widespread overall fluctuations in the trade conducted through Peshawar with Afghanistan and Central Asia (after 1850, the Khyber route accounted for the bulk of the trade between India and Central Asia), a peak being reached in the mid-1870s, to be followed by a decline. No reliable estimate exists regarding the share of that trade which was conducted with Bukhara. However, it

[32] It fell from 42,496 to 42,004, the only significant town in the Bombay presidency with Surat to have experienced such a decrease during the intercensal period. See *Census of India 1891*, vol. VII, *Bombay and its Feudatories*, part I, *Report*, W. W. Drew, Bombay, 1892, p. 33. The stagnation was explained by the flight of labour from outside which had been attracted to the town in a previous period. There was no mention of the impact of outward migration.

cannot have accounted for more than half the value of the trade in 1860–61, i.e. a maximum value of £285,000 (probably an overestimate). On the other hand, an estimate from a Russian source puts the value of the trade between India and Bokhara in 1887 at 5,500,000 roubles (i.e. approximately £550,000),[33] thus suggesting that the value of the trade doubled during a twenty-five-year period. This estimate is to be taken with due caution, and as only indicative of a broad trend.

Somewhat more reliable demographic data dispersed across various sources point to a fairly spectacular increase in the size of the Shikarpuri community in Central Asia. Prior to the 1860s, the only estimate available relates to the number of Shikarpuris in Bukhara proper: according to J. Wolff, who visited the town in the 1840s, there were in Bukhara 'three hundred merchants from Scind'.[34] In 1863–64, the Hungarian traveller Arminius Vambéry reported that in the khanate of Bukhara there were 500 Hindus dispersed between the capital and the provinces.[35] Censuses taken by the Russian authorities in 1868 in newly annexed territories revealed the presence of 93 Hindus in the old city of Tashkent and of 214 Hindus in the Zarafshan valley, of whom about 100 were in the town of Samarkand.[36] Five years later, the American consular official Eugene Schuyler reported the presence of 140 Hindus from Shikarpur in Tashkent,[37] where they occupied three caravanserais.

From this scattered evidence, it is clear that Shikarpuris in Central Asia, at the time of the Russian conquest, were increasing in numbers and spreading to new localities. Partly on the basis of later estimates, I suggest that the Shikarpuri population of the khanates of Khokand and Bukhara (there were apparently no Shikarpuris in Khiva), which were annexed or placed under Russian protectorate between 1865 and 1876, rose from around 500 in 1850 to around 3,000 in 1890. These figures may not appear very impressive, but let us recall that all the Shikarpuris in Central Asia were adult Hindu males. The adult Hindu male population of Shikarpur at the 1891 Census was not more than 7,000 to

---

[33] Quoted in S. Becker, *Russia's Protectorates in Central Asia: Bukhara and Khiva, 1865–1924*, Cambridge, MA, 1968, p. 276.
[34] J. Wolff, *A Mission to Bokhara*, ed. G. Wint, London, 1969 (1st edn, London, 1845), p. 150.
[35] A. Vambéry, *Travels in Central Asia, Being the Account of a Journey from Teheran across the Turkoman Desert on the Eastern Shore of the Caspian to Khiva, Bokhara and Samarcand*, London, 1864, p. 372.
[36] Quoted in H. Lansdell, *Russian Central Asia, including Kuldja, Bokhara, Khiva and Merv*, London, 1885, vol. I, pp. 440, 541.
[37] E. Schuyler, *Turkistan, Notes of a Voyage in Russian Turkistan, Khokand, Bukhara and Kuldja*, London, 1876, p. 184.

8,000,[38] which means that the Central Asian diaspora represented 40 per cent of the resident adult male Hindu population of the town. Information gathered in the Bombay Political Proceedings reveals that, around 1890, 150 passports were given annually to male Hindu Shikarpuris for travel to Russian Central Asia. This, of course, does not give a net figure for migration, since there are no data on the numbers who returned to Shikarpur annually. However, it means that every year, approximately one out of fifty male Hindu Shikarpuris travelled to Central Asia on business. Given the fact that these men often stayed in Central Asia for long periods, it means that there was a big turnover. An important fraction of the adult Hindu male Shikarpuri population travelled at least once to Central Asia.

The political change that the region underwent with the imposition of Russian direct or indirect domination does not seem to have had a negative impact on the migration of Shikarpuris, in spite of occasional expulsions, such as that of thirty merchants expelled by the Russian authorities in 1878 from Samarkand, Khokand, Khodjend and Tashkent.[39] There is even some evidence that the Russian conquest acted as an incentive to further migration, at least for a few years, as there were opportunities for business in supplying the Russian garrisons with the necessities of life and generally an expansion in trade. Russian policy *vis-à-vis* trade between Central Asia and India was at first hesitant and contradictory.[40] It is only from 1881 onwards that measures to limit the entry of Indian goods into the territories under direct Russian administration, the guberniia of Turkestan, were taken. The khanates of Khiva and Bukhara were, however, not concerned by these measures and trade with Bukhara remained, therefore, largely unimpeded, although re-exports from Bokhara to the guberniia were made more difficult. Serious obstacles to trade between India and Bukhara were imposed only in 1894–95 when the Russian customs frontier was extended to Bukhara.[41]

[38] The total Hindu male population of the town was 12,550. *Census of India, 1891*, vol. VIII, Table V.
[39] See Confidential Newsletter, 29 October 1878, Political & Secret Correspondence with India 1875–1911, L/P&S/7/20.
[40] This comes out clearly from a perusal of the collection of papers assembled by the Foreign Department of the Government of India in 1872. See chapter 3, 'Correspondence and memoranda about the trade between India and Western Toorkistan. Question how far it is impeded by the action of the Russian authorities', in *Précis of Papers Regarding Affairs in Central Asia, 1867–1872*, compiled by H. Le Poer Wynne, under-secretary to the Government of India, Foreign Department, Simla, 1872, pp. 75–94. Reports sent to Peshawar by various 'confidential agents' gave very contradictory accounts of the policy followed by the Russian authorities in relation to trade with India.
[41] Becker, *Russia's Protectorates*, p. 152.

Detailed evidence on the Shikarpuri community in Central Asia was provided incidentally by the emergence of a legal problem regarding the estates of merchants who died in Russian territory. This legal archive is the main source upon which I have reconstructed a profile of the Shikarpuri community as it lived and toiled in Russian Central Asia in the period between 1881 and 1917.

The Shikarpuris in Russian Central Asia, c. 1880–1917

The existing literature in Western languages on Russian Central Asia makes some passing references to the presence of a community of Hindus from Shikarpur, who are described as a group of particularly greedy moneylenders,[42] but is not very informative on their life and activities in the region. The best account remains the one by Schuyler, and later travellers had little to add to his observations. The vast Russian and Soviet literature does not appear either to have taken much notice of this group.[43] A recent Russian compilation based on photographic archives, however, includes a few pictures of Indian merchants in the khanate of Bukhara.[44] The discovery of a fairly large and in some ways very detailed archive in the India Office Records is therefore an important breakthrough, although its exploitation is not devoid of problems.

This archive was gradually constituted by the British authorities in a very *ad hoc* manner, as they were confronted, from the early 1880s onwards, with a delicate problem regarding the successions of Shikarpuri merchants who died intestate in Russian Central Asia and without their heirs being present. It could be observed that, since there were Shikarpuris in Central Asia from at least the end of the eighteenth century, scores of them must have died before the 1880s. Their estates did not however give rise to official exchanges before the early 1880s. The reason is that, prior to 1876, these estates occurred in a political context which was different: Central Asia was still under the formal rule of Uzbekh khans in Khiva, Khokand and Bukhara, and in these Muslim states it appears that when Hindu merchants died without their heirs being present, their estates were simply confiscated by the state, a practice which apparently was considered perfectly normal. The only way for Hindu merchants to transmit their estates to their heirs in Shikarpur was either to return in time to die in their native city, or, if

---

[42] See for instance A. M. B. Meakin, *In Russian Turkestan, A Garden of Asia and its People*, London, 1903, p. 191.
[43] See, however, P. N. Rasulzade, *Is Istorii Sredne-Indiisiskh Svyazei*, Tashkent, 1966, where the role played by Indian moneylenders in the Ferghana Valley is mentioned.
[44] A. G. Nedvetsky (comp.), *Bukhara: Caught in Time*, Reading, 1993.

travelling was made impossible by ill-health or any other cause, to arrange for the transfer of the maximum amount of money through the existing channels, i.e. the Shikarpuri bankers. Doing business in the khanates was, therefore, a gamble, and it was very much integrated within the merchants' calculations of the costs and benefits of operating in Central Asia.

With the advent of Russian rule in the 1870s, and the division of the region between the directly administered guberniia of Turkestan, including the ex-khanate of Khokand and a part of the khanate of Bukhara, and the surviving khanates of Khiva and Bukhara, which became 'native states' under Russian protection, the question of the successions of British subjects took a different aspect. Given the growing tension in Anglo-Russian relations over Central Asia in the early 1880s (culminating in the famous fit of 'Mervousness' of 1884), Russian authorities became wary of giving pretexts to the British to interfere too much in the affairs of their Central Asian dominions. To prevent the British from using the question of successions as a pretext, they tried to appear as respectful of legal proceedings as possible. That is why, from 1883 onwards, Russian authorities in the guberniia, when informed of the death of a British-Indian subject without his heirs being present, tried to enrol the help of the British authorities in tracing the heirs to India.[45] Thus, the Bombay government and the India Office started assembling files regarding cases of successions of Indians dying in Central Asia, who were almost exclusively Shikarpuri merchants. From the late 1880s, cases of Shikarpuris dying in the khanate of Bukhara were added.

The legal problems involved were, however, daunting, and it took the two governments more than twenty years to reach some kind of understanding, which did not prevent feuds from arising. The difficulties stemmed from the fact that, first, Shikarpuri merchants, like most Hindus, were not in the habit of leaving a will, and therefore died intestate, and secondly, that, at the time of their death, in most cases, their heirs were in Shikarpur and not in a position to travel to Central Asia to reclaim their inheritance in person. The problem for the Russian authorities, who were unaware of the intricacies of Hindu personal law as it was administered in British India, and more specifically in the

[45] The first mention of the death of a Shikarpuri merchant in Russian territory occurred in a letter from the Foreign Office to the India Office, 10 April 1883 transmitting copy of a letter from the British Embassy in St Petersburg, enclosing a letter from the Russian Ministry of Foreign Affairs to the Russian Embassy in London, informing of the death in prison in the town of Novo-Margellansk of a merchant from Shikarpur known as Bay Tillja Takover. Enclosed in IOR, Public & Judicial Department Records, Departmental Papers: Annual Files 1880–1930, File J&P 631/1883, L/P&J/6/96.

Bombay presidency, where a variant of the *Mitaksara* system was in force, was to establish who the legal heirs were, and having done that, to apply the existing laws of Russia to those cases. They asked for British help regarding the first point, and it became the practice for the presumptive heirs to send documents, i.e. heirship certificates, establishing their position as legal heirs to the deceased merchant. Another problem arose regarding representation. Russian law demanded the presence of the heirs or of their attorney at the legal proceedings. Travelling to Russian territory at short notice was impossible for most claimants: Shikarpuri women, who were the claimants in many cases, never travelled to Central Asia (a point to which I shall come back later), and even for men, it was difficult to contemplate such a trip, unless there was the prospect of a very large estate. Appointing an attorney was not an easy course, because he would have to be cognizant of Russian law, which few people in British India, even in Shikarpur, were. Therefore the solution which evolved was for the presumptive heirs to give a British consular official a power of attorney to represent them before the Russian courts. Even then, problems remained, as there was no British consular representation in Central Asia; the nearest British consulate was at Tiflis, and it was a small and understaffed consular post, unable to undertake such tasks. Following some exchanges between Bombay, London and St Petersburg, it was decided that the British consul general in St Petersburg would be the official in charge of the delicate question of the inheritances of British Indian subjects dying in Central Asia. It is no surprise then that in April 1894 the ambassador in St Petersburg wrote to the Foreign Office: 'There are no cases which give us more trouble and entail more delay than those relating to the claims of Indian subjects to property left by their relatives dying in Russian Central Asia'.[46] Besides the sheer complexity of the legal position in many cases, there were complications and delays in getting the right documents duly translated and forwarded to Central Asia, including the necessity of employing Russian lawyers. For a while in the late 1880s and early 1890s the system seemed to be working reasonably well, the documents of the British Indian courts being generally accepted by the Russian courts as legal proof of rights to inheritance, but a crisis occurred in the late 1890s, as, following a decision of the Russian Senate, the Russian courts stopped recognizing the legal validity of the documents issued

---

[46] St Petersburg despatch no. 78, 9 April 1894, to Foreign Office enclosed in Foreign Office to India Office, 19 April 1894, enclosed in public despatch to India no. 46 of 17 May 1894, in *Selections from Despatches to India January–June 1894*, London, 1894, pp. 319–22.

by British Indian courts.[47] Deadlock ensued as far as successions in the guberniia were concerned, which seems to have lasted for a few years, during which practically no cases of successions in that part of the Russian dominions came to the knowledge of the British authorities. In spite of the rapprochement between England and Russia in 1907, difficulties remained and the question was one of those Sir Edward Grey, the secretary of state for foreign affairs, raised with his Russian counterpart Sazonov during their conversations in 1912.[48]

The situation was quite different in the khanate of Bukhara. There, Russian law was not in force, except for Russian subjects and Christian foreigners who were assimilated to them. Non-Christian foreigners, whether Muslims or Hindus, were subjected to local laws,[49] which were a mixture of customary law and *sharia*. The law was, however, administered by the local *kazis*[50] in a fairly arbitrary fashion, and it seems that, as far as the inheritances of Hindu merchants were concerned, the *kazis* allowed the local Hindu *panchayats* to decide the matter according to Hindu law, or their interpretation of it. In Bukhara therefore, as Lord George Hamilton, the secretary of state recognized in 1900,[51] there

---

[47] A Russian memorandum dated 2/15 January 1901 stated the legal position as it stood from the Russian point of view. Annex 4 in Foreign Office to India Office, 29 January 1901, enclosure no. 3 in public despatch no. 34 of 1901, in *Selections from Despatches to India January–June 1901*, London, 1901, pp. 453–9.

[48] See 'Copy of Cabinet Paper containing record of conversation with Russian Minister for Foreign Affairs at Balmoral', in Sir Edward Grey to Sir G. Buchanan, British ambassador at St Petersburg, 4 October 1912, Russia and Central Asia Confidential, 8 October, in IOR, Political and Secret Department Records, Departmental Papers: Political and Secret Annual Files 1912–1930, L/P&S/11/36, enclosing 'Memorandum respecting conversation at Balmoral between M. Sazonof and Sir Edward Grey'. Under the heading 'Grievances of British Subjects in Russian Central Asia', three main points were raised: (1) the delay caused to trade agents, and the consequent loss to business, entailed by the new passport regulations introduced in 1909; (2) the hardships suffered by British Indian subjects owing to the procedure adopted for dividing among creditors the estates of deceased or bankrupt debtors – a procedure which placed British Indian creditors at a disadvantage as compared with those of Russian nationality; (3) the difficulty in realising the estates of deceased British subjects. Regarding the latter point, the memorandum stressed that the difficulty was mainly due to the decision of the Russian government in 1909 to insist on the strict observance of the law requiring claimants to appear before the proper district courts in Russia, either personally or by attorney. To tide over the difficulties, the Government of India had proposed a reciprocal arrangement with Russia, but no answer had been received from the Russian side.

[49] As the above-quoted Russian memorandum stated: 'Foreigners, non-Christians, and consequently Hindoos do not come within the jurisdiction of Russian judicial procedures and all cases concerning them are conducted on a par with those of natives, by the Bokharian Authorities.'

[50] On the judicial powers of the *kazis* in matters of inheritance in the emirate of Bukhara, see D. I. Logofet, *The Land of Wrong: the Khanate of Bokhara and its Present Condition*, Simla, 1910 (translated from Russian edn, St Petersburg, 1909), p. 29.

[51] The India Office wrote to the Foreign Office in a letter, 24 July 1900, J&P 1209/1901,

were no legal difficulties involved in the transmission of the estates of British Indian subjects. The major problem in the Emirate was the short time allotted to presumptive heirs to present their claim. The authorities imposed a time limit of one year, after which the estates reverted to the state. Given the time involved in getting the necessary legal documents in India, in having them translated into Persian and Russian, and in transmitting the whole to Bukhara, it was practically impossible for the presumptive heirs to present their claim within the prescribed period. Following British representations and a bit of arm-twisting by Russia, the Bukharan government was persuaded to extend the period to two years, but even then it was a real race to get all the necessary legal documents in time, and the expense involved was not insignificant.

For the historian of international private law, the story probably stands as an instance of the inadequacy of the state of the law in that period.[52] However, the legal difficulties are the main reason why the archive was constituted in the first place, and the economic and social historian looking for data on the Shikarpuri community finds in the voluminous correspondence generated an unparalleled trove of fascinating material. This correspondence involved many layers in what were probably at the time the two most intricate bureaucracies in the world, that of czarist Russia and British India.[53] The official correspondence

enclosure no. 1 in public despatch no. 34, *Selections from Despatches*, pp. 453–9: 'Lord George Hamilton understands that no legal difficulties in connection with the recovery of estates exist in the khanate of Bukhara, so long as claims are presented within two years of death, and that duly authenticated Indian certificates of heirship are still received in evidence by the Bukharan authorities.'

[52] Interestingly, it is in the 1870s that efforts were first made by jurists to evolve a body of international private law, efforts which culminated in the first Hague Conference which took place in 1893. See T. M. C. Asser Institut, *The Influence of the Hague Conference on Private International Law*, Dordrecht, 1993.

[53] The main agencies involved on the Russian side were the military authorities of the guberniia of Turkestan and the Russian political agent in Bukhara, both hierarchically subjected to the Asiatic Department in the Russian Ministry of Foreign Affairs. The Asiatic Department corresponded with the British Foreign Office largely through the channel of the Russian Embassy in London. All the Russian diplomatic correspondence was conducted in French, and reproduced in the original language in the India Office documents. On the British side, the India Office, in both the Public and Judicial and the Political and Secret Departments, did not correspond directly with the Russian authorities, but had to go through the Foreign Office. The latter conducted a fairly large correspondence with the British Embassy in St Petersburg on the question of the estates of Indian merchants dying in Russian Central Asia. On the other hand, the India Office corresponded regularly on the question with the Bombay government, largely bypassing the Government of India in the Foreign Department. Why the Government of India was largely sidelined in the process remains a matter for speculation. The most plausible reason is that the Foreign Department was too busy with the *haute politique* of the Great Game to devote attention to such mundane matters as the inheritances of Indian merchants, and preferred to let the Bombay government look after this complicated and unrewarding problem. Another possible reason is that the Bombay

regarding the estates of Shikarpuri merchants who died in Russian Central Asia between 1881 and 1917 is therefore a diversified archive which includes many documents produced by the Shikarpuris themselves, of which there is no trace elsewhere. It is the main source available for reconstructing the profile of the Shikarpuri community of Russian Central Asia during this period.

All in all, between 1883 and 1917, 131 cases of Shikarpuri merchants dying in Russian Central Asia (or, in a few cases, dying in other parts of Russia, in Persia or Afghanistan while on their way back from Central Asia to Shikarpur) came to the knowledge of the British authorities. It would, of course, be interesting to be able to assess the representativeness of the sample, by comparing the number of deaths known to British authorities with the total number of Shikarpuris dying in Russian Central Asia during this period. However, such an exercise is impossible, due to the lack of demographic data on the Shikarpuri population in Central Asia. A gross estimate of their number around 1890 has been presented, and there are indications that, between 1890 and 1917, the number of Shikarpuris tended to decrease. This assessment is based on data regarding the number of passports delivered annually by the collector of Shikarpur to Shikarpuris for travel to Russian Central Asia (by a notification of 1863,[54] the collectors in Sind were empowered to issue certificates of nationality in lieu of passports to British Indian subjects travelling west of the Indus). During 1890–92, the average number of passports issued annually was 150,[55] while in 1900–2, it was

government, thanks to its voluminous correspondence with the commissioner in Sind, was better informed of the problems of this particular province. The commissioner himself, however, served mainly as a relay between the collector of Shikarpur district (since 1883 resident in the neighbouring town of Sukkur), who was really the man who knew the Shikarpuri merchants, and the Bombay government. It is through the collector that the Shikarpuri merchants and their families made their views and demands known, through petitions which were regularly submitted to him, and which he duly transmitted to his superiors. These petitions are the most interesting documents found in the archives, because they were based on information which the families of merchants had directly received from Central Asia, through the *mazhar* (public declarations) regularly exchanged between the Shikarpuri *panchayats* in Central Asia and the Shikarpuri *panchayats* in Shikarpur. Some of these *mazhars* were even reproduced as accompaniments to petitions, and are of course particularly interesting.

[54] Notification no. 71, dated Camp Delhi, 3 March 1863: 'As British subjects travelling or residing in Persia and other foreign countries, are frequently subjected to much inconvenience and loss for their inability to prove their claim to British consular protection, all British subjects intending to proceed into foreign territory, west of the Indus, are hereby advised to provide themselves with Passports ...'. District magistrates in Sind and the Punjab Frontier were specifically empowered to deliver those passports. Notification reproduced in India Proceedings, Foreign Department, Political, March 1863.

[55] See 'Statement of Indian British Subjects proceeding to Central Asia to whom passports were granted during years 1890, 1891 and 1892', enclosed in Political Despatch from

only 100, the level at which it remained until the First World War.[56] Of course no comparable data are available regarding the number of Shikarpuris returning each year to Shikarpur, but it was probably slightly higher. After 1890, the Shikarpuri community stopped expanding. A reasonable estimate for 1917 is that there were about 2,000 Shikarpuris in Russian Central Asia.[57] The Shikarpuris were not the only merchant community from British India present in the region: there was a community of Peshawari Muslim merchants which was approximately 500-strong,[58] and also merchants from the Punjab, Hindus, Sikhs and Muslims, as well as Kashmiris (who were engaged in

Bombay no. 7, 17 February 1894, IOR, Political & Secret Correspondence with India 1875–1911, L/P&S/7/305. According to this statement, 125 passports were delivered in 1890, all to Shikarpuri Hindus, excepting one to a Muslim resident of Sukkur, 157 in 1891, all to Shikarpuri Hindus, except 2 to Hindu residents of Sukkur taluka, and 147 in 1892, all to Shikarpuri Hindus.

[56] In 1898, 1899 and 1900, the respective number of passports delivered was 94, 127 and 95, according to memorandum no. P/O1, 16 November 1900 from commissioner in Sind to secretary to government in Political Department, Bombay, enclosed in Bombay Political Proceedings (henceforth BPP), December 1900, Serial no. A 72. During 1912–14 an average of 100 passports a year was delivered, according to letter no. 803, 21 September 1914, commissioner in Sind to secretary to government in the Political Department, Bombay, enclosed in BPP, December 1914, Serial no. A 53.

[57] It is based on two estimates of Shikarpuri source found in the archives. The first one, dated 1903, found in the diary of the *munshi* of the British agency in Kashgar, in neighbouring Chinese Sinkiang (where there was also a Shikarpuri community, of which later), is an estimate given by a Shikarpuri merchant having returned to Kashgar from a visit to Russian Turkestan. He estimated the strength of the Shikarpuri community in the guberniia of Turkestan to be in the neighbourhood of 600. See 'diary of British agency at Kashgar (henceforth Kashgar diary) for the ten days ending on 10 July 1903', copy in IOR, Secret Correspondence with India 1875–1911, Political Letters from India 1903, L/P&S/7/157. The second information, found in a successional document of 1909, is an estimate of the strength of the Shikarpuri community in the town of Bukhara and its immediate surroundings, which is put at approximately 500. See petition to the collector of Sukkur, 6 February 1909, enclosed in 'Application from Mussamat Bhojbai for the recovery of the estate of her deceased husband Dhramadas alias Sherdil walad Premchand who died at Bahadin in the Bukhara district in the Russian territory', BPP, April 1909, Serial no. A 21. Extrapolating from these two pieces of information which appear reliable, I have come to the conclusion that the total strength of the Shikarpuri population in Russian Central Asia, i.e. the guberniia of Turkestan and the khanate of Bukhara (there were apparently no Shikarpuris resident in the khanate of Khiva, although Shikarpuri merchants are known to have travelled to Khiva and Urganc) cannot have been more than 2,000 on the eve of the Russian Revolution.

[58] See the petition dated Peshawar, 18 October 1910, addressed to the deputy commissioner, Peshawar District by thirteen big Peshawari Muslim merchants having dealings in Central Asia in which they claim that they have been trading in Turkestan for sixty years, and, after having exposed some of their grievances against the Russian authorities end with the following: 'We trust due consideration will be given to our legitimate request which is from about 500 Indians now engaged in trade in Bokhara, Russia and Turkistan.' Petition enclosed in IOR, Political & Secret Department Records, Departmental Papers: Political & Secret Separate (or Subject) Files 1902–1931, File 947/1912, L/P&S/10/247.

the shawl trade) and the occasional Marwaris, Gujaratis and other north Indian merchants. Knowing the approximate number of Shikarpuris (who were all adult males between the ages of 15 and 55) does not, however, allow us to derive a theoretical number of deaths, given firstly that the exact age composition of this population is not known, and secondly, that detailed mortality tables for both Central Asia and Sind are not available. Hazarding a guess, I would say that the total number of deaths during the years 1881 and 1917 must have been somewhere between 500 and 1,000, which means that the sample found in the archives represents at best one-fourth and at worst one-eighth of the total number of deaths which occurred in Central Asia. The sample appears therefore representative; it is not random since it includes all deaths traced by the British authorities and dealt with by them. It has, however, an inbuilt bias, a point which will be discussed later.

This sample can firstly be used to reconstruct the exact geographical contours of the Shikarpuri diaspora in Russian Central Asia. The first point to note is that, of the 131 successions, 81 occurred in the khanate of Bukhara and 50 in the guberniia of Turkestan, the growing preference of the Shikarpuris for the khanate being due to the fact that there they met with a lower level of official hostility. Out of 81 successions in the khanate, 22 took place in Bukhara town, and the other 59 in a total of 22 localities, of which only 9 can be considered as urban (mostly small towns), thus revealing the widely spread-out nature of the Shikarpuri network in the khanate and its penetration of the rural areas. Of the 50 successions in the guberniia, 35 took place in the province (oblast) of Ferghana, of which 24 in the six principal towns, and 11 in smaller rural localities; 9 took place in the Samarkand oblast, of which one in Samarkand town, 5 in other urban centres and 3 in smaller localities; and, lastly, 6 occurred in the Syr-Daria oblast, of which 4 in Tashkent and 2 in small localities. The files reveal the existence, in most localities of Central Asia, of Shikarpuri *panchayats*, thus indicating the presence of sizeable colonies of Shikarpuri merchants. Some small localities in the khanate of Bukhara had a Shikarpuri colony of ten to twenty merchants, which must have totally dominated local trade. On the other hand, in the larger localities, Shikarpuri merchants competed with various other merchant groups, and there is no evidence that they occupied a clearly dominant position. The contention in the 1910 edition of the *Encyclopaedia Britannica* that 'most of the trade of Bukhara was in the hands of a colony of merchants from Shikarpur'[59] seems therefore exaggerated. Looking at the spread of the network on the map, one notices that it

---

[59] 'Bokhara', in *Encyclopaedia Britannica*, 11th edn, 1910–11, vol. IV, Cambridge, 1910, pp. 156–7.

encompassed most of Central Asia. Its westernmost point was Kurakol, west of Bukhara and its easternmost one Osh, at the end of the Ferghana valley, fairly close to the Sinkiang border, that is a distance of less than 1,000 kilometres; its north–south extension was less: the northernmost point reached by the Shikarpuris appears to have been Chimkent (in the extreme south of present-day Kazakhstan) and its southernmost point Guzar in the central region of the khanate of Bukhara. This survey includes only the localities in which there were colonies of resident Shikarpuri merchants. But there is evidence elsewhere that Shikarpuris travelled on business to other areas of Central Asia, such as the khanate of Khiva, where they did not, however, establish residence for any length of time. This area may not appear very extensive, especially when compared to that in which the Hyderabadi merchants, the Sindworkies, circulated, but the impression is slightly misleading. In the late nineteenth century it was much easier to travel by sea between India and many parts of the world than to travel by land between Shikarpur and the fastness of Central Asia. The latter trip involved not only crossing high mountain ranges and deserts, but also enduring the dangers of travelling through Afghanistan and southeastern Iran, where insecurity was endemic and banditry rife.

The successional documents, supplemented by other sources, give some interesting information on the routes used by Shikarpuri merchants to travel between their home town and Central Asia. The traditional route via the Bolan Pass, Quetta, the Khojak Pass, Kandahar, Kabul, Balkh and Karshi to Bukhara was still in use at the end of the nineteenth century, but was increasingly superseded by other routes. Many Shikarpuris seem to have used the Khyber Pass from Peshawar to Kabul and then Bukhara, but three other routes were also in increasing use. Two went through Persia: the first involved a sea voyage from Karachi to Bandar Abbas (regular steamer services from Karachi to the Gulf ports started after 1860), the second was a land route via Meshed; some Shikarpuris went by train to the Persian border via Quetta, Nushki, and Zahedan (then called Duzdap), and from there by caravan. Routes through Persia were not however very safe: a rich Shikarpuri merchant travelling from Tashkent to Shikarpur was murdered in 1889 near Meshed and his considerable fortune looted. The last route to develop, with the encouragement of the Russian authorities, was the most circuitous, but by far the safest. It meant travelling by ship from Bombay to Batum on the Russian shore of the Black Sea, after having changed ship once either at Constantinople or at Odessa, transferring to a train from Batum to Baku, crossing the Caspian Sea between Baku and Krasnovodsk, and using the new Transcaspian railway line to

Bukhara and beyond. By either of these routes, the minimum travel time between Shikarpur and Bukhara was about two months. Besides, travel within Central Asia, apart from the main axis, was slow and not necessarily very safe. Keeping the network going from Shikarpur was undoubtedly a strain, stretching to the limit the resources of the Shikarpuri merchants. If men did not circulate easily between Shikarpur and Central Asia, the same was true of information, this most precious commodity to merchants. The telegraph reached Bukhara only in the late 1880s,[60] and few areas of the khanate were linked by telegraph at the time of the Russian Revolution. Besides, there were no direct telegraphic communications between Bukhara and India: telegrams had to be routed through Moscow, Teheran and Karachi, and were expensive. This explains that letters, or more precisely *mazhars* sent by courrier, remained the preferred mode of communication between Shikarpur and the widely dispersed colonies of Shikarpuri merchants in Central Asia.

What were these men doing in Central Asia? On this point, the successional documents help correct the somewhat unilateral view taken by most contemporary observers of the Shikarpuris as exclusively a community of moneylenders, who were involved in trade only as a subsidiary activity. An analysis of fifty-five estates (those for which an inventory of contents is furnished) reveals that stocks of cereals, mostly wheat, and other commodities, such as silk, accounted for some 10–15 per cent of their total value. Part of the cash, which accounted for some 30 per cent of the total, must also have been derived from the sale of goods; besides, there is also often mention in the inventories of shops in the bazaars. More detailed evidence of the commercial dealings of the Shikarpuri *banias* has come to light in other documents, leading to an overall assessment that trade was an important activity of the Shikarpuris, particularly in the khanate of Bukhara. Of course, the close connection between grain-trading and rural moneylending has been already noted in the case of Sind itself. It would seem that some of the Shikarpuris in Central Asia more or less conformed to the model of the 'merchant-moneylender', who used moneylending as a way of procuring grain at a low cost and derived his profits mainly from speculating on the sale of grain. A closer look reveals, however, that the situation in Central Asia was different from that which prevailed in Sind. Cheesman's work shows that in Sind the *banias* often did not recover either the principal or the interest on the loans they had extended to the *waderos* or the *haris*. In Central Asia, on the other hand, the local population was generally

[60] Becker, *Russia's Protectorates*, pp. 162–3.

considered a good risk. There was apparently a saying among Shikarpuris that 'the Turks . . . repay their debts even in 50 years'.[61] Whether it had to do with the capacity of the authorities, in the person of the *kazis*, to coerce the peasantry into repaying their debts, or with other reasons, the fact is that moneylending in Central Asia was generally a more profitable activity than in Sind. It is not, therefore, possible to classify Shikarpuris neatly between the two different categories of 'usurers' and 'merchant-moneylenders'. Most Shikarpuris in Central Asia were probably a bit of both.

Within the network itself, there was a hierarchy of moneylenders. An upper layer consisted of bankers in the major towns, such as Bukhara and Khokand (in the Ferghana valley) who did banking on a fairly large scale. Although none of the men in the sample belonged to that category, some idea of their dealings can be gathered from scattered evidence. Originally, they must have been agents of the Shikarpur bankers whose main function was to facilitate the trade between India and Central Asia; they provided credit to the Indian merchants buying goods in Central Asia and to the Central Asian traders buying the Indian goods brought by the caravans. They also did the business of *sarrafs*, i.e. money changers. They got their funds from their principals in Shikarpur, and repaid them out of the profits they made on their operations in Central Asia. However, as trade between India and Central Asia declined, especially from the 1890s onwards, and as Russian banks expanded into Central Asia from the 1870s, the nature of their business changed. They increasingly borrowed funds from Russian banks which they lent to other Shikarpuri moneylenders at a higher rate. The second layer consisted precisely of these moneylenders who borrowed from the big bankers, and lent at a higher rate both to other Shikarpuris and to the indigenous population. These men generally operated in towns, but had dealings in the neighbouring countryside. They often mixed trading, especially grain trading, with their moneylending operations. At the bottom end of the system were the smaller rural moneylenders, who lent, almost exclusively to the local peasantry, funds which they borrowed from the previous group. The existence of such a chain of lenders was made possible by the huge differences in interest rates charged by the Russian banks, which were around 6 per cent per year, and those actually paid by the peasants which often reached 40 to 60 per cent.[62] By using intermediaries such as the

[61] Quoted in a statement submitted by Mussamat Rukmanbai, a Shikarpuri widow whose husband had died in Central Asia, to the collector of Sukkur, 15 March 1915, enclosed in BPP, July 1915, Serial no. A 304.
[62] On the question of the actual rates of interest paid by agriculturists in Russian

Shikarpuris, the Russian banks spared themselves the cost of assembling and processing information on a myriad of small borrowers, who often could not provide any collateral except their tiny plots of land. They also limited their risks in case of default. The Shikarpuris, on the other hand, had direct or indirect access (through the *panchayats*) to all the information needed on the borrowers, and in the last resort they foreclosed on defaulting debtors. Quite a few Shikarpuris in the sample had some land, which they had acquired as a result of such foreclosures, although legally they were not allowed to own land in Turkestan.

We do not know the details of the process by which the Shikarpuris, described in early nineteenth-century sources as a group of international bankers-cum-traders, transformed themselves into a community mostly engaged in rural moneylending, a process we might call 'Chettiarization' by comparison with the role played by the Chettiars in rural moneylending in British Burma, British Malaya and French Cochin-China. An important factor in the reorientation of their activities was certainly the dramatic fall in the value of the rupee throughout the 1870s and 1880s, linked to the depreciation of silver in relation to gold. It must have affected very directly their trading operations between Russian Central Asia and India, leading them to seek new sources of profits. It is certain that their move towards rural moneylending was not the result of political encouragement from the Russian authorities. The latter, on the contrary, showed a certain degree of hostility toward the moneylending operations of the Shikarpuris, which they viewed in the same unfavourable light as the usury practised by their Jewish subjects in the Pale. In the guberniia of Turkestan, usury was a punishable offence and some Shikarpuris fell foul of the Russian law; a few were even deported to Siberia.[63] However, independently of the wishes of the authorities, the economic facts, i.e. the growing commercialization of agriculture, mostly in Ferghana, and the increasing need for credit for tools, oxen, etc. by the peasantry, created the conditions for the Shikarpuris to thrive as rural moneylenders, although they were not the only ones. The attitude of the Bukharan authorities to usury appears, however, to have been much more lenient, and the economic trends in the emirate, although less pronounced, were also in the direction of growing commercializa-

---

Turkestan, see R. A. Pierce (ed.), *Mission to Turkestan, Being the Memoirs of Count K. K. Pahlen 1908–1909*, London, 1964, pp. 101–2, and A. Woiekof, *Le Turkestan Russe*, Paris, 1914, p. 145.

[63] Mentioned in the above-quoted entry in the Kashgar diary for 8 July 1903: (Meng Raj states): 'that during the course of last fifteen years, three Shikarpuri Hindus had been awarded the punishment of transportation for life to Siberia for exactions in moneylending transactions'.

tion and monetization.[64] Most of the detailed evidence in the successional documents concerns rural moneylending, but Shikarpuris were also active in lending money in the towns. They also lent money to the soldiers of the Bukharan army.[65]

The connection between the different layers of Shikarpuri moneylenders was largely ensured by a system of partnership known in Shikarpur as the *shah–gumastha*. Under this system, a capitalist partner, called *shah*, advanced the funds to one or several working partners called *gumasthas*, for a specific kind of business operation for a certain duration of time, and was remunerated by a share of the profits. No partnership document for Shikarpur has been found in the archives, although some have come to light from Hyderabad. It is, therefore, not known whether partnership agreements were generally written or oral. Detailed discussion of the system will be taken up at a later stage.

The aspect best documented in the successional documents is of course wealth. Through the information given about the value of the estates left by Shikarpuri merchants dying in Central Asia, one can form some idea of the gains they made and of the contribution of the Central Asian venture to the economy of Shikarpur.

At this stage, a brief description of the official way in which the residue of the estates was transferred to the heirs is in order. We shall take the instance of an estate in the khanate of Bukhara, since that is where two-thirds of the successions occurred. The *kazi* of the locality where the merchant who died was resident proceeded to realize the outstanding debts, settle accounts with the creditors, sell the goods which were in stock and thus produce a sum in Bukharan currency, the tenga, which was transferred to the state Treasury. This sum, having been exchanged for Russian roubles at the bazaar rate of the day (it is only in 1901 that a legal rate of 1 tenga for 15 kopecks was introduced) was then transferred to the Russian political agent in Bukhara who sent it to the Russian Imperial Treasury in St Petersburg. The Imperial Treasury, having converted the sum into sterling, sent a cheque for the amount to the British Embassy in St Petersburg. It was then transferred to the Foreign Office, and, through Her Majesty's Treasury, to the India Office, and included in the account between the secretary of state and the Government of India. The Government of India credited the sum converted into rupees to the account of the Government of Bombay, which, through the commissioner in Sind, put it at the disposal of the collector of Sukkur. So there it lay at the Huzur Treasury in Sukkur for the heirs to encash if they wished.

[64] See Becker, *Russia's Protectorates*, pp. 180–6.
[65] Nedvetsky, *Bukhara*, p. 59.

However, the road between Sukkur and Shikarpur being not very safe to travel, especially with a large amount of money in cash, the heirs often asked for the sum to be transferred to the account of the *mukhtyarkar* in Shikarpur, where they could at last lay their hands on it. The entire process from Bukhara to Shikarpur, which entailed the signature of some twelve different Bukharan, Russian and British officials, as well as three operations of change, took an average of one to two years to be completed, when all went smoothly.

There was also a parallel system, through which the majority of estates were transferred to Shikarpur. In this matter, a difference existed between the guberniia and the khanate of Bukhara. In the guberniia, affairs of Hindus were not dealt with by *kazis*, but by Russian judges, who, though probably as corruptible, were not used to the ways of the Hindu merchants and were probably not willing to cooperate with the *panchayats* to the same extent as in Bukhara. In the guberniia, therefore, the only way to avoid the cumbersome official channels was for the presumptive heirs themselves to travel to Central Asia or to entrust their interests to an attorney, generally a local Indian, and themselves organize the transfer of the money to Shikarpur. In Bukhara, a much more important role was played by the *kazis* and the Shikarpuri *panchayats*. A description of the 'unofficial' system is enclosed in a report sent in 1904 by the collector of Sukkur to the commissioner in Sind.[66] Following widespread allegations of misappropriation in the case of several successions of Shikarpuri merchants in Bukhara, the collector, Jean-Louis Rieu, who was a good linguist, conducted an unofficial inquiry in Shikarpur among the milieu of the merchants connected with Bukhara, which produced some startling findings. He explained that when a Shikarpuri died, the *kazi* took charge of his moveable and immoveable property and impounded his account books. 'The local Shikarpuri panchayat', he added, 'generally intervenes for the purpose of securing the administration of the estate. A real or fictitious heir to the estate is put forward, the Panchayat undertake to pay from the estate the death duties and other fiscal dues which the Bokharan authorities demand.' The property was then handed over by the *kazi* to the *panchayat*, who put up the whole concern, known as a *mamlo*, to auction. 'The purchase of these estates by auction', he commented, 'appears to be a recognized and highly profitable line of business.' A kind of dual transaction ensued: on the one hand, the heirs in Shikarpur were approached and offered a lump sum, based on an estimate of the value that the auction was expected to fetch. They generally accepted the offer, because it

[66] Collector of Sukkur to commissioner in Sind, no. 3,600, 5 June 1904, enclosed in BPP, June 1905, Serial no. A 102.

presented them with 'the prospect of an immediate realization of their claims free from the otherwise inevitable trouble and delay', although the sum offered was often less than the amount for which the estate was put up to auction. Then the auction sale took place, and due to combination amongst the bidders abetted by the *panchayat* resulted in the estate generally being sold far below its real value. Rieu emphasized that, in that way, a 'double profit' was realized to the detriment of the heirs. He added,

> Only in a comparatively small proportion of cases are the estates administered officially and their proceeds remitted to the heirs through the official channels. Such cases occurr either when the *Panchayat* have not for some reason or other taken any action with a view to, or have not succeeded in, inducing the Bokhara authorities to surrender to them the administration of the estate, or, more frequently when the heirs of the estate do not accept the settlement effected by the *Panchayat*, claiming a larger amount than that realized by the auction sale.

Although a tone of moral indignation was perceptible in Rieu's account, he underlined the fact that merchants declared themselves satisfied with matters as they stood, 'their explanation being that formerly, before the State of Bokhara came within the Russian sphere of influence, the authorities used to confiscate the entire property of British subjects dying within their jurisdiction, so that the present state of affairs was a great improvement on the past'.

Rieu's information is corroborated in numerous instances. Thus in one case, the *panchayat* of Guzar, a locality in the khanate, themselves advised the heirs to an estate to try the official channels, as they had failed to reach an agreement with the *kazi*.[67] Cases which came to the knowledge of the British authorities in the khanate are often characterized by recriminations against the *panchayat* and some individuals who are supected of manipulating the said *panchayat* for personal reasons. It would therefore appear that heirs in Shikarpur used the official system

---

[67] In a *mazhar* addressed to several merchants in Shikarpur, the Shikarpuri *panchayat* of Guzar, a locality in the khanate of Bukhara, having announced the death of a Shikarpuri merchant of the locality, went on to state: 'You may know that the Panchayat here have named Bhai Udhamal Gurbamal Chugh to be the brother of the deceased to Government here. He has now settled disputes and accounts. The Government have taken eleven thousand tangas by force. We have also applied to the Pej Patshah (the government of the Amir) and have received a reply to recover the money according to law. We are unable to recover even according to law here. Therefore the amount of eleven thousand tangas is with the Sirkar and we could not recover, which please note. You will try to get back the amount through British Government. You may try your utmost there so as to get the amount back. You may submit an application and get heirship certificate, when the amount will be recoverable from the Patshah.' True translation of *mazhar* enclosed in memorandum no. 294, 4 April 1900, commissioner in Sind to secretary to government, Political Department, Bombay, BPP, July 1900, Serial no. A 93.

as a last resort when all other channels had failed. There seems to have been a kind of pattern at work in determining who used the official channels. A common characteristic of most of the heirs involved in the 'official' successions was the fact that they had little or no kin; they were often widows, or daughters of the deceased, and found themselves at a disadvantage when negotiating with the *panchayat*. One can surmise *a contrario* that heirs who belonged to large families with extended kin, some of whom were probably on the spot, had a better chance of reaching a satisfactory agreement with the *panchayat*. There was an inverted correlation between size of kin and inclusion in the sample of 'official' successions. On the other hand, there is no evidence that those successions which figure in the official records were smaller than the others. So the bias in the sample has probably more to do with the size of kin than with the value of the estate. It should be added that the official system, although extremely cumbersome and unsatisfactory, nevertheless offered a better chance of recovering the totality of the estate. Provided the heirs were not in a hurry to get money, it was probably a more rational decision to go through the official system rather than to deliver oneself into the hands of the brothers of the *panchayat*. That the majority of heirs in Bukhara chose the unofficial channels can be therefore explained firstly by the fact that most of them needed the money urgently and secondly by a 'cultural' preference for operating within the Shikarpuri network, so as to avoid the prying eyes of the Sarkar. However, for the minority who chose to use the official channels, it could be argued that the colonial state became a substitute for the absent or insufficient kin, thus giving a very concrete meaning to the well-known metaphor of the 'ma-bap' (in which the government was mother and father).

Data are available regarding the value of 113 of the 131 estates in the sample. For methodological reasons, it seemed sensible to include the value of the estate left by the dead man in Shikarpur, as most of it consisted in monies transferred from Central Asia during the lifetime of the merchant and deposited with bankers in Shikarpur. The value of the estate has been taken to be the cumulated value of the estate left by the dead man in Shikarpur and of the amount transferred from Central Asia. All sums have been converted into rupees.

The 113 estates of Shikarpuri merchants who died in Central Asia between 1881 and 1917 have been divided into four groups, according to their worth. In five cases, there was no estate, meaning that the man died a pauper. There were 47 'small' estates, i.e. inferior to Rs 1,000, 49 'substantial' estates, worth between Rs 1,000 and 10,000, and 12 'large' estates, the value of which was superior to 10,000 rupees. Adding the last two categories, one could conclude that the majority of the deceased managed to leave 'substantial' or 'large' estates to their heirs. No very large estate, however, figures in the sample; the biggest was valued at Rs 40,000. This was a very sizeable amount in early twentieth century Sind (where a sum of 1,000 rupees was deemed 'considerable'), but is nothing much compared, for instance, with the estates left by Parsi merchants of Shanghai and Canton in the late nineteenth and early twentieth centuries, which could reach lakhs of rupees.[68] A caveat should however be entered here. The Shikarpuris who travelled to Central Asia were not the richest merchants of the town, but generally *gumasthas* working for a big merchant of Shikarpur. In the sample, there is only one clear case of a *shah* from Shikarpur having travelled to Central Asia for the specific purpose of settling his accounts with his *gumasthas* in Bukhara, where he had the misfortune to die just before he was due to return.[69] He left an estate in Central Asia worth Rs 12,000, but his estate in Shikarpur was not very large, and he is probably not very representative of the class of *shahs* as a whole. All the other merchants included in the sample appear to have started their career as *gumasthas*, even if some then managed to become *shahs* in their turn. They were, therefore, a group of men who left for Central Asia without their own capital, and had to build their fortune from scratch. Considering this, it was no mean achievement for the majority to have been able to leave substantial estates. It should be added that often the amount transferred from Central Asia to Shikarpur represented only part of the value of the estate; in some cases, the entire value of the estate had been misappropriated or confiscated by the authorities. So the realized value of the estate was not necessarily a good benchmark of achievement. Taking into account the value as declared by the heirs to the authorities would lead to a different result; the problem is that there

---

[68] Thus three large Parsi estates in Shanghai in the late nineteenth and early twentieth centuries respectively amounted to £26,750, £10,900 and £8,903. See Public Records Office (PRO), Foreign Office Records, Embassy and Consular Archives: China, Shanghai Supreme Court Probate Records, FO 917/278 (estate of Dorabjee Nusserwanjee Camajee, 1882), FO 917/370 (estate of Hormusjee Dorabjee Camajee, 1886), FO 917/1199 (estate of Jwanbai Bomanji Karanjia, widow of Bomanjee Pallanji Karanjia, 1906).

[69] See petition, 26 June 1901, Kuden, widow of Notandas walad Jamandas who died in Bukhara on 16 June 1900 to collector, Shikarpur district, in BPP, March 1902, Serial no. A 17: 'My husband . . . had dealings in Bukhara. He had the following three agents in that territory; 1) Gobindomal valad Notandas at Kurakol, 2) Hukmat valad Notandas at Girdiwan, 3) Moorijmal valad Sobhraj at Bookharo-Khojejan. In order to settle his accounts with these men and recover the amount of his profits due to him, he proceded to that country three years ago. Having transacted his business there he made preparations to return home with what fortune he obtained, but unfortunately, died all of a sudden . . .'.

is no way of knowing how correct these assessments, often based on hearsay, were.

The total worth of the 113 estates was Rs 388,138. Of this amount, Rs 198,864 had been transferred from Central Asia through official channels on account of 76 estates, the residue being the value of 78 estates in Shikarpur according to heirship certificates, the bulk of which consisted of monies transferred from Central Asia before the death of the merchant and deposited with a few firms of Shikarpuri bankers (because of overlapping, the figures do not add up).

Focusing on some individual estates will help put things in perspective. The largest estate in the sample was that of a man named Mohandas, walad (son of) Janjimal,[70] who died in 1907 in the town of Kitab, in the central region of the khanate of Bukhara, where he had resided for thirty-eight years, which means that he must have been in his fifties or sixties at the time of his death. The estate as descibed by his presumptive heir in Shikarpur, who was his nephew, was indeed considerable. He was owed over 120,000 Bukharan tengas, i.e. Rs 30,000, consisting of: debts owed to him by 'banias of Kitab', i.e. other Shikarpuris of the place, monies due by 'Turks and Pathans', probably landlords who had estates in the vicinity of Kitab, and lastly, debts owed to him by his three *gumasthas*. There was also a certain amount of cash, in tengas and in tillas (Bukharan gold coins), 'ornaments and silken cloths' which were with his *gumasthas, hundis* and receipts, the value of which was unknown, 'lands and gardens and *sarais* in the above mentioned place and surroundings of great value', as well as 'a great stock of woollen and silken goods'. This was the portfolio of a large urban trader-cum-moneylender, accumulated over an entire lifespan. Interestingly, his estate in Shikarpur, also large, consisted almost exclusively of money deposited with two local bankers, fetching high interest, which meant that it had been transferred over a long period of time. The actual sum transferred to India, amounting to £1,885 (Rs 28,500), corresponded more or less to the amount claimed by the heir, which means that in this case the official system functioned quite efficiently. It is worth noting that the man had spent all his adult life in Central Asia, and died unmarried and issueless, leaving his large fortune to a nephew in the paternal line. What is remarkable is that, apart from the money transferred from Central Asia at regular intervals, his estate in Shikarpur consisted only of a share in ancestral property worth Rs 200. It is highly probable that Mohandas left Shikarpur in the late 1860s as the *gumastha*

---

[70] See 'Application from Tikamdas walad Parmanand for the recovery of the estate of his uncle Mohandas walad Janjimal, a British Indian subject who died at Sahar Kitab Zilla Sur Sabz Bokhara in August 1907', BPP, April 1909, Serial no. A 82.

of a Shikarpuri merchant, without capital of his own; he was most probably a younger son of a relatively poor merchant family. Therefore, his is an exemplary success story, not very often repeated.

The same year, 1907, in another part of the khanate of Bukhara, in a village called Kislak Kazan, a man called Hemraj walad Bhojraj,[71] who also left a large fortune, died. He was the only Hindu resident of the village, where he had lived for thirty years, and was murdered by local Muslims, following a quarrel over money (or a woman?). His estate, consisting of some 67,000 tengas, was half in the form of cash, and half in grain and real estate, which probably meant both agricultural land and buildings. His grain stock, which was large, consisted of wheat, barley and other grains. He was clearly a rural moneylender living isolated in a village, a situation which was not without danger. Like the previous one, he died unmarried and issueless, leaving over Rs 15,000 to an elder brother in Shikarpur. His estate in Shikarpur was small, consisting only of a deposit worth Rs 400, and he had not apparently remitted money on a regular basis.

These are two cases of 'long-term sojourners' who spent a whole lifetime in Central Asia and died in possession of large estates. The second one was probably planning to go back to Shikarpur when he was murdered, judging from the fact that he had no debts to recover.

Others managed to accumulate respectable fortunes over shorter periods of time. Thus a man called Dipusing walad Jethasing,[72] who died in 1902, had been a resident of the town of Chirakchi in the khanate of Bukhara for only six years at the time of his death. His estate, worth 37,000 tengas, consisted for half of wheat and barley, the rest being mostly outstanding debts, the typical portfolio of a merchant-moneylender. The shorter length of his stay is easily explained by the fact that he was married and had seven sons, all adults, a clear indication that he had come to Central Asia during the years of his maturity, hoping to make a quick fortune. His estate at Shikarpur was worth only Rs 1,000 and the estate he left in Chirakchi, although worth some Rs 7,000, was not very large for a big family. Some who stayed for very long periods did not achieve as much. Thus a man called Naraindas walad Murjimal,[73] who spent forty years in the town of Katerji in Bukhara,

[71] BPP, October 1908, Serial no. A 78, 'Relative to the recovery of the estate of Hemraj alias Tulo or Tilo walad Bhojrarj Peshawari, who is reported to have been murdered at Kasan or Kaskan in the District of Bukhara'.
[72] BPP, March 1903, Serial no. A 15, 'Claim of Mulsing walad Jethasing to the estate of his brother Dipusing alias Sophua walad Jethasing of Shikarpur who died at Bokhara on 14 May 1902'.
[73] BPP, January 1900, Serial no. A 42, 'Recovery of estate of Naraindas alias Shami walad Murjimal, alias Murich, a British Indian subject who died in Bukharan territory'.

where he died in 1898 (the longest sojourner in the sample), left only some Rs 5,000 to a nephew. His estate consisted mostly in outstandings recovered from 'various Hindus', as well as cash and ornaments. His profile was more specifically that of a typical moneylender.

There were also some who failed, leaving no estate (in very few cases), or estates which were so small that they did not cover the expenses their heirs incurred in trying to recover them. In some cases, the heirs could recover only a small part of the estate they claimed, for a variety of reasons. One could give the example of a man known from Russian sources as Bay Souba Bay Djouba,[74] who was murdered in Khokand, in Ferghana, in 1882, and whose assets, consisting of various documents, were less than his liabilities. He was probably a *gumastha*, and his *shah*, claiming that he was indebted to him to a larger amount, actually laid his hands on the estate. Sometimes detailed inventories of personal effects are included in the documents, and they sound an almost pathetic note, throwing light on a world of men living with very few personal possessions, a fact which one does not know whether to ascribe to actual poverty or to self-denial.

Keeping in mind that successions realized through the 'official' channels were, at least in Bukhara, only the tip of the iceberg, one can only guess what the amount actually transferred could have been. Large sums of money were undoubtedly sent each year from Central Asia to Shikarpur, either on account of transfers of estates of merchants who had died, or of remittances sent by merchants to their families and their principals. Most of the money was probably sent by the way of *hundis* drawn by Shikarpuri bankers in Central Asia on their principals in Shikarpur. But, at least prior to the 1890s, merchants also brought back bullion; the Bukharan tilla was a gold coin of exceptional purity, which fetched a premium in Shikarpur. On the other hand, nothing is known of possible transfers of funds from Shikarpur to Central Asia. *Gumasthas* who left the town for Central Asia generally had money only for their travel expenses; they left with *hundis* from their principals with which they obtained credit in Central Asia to operate. The operations of the Shikarpuris in Central Asia appear to have been sufficiently profitable to be largely self-financing, except for the money borrowed from the Russian banks and repaid from the profits made locally. The operations of the Shikarpuris in Central Asia do not appear to have been the cause of the 'steady leakage' of gold across the land frontier mentioned by

[74] Letter from Russian Ministry of Foreign Affairs enclosed in despatch no. 156 from St Petersburg to Foreign Office, 20 June 1883, enclosed in Foreign Office to India Office, 3 July 1883, IOR, Public and Judicial Annual Files 1880–1930, File J&P 1127/1883, L/ P &J/6/101.

Keynes in 1913.[75] Gold exports from India are reported to have entirely financed the deficit in the transborder trade, which was estimated at Rs 30 lakhs in 1911–12. On the other hand, it is highly probable that the Shikarpuri bankers of Peshawar, in relation with those of Kabul and Kandahar, were very much involved in the export of gold to pay for imports from Afghanistan into India. The importers, however, were mostly Muslim merchants from Peshawar, who were also involved in the export of tea to Central Asia. This suggests a certain amount of segmentation in the Shikarpuri network between Central Asian operations on the one hand, which remained closely controlled from Shikarpur, and financing of trade between India and Afghanistan on the other hand, which was organized from Peshawar by local bankers of Shikarpuri origin.

Successional documents allow only a glimpse into the actual operations of the network, but they reveal that it was still in full operation on the eve of the Russian Revolution. The revolutionary period itself led to the production of new kinds of documents, which were mostly claims filed by Shikarpuri merchants with the British authorities in the hope of being compensated at a later stage by the Russian authorities. Although such claims have to be taken with a certain amount of caution, since there is no way of checking their accuracy, they nevertheless offer an insight into the dynamics of the Shikarpuri network, as it was at work even in the middle of the revolutionary troubles. Thus a series of claims filed in 1918–19 by merchants who were caught in the fighting around Kermineh in the khanate of Bukhara, which was at one point the front line in the war between the Red Army and the Bukharans allied to the Whites, shows that some Shikarpuri merchants were travelling with very large stocks of goods. Six claims for compensation filed with the authorities in 1918,[76] of which five emanated from the Kermineh area, amounted to a total of more than Rs 5 lakhs, of which goods in stock accounted for some Rs 350,000. Considering that the conditions were disturbed in 1918, it gives an idea of the amount of trading which could

---

[75] J. M. Keynes, *Indian Currency and Finance*, London, 1913, p. 75.

[76] Thus two merchants claimed losses of 76,000 roubles (i.e. Rs 1 lakh), of which 40,000 consisted of a stock of goods such as tea, sugar, soap and flour. See petition, 14 August 1918 from Messrs Dooloomal and Radhamal of Shikarpur (Sind) to under-secretary to government of Bombay, Political Department, BPP, October 1918, Serial no. A 385. Another merchant reported losses of over 200,000 roubles (i.e. over Rs 3 lakhs), of which 100,000 was accounted for by one single diamond (a claim the plausibility of which is of course impossible even to assess), and 20,000 by various kind of foodstuffs (potato, jam, flour, rice and tea). See petition, 29 August 1918, from Mr Khemchand Udhavdas of Shikarpur to same, BPP, December 1918, Serial no. A 498. A third one claimed to have lost 70 cases of matches worth 8,400 roubles. See petition, 12 November 1918, from Mr Dulabmal Nevendram of Shikarpur to same, *ibid*.

be going on in normal circumstances. The goods the Shikarpuris traded in were varied in kind and of diverse provenance. Incidental information found in another document tells us of a Shikarpuri commercial firm in the town of Jizak near Samarkand. It appeared to have been founded in the 1860s to deal in grain and cotton, and was still active in 1914 when the Russian authorities took measures against it, which led to a complaint to the Privy Council in London by the principal of the firm.[77] There are thus indications that, apart from moneylending operations and the attendant trade in grain, Shikarpuris were involved in a wide range of trading activities in the khanate of Bukhara and the guberniia of Turkestan. An estimate by the collector of Shikarpur in 1900[78] was that the annual total income of the Central Asian traders of Shikarpur was Rs 1.5 lakh. Shikarpuris in the region were not, however, confined to Russian Central Asia. They were also active in Afghanistan, in Southeastern Iran and in southern Sinkiang (Kashgaria).

Other areas of Shikarpuri activity: Iran, Afghanistan and Sinkiang

No corpus of documents regarding Shikarpuri activities in these areas comparable to the successional documents from Russian Central Asia has come to light. The most useful source on Shikarpuri activities outside Russian Central Asia is to be found in the diaries of the Kashgar agency, which became at some point the Kashgar consulate. It gives a fairly detailed, although extremely hostile account of the activities of Shikarpuri moneylenders in southern Sinkiang, or Kashgaria (there is no evidence of a Shikarpuri presence in the rest of this huge territory), from the 1890s to the 1940s, which saw the last Shikarpuris leave the region.

Although Burnes, in his 1837 text, listed Yarkand as one of the places where the Shikarpuri merchants had agents, subsequent British documents, such as the account of the mission which visited Yarkand in 1873,[79] do not mention their presence. It is only in the 1890s that Shikarpuris became a noticeable presence in the southern parts of the

[77] Petition by Ramdas alias Dilaram, Shikarpur 3 June 1914, enclosed in Privy Council to under-secretary of state for foreign affairs, 23 June 1914, IOR, Political and Secret Annual Files 1912–1930, File P 2785/1912, L/P&S/11/24.

[78] Memorandum no. P/01, 16 November 1900. See above, note 56.

[79] See *Report on a Mission to Yarkand in 1873, with the comment of Sir T. D. Forsyth with historical and geographical information regarding the possessions of the Ameer of Yarkand*, Calcutta, 1875, in particular Appendices, pp. 496 ff., giving list of principal merchants. No mention of the Shikarpuris occurs either in James A. Millward, *Beyond the Pass: Economy, Ethnicity and Empire in Quing Central Asia 1759–1864*, Stanford, 1998, a detailed study of the Sinkiang economy.

'New Dominion'. They were not the only, or even the principal, Indian traders in that area. The actual trade between India and Sinkiang via the high Karakoram Pass[80] was controlled by Punjabi Hindu merchants from the town of Hoshiarpur. Kashmiri Muslim merchants also travelled regularly to Sinkiang. It is not known whether the Shikarpuris who entered Sinkiang in the 1890s came from neighbouring Russian Turkestan, following the trail which led from Osh, the easternmost town in Ferghana, to Kashgar and Yarkand, or whether they came directly from Shikarpur via Kashmir, attracted by the opportunities offered by British protection in this western march of the Chinese Empire. When Macartney, in 1900, took his post as special assistant for Chinese affairs in Kashgar under the resident in Kashmir, he wrote to his superiors a detailed report on British interests in the area, in which he mentioned the presence of 130 Shikarpuri moneylenders.[81] Five years later, their number had reached 400, and in 1907 they numbered 500.[82] According to information given to Shuttleworth, who was Macartney's assistant, some 60 per cent of them were *gumasthas* employed in the collection of debts and who had no capital of their own.[83] Some of these *gumasthas* were described as 'bad characters', men against whom there were court cases in Shikarpur for 'house-breaking'. Their exactions against the local population in the course of collecting debts, in particular their seizing of women and children as sureties, led to a string of protests from the Uighur peasantry[84] which were relayed by the Chinese authorities to the British consular authorities. Dealing with the affairs of the Shikarpuris became a large part of the routine activities of the local British representative. Shuttleworth wrote in exasperation: 'Shikarpuris will never meet the Chinese (i.e. the local Chinese magistrate in charge of settling civil disputes) half-way, and the amount of trouble they are giving to the magistrate is considerable. The Chinese and I are only too ready to help them to collect their debts, but there is no satisfying these vultures. I have seldom come across a race with so few good points; they

---

[80] See J. Rizvi, 'The Trans-Karakoram Trade in the Nineteenth and Twentieth Centuries', *The Indian Economic and Social History Review* (IESHR), vol. 31, no. 1, 1994, pp. 27–64.

[81] See C. P. Skrine and P. Nightingale, *Macartney at Kashgar: New Light on British, Chinese and Russian Activities in Sinkiang, 1890–1918*, London, 1973, p. 116.

[82] *Ibid.*, p. 148.   [83] *Ibid.*, pp. 158–9.

[84] In the Kashgar diary, under the entry for 5 November 1908, copy in IOR, Political & Secret Correspondence with India 1875–1911, Political & Secret Letters from India 1908, L/P&S/7/224, Macartney's deputy, Shuttleworth wrote from Karghalik, a locality in Kashgaria: 'I have received number of petitions by Kashgaris against the Shikarpuris of this place. I have heard over 25 cases today. The chief grievances are: (i) exorbitant interest; (ii) bonds not being returned, although the money has been fully paid up; (iii) being made to sign back for larger sums of money than those received; (iv) being forcibly kept in confinement until the money is paid or a fresh bond signed for a larger amount.'

are indeed an unlovable lot'.[85] Attempts were made to limit their influx, and even to send some of them back to India. Thus in 1908–09, up to half of them were sent back, and, although some of them came back later, the Shikarpuri community in Kashgaria seems to have ceased expanding. However, it remained active till the early 1930s, when an anti-Chinese rising in 1933, leading to the death and ruin of many Shikarpuris, almost put an end to that chapter of history.

The Shikarpuri venture into Sinkiang in 1890–1933 seems an interesting instance of a purely opportunistic operation. Shikarpuris appear to have been attracted to Sinkiang by the combination of a demand for credit, apparently in part for gambling purposes, which was not entirely satisfied by the local Muslim merchants and the immigrant Afghan and Kashmiri Muslim merchants, and of the legal protection offered to foreign subjects by the capitulation system. They specialized in small loans at very high rates of interest to a multiplicity of small borrowers, which was a way of spreading risk. According to the account of a British traveller,[86] who expressed the usual hostility to their practices, but observed them at close quarters, they used the opportunity of temporary bazaars all over the country, to lend sums varying between 4 annas and 5 rupees to merchants 'and other who were temporarily pressed'. This would explain how they were spread out extensively throughout the whole of southern Sinkiang, not only along the main route of the oasis which went from Kashgar to Keriya through Yangi Hissar, Yarkand, Kargalik, Posgam and Goma, but also along the less important road linking Yarkand with Aksu via Merket and Maralbashi, as well as in smaller mountain localities such as Khanarik. They were constantly on the move, trying to recuperate small amounts of money they had lent to borrowers in various small localities. Although the local peasantry was very poor and little inclined to repay its debts, Shikarpuris, by bribing local *kazis* and Chinese officials and pressurizing the local British representative, managed to achieve a rate of repayment which was superior to the one obtained in Sind. In Sinkiang the Shikarpuris appear to have been almost pure 'usurers', employing coercion to obtain repayment of short-term loans. Some of them, however, also did some trading, mostly dealing in Russian and local products rather than in Indian goods.[87] In the absence of estate documents comparable to those

[85] Kashgar diary, entry for 15 February 1909, copy IOR, Political and Secret Letters from India, 1909, L/P&S/7/227.
[86] D. Fraser, *The Marches of Hindustan, the Record of a Journey in Thibet, Trans-Himalayan India, Chinese Turkestan, Russian Turkestan and Persia*, Edinburgh and London, 1907, pp. 272–3.
[87] See Kashgar diary entry for 17 August 1903, IOR, Political & Secret Letters from India 1903, L/P&S/7 157: 'Meng Raj (a prominent local Shikarpuri) says he used to buy 200

concerning Russian Central Asia (the reason being that there were apparently no particular problems in transferring to India the residue of the estates of those Shikarpuris who happened to die there), it is difficult to produce an estimate of the balance sheet of the Shikarpuri venture in Sinkiang. There is some evidence that the operations of the Shikarpuris contributed to the drain of precious metals from Sinkiang under the regime of governor Yang Tseng-Hsin (1911–28).[88]

More precise indications are provided by the documents concerning the 1933 rising in southern Sinkiang which led to the proclamation of an ephemeral Republic of Eastern Turkestan.[89] In the course of the rising, which was directed mainly against the Chinese administration, Shikarpuris in some localities became a target for the mobs: some were killed and others saw their properties looted. When order was reestablished, an estimate of the losses endured by British subjects was presented by the British consular authorities to the Chinese authorities.[90] In all, twenty-five Shikarpuris lost assets worth some Rs 2 lakhs, consisting partly of cash, partly of goods, houses and personal effects. This reflected some shifting from 'pure' moneylending to 'trading-cum-moneylending' after 1909, following pressure applied by the local British representative. The most compact evidence comes from the town of Karghalik.[91] The eight Shikarpuris killed there, whose entire property was looted by the rioters, had assets worth Rs 132,000, i.e. some 16,000 per head, which is not a negligible figure. It is not known over how many years they had accumulated that amount or how much had been remitted to Shikarpur.

The evidence from the Kashgar diaries shows that, as in Russian Central Asia, the Shikarpuris in Sinkiang lived in small colonies, mostly in their own *sarais*, and that they had a similar *panchayat* organization. Where the Shikarpuris represented the bulk of the British Indian population, the Indian *Aksakal* (headman) was a Shikarpuri, but in some large localities he was generally a Kashmiri Muslim or a Hoshiarpuri.

---

maunds per week of wheat flour in Yarkand for export to Fyzabad (a neighbouring town).'

[88] L. E. Nyman, *Great Britain and Chinese, Russian and Japanese Interests in Sinkiang, 1918–1934*, Lund, 1977, p. 30.

[89] On the events of 1933–4 in southern Sinkiang, see A. K. Wu, *Turkistan Tumult*, London, 1940, pp. 240–53 and A. D. W. Forbes, *Warlords and Muslims in Chinese Central Asia: a Political History of Republican Sinkiang 1911–1949*, Cambridge, 1986, pp. 63–96.

[90] See British consul, Kashgar to foreign secretary, Government of India, in the Foreign & Political Department, 23 January 1936, enclosed in F 1439/2/10, PRO, Foreign Office Records, Foreign Office General (Political) Correspondence, Far East 1936, FO 371/20 220.

[91] Appendix 'C', 'List of losses of British subjects murdered in Kargalik', in *ibid*.

A difference with Russian Central Asia is that Shikarpuris in Sinkiang had local 'common law' wives (and presumably therefore children). The only successional document which has come to light regarding Sinkiang thus includes an interesting clause. In the will which a Shikarpuri of Yarkand drafted in favour of his partner, it was specified that the partner had to provide for the woman he kept.[92] The difference in the 'sexual economy' of the Shikarpuri diaspora in Sinkiang as compared with Russian Central Asia will be taken up later.

The story of the Sinkiang venture of the Shikarpuris shows how quickly information circulated within the network. As soon as a British agency was established in Kashgar, the Shikarpuris, whose links to the area appear to have been at best tenuous, were there scouting opportunities. Nor does the sheer length and difficulty of the voyage, which involved the crossing of several very high passes, appear to have been a discouraging factor, or the absence of communications by telegraph. As to the origins of funds, it seems that they must have come at first either from Shikarpur or from Russian territory, but that very rapidly the network became self-supporting, as part of the profits generated were reinvested in new loans. Given the small size of most loans, the initial investment from outside need not have been of any magnitude. The extension of Shikarpuri operations into Sinkiang was facilitated by the fact that the currency system was the same as in Russian Turkestan, with both Russian roubles and local tengas being legal tender, while Chinese taels seem to have been used only as a counting currency. Regarding the Shikarpuri venture into Sinkiang, one can conclude that it was an opportunistic offshoot of British attempts at establishing a foothold in the region so as to keep a close watch on Russian movements, but did not have a lasting local impact (except through the emergence of a category of half-castes, the product of temporary unions between Shikarpuris and local Uighur women, a group whose fate has not attracted any attention in the literature).

In Afghanistan and Iran, Shikarpuri involvement had a much longer

[92] See consul at Kashgar to resident in Kashmir, enclosed in resident in Kashmir no. 422–G, 23 May 1917, to foreign secretary to the Government of India in the Foreign and Political Department, BPP, October 1917, Serial no. A 572, in which the consul stated that on 23 March 1916 the Indian Aksakal at Yarkand reported the death, one month earlier, of Dwarkadas walad Kundandas, a Shikarpuri merchant of Islambagh near Yarkand. The Aksakal sent copies of two 'deeds of conveyance' dated 1915. 'In the former', the Consul wrote, 'Dwarkadas said that as he was no longer able to carry on business owing to ill-health, he gave all his property, which consisted of one Sarai and four rooms in Da-Shambi(?) Bazaar, of one shop and one room at Kancheng, and of his money-lending account books and bonds to Talia Ram in consideration of Talia Ram maintaining him and a woman named Mariam Bibi kept by Dwarkadas, as long as Dwarkadas was alive in Turkestan.'

history. Actually it has been mentioned already that the Shikarpuri network started as an 'Afghan' network at the time of the Durrani Empire, and it appears that connections with Afghanistan remained close throughout the nineteenth century and even the first half of the twentieth century. However, only incidental evidence has come to light regarding Shikarpuri activities in Afghanistan. It seems that all important Afghan cities, and a certain number of lesser localities had a Shikarpuri bazaar. Kandahar, as the closest to Shikarpur, appears to have sheltered the largest, richest and most active of Shikarpuri communities in Afghanistan. An account of a tour of Afghanistan by the amir written in 1907 by the British agent at Kabul[93] gives some interesting information. Six 'leading men' among the Hindus of Kandahar are mentioned, of whom five, judging from their name, appear to have been Shikarpuris. The richest, one Faqir Chand, was said to be worth 6 lakhs in cash, indicating his function as a banker. According to Gregorian, in the early twentieth century, the Hindus (amongst whom the Shikarpuris figured prominently, though the appellation applied also to Punjabi Sikhs and Hindus) were still the most numerous and wealthiest merchant class in Herat (with some 700 Hindus), Kabul and Kandahar, and they had trading colonies in Balkh, Ghazni, Sabzawar, Tashkurgan and Maimana, controlling most of the export trade.[94] What is not very clear is the amount of actual circulation between Shikarpur and Afghanistan, especially when other routes between Shikarpur and Central Asia became popular. Shikarpuris must have suffered from the measures taken under Abd-ur-Rahman to increase the taxation and control of the merchants by the state. However some evidence regarding repatriation of Shikarpuris from Russian Central Asia after the Russian Revolution indicates that the Shikarpuri network was still active in the kingdom in the early 1930s.

The spread of the Shikarpuri network in southeastern Iran is an altogether different story. Stephen Dale mentions large-scale Multani activities in Iran in the seventeenth century, centred particularly around Isfahan. In the late eighteenth century, according to George Forster, these activities were largely confined to the eastern part of the country, and Turshish was the westernmost outpost of this Multani network, other colonies being at Murchid, Yezd, Kachan, Casbin and some ports of the Caspian shore. On the other hand, Shikarpuri activities in Iran

[93] *Report on the Tour in Afghanistan of His Majesty Amir Habib-Ulla Khan in 1907 by Fakir Sayid Iftikhar-ud-Din, British Agent at Kabul*, Simla, 1908, pp. 16–17, enclosed in Secret Letter from India no. 511, 4 February 1909, IOR, Political & Secret Letters from India 1909, L/P&S/225.
[94] V. Gregorian, *The Emergence of Modern Afghanistan: Policies of Reform and Modernisation, 1880–1946*, Stanford, 1969, pp. 62–3.

in the late nineteenth and early twentieth centuries appear to have been even more restricted in their geographical scope, and to have been largely concentrated around Bandar Abbas and Kirman. The Hindu community in Bandar Abbas whose number was 66 around 1900[95] appears to have consisted mostly of Shikarpuris, who were agents for Shikarpur firms, and the twenty British-Indian merchants of Kirman mentioned by Sykes, the local British consul, in 1902 were all Shikarpuris.[96] I have not been able to discover when exactly Shikarpuris started operating along this route. One judicial document[97] mentions the existence of a 'millionaire' firm from Shikarpur which had been operating in Persia for 'a century', which would indicate that it was founded around 1830. It appears that, by the early twentieth century, this particular branch of the Shikarpuri network was acting mainly in the position of agents for big British firms in Karachi and Bombay (such as Forbes, Forbes, Campbell) to sell British and Indian textiles on the markets of southern Persia. There was a group of merchants in Shikarpur called the Persian Gulf merchants, who were specifically engaged in this trade through the agents they had at Bandar Abbas and Kirman.[98] This trade, which appears to have been on a rather considerable scale,[99] was ultimately controlled by British firms.[100] The connec-

[95] *Lorrimer's Gazetter of the Persian Gulf, Oman and Central Arabia*, vol. II, *Geographical and Statistical*, Calcutta, 1908, p. 10.

[96] P. M. Sykes, *Ten Thousand Miles in Persia or Eight Years in Iran*, London, 1902.

[97] Petition of Gangaram Shewaram, Shikarpur 18 January 1928, to British vice-consul at Duzdap, enclosed in Foreign Office to India Office, 13 February 1928, IOR, Political and Secret Annual Files 1912–1930, File P/840/1928, L/P&S/11/288: 'I Gangaram son of Shewaram, merchant and banker of Duzdap (East Persia) now at Shikarpur (Sind) must humbly... beg to state that I had a firm of moneylending business and other trade at Duzdap, and am an agent working partner of Messrs Tharoomal Ramdas Khemchand a millionare [sic] firm whose business is extended in many places in Persia since the last one century from the day of his [sic] ancestors.'

[98] See letter, Shikarpur, 9 October 1914, addressed to secretary, Foreign Department, Government of India, by eight Shikarpuri merchants giving their address as 'The Persian Gulf Merchants', c/o Seth Dayaram Menghraj, Shikarpur. They complained about the lack of telegraphic facilities for the remittance of money from Kirman to Bombay. IOR, Political and Secret Separate (or Subject) Files, File 283/1912, L/P&S/10/214.

[99] In a letter, 16 September 1912, from the collector of Sukkur to the undersecretary in the government of Bombay in the Political Department, enclosed in ibid., it was mentioned that 'the Shikarpur merchants who trade in Persia had borrowed to the extent of about Rs 3 million for investment in their trade'.

[100] See letter, 29 June 1912, from M. de P. Webb, chairman of the Karachi Chamber of Commerce to the secretary to the Government of India in the Foreign Department, in ibid. He wrote to give his support to the demand by Shikarpuri merchants to be protected by armed escorts on the route between Bandar Abbas and Kirman, where attacks by bandits on caravans were frequent, and he added: 'these Indian merchants are directly connected with members of this Chamber in matters of exports, imports and finance'.

tion with the Shikarpuri network was through Karachi, where Shikarpuris were known to be very active, and it was through British firms in Karachi that they ordered the goods which were sent directly from Europe to Bandar Abbas. The reason why British firms traded through Shikarpuri agents rather than directly has probably to do with questions of cost and also with the fact that it was difficult to induce Britishers to reside for any length of time in such places as Bandar Abbas or Kirman which were neither pleasant nor safe. An official report of 1906 clearly said: 'Our chief hope lies in persuading Indian traders . . . to settle in Persia'.[101] The expansion in the trade after 1907 resulted in a further influx of Shikarpuris: the community in Bandar Abbas grew to 100 in 1913 and that at Kerman to 50.[102] This occurred in spite of the fact that the caravan route between Bandar Abbas and Kirman was often under attack from bandits, which led to an accumulation of claims by Shikarpuri merchants against the Persian authorities, which gives some idea of the scale of their operations.[103]

Trade and politics were very closely intertwined in Persia in the late nineteenth and early twentieth centuries, as Britain was vying for supremacy with Russia, leading to the 1907 agreement, which divided the country into two 'spheres of influence', southern Persia being in the British sphere. The close relationship between trade and politics and the way in which Shikarpuri merchants were used by the British to advance British and Indian trade in southern Persia (and the way in which the Shikarpuris in their turn made use of the British connection to enhance their own interests) come out even more clearly from the story of the land route developed between India and Persia in the early twentieth century. A rail link, mostly geared to strategic purposes, was constructed between Nushki in Baluchistan and the Persian border at Duzdap (now known as Zahedan). British authorities then tried to make it profitable by encouraging the development of trade between Quetta and the Iranian border province of Seistan, which was poor and isolated. Since

[101] *Report on the British Indian Commercial Mission to South-Eastern Persia during 1904–05*, A. H. Glendowe-Newcomen, Calcutta, 1906.
[102] As mentioned in the 'Report on the trade and commerce of Bandar Abbas for 1912–13', enclosed in H. V. Biscoe, consul, to the secretary to the Government of India in the Foreign Department, 20 December 1913, India Foreign Proceedings, External, February 1914, Pro No. 5.
[103] A list of seventy-five claims on behalf of British Indians was submitted to the Persian authorities by the British in 1933. They mostly referred to outrages committed before 1914. Although the fact that the merchants were Shikarpuris was mentioned in only one claim, the evidence of onomastics suggests that the vast majority of the claimants were Shikarpuri merchants based in Bandar Abbas or elsewhere. The amounts claimed could reach large sums. PRO, Foreign Office Records, Foreign Office General (Political) Correspondence, Political (Eastern) Persia 1933, 'List of claims of British subjects against Persian government, Bander Abbas claims', FO 371/16949.

British traders were understandably reluctant to embark upon a venture with such uncertain prospects, the British authorities tried to induce Indian traders to step in, but they were equally reluctant to do so. Various groups of traders, Muslims of Quetta, Punjabi Sikhs from Rawalpindi and Campbellpore, were solicited, and the British also sought to enrol the Shikarpuris in that new venture. In 1901 the Government of India advanced a loan of Rp 1 lakh, not a negligible sum, to a big Shikarpuri firm to induce them to develop trade in Seistan.[104] It was to prove a disappointing venture, but one in the course of which some interesting documents were produced, which throw a crude light on state-sponsored trade in southern Persia in the early twentieth century.

The firm, known as Messrs Chiman Singh Ram Singh and Co., owned in partnership by two brothers, who were well established and held the opium farm for the whole of Sind, started operations in Seistan in 1901, but the account books shown to the British consul and reproduced by him in his correspondence with the Foreign Department of the Government of India[105] show that the firm purchased goods in India for a total value of only 260,000 Persian krans, i.e. less than Rs 80,000, which means that the loan was not entirely used up and that the firm avoided engaging any of its own capital in the venture. The account books for the period November 1900–July 1902 indicate a net loss of some 25,000 krans, most of the losses being on sales of wool and indigo, as well as on exchange and on debts unpaid. During the following period, July 1902–April 1904, things improved a bit, as a net profit of some 20,000 krans was recorded, though this was not sufficient to compensate the losses of the previous period. There are reasons nevertheless to think that the account books presented to the consul gave only a partial picture of the truth. The officiating consul in Seistan wrote in December 1903[106] that to his knowledge the agent of the firm had

[104] See 'Indenture made on 23 September 1901 between Collector of Shikarpur on behalf of the Secretary of State for India in Council of the one part and Seths Chimansing and Gulabsing contractors sons of Seth Ramsing of Shikarpur of the other part. Whereas the Government of India have been pleased to advance to the executants one lakh of rupees with a view to enabling them to carry on trade in Seistan, Birjand and Meshed by establishing shops for the sale of English and Indian goods at these places on the condition of payment of interest at the rate of 4 per cent per annum', reproduced as Appendix to Serial no. A 58, BPP, July 1904, 'Request of the Government of India to be furnished with a copy of the security-bonds taken from Messrs Chiman Singh Ram Sing & Co of Shikarpur and their sureties on the occasion of the loan made to them by Government in 1901'.

[105] Letter no. 293, 9 June 1904 from Captain A. D. Macpherson, His Britannic Majesty's consul at Seistan and Kain to Louis W. Dane, secretary to the Government of India in the Foreign Department, enclosed in Serial no. A 84, BPP, July 1904.

[106] Letter no. 717, 15 December 1903, from Captain A. D. G. Ramsay, officiating consul

remitted some rupees Rs 20,000 during the previous two months, 'which were certainly not sale-proceeds of his shop during that period'. He strongly suspected the agent of having made his profits in moneylending, although the contract with the government specifically provided that the loan had to be used for trading purposes. The same accusation was levied by the consul in Khorrassan against the agent of the firm in Meshed.[107] The firm appears to have closed its business in Seistan in 1906, following a dispute between the partners.

State-sponsored trade proved a disappointing experience in Southeastern Persia, both for the colonial state, which did not succeed in stimulating the sale of British and Indian goods in the area on the scale expected, and for the merchants who did not find the venture sufficiently profitable and had to recoup their losses by resorting to moneylending. It is interesting to note that the agents of the Shikarpur firms in Kirman, who traded more successfully in goods they received from Bandar Abbas, were also accused by a British official of indulging in moneylending on the side.[108] It is obvious that, given the undeveloped state of the credit market in Persia, there was more profit to be made in moneylending than in trading, in spite of the high risks of not recovering one's money. Another unrecorded activity of the Shikarpuri merchants in Persia, from which substantial profits could be derived, was the trade in the turquoises produced in Nishapur in Khorrassan,[109] over which the Shikarpuris seem to have enjoyed a kind of monopoly. Well into the twentieth century, Shikarpur was known as a place where high quality gems could be procured at attractive prices.[110]

Iran was where the Shikarpuri presence endured longest, and where the greatest of all Shikarpuri fortunes was started. The reasons why it was so are not obvious, but they may have to do with cultural affinities. Shikarpuri Hindus lived in a cultural world which was persianized, even if few of them knew High Persian. Their commercial terminology was

in Seistan to Louis W. Dane, enclosed in letter no. 1997, 17 May 1904, from E. H. S. Clarke, assistant secretary to the Government of India, Foreign Department, to S. W. Edgerley, acting chief secretary to government, Political Department, Bombay, Serial no. A 83, BPP, May 1904.

[107] Letter no. 149, 12 March 1904, from Lt.-Col. C. F. Minchin, HBM's consul-general and agent of the Government of India in Khorrassan to Louis W. Dane, *ibid.*

[108] P. M. Sykes, *Ten Thousand Miles*, p. 198: 'their trade flourishes, but as money-lenders of the most voracious kind, they are unsurpassed'.

[109] The consul in Khorrassan, in the above-quoted letter, mentioned that the agent of the firm in Meshed, one Chooharsingh, 'took away with him to India turquoises worth a considerable sum of money'.

[110] An official survey written in 1919 mentioned that 'pearls from the Persian Gulf, rubies from Burma and other gems of all kinds are sold at Shikarpur and that their reputation for quality and cheapness is not undeserved'. *Gazetteer of the Province of Sind 'B'*, vol. III, *Sukkur District*, Bombay, 1919.

Persian and may have been originally imported from that country. In spite of a certain degree of political instability, Iran in the twentieth century was spared the massive upheavals which resulted in the uprooting of the Shikarpuris from Russian Central Asia and Sinkiang and their gradual wilting away in Afghanistan.

In the history of the Shikarpuri Hindu *banias* in the twentieth century the two defining moments were, firstly, the Russian Revolution which resulted in their expulsion from Central Asia and, secondly, the Partition of 1947. Between 1917 and 1947, the Shikarpuri network went through a process of reorientation which, in some ways, laid the basis for the post-1947 developments.

The Shikarpuri network betweeen 1917 and 1947

The Russian Revolution, and especially the fall of the khanate of Bukhara to the Red Army in September 1920, and the proclamation of the Bukharan Soviet Republic (which was later divided between the Soviet Republics of Uzbekistan and Tajikistan), resulted in a massive exodus of Shikarpuris from Central Asia. Little is known about its exact modalities, nor did all Shikarpuris immediately leave Soviet territory. Some of them remained stranded there and had to survive in very difficult circumstances. In the official records some individual stories have been preserved which show the resilience of these merchants in the face of a hostile environment. A petition presented in April 1921 to the deputy commissioner of Peshawar by a rich Peshawari Muslim merchant, K. B. Haji Karimbaksh[111] enclosed a vivid description of the entry of the Red Army into Bukhara, which is worth quoting:

In the attack that took place at 2 o'clock at night, the invaders wrecked [sic] their vengeance on His Majesty's British subject [sic] to their hearts content. They spared neither life nor property of the British subject and duelled [sic] all the operations, against Sarai Kazi Kalan which is the commercial quarters of all the Indian, His Majesty's subjects. Incendiary bombs were dropped from Aeroplanes and the place was completely burnt to ashes.

Although the *sarai* here mentioned appears to have been the *sarai* of the Peshawari Muslim merchants, and not the main Shikarpuri *sarai*, which was known as the Kanchhi *sarai*, it is most likely that the Shikarpuri *sarais* knew the same fate. No estimate of loss of life in the war from amongst the Shikarpuri community has come down to us, but it was

[111] Petition, 23 April 1921, enclosed in chief commissioner North West Frontier Province to foreign secretary, Government of India, Foreign & Political Department, memo no. 193/D. W., 18 May 1921, IOR, Political and Secret Annual Files 1912–1930, File P 2696/1922, L/P&S/11/216.

probably not negligible. Most Shikarpuris, however, apparently managed to make their escape from the territory conquered by the Red Army through Afghanistan, the route also followed by thousands of Bukharan Muslims, and the amir of Bukhara himself. Shikarpuris continued to surface in Afghanistan until the early 1930s, often telling harrowing tales of harassment and claiming huge losses of property which they registered with the authorities, in the naive hope that they would one day get compensation. The most interesting of these narratives was a petition presented in December 1931 to the British consul in Kabul by two Shikarpuris, known as Lala and Nicha, who had reached Kandahar.[112] They had gone to Bukhara in 1905, and had apparently prospered. They wrote:

In 1920, some Bolsheviks forcibly took away our cash and all our articles of merchandise that we had approximately valued at 124,000 *Sumbs*, equal to between 60,000 and 70,000 Indian rupees and then in our presence set fire to our shop. Our miseries did not end there but they took us prisoners and carried us to Samarqand where we were set free after a month's terrible tortures which human tongue cannot describe nor can even a hardheaded man dare hearing them. We then returned to Bokhara in most indigent circumstances and approached the authorities but in vain . . . As we had nothing with us, the only alternative we had was to take petty loans and carry on our business afresh till such time as we had repaid all our loans and had sufficient money to return to India. Accordingly we availed of this opening and in April last had some 9,000 *Sumbs* with us when we made up our mind to leave for India.

They complained that most of their belongings had been confiscated by the Soviet border guards at the Afghan border, and registered a claim. They eventually left for Shikarpur in January 1932. Leaving aside the rhetoric, which may have been a bit overblown in the hope of attracting the sympathy of the British representatives to men who had been victimized by the Bolsheviks, this testimony allows us a glimpse into the life of those Shikarpuris who had stayed behind in 1920 and had to start again from scratch. It shows that under the Soviet regime, including in the post-NEP phase (but full-scale collectivization of the economy in Central Asia occurred only after 1936), they were able to continue petty trading activities which allowed them to survive and even to accumulate capital on a small scale. Shikarpuris continued to be repatriated from the Soviet Union up to the late 1930s. It is probable that some, who had married local women, just merged into the Uzbek population, but as a

[112] Petition 27 December 1931 enclosed in memo no. 531, 28 December 1931, from HBM consul Kandahar to counsellor, British Legation, Kabul, enclosed in counsellor, British Legation, Kabul, memo no. 194, 9 January 1932, to deputy secretary to the Government of India, Foreign & Political Department, copy in IOR, Political & Secret External Files and Collections, Collection 32/5, 'Position of British subjects in Russia and their protection' L/P&S/12/4007.

distinct group the Shikarpuris had apparently disappeared by the late 1930s. Thus ended a venture which had started in the late eighteenth century and had for a century and a half played an important role in the economy of the region.

The sudden return of so many men who had spent long periods abroad must have had an impact on the Shikarpuri economy, by closing an important source of remittances. After 1920, most of the surplus male population in Shikarpur who had come back from Central Asia appear to have moved to other localities in India. Karachi was certainly a major destination for the Shikarpuris: they were already a well-established merchant community there and there is evidence that their role in the commodities trade of Karachi increased in the 1920s. Other areas of activity in India for the Shikarpuri *shroffs* were Bombay, where their presence was of long standing, but where in the 1920s they emerged as one of the major groups of 'indigenous bankers',[113] and south India where, under the appellation of Multanis, they also started to attract attention for their activities in indigenous banking and in extending loans to small industries. South Indian material shows clearly that in south India in the 1920s the so-called Multanis were newcomers,[114] not familiar with the language and the society, which confirms the hypothesis of a shift of personnel from Central Asia to south India by some Shikarpur firms. In the same period, the Shikarpuris appear also to have reached Burma, where they specialized in rediscounting bills with banks in India,[115] and in Ceylon. Their presence in Malaya is also sometimes mentioned. The interwar period saw the Shikarpuris successfully manage a redeployment of their activities from Central Asia towards South Asia.

During the inter-war period the most significant area of Shikarpuri involvement outside India appears to have been Iran. The foremost merchant there was Srichand Hinduja who started business in 1919. A textile merchant in Shikarpur, he dealt in a diversified line of products in

---

[113] See L. C. Jain, *Indigenous Banking in India*, London, 1928, p. 45, where the Multanis are mentioned as one of the two examples of 'bankers qua bankers' (the others being the Chettiars), as opposed to 'bankers-cum-traders'.

[114] See C. J. Baker, *An Indian Rural Economy 1880–1955: the Tamilnad Countryside*, Delhi, 1984, p. 291, on those he calls 'Shikarpuri Multanis' (all Multanis were actually Shikarpuris, but this kind of mistake is fairly common). He writes: 'they came rather later (than the Marwaris), were barely settled by the 1920s, and tended to use local sub-bankers because their lack of local knowledge placed them in some danger. By the early 1930s, there were 45 Multani firms in the province with about 110 branches.' On the Multanis in South India, see also *The Madras Provincial Banking Enquiry Committee 1929–30*, vol. I, *Report*, Madras, 1930, pp. 190–2.

[115] See *Report of the Burma Provincial Banking Enquiry Committee 1929–30*, vol. I, *Banking and Credit in Burma*, Rangoon, 1930, pp. 187–8.

Table 3.2. *Population of Shikarpur and Sukkur 1891–1931*

Year	Shikarpur	Sukkur
1891	42,004	29,302
1901	49,491	31,316
1911	53,944	35,294
1921	55,503	42,759
1931	62,505	69,277

Source: Census of India, 1931, vol. VIII, part I, *Bombay Presidency, General Report*, Bombay, 1933, p. 45.

Iran (spices, fruits and vegetables, cutlery, etc.). He made a fortune and invested it mostly in real estate,[116] laying the basis of one of the great South Asian business firms of the twentieth century, although his real 'take-off' occurred only in the 1960s. After 1930 the trading restrictions and currency regulations adopted by the new Pahlavi regime made life difficult for the Indian traders, but the Indian commercial presence in Iran received a new boost from the British occupation of the southern part of the country in 1941.[117] Although Shikarpuris were by no means the only Indian traders in Iran in the late 1940s, they nevertheless appear to have still counted amongst the most active.

By the 1930s Shikarpur appeared undeniably as a kind of backwater, and it had been clearly supplanted by the neighbouring town of Sukkur, which, having been made the headquarters of the district in 1883, benefited from the construction of the big dam on the Indus which was inaugurated in 1932. The Table 3.2 presents the growth of the population in the two towns of Shikarpur and Sukkur between 1891 and 1931.

From 1901 onwards, Sukkur grew more quickly and in the 1920s it clearly overtook Shikarpur. The latter however maintained a regular growth rate during the period, which seems to reflect some economic dynamism linked to agriculture. In spite of its growing isolation and the end of the Central Asian connection on which it had thrived for almost two centuries, it remained the seat of important banking firms, which

---

[116] On the origins of the fortune of the Hindujas, see C. Cragg, *The New Maharajahs: The Commercial Princes of India, Pakistan and Bangladesh*, London 1996, pp. 33–4.

[117] According to the evidence of a letter sent by a member of the Hinduja family to the Government of India in 1948 to protest restrictions imposed by the Iranian government on the activities of Indian traders, the latter had taken over most of Iran's foreign trade, which was mostly conducted with India (except for oil), and some had settled permanently there, including his own brother, who conducted trade in the main cities, i.e. Tehran, Ahwaz and Zahedan. Letter from Kanayalal Deepchand Hinduja, Bombay, to the secretary, Ministry of External Affairs, New Delhi, 29 June 1948, Nehru Memorial Museum and Library, New Delhi, Indian Merchants Chamber Records, File no. 17, 'Indians overseas, 1948'.

had operations extending from Dubai to Singapore, and played a particularly important role in the financial life of Maharashtra and the Madras Presidency. The case of the Shikarpuris is that of a 'frontier' community of the Indo-Afghan confines which knew its greatest days of glory during the years of Durrani rule, but was able to survive Durrani collapse and continue to play a role, be it reduced, in Central Asian trade and finance up to 1917. Only the Russian Revolution, this cataclysmic event, was capable of putting an end to the operations of a merchant network which had become an integral part of the economic life of a vast region. But neither the Russian Revolution nor the Partition of 1947, which led to a massive exodus of Shikarpuri Hindus towards Bombay and other parts of India, did sound the death knell of a merchant community which, throughout the vicissitudes of a chequered history, always showed a capacity to rebound and to recreate itself.

This broad presentation of the history of the Shikarpuri network has of course left many questions unanswered. One of the most puzzling is that of the spatial extent of the network. Why is it that, at the time of its maximum extension in the first decade of the twentieth century, the Shikarpuri network had as its westernmost outpost Kirman in Southeastern Iran and as its easternmost one Keria in eastern Kashgaria, as its northernmost one Chimkent in Turkestan and as its southernmost one Aden in Arabia? Such a space does not correspond to any political unit, past or present, or to any well-defined economic region or group of regions. One of its keys however is to be found in the conception the Shikarpuris had of their ecumene. For them the world, i.e. their world was divided into three areas: Hind, Khorrassan and Turkestan. Shikarpur was the frontier between Hind and Khorras/basan. The latter area meant Baluchistan, southeastern Iran and southern Afghanistan. Turkestan meant Afghan Turkestan, the Uzbek khanates and presumably, although it is not entirely clear, eastern Turkestan, or at least the part of it which was known as Altishahr. What is remarkable is that such a conception was able to survive the momentous political and economic changes the area underwent between the collapse of the Durrani Empire, i.e. *circa* 1810, and the establishment of Russian and Chinese domination over the whole of Turkestan by the early 1880s.

We have here an interesting example of the difference between the logic and the temporality of a network and the logic and temporality of empires. The Shikarpuri merchant network showed a remarkable capacity to adapt to and espouse the twists in the fortunes of the various empires which divided the region between themselves, leaving only Afghanistan as a kind of semi-independent buffer state between Russia and British India. While the 1810–50 period was one of dispersal and relative decline, Shikarpuris used the advent of Pax Britannica and the enhanced safety it brought to some of their trading routes to strengthen their Central Asian connections and to extend their operations into the heart of Central Asia. The Russian conquest of 1864–76 also offered short-term opportunities which they seized upon to consolidate their position. So that when, in the 1880s the Russians established a real economic domination over the area and adopted an attitude of hostility towards all the British-Indian traders, whom they saw as dangerous commercial rivals as well as potential British spies, the Shikarpuris were already too entrenched to be eliminated. They reacted to Russian measures aimed at limiting trade with India by shifting to rural money-lending on a big scale, a shift which the Russian policy of encouraging commercial agriculture made possible. Subsidiarily they also benefited from the fact that the Bukharan authorities were less hostile to them than the authorities in the guberniia, which explains why the network became particularly active in the khanate.

While in Afghanistan, the Shikarpuri presence could be seen as in some ways residual, in Iran the Shikarpuris managed to make themselves indispensable auxiliaries of the British in their attempt at consolidating their commercial position in southern Persia in the face of growing Russian inroads, On the other hand, in Sinkiang, or more precisely Kashgaria, the Shikarpuri presence was a completely unintended consequence of the establishment of a British agency in Kashgar, which in turn resulted from the official annexation of the region to China in 1884 under the name of 'New Dominion'.

Apart from these political considerations, the spatial configuration of the network has also to be understood in relation to demographic factors. A limited Hindu male population such as that of Shikarpur was already stretched to the limit to control a network of such magnitude, given the primitive state of communications in the area taken as a whole. Any further spatial extension of the network would have meant bringing in 'outsiders', a move that the principals of the Shikarpuri firms never appear to have contemplated. Its self-contained nature is one of the most enduring characteristics of the Shikarpuri network, one which will be found also in Hyderabad. However the Hyderabadi network distinguished itself by its linkage with one of the most dynamic sectors of the world economy in the 1850–1914 period, that of maritime transport and travel. Which explains why, unlike the Shikarpuri network, which remained limited to a specific region of Asia, the Hyderabadi network became a worldwide network.

4 From Kobe to Panama: the Sindworkies of Hyderabad

While the Shikarpuri network developed during the second half of the eighteenth century in relation to the caravan trade of Central Asia at the time of the expansion of the Durrani Empire, an international trading network developed in the second half of the nineteenth century in another of the main towns of Sind, Hyderabad, in relation to international maritime trade and within a context which was colonial. As a result of its reliance upon the new technologies of the steamship and the electric telegraph, the network built after 1860 by the Hyderabadi merchants known as Sindwork merchants or Sindworkies came, by the late nineteenth century, to encompass most of the colonial and semi-colonial world. The origins of the network, as in the case of Shikarpur, are somewhat obscure, but an analysis of the socioeconomic context of post-annexation Hyderabad can provide some clues.

The context: Hyderabad in the post-annexation era

By the time Sir Charles Napier defeated the Talpur army at the battle of Miani and proceeded to the annexation of Sind to British India, Hyderabad, a recent urban foundation of the Kalhoras, had been for sixty years the seat of the court of the main branch of the reigning Talpur dynasty of Sind. It was a town of some 20,000 inhabitants, described as unprepossessing by most contemporary travellers,[1] except for its imposing fortress and the tombs of the Mirs situated in the immediate vicinity. Its functions were primarily political, as the headquarters of the main administrative establishment of the Talpurs, but it

---

[1] Thus Postans wrote that, 'although the capital, [it] is of the most poverty-stricken and miserable appearance'. See T. Postans, *Personal Observations on Sindh, the Manners and Customs of its Inhabitants and its Productive Capabilities*, London, 1843, pp. 27–8. Another Britisher, Keith Young, wrote: 'The town of Hyderabad, for city one cannot call it, is a collection of mean mud hovels, and the Grand Bazaar does not deserve the name of one. Our third-rate towns in India would be ashamed of it.' See A. F. Scott (ed.), *Scinde in the Forties: Being the Journal and Letters of Colonel Keith Young, CB, sometime Judge-Advocate-General in India*, London, 1912, p. 47.

was also an important garrison town, where much of the Baluch soldiery which formed the backbone of the Sindhian army was quartered. Other elements in the Muslim population were a community of Khoja merchants, and various groups of artisans and day labourers. The majority of its civilian population, however, appears to have consisted of Hindus, mostly, of course, Lohanas. Hyderabad, as the political capital of Sind, had the largest concentration of Amils in the province, who were themselves divided into two main classes, the Khudabadi Amils, supposed to originate from the ancient Kalhora capital of Khudabad near present-day Sehwan, and non-Khudabadis whose status was deemed to be slightly inferior to that of the former. Apart from the Amils who were clearly the dominant social group among the Hindus and of Saraswat and Pushkarna brahmins, there were mostly the *banias* or Bhaibands, who were themselves a varied lot. At the top was a small aristocracy of bankers, who specialized in loans to the state and the mainly Baluchi courtiers who formed the core of the entourage of the reigning Mirs. Other merchant-bankers were engaged in financing trade and craft production. At the bottom of the scale, there was a large strata of small merchants and shopkeepers who were engaged in the retailing of local produce and imported goods. It is from among the second category that the Sindworkies were to evolve.

In many ways the British annexation dealt a severe blow to the existing economic and social fabric of Hyderabad. Of particular consequence was the decision taken by Sir Charles Napier in 1843 to move the capital to Karachi, on account of it being healthier and closer to Bombay than Hyderabad. It meant that the disappearance of the court and administrative apparatus of the Talpur regime was not compensated by the arrival of a new establishment. In the military field, Hyderabad remained the seat of the major garrison in Sind, but the British and Indian troops which took their quarters in the town were largely supplied by Parsi contractors who moved up from Bombay and Karachi. The loss of the town's political functions affected its merchants in many ways. Those bankers who were specialized in lending to the state lost their business entirely as the British came to Sind with an established treasury system and did not need advances from the local bankers. One such banking firm, founded around 1830, was still active in 1930, but its operations were on a limited scale and it complemented its business of deposit banking with bullion trading and commission business.[2] The merchant-bankers who were mostly engaged in financing trade and craft

---

[2] See the evidence of Mukhi Dayaram, of Hyderabad, in *Bombay Provincial Banking Enquiry Committee 1929–30*, vol. IV, *Evidence, Calcutta, 1930*, pp. 229–35. He was the head of the banking firm of Hiranand Tarachand which used to lend to the Mirs.

112   Indian merchants, 1750–1947

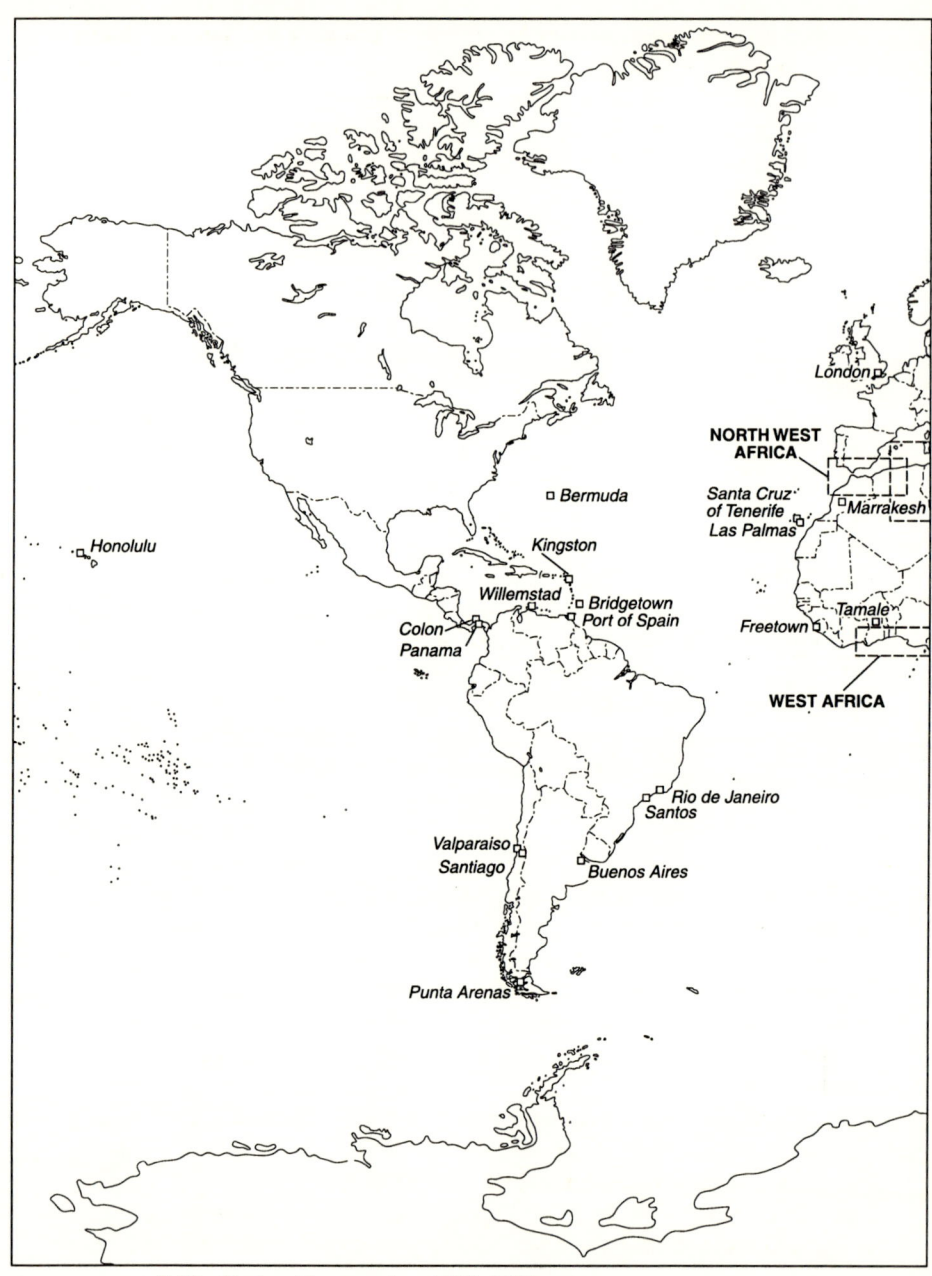

3 The Sindworkie network, *c.* 1890–1940
Source: *Base Mondiale* ESRI (DWC), C. Markovits, M. Legrand and F. Pirot, 1998

From Kobe to Panama

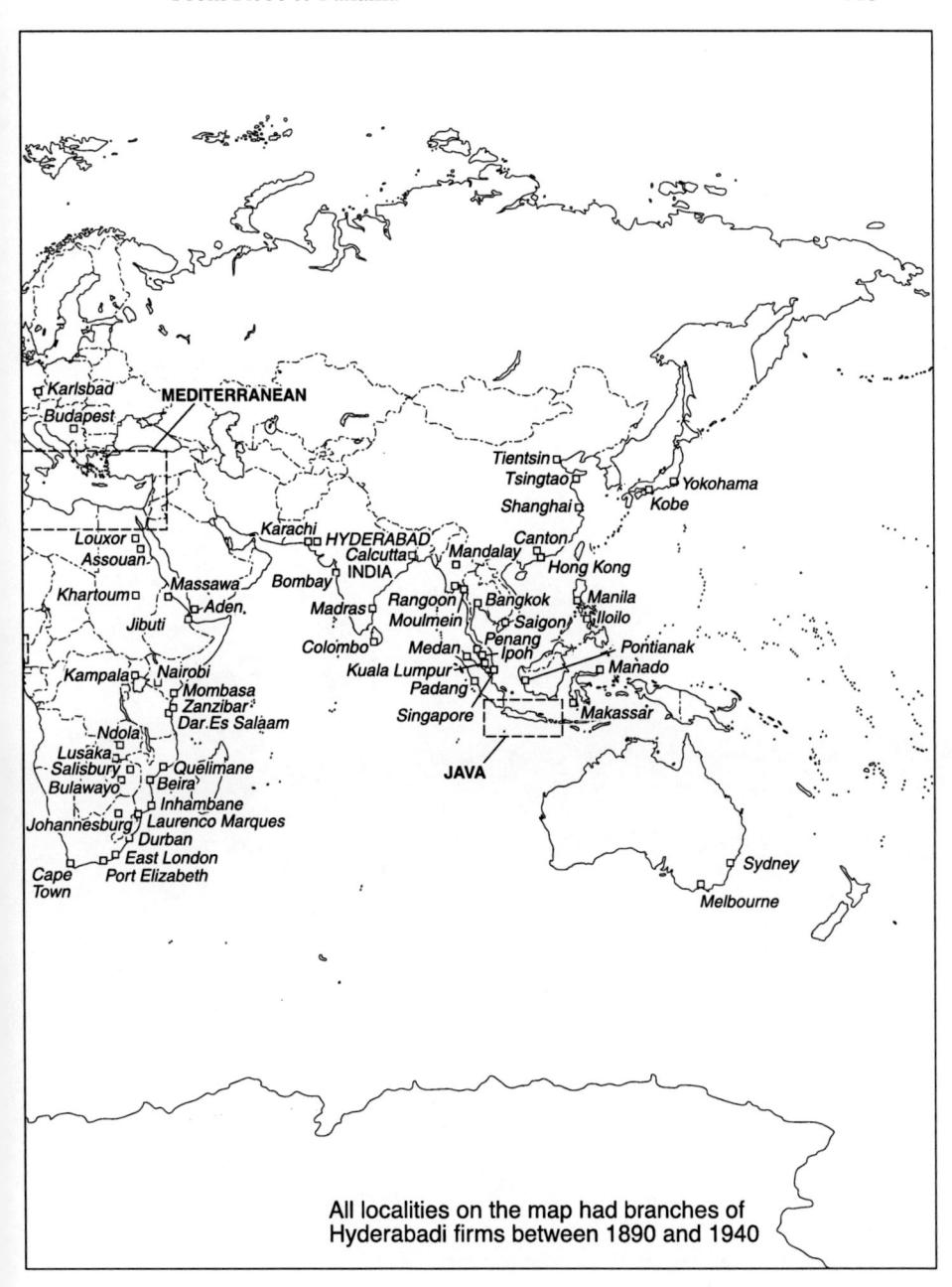

All localities on the map had branches of Hyderabadi firms between 1890 and 1940

NORTH WEST AFRICA

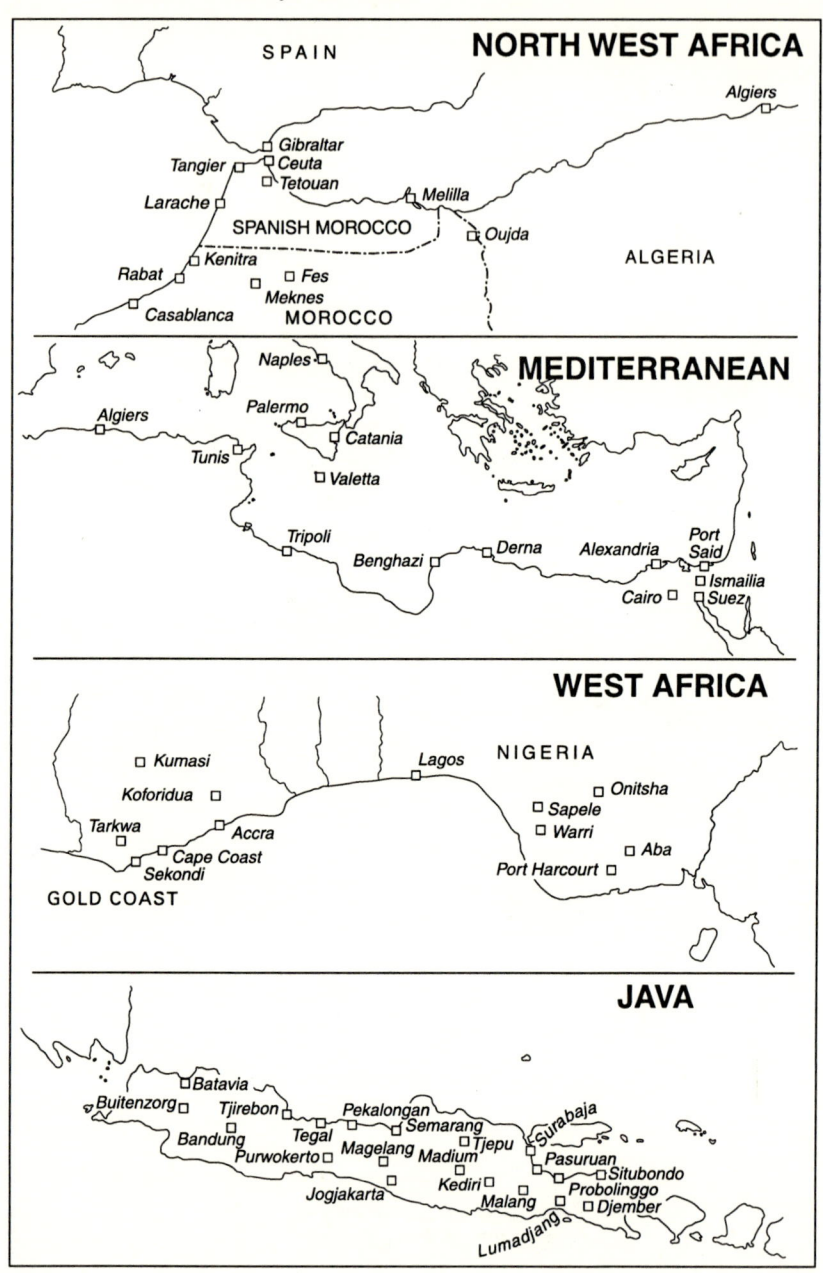

SPAIN

Algiers

Gibraltar
Tangier, Ceuta
Tetouan
Larache
Melilla
SPANISH MOROCCO
Oujda
ALGERIA
Kenitra
Rabat
Fes
Meknes
Casablanca MOROCCO

MEDITERRANEAN

Naples
Palermo
Algiers
Catania
Tunis
Valetta
Tripoli
Benghazi Derna Alexandria Port Said
Ismailia
Cairo Suez

WEST AFRICA

Kumasi
Lagos NIGERIA
Koforidua
Onitsha
Tarkwa
Sapele
Accra
Warri
Cape Coast
Aba
Sekondi
Port Harcourt
GOLD COAST

JAVA

Batavia
Buitenzorg Tjirebon
Pekalongan
Bandung Tegal Semarang Surabaja
Purwokerto Magelang Tjepu
Madium Pasuruan
Kediri Situbondo
Jogjakarta Malang Probolinggo
Djember
Lumadjang

production were also affected, as they lost the profitable business of the Malwa opium trade and suffered from the rerouting of part of the trade with northern India, previously carried by caravan across the Thar desert, via the sea-route through Karachi. As far as local craft production was concerned, which consisted mainly in textiles, embroidery,[3] lacquerwork and weapons, for which the court and the army had been an important market, it got exposed to the full force of competition from British and Indian products entering the province through Karachi and was therefore going through difficult times. The annexation had thus largely negative consequences for the bankers and merchants of Hyderabad, and they were forced to look for new outlets.

Opportunities in the rural sector were limited. Although Hyderabad was situated in the centre of one of the most fertile tracts of the Sind countryside, irrigated by the Fuleli canal which was parallel to the Indus, the poor maintenance of the canal during the last period of Talpur rule and the first decades of British domination made for slow growth in agriculture. Besides, Hyderabad district was always characterized by a high degree of dacoity and rural crime,[4] which tended to specifically target the *banias*. The town itself, with its particularly narrow lanes, was known to be infested by thieves,[5] which means that merchant property was constantly at risk.

Restricted opportunities in local trade, finance and agriculture in the immediate post-annexation period explain that Hyderabad merchants looked for opportunities outside their home town and even outside their

---

[3] One specific type of embroidery, with silver or golden thread, on velvet or other kind of cloth with buff, was known as 'Zardozi', and in Hyderabad, hundreds of craftsmen practised that art prior to the British conquest. See Mumtaz Mirza, 'The Zardozi Art of Embroidery', in N. A. Baloch (ed.), *The Traditional Arts and Crafts of Hyderabad Region*, Hyderabad, 1966, pp. 41–2.

[4] Statistics on crime in the Bombay Presidency always placed Hyderabad district ahead of all other districts in the Presidency, except Shikarpur. See, for instance, 'Annual Report on state of crime and working of police in Sind and in Northern, Central and Southern divisions of Bombay Presidency for year 1895', enclosed in despatch no. 22, from Judicial Department of the Government of Bombay to the secretary of state for India, 5 December 1896, IOR, Public and Judicial Annual Files 1880–1930, File J&P 2301/96.

[5] The district superintendent of Hyderabad police wrote to the commissioner of police in Sind, 8 March 1870: 'The City of Hydrabad [*sic*] itself will, I fear, always show badly in respect to the detection of thefts. There it is not with outside thieves that the Police have to contend but with Hindoos of the town, the cleverest of burglars. There is no passage that can be properly called a street in all the Hindoo quarters of the Town, which are full of narrow, winding lanes, in which are doorways leading into narrower passages still, in which are crowded the Hindoo abodes . . . The burglars are of the same class of people as those upon whom they prey, and the thefts are committed, and the property disposed of, all, as it were, among themselves. In short, until the city be rebuilt, and the morality of its inhabitants improved, despite the vigilance of any Police, thefts will occur and remain undetected.' *Selections from the Records of the Bombay Government*, no. CXXII, new series, Bombay, 1871, p. 31.

home province. Unlike their brethren in both Thatta and Shikarpur, who had a long history of involvement in international trade and finance, Hindu merchants of Hyderabad do not appear to have nurtured such traditions in the pre-colonial period. The only merchants of Hyderabad who had a tradition of outside involvement were the local Khojas who were particularly active in the trade of Masqat from the end of the eighteenth century. It is possible that information on outside opportunities came to Hyderabad via this particular network. Of greater importance, however, in directing the attention of the Hyderabadi Hindu merchants to international trading was probably the establishment of a direct connection between Hyderabad and Bombay, particularly after Sind had been made part of the Bombay Presidency in 1847. Commercial links between Hyderabad and Bombay actually predated the British annexation, and Burnes reported in 1837 on the regular visits to Hyderabad by Bombay merchants.[6] A linkage also existed through the Malwa opium trade. The novelty was that during the 1850s some Hyderabadi merchants who were dealers in local craft products, which they bought from Muslim artisans, started going to Bombay on regular visits to sell these products, as they found ready-made custom among the European population of the great metropolis of Western India. The discovery that some of the craft productions of Sind appealed to European taste seems to have been made during the 1840s[7] when it was noticed that European officers and administrators took a fancy to some of the local products, probably because they appeared more 'authentic' than what was then produced in the workshops of the rest of the Bombay Presidency. The kind of goods the Hyderabadi pedlars sold in Bombay became known as 'Sindwork' and the merchants who sold them as 'Sindworkwallas' or 'Sindworkies'. Among those goods, lacquer work on wooden articles from Hala and the village of Lukman, *kashi* work, that is painting work on flower vessels, jugs and jars, also from Hala, *lungis* from Thatta, *ajrak*, a kind of quilt cover from Dadu, embroidery work from Nawabshah, brass and *kansa* work of Larkana are described as the most popular items.[8] Reports written in the late nineteenth century mention continuing production of embroidery and lacquerware at Hyderabad, as well as lace manufacture, but all emphasize the

---

[6] See *Reports and Papers, Political*, etc., p. 19.
[7] Travellers in Sind all commented on the sumptuous turbans, scarves and sashes that were patronized by the Talpur Mirs, and the *lungis* they wore were also considered of high quality. See N. Askari and R. Crill, *Colours of the Indus: Costume and Textiles of Pakistan*, London, 1997, p. 55.
[8] See P. Bharadwaj, *Sindhis Through the Ages*, Hong Kong, 1988, pp. 246–7. I am grateful to Mr P. Lachman of Bombay for having kindly supplied me with a copy of this book.

rapid decline of traditional crafts in Sind.[9] Regarding the art of lacquering wood, which seems to have survived better than others, the *Gazetteer* reported in 1907 that 'this kind of work is hawked all over India as "Sind-work-bokkus", in the form chiefly of nests of round boxes fitting one inside another and all beautifully lacquered in red, yellow, black and green'. It added that 'the principal indigenous application of the art is to the glorification of bedsteads and of those swinging cots and cradles which are found in the house of every prosperous Sindhi gentleman'.[10]

Had the Hyderabadi pedlars limited themselves to Bombay and other Indian cities, it is probable that the network would have long fallen into oblivion as one of the many networks of hawkers which crisscrossed the subcontinent for many centuries. However, around 1860, some Hyderabadi merchants took the momentous initiative of extending their peddling operations outside India. Their first destination was Egypt, and this was to shape the network in a very specific way, as Egypt emerged at that time as the first destination of 'tourists' in the modern sense of the term. In the following five decades, this network which had had such humble beginnings in the peddling of the native craft products of a medium-sized town in Sind was to transform itself into a full-fledged international trading network, while it continued to be financed and controlled from Hyderabad.

The expansion of the network until the First World War

Between 1860 and 1914, the Sindwork merchants of Hyderabad gradually expanded their operations to a large part of the world. In the process, the character of the network was profoundly transformed. The merchants started with marketing the native crafts of Sind to an international clientele, but, as they progressively enlarged the size of their operations, the small-scale workshops of Sind became increasingly incapable of supplying the needs of a constantly expanding network. That is why, from the 1870s onwards, the Sindwork merchants started procuring goods from other sources, both within India, in the Punjab, in Kashmir, in Benares, and outside India, mostly in the Far East, in China and Japan. The expansion of the network basically was driven both by

---

[9] See G. C. M. Birdwood, *The Industrial Arts of India*, London, 1880, pp. 226, 282; T. N. Mukherji, *Art Manufactures of India*, Calcutta, 1888, pp. 257–8, 363, 380; Sir George Watts, *Indian Art at Delhi: Being the Official Catalogue of the Delhi Exhibition 1902–03*, Calcutta, 1903, who writes about lacquerware, p. 217: 'although this art attains its highest perfection in Hyderabad (Sind) . . . in fact the beautiful art of lac painting has for years past been steadily disappearing from Sind'.

[10] *Gazetteer of the Province of Sind*, p. 397.

demand and by supply factors, which in their turn determined its spatial configuration.

At the level of demand, the main factor was the enormous increase in the extent of international travel between 1860 and 1914, as steam navigation and the opening of the Suez and Panama canals led to an unprecedented expansion in the number of sea voyages for purposes of work as well as of rest and recreation. Although this expansion was largely limited to Europe and North America, it fed a growing demand for a certain type of goods which became known as 'curios', as well as for certain kinds of textiles with an Oriental flavour, particularly silk cloths. The origin of the fashion for 'curios' has to do both with the increase in the range and frequency of travel, and with the expansion of European imperialism. 'Orientalism' existed also in marketing, as there was a growing interest in products which could be perceived as 'different' from those turned out by the factories of the West.

Changes in the intellectual climate of Europe and North America in the second half of the nineteenth century had a direct impact on consumer tastes. As John Mackenzie writes: 'The high noon of imperialism, far from coinciding with a downgrading of the arts of the subordinate people of the East, actually coincided with a new appreciation.'[11] In England in particular, a group of critics and writers, of whom the most prominent were Owen Jones, Christopher Dresser and George Birdwood, contributed to an increased appreciation of the craft productions of Asia, more particularly those of India, China and Japan.[12] While appreciation for Indian textiles and other craft productions already had a long history in the West, 'japonisme' was an entirely new fad which swept Europe and North America at regular intervals between the 1860s and the 1920s. The Japanese exhibits at the various international exhibitions held between 1862 and 1893 were ecstatically received and they provoked a surge of interest in everything Japanese.[13] Photographers travelled to Japan and Christopher Dresser's richly illustrated account of his visit, published in 1882,[14] had a considerable impact. 'Japonisme' did not remain limited to aesthetic circles and an aristocratic elite, but quickly spread to the middle classes. Japanese objects increasingly became part of the décor of many middle-class homes in Britain, continental Europe and the United States. Firms were created specifically to import directly from Japan and specialized shops were opened in

---

[11] J. M. Mackenzie, *Orientalism, History, Theory and the Arts*, Manchester, 1995, p. 107.
[12] *Ibid.*, p. 119.
[13] See P. Greenhalgh, *Ephemeral Vistas: the Expositions Universelles, Great Exhibitions and World's Fairs, 1851–1939*, Manchester, 1988, p. 148.
[14] C. Dresser, *Japan, its Architecture, Art and Art Manufactures*, London, 1882.

London, the best known being Liberty's, which was started in 1875, where silks, embroideries, furniture, carpets, porcelain and curios of Oriental provenance were displayed grandly and attracted considerable custom, from fashionable aesthetes as well as from middle-class women.[15] One consequence of the spread of 'oriental' fashions in the West was that cheap imitations of 'oriental' goods were produced which catered to a lower-middle-class market. This created a potentially vast market for 'true' Oriental craft productions which the importers in Western countries could not entirely satisfy. For members of the upper-middle class, having the 'real thing' rather than a cheap imitation became a matter of social distinction. Hence the growth of travel purchase, which seemed to offer greater guarantees of 'authenticity'. Well-heeled Westerners travelling to the East saw the acquisition of authentic Oriental objects as one of the perquisites of travel. This created a specific niche market in which the Hyderabadi merchants were quick to specialize successfully. International travellers could be most easily contacted at the main ports of call of the steamers plying the major international sea routes. That is why the Sindwork merchants tended to follow these routes and to establish operations at the major ports. They usually started with peddling, and, once they had tested the waters and concluded that the demand for their goods was steady enough, they opened shops. These shops appear to have been modelled on the new 'Oriental' shops which had started opening in London and other major European and North American cities, so that travellers had the impression of being on familiar ground there. Culturally, this is an interesting example of 'Oriental' merchants learning from Western merchants about trading in 'Oriental' goods.

At the level of supply, the main factor behind the expansion of the network was the need to tap new sources of materials in order to cater to the growing demand of European consumers for Asian craft products. Increasingly, given the rapid decline of craft production in Sind,[16] these sources were elsewhere in India, as well as in the Far East, more specifically in Japan, and to a lesser extent in China. India remained an essential source for curios, but the modest size of its silk industry inevitably led the merchants to seek other sources of silk goods in the Far East, where the silk industry was going through a period of rapid expansion. So, from the 1870s onwards, Sindwork merchants started

---

[15] See A. Adburgham, *Liberty's: A Biography of a Shop*, London, 1975.
[16] See above, note 9. It is further documented in *Gazetteer of the Province of Sind*, pp. 395–6. Instances of declining crafts are the embroidery known as Chikimdozi (which seems to be the same as Zardozi), the making of daggers and scabbards, that of inlaid gold and silver ornaments, etc.

opening branches in the Far East for the purpose of buying goods which they marketed across the colonial and semi-colonial world, in all the ports and emporia where the steamers plied.

Apart from well-known centres of craft production in India such as Kashmir, the Punjab and Benares, Sindwork merchants also bought goods from itinerant Indian craftsmen, who travelled across the world, selling their products to specialized dealers. The existence of that category of itinerant craftsmen is revealed in a letter one of them wrote to the secretary of state for the colonies to protest Australian immigration restrictions.[17] The writer, a Punjabi from Ludhiana, described himself as a carver of ivory, tortoise shell, ebony, jade stone, bone and wood, and claimed that he sold his goods to wholesale dealers who in turn retailed the goods to shops and pedlars. The map of his travels largely coincided with that of the network of the Sindwork merchants.[18]

These merchants were thus increasingly becoming 'global middlemen' between the Far East and India, where they procured the goods, mostly silk and 'curios', and other regions of the colonial and semi-colonial world, such as Africa, Southeast Asia, the Mediterranean and Central and South America where they sold them to a mostly European clientele of international travellers as well as of settlers. Why merchants from a medium-sized inland town in a province of British India found themselves particularly well placed to exploit these opportunities will always remain something of a mystery. There remains in particular the question as to why Far Eastern merchants, both Chinese and Japanese, were not in a position themselves to exploit these opportunities and to directly market their goods to international travellers. The answer is largely political: Chinese and Japanese merchants had to contend with political obstacles when they moved abroad, outside their traditional regions of operation (the Nanyang for the Chinese merchants, and parts of East Asia for the Japanese). On the other hand, the Sindwork merchants, being British Indian subjects, benefited from the protection given to them by their status and could move freely more or less anywhere.

The reconstruction of the main stages in the global expansion of the network proved, however, a difficult task, as the movements of the merchants remained largely unnoticed by British authorities prior to the

[17] Petition of J. Heera Singh to Joseph Chamberlain, 29 March 1899, IOR, Public & Judicial Annual Files, File J&P 1004/99.
[18] He claimed to have resided 'for the purposes of trade' in Mozambique, Madagascar, Dar-es-Salaam, Massawah, Japan and China, and Manila, all places, except Madagascar, where Sindwork firms were actively engaged in the curio trade. He arrived in Melbourne from the Philippines 'with the object of purchasing . . . emu eggs and different Australian woods and pearl-shell'.

First World War, and no statistical record of them is therefore extant. That such a wideranging dispersion of merchants largely escaped notice appears surprising, but it can be explained partly by the fact that the Sindwork merchants were generally known in their places of business as 'Bombay merchants' and were thus largely indistinguishable from other traders hailing from Western India. A sudden influx of traders from Hyderabad into Egypt around 1907 and a corresponding increase in the number of court cases before the consular court in Cairo, however, led the local British consular authorities to question the Government of India as to its causes and possible ways to limit it,[19] thus attracting for the first time the attention of the authorities in India to this specific commercial migration. At the same time, a first estimate of the size of the Hyderabadi diaspora was given in the 1907 edition of the *Gazetteer of the Province of Sind*; the compiler, E. H. Aitken, who was generally well-informed, put its strength at 5,000.[20] The detailed story, in which many gaps remain, had to be pieced together from a multiplicity of sources: dispersed demogaphic data in various censuses, commercial directories, firm histories and a community history, which is not a particularly good source, although it is informative.[21] In the interwar period, this community of dispersed merchants started attracting more attention from British and Indian observers. C. F. Andrews, in particular, who came across them in the course of his voyages in the 1920s and 1930s, devoted a few pages to them in his *India and the Pacific*.[22]

[19] See Letter, 10 May 1907, from British consul, Cairo, to secretary to the Government of India, Foreign Department, Calcutta: 'The number of British Indian merchants trading in curios and Indian stuffs has increased of late years. Formerly there were only two or three old established firms . . . Now, however, a number of other firms have shops here . . . At the present time considerable trouble is caused to this Consulate and Consular Court by the constant disputes arising out of these circumstances . . .'. Copy in Bombay General (Miscellaneous) Proceedings Emigration, November 1907, Serial no. A 112. R. E. Enthoven, acting secretary to the government of Bombay, in a letter no. 6650, 8 November 1907, to the Government of India, Department of Commerce and Industry, wrote: 'The trouble complained of appears to be due to the action of dealers from Hyderabad (Sind) who have established themselves at Cairo and who are in the habit of importing young and irresponsible Hindus to help in their shops.' Copy in *ibid*. See also India Commerce and Industry (Emigration) Proceedings, July 1907, Serial no. A 1, 'Emigration of Indian shop assistants to Egypt under contracts'.

[20] He wrote in *Gazetteer of the Province of Sind*, p. 395: 'Fifty years ago the "Sind-work-walla" was a familiar figure in Bombay, whence he travelled as far as Egypt and Malta and established imposing shops . . . There are said to be 5,000 of these Sind merchants at this time in different parts of the world, and the money that they bring or send home has contributed much to the present wealth of Hyderabad city; but they sell the curios of China and Japan, Benares, Amritsar and Madras, rather than the productions of Sind, which are passing away'.

[21] Bharadwaj, *Sindhis through the Ages*.

[22] He wrote in *India and the Pacific*, London, 1937, p. 159: 'The Indian merchants in the Pacific have come mainly from Hyderabad, Sind, which is the one town in India that

Two main routes were followed by the Sindwork merchants: one led westward from Bombay, the other eastward, either from Bombay with transhipping at Colombo where most steamers to the Far East called, or alternatively from Calcutta. West of Bombay, the main route followed by the Sindworkies led them first to Egypt. They found themselves in Egypt precisely at the time when that country was becoming the first destination of modern 'tourists'. They were not actually the first or even the main participants in the trade in tourist artefacts in Egypt: Armenian, Levantine and Jewish merchants had preceded them and remained always dominant in the field. But the rapid growth of tourism in Egypt between the 1860s and the First World War[23] offered sufficient possibilities for a small group of Indian merchants to carve for themselves a niche in that kind of trade and to acquire the expertise and the capital which fed their further expansion to other places.

From the evidence of cases in the British consular courts in Egypt involving Sindhi merchants, it appears that the Sindwork trade had modest beginnings in the 1860s and 1870s, when merchants from Hyderabad came to Egypt only for the duration of a trading season and were involved in hawking goods they had brought with them from India. It was only in the 1880s that permanent shops were established, with a large stock-in-trade of goods, which were still mostly from India, but included a growing proportion of Far Eastern imports. This decade coincides with the British occupation of Egypt, and it is no fortuitous coincidence: the security afforded by British rule to the Sindwork merchants, who were themselves British subjects, played probably no little role in encouraging them to step up their investments in Egypt and to establish permanent shops. The presence of an important British garrison and the rise of a population of British civilians with high incomes were also important incentives. The probate inquiry into the goods of one Nanikram Gehimall Tolaram, a merchant of Hyderabad who died in 1888 in Alexandria,[24] possessed of two substantial shops in Cairo and Alexandria, gives a fairly precise idea of the volume and composition of the stock-in-trade of a Sindwork merchant. The detailed

sends out far more emigrants than any other . . . I have found them, not only in every large town on the Pacific coast, but in places as far distant as Capetown, Panama, the Bermudas, and Port Said.'

[23] The number of tourists, which was a few hundreds in the 1860s, reached 5,000 to 6,000 around 1900 and 10,000 in 1913–14. Their annual expenses at the latter date were estimated to reach 10 million French francs. G. Lecarpentier, *L'Egypte Moderne*, Paris, 1920, p. 88.

[24] 'Inventory of the effects of the late Gehimall Nanikram Tolleram contained in a shop situated in Lombard Street, Alexandria, taken on 7 September 1888', in 'Estate of Gehimall Nanikram Tolleram', PRO, Foreign Office Records, Embassy and Consular Archives: Egypt, Alexandria Consular Court Records, File no. 11 of 1888, FO 847/16.

inventory of the shop situated in Lombard Street, Alexandria, shows the variety and diverse provenance of the goods sold. The total value of the goods was estimated at £637, i.e. some Rs 10,000, not a negligible amount in 1888, mostly silk cloth and other kind of cloth, as well as brassware, silverware and various other items. The deceased was obviously a prosperous merchant, who used to transfer weekly remittances to Hyderabad via Bombay and willed his entire property to two minor nephews. Nanikram's case testifies to the fact that in the 1880s the Sindworkies were becoming an established group in Egypt. The 1890s and early 1900s saw a considerable influx of Sindwork merchants and commercial employees into Egypt. A combination of push and pull factors were at work. A serious cholera epidemic in Hyderabad in the early 1890s led to a spate of departures, and the attraction of Egypt seems to have been, apart from its easy accessibility from India, the rapid expansion in the tourist trade. The new arrivals, unlike the earlier ones, appear to have been often men of limited means who had neither capital of their own nor contracts with an employer, and took to hawking as the only way to earn a livelihood.

From Egypt, some firms which had made big profits expanded into the Mediterranean, establishing branches in Malta, Algiers and Gibraltar by the 1890s, and at a later stage in Naples, Sicily, Tunis, Tangier, Tetuan, Ceuta and Melilla. Beyond Gibraltar, some Sindworkies followed the steamer routes to West Africa, reaching Sierra Leone[25] and the Gold Coast by the 1890s, and Nigeria at a slightly later date. Others followed the Cape route to West Africa via East Africa[26]

---

[25] For a detailed account of the history of the Sindhis in this West African country, see H. V. Merani and H. I. Van der Laan, 'The Indian Traders in Sierra Leone', *African Affairs*, vol. 78, no. 311, 1979, pp. 240–50. According to these authors, the first firm to reach Sierra Leone was M. Dialdas & Sons in 1882, but this date seems to refer to an exploratory voyage. The *Sierra Leone Handbook* of 1925 gives 1901 as the date of foundation of the branch of the firm in Freetown, which appears more plausible. The first firm to have opened a branch was actually J. T. Chanrai, in 1896.

[26] In East Africa, the presence of Sindhi traders goes back to the period of Omani domination of the coast. A 'Census of British Indian subjects in the dominions of the Sultan of Zanzibar' taken in 1887 by the British consul enumerated 378 Sindhis out of a total of 6,345 British Indians. They were the largest community in Mombasa, where they accounted for almost half the local Indian population (255 out of 533) and were also significantly represented in Bagamoyo. See R. G. Gregory, *India and East Africa: A History of Race Relations within the British Empire 1890–1939*, Oxford, 1971, Table I, p. 37. These Sindhis appear to have been mostly Bhatias of Thatta, who had longstanding connections with the Omani rulers of Zanzibar. It is not known, however, why they were specifically concentrated in Mombasa. This community seems to have gradually faded away during the first half of the twentieth century. The presence of Sindwork merchants from Hyderabad seems to date back to 1880, when the firm of B. Choithram, which specialized in the sale of curios in the main cities of East Africa, was established. A few other Sindwork firms also established branches in the major

and South Africa, where they started operating in the late 1890s.[27] An offshoot of this trading route covered the Canary Islands, where some started frequenting Tenerife and Las Palmas in the late 1890s. From the Canaries they followed a route which led them to South America, where they reached Rio, Buenos Aires and Chile by the late 1890s and to Panama where they started operating around 1905.

Eastward, the main thrust of expansion was from Colombo or Calcutta to Singapore where the first Sindworkies made their appearance in 1873, and from there to the Dutch East Indies. The pioneering firm was Wassiamall Assomull, which opened a branch in Singapore in 1873 and one in Surabaya around the same time.[28] In the 1880s, more Sindworkies came to Java; another popular destination in the Indies was the Ost-Kuist of Sumatra near Medan. A significant Sindwork firm, still in existence, Jhamatmal Gurbamall, traces its origins to the arrival from Singapore to Medan, in the 1880s, of a merchant called Jhamatmal Gurbhamal Melwani who earned a fortune in the textile trade and created one of the largest firms in Medan.[29] Another well-known firm, Khemchand & Sons (then known as K. Hoondamall & Sons) was also founded in Medan in the late 1880s by a merchant called Bhai Khemchand Hundamal Mahtani, who then opened a branch in Kobe and specialized in the trade between Japan and the Dutch East Indies.[30] Sindwork merchants also travelled to the Outer Islands of the archipelago: in 1887 a merchant from Hyderabad died in Manado in North Celebes, leaving a succession in Macassar.[31]

cities of East Africa, but the Sindhi element never gained prominence in a region dominated by Gujarati capital.

[27] Detailed biographical entries in commercial directories allowed the entry of Sindwork merchants into South Africa in the late 1890s to be traced. Natal and the Transvaal were their preferred destinations at first, but the Boer War led to a temporary exodus from the Transvaal to the Cape Province. Thus the most successful Sindwork firm in South Africa, Trikamdas Bros., transferred the seat of its operations to Port Elizabeth, where it was by far the largest Indian trading firm, in command of the local silk market. See *The South African Indian Who's Who and Commercial Directory 1936–37*, Pietermaritzburg, 1935.

[28] A. Mani, 'Indians in Jakarta', in A. Mani and K. S. Sandhu (eds.), *Indian Communities in South East Asia*, Singapore, 1993, pp. 98–130.

[29] Bharadwaj, *Sindhis through the Ages*, p. 367.

[30] *Ibid.*, pp. 372–3.

[31] Letter from colonial secretary, Straits Settlements no. 2240–88, Consuls, 12 March 1888, forwarding copy of letter dated 29 February from vice-consul in charge of Netherlands consulate-general at Singapore regarding a native of India named Uthomal Rupomal who died in Manado (Celebes) on 24 August 1887; Memorandum from commissioner in Sind no. 403, dated 19 October 1888, forwarding letter from collector of Hyderabad, stating that deceased left heirs in Hyderabad district; letter from colonial secretary, Straits Settlements, no. 136–91, Consuls, 8 January 1891, informing that a sum of Rs 790.80 has been forwarded to commissioner in Sind for payment to the widow. Bombay General Proceedings, February 1891, Serial no. A 52.

China was reached in the late 1870s or early 1880s, and Japan, Siam, the Philippines and French Indochina in the 1890s. One firm of Sindwork merchants even had a branch at Honolulu in Hawaii before the First World War.[32] Another firm established a branch at Melbourne as early as 1876, and again in 1892, followed by one at Sydney. Thus on the eve of the First World War, Sindwork merchants were dispersed throughout the colonial and semi-colonial world. They did not however reach Western Europe or the North American continent, except in the form of peddling forays which did not result in the establishment of permanent branches of their firms.

These merchants established branches of their firms in the major ports along the various maritime routes. They operated through a system of partnership which was a variant of the *shah–gumastha* system of Shikarpur, although the same terminology was not always used. There was generally a contract between a principal in Hyderabad, who was called the capitalist partner or the *shah*, and one or several working partners or *gumasthas* who went abroad to sell goods supplied by his principal or bought from suppliers with credit supplied by the same principal. Over time many of these partnerships consolidated themselves into more or less durable firms. Another important development was the gradual emergence of a category of salaried employees.

Due to the tendency of firms to split, either because of the partition of a joint family, the classical case in Indian business, or because the manager of a branch of a firm separated from the principals and set up his own firm, the network could grow and diversify rapidly over some four or five decades from small beginnings. There were a few 'mother firms' from which the entire network sprang. The two most important of these 'mother firms' were the firm of Pohoomull Bros, created in 1858, from which a good part of the western branch of the network originated, and the firm of Wassiamall Assomull, created in 1866, which played a pioneering role in the eastward expansion.

Little quantitative data is available on the size of the outward migration from Hyderabad as the decennial censuses do not give figures of migration. The only detailed figures on the age, sex and marital status of the population of Hyderabad are found in the 1901 Census. They reveal a surplus of married females over married males among Hindus in Hyderabad of around 1,500.[33] Since polygamy was almost non-existent

---

[32] Mentioned by British vice-consul at Honolulu in a letter, 2 July 1915, about British Indian subjects resident in Hawaiian islands, copy in IOR, Public & Judicial Department Annual Files, File J&P 3153/1915.

[33] *Census of India 1901*, vol. IX A, *Bombay*, part II, *Imperial Tables*, R. E. Enthoven, Bombay, 1902, Table VII, p. xv, Cities, Age, Sex and Civil Condition. In Hyderabad, among Hindus, there were 9,081 married females and only 7,465 married males.

(except among Amils), this pattern of 'absentee husbandship' can only be ascribed to the residence outside Hyderabad, elsewhere in India as well as abroad, without their spouses, of some 1,500 married male Hindus. Given the fact that married men represented only a minority of the merchant diaspora from Hyderabad, which was mostly a diaspora of young unmarried males, census data tend to give plausibility to Aitken's estimate of the size of the diaspora.

Although no official figures exist of the number of commercial migrants who left Sind annually for destinations abroad prior to the late 1930s, it has been possible to reconstruct those movements, thanks to the existence, in the records of the Public and Judicial Department of the India Office, of duplicates of certificates of identity which were delivered in lieu of passports by the district magistrate of Hyderabad. For the period between January 1915 and January 1916, a complete set of duplicates is available. During that one-year period, 572 certificates of identity were delivered by the district magistrate of Hyderabad to men from Hyderabad district going abroad for purposes of trade.[34] It is not a random sample, but, as far as can be ascertained, a complete series. It should be noted that it does not include those who departed for Burma and Ceylon, for whom no documents were required. Due to the First World War, there were of course no departures for countries with which the British Empire was at war, that is Germany, Austria-Hungary and the Ottoman Empire. From whatever information is available from other sources, it appears that these countries were never important destinations for Sindwork merchants (though a few have been known to reside in Budapest and Karlsbad, in Austria-Hungary, in the Ottoman Empire and in German East Africa prior to the war). Therefore the data for 1915–16 can be considered fairly representative of the situation as it existed during the immediate pre-war years.

These certificates (of which duplicate copies are preserved in the India Office Records, while it is not known whether the originals still exist) provide information on several aspects. They give the name of the applicant, his father's name, his age, his 'social status' (i.e. the profession of the next of kin who stood guarantor, in case of the applicant having to be repatriated at government's expense), the destination and the purpose of the trip (only the applicants whose declared purpose was trade have been included; there were also a few certificates given to persons, generally Amils, who travelled for recreation and pleasure).

[34] Duplicate certificates are in IOR, Public & Judicial Department Annual Files 1880–1930, Files J&P 1174/15, 1643/15, 2428/15, 2669/15, 3023/15, 3137/15, 3242/15, 3370/15, 3466/15, 3565/15, 3681/15, 3759/15, 4268/15, 4431/15, 4548/15, 4742/15, 5301/15, 958/16.

Table 4.1. *Destinations of applicants for certificates of identity in Hyderabad district 1915–1916*

Destination	Number of applicants
Mediterranean and Atlantic	222
Gibraltar	104
Naples	7
Sicily, Catania	3
Egypt	69
Tripoli	2
Tunis	2
Algeria, Algiers	9
Ceuta, Melilla, Tetuan	4
Casablanca	2
Canary Islands	8
Vigo	1
Malta	11
Far East	293
Dutch East Indies	108
Philippines	51
Straits Settlements	79
Japan	23
China	18
China and Japan	2
Saigon	8
Bangkok	4
East and South Africa	28
Eritrea	2
Jibuti	1
Mombasa	1
Portuguese East Africa	10
South Africa	10
Salisbury	4
West Africa	10
Sierra Leone	8
Lagos	2
Central and South America	15
Panama	7
Chile	6
Trinidad	2
Persian Gulf	3
Australia	1
Grand Total	572

Another interesting indication is the signature. Most of the applicants were able to sign and can be divided into three groups: those who signed in English, those who signed in Sindhi (either in Arabic Sindhi or, in a few cases, in *'bania'* Sindhi, i.e. a variant of *devanagri*) and those who signed in the two scripts. Another interesting feature of the series is that the applications are generally arranged by firm. Thus, out of 572 applicants, 492 were in the employ of a total of 58 firms. Of the other 80, some may also have been in the employ of a firm, but the majority left without a contract, which does not mean that they did not have connections with firms.

Table 4.1 presents the destinations of the applicants arranged by major geographical regions, with the purpose of discovering the spatial logic behind the expansion of such a network.

From a reading of the table, it comes out clearly that two areas, the Mediterranean (including the Canary Islands and Atlantic Morocco) and the Far East attracted the bulk of the departing Sindworkies. This illustrates their role as middlemen linking those two areas through webs of trade, although in the detail the pattern was more complicated. Other areas played a rather subsidiary role. Although there is an element of randomness in this table, on the whole it appears to reflect the actual spatial configuration of the network.

In contrast with widely held ideas about the general nature of Indian merchant networks during the colonial period, only a little more than half the applicants were going to countries and territories which were part of the British Empire (exactly 302 out of 572). The remaining 270 went to territories under various sovereignties, mostly Dutch, but also American, Spanish, French, Italian, Portuguese, Chinese, Japanese and Siamese. If it is added that most of the applicants who gave Gibraltar as their destination were at a further stage dispatched from there to various destinations in North Africa, the Canary Islands and West Africa, it will appear that the Hyderabadi network was not a classical British imperial network. This is a characteristic it shared with the Shikarpuri network.

Looking in more detail at the geographical spread of the network, five areas stand out as of particular importance as destinations for the departing Sindworkies: Gibraltar and North Africa, Egypt, Java, the Straits Settlements and neighbouring Sumatra, and the Philippines. In all these areas, it was the existence of a sizeable demand for the kind of goods the Sindwork merchants traded in which was the main 'pull' factor. On the other hand, the area which was the major source of the goods traded, i.e. Japan and China, attracted less than 10 per cent only of the total manpower movement from Hyderabad to the outside world.

Table 4.2. *Annual emigration of skilled labour registered in Karachi 1928–1946*

Year	Total of skilled labour	Commercial personnel
1928	456	n.a.
1929	536	n.a.
1930	425	n.a.
1931	320	n.a.
1932	368	n.a.
1933	440	n.a.
1934	429	401
1935	401	382
1936	460	438
1937	439	417
1938	710	549
1939	574	501
1940	419	383
1941	407	n.a.
1942	110	n.a.
1943	145	n.a.
1944	251	n.a.
1945	247	n.a.
1946	448	n.a.

Sources: For 1928–33 and 1941–46, 'Yearly returns of skilled workers who proceeded to various countries', enclosed in IOR, Public & Judicial Collections, Collection 108 1 E, L/ P&J/8/185; for 1934–40, *Consolidated Annual Report on the Working of the Indian Emigration Act for the year ending on 31 December 1934*, New Delhi, 1935, and for year 1935, *ibid.*, 1936; *Annual Report on the Working of the Indian Emigration Act, 1922, in Sind, for the year 1936*, New Delhi, 1937, and for years 1937, 1938, 1939 and 1940, *ibid.*

This is not surprising in view of the fact that retailing operations are more demanding in manpower than wholesaling.

Descending to the level of localities, some fifty are specifically mentioned in the certificates. Leaving aside the case of Gibraltar, which was largely a redispatching centre for Sindwork firms towards Morocco, the Canary Islands and West Africa, the localities which attracted the largest number of applicants were Singapore (55), Surabaya (53), Manila (49) and Cairo (44). Other significant destinations were Penang (24), Yokohama (18), Port Said (14), Hong Kong (11) and Malta (11). Thus the Hyderabadi network clearly appears as a worldwide network. At the same time, it was entirely recruited from Hyderabad proper and a few neighbouring localities in Hyderabad *taluka*. Of the 572 applicants, only 17 were residents of localities outside Hyderabad, including 1 resident of Karachi and 2 of Kotri. The remaining 555 were recruited in Hyderabad town. They were all males, all Hindus and all but 21 were aged between 15 and 45. Therefore, to assess the demographic importance of that yearly migration, one would have to measure it against the Hindu adult male population of age 15–45 of Hyderabad. The 1901 Census gives a figure of 10,092. No detailed figures were included in the 1911 Census, but, given that the overall Hindu male population of the town increased by only a little over 10 per cent during the intercensal period, the figure cannot have been much higher than 11,000. Thus the 534 applicants aged between 15 and 45 represented almost 5 per cent of the male Hindu population of the same age group. Since practically all those who departed were Bhaibands (although there were one or two Brahmins and a few Amils), while Bhaibands probably accounted for not more than half of the Hindu population of the town it can be said that every year a significant fraction, amounting to almost 10 per cent, of the adult male Bhaiband population of Hyderabad aged between 15 and 45 left for various destinations abroad 'on Sindwork'. However, since we have no data on the number who returned to Hyderabad during the same period, we are left to guess whether there was actually a net migration process from Hyderabad. Comparison of census data at various dates does not lead to that conclusion. It seems, therefore, reasonable to assume that, by the time of the First World War, the network was not expanding much and that most of the movement of people consisted in a circulation meant to replace returning personnel. It seems highly probable that most of those who left with contracts from firms were replacement staff and that the 'new migrants' were mostly those who left without contracts, i.e. 80 out of 572.

Regarding the size of the annual movement from Hyderabad, further indications are given by emigration statistics, following the passing of the 1922 Indian Emigration Act, under the purview of which the emigration of skilled labour, including commercial personnel, fell. The series available for the 1928–46 period gives the annual figures of emigration of skilled labour registered in Karachi. For a few years in the late 1930s, there are even detailed statistics of the emigration of commercial personnel, meaning Sindworkies. Table 4.2 presents the data on emigration of skilled labour and, when available, commercial personnel registered in Karachi between 1928 and 1946.

During the 1928–40 period, the annual outward movement of commercial personnel from Hyderabad was in the range of 400–500, i.e. less than in the immediate pre-war and early First World War years, representing therefore a diminishing drain on the demographic resources of the Bhaiband community. The absence of reliable statistics on returning emigrants makes it impossible to assess the demographic balance of these movements.

Table 4.3. *Destinations of employees of six major firms in Hyderabad 1915–16*

Firm	D. Chellaram	M. Dialdas	Pohoomull	J.T. Chanrai	W. Assomull	Chotirmall
Naples	4				1	
Gibraltar	32	23	24	4		
Cairo	9		17	1		
Algeria	3		1			
Yokohama	1		2		4	
Singapore	6		1		2	13
Manila	21		7		12	
Saigon	4		2			
Alexandria	4		3			
Catania	2					
China	4					
Egypt	3					
Hong Kong	1	2			3	
Sierra Leone		3		5		
Port Said		2				
Java (unspecified)		3				
Colon		1	2	3		
Tenerife		1	3	1		
Beira			6			
Tunis			2			
Malta			3			
Panama			1			
Salisbury			3			
Trinidad			2			
Shanghai			1			
Canton			1			
Melilla				2		
Lagos				2		
Casablanca				2		
Vigo				1		
Ceuta				1		
Las Palmas				1		
Tetuan				1		
Punta Arenas				2		
Chile (unspecified)				1		
Japan (unspecified)				1		
Penang					6	
Batavia					4	
Bangkok					3	
Surabaya					3	
Macassar					1	
Total	94	35	81	28	39	13

The only global post-1907 estimate of the size of the Sindworkie network is given in a document of the Sindwork Merchants Association of 1937[35] at the time of the Spanish Civil War, in which it was claimed that the total manpower employed by the network was 25,000. Assuming that half this personnel was employed in Hyderabad itself and in other locations in India, it would put the size of the global Hyderabadi worldwide diaspora close to 12–13,000, i.e. more than double the estimate given by Aitken in 1907. Most of the expansion must have taken place in the 1907–27 period, but it would be futile to try to guess the exact chronology.

The second kind of information given by the certificates concerns the size of firms. The 492 applicants known to have been employed by firms were not equally spread between the 58 firms; 6 major firms employed 290 of them, while the remaining 202 were employed by 52 firms. It thus appears that the 6 firms of the first group sent an average of 48 men, while the 52 firms of the second group sent an average of 4 men. These figures do not necessarily reflect exactly the respective size of the different firms in terms of employees, depending on whether in the particular year under consideration firms were having to replace personnel or not. However, the divide between two types of firms is clear and will be elaborated upon at a later stage. Table 4.3 shows the destinations of the employees of the six major firms.

Even among the six largest firms, there was a clear distinction between two subtypes: the 'global' firm, with branches across the world, of which D. Chellaram and Pohoomull Bros. were the two most conspicuous examples, although M. Dialdas also answers the definition, and firms with a more regional network, of which one, J. T. Chanrai, was mostly a 'Western' firm, while the other two, Wassiamall Assomull, and K. A. J. Chotirmall were 'Eastern' firms.

Given the wide differences between even the big firms, the question arises as to what extent can the Sindwork merchants be seen as a network. Sindwork firms constituted a network both economically and socially, because they all traded in the same kind of goods, using the same commercial techniques, sharing information and recruiting staff from the same local pool of labour. The unity of the network came from

---

[35] Telegram from Sindwork Merchants Association, Hyderabad, Sind, to Government of India, Foreign & Political Department, 9 February 1937, which said: 'Entire Sind Work business, worth 20 crores, affecting 25,000 men, nearly paralysed.' Enclosed in PZ 1086 1937, telegram from Government of India, Foreign and Political Department to secretary of state for India, 15 February 1937, IOR, Political & Secret Department Records, Departmental Papers: Political External Files and Collections, *c.* 1931–1950, 'Spanish Civil War: protection of British Indian lives and property in Spain, Spanish Morocco and Canary Islands 1936–40', L/P&S/12/210.

its extreme centralization at Hyderabad. The headquarters of all the firms were situated in the narrow lanes of the bazaar, and telegrams kept circulating to and from the branches dispersed across the world. It was in Hyderabad that the yearly accounts of all the branches were settled, and the principals of the firms all resided in the same locality, Hirabad.

Besides, credit circulated a lot within the network, although the Sindworkies, unlike the Shikarpuris, were not a banking community, and chains of suppliers also existed. At the same time, individual firms played a larger role in Hyderabad than in Shikarpur. Most of the major firms were created between 1858 and 1875, and only one large firm was founded at a later stage.

A quick look at the history of the six big firms of 1915 is in order here. The oldest was the firm of Pohoomull Brothers, which traced its origins to 1858, although it is difficult to know whether it actually started trading in Sindwork at that early date. It was founded by four brothers of the Khiani family, one of whom, not the most active, was called Pohoomull, and the firm was named after him following the advice of the family pandit-astrologer.[36] The firm became active in the 1870s in Egypt, where it seems to have been extremely successful and to have made large profits which fed its further expansion. By the 1890s it was trading all over the Mediterranean between Port Said and Gibraltar and had started expanding into the Far East with branches in China, Japan and the Philippines. In 1911, an entry in a directory gave a list of twenty-two branches outside India: Cairo, Alexandria, Algiers, Tenerife, Las Palmas, Budapest, Karlsbad, Gibraltar, Malleija (Malta), Beira, Salisbury, Durban, Johannesburg, Cape Town, Hong Kong, Canton, China (?), Manila, Iloilo, Yokohama, Kobe and Kuala Lumpur.[37] It was probably the largest of all the Sindwork firms in terms of turnover, although D. Chellaram had a more extended network of branches. It was also the most 'classical', purchasing in India through its Bombay branch and its Madras and Calcutta agencies, and in the Far East through its five branches in China and Japan, vast quantities of silk cloth and different kinds of curios which it sold in its retailing outlets in the Philippines, in Southern Africa, in Egypt (by far its largest branch), all over the Mediterranean and even in Central Europe. Very similar was the firm of D. (Dhanamal) Chellaram, founded in 1860, whose founder, Seth Dhanamal Chellaram Chulani is said to have been the first Hyderabadi merchant to travel westward to Egypt in 1860.[38] The firm of J. T. Chanrai, founded in 1860, had a more 'Western' orientation,

---

[36] Interview with Mr L. Khiani, Gibraltar, 4 September 1992.
[37] *The Singapore and Straits Directory 1911*, pp. 188–90.
[38] Bharadwaj, *Sindhis Through the Ages*, p. 292.

and acquired branches in the Far East only at a later stage. A document of the firm, dated 1916,[39] gives a list of eighteen branches outside India, of which six were in Morocco, one in Gibraltar, two in the Canary Islands, four in West Africa, two in South America, two in Panama and one in Japan (Yokohama). That particular firm appears to have pioneered the expansion of the network westward from Gibraltar, into the Canary Islands and South America by the late 1890s, to Panama by 1905 and into Morocco on the eve of the First World War. The firm of Wassiamall Assomull, founded by Wassiamall Assomull Mahtani in 1866, followed a slightly different trajectory. It played a major role in the expansion of the network in the Far East, being the first to operate in Singapore from 1873 onwards, and thence in the Dutch East Indies. It also appears to have been one of the earlier firms to have established branches in China and Japan. It established a branch at Melbourne in Australia as early as in 1876, and after a period of closure, reopened it in 1892.[40] In an early phase, it had branches in the Mediterranean, in Egypt and Algiers, but seems to have sold them by the late 1890s to concentrate on its Far Eastern operations. The firm of M. Dialdas & Sons, founded in 1870 by Seth Mulchand Dialdas Nandwani, was very similar in its spread to Pohoomull Bros. and D. Chellaram. The latest among the 'big six', the firm of K. A. J. Chotirmall,[41] was the only Sindwork firm which was actually founded outside Hyderabad, having been established in Batavia in 1875 by a member of a family of five brothers, one of whom was an employee of the firm of Wassiamall Assomull in Singapore. The firm was at first unsuccessful, and, following various vicissitudes, was established for good as a partnership in 1887 with branches at Batavia, Semarang and Surabaya.[42] Afterwards the firm expanded all across the Far East, opening branches at Saigon, Hong Kong, Bangkok, Yokohama, Shanghai, Tsingtao and Port Arthur by the end of the nineteenth century. It continued however to be controlled from Hyderabad by members of the Chotirmall family.

It is not easy to explain how such a sudden spurt of entrepreneurship,

---

[39] Letter of J. T. Chanrai & Co, Gibraltar, 5 June 1916, to Pribhdas Roopchand, Cairo, enclosed in 'J. T. Chanrai vs. Pribhdas Rupchand', PRO, Foreign Office Records, Embassy and Consular Archives: Egypt, Cairo Consular Court Records, civil case no. 38 of 1918, FO 841/170.

[40] Letter from Tejumull Gaganmall, manager of the firm, Melbourne, February 1899 to the secretary to the Government of India in the Foreign Department, copy in India Revenue and Agriculture (Emigration) Proceedings, June 1899, Serial no. A 1. He states that the firm first established business in Melbourne in March 1876, and that the existing branch was opened in October 1892.

[41] See the history of the firm, privately printed, *Chotirmall Group of Companies: A Century of Perseverance, 1875–1975*, Jakarta, 1975.

[42] Mani, 'Indians in Jakarta' pp. 100–1.

with the creation of so many firms, was possible in a small inland town of a peripheral province of British India. In particular, questions arise as to the finance which was available to those budding entrepreneurs to help them launch their ventures. The first source of finance must have been the family wealth of those Bhaiband families. While there is no detailed information as to their areas of operations before they became Sindwork merchants, evidence given by a Sindwork merchant to the Bombay Banking Inquiry Committee in 1930 shows that most Sindwork firms had banking as a subsidiary line of activity.[43] It is therefore probable that some of those families had been engaged in banking and had thus accumulated funds which they could invest in the new enterprises. They appear also to have been in the habit of taking deposits from middle-class Hindus of Hyderabad, both Amils and Bhaibands, which provided another source of finance. Once this trade had been established on a successful footing, it could then develop on the basis of the ploughing back of the profits accrued, which often appear to have been considerable during the early years, particularly in Egypt, especially because the firms, being partnerships, did not have to bother about paying dividends to shareholders. Participation in international trade, however, necessarily involved using the services of the exchange banks, and it would be interesting to know how these merchants, who were unknown in the world of international trading finance prior to 1860, managed to establish their credentials so as to obtain the necessary lines of credit for their operations. The forging of early links with Bombay was essential to that side of their business, as all the finance of international trading operations had to be arranged from Bombay, where the exchange banks had their branches, and not from Hyderabad. That is why all the important Sindwork firms had a branch in Bombay. Not all merchants, however, used letters of credit from banks to finance their trading operations. Some operated on the basis of documentary credit only, which could be extended by private firms. Thus smaller merchants who bought goods from big firms received credit from them. This credit was extended through *hundis*,[44] and the *hundi* business was therefore a sideline business for the big firms. Only the latter had extensive direct dealings with the exchange banks. They increasingly used the services of the non-British exchange banks, in particular the Japanese banks. In the 1920s and 1930s, Japanese banks like the Bank

[43] Evidence of K. Bulchand, chairman of the Khudabadi Bhaiband Cooperative Credit Bank, Hyderabad, in which he stated that 'Most of the Hyderabad bankers have other lines of their own in addition to banking . . . Many have business in foreign countries (Sind workers)', and in his oral evidence he admitted belonging to the Sind-work merchants' line. *Bombay Provincial Banking Enquiry Committee*, vol. IV, pp. 268–74.

[44] Oral interview of P. Lachman, Bombay, 22 December 1992.

Table 4.4. *The population of Hyderabad 1872–1941*

Year	Total population	Hindu population
1872	43,088	18,609
1881	45,195	n.a.
1891	54,569	33,130
1901	64,790	43,499
1911	69,140	49,678
1921	73,951	55,176
1931	96,021	70,404
1941	134,693	93,929

Source: Census of India, for relevant dates.

of Taiwan played a big role in financing the Sindwork merchants' global trading operations. Some firms, however, continued to have a close connection with British banks, in particular with the Hong Kong and Shanghai Bank in the Far East and with Barclays Bank, which widely financed Sindwork traders in Egypt or in West Africa.

The sudden rise of the Sindworkies after 1860 is an interesting example of a successful 'niche' operation, that is, of the exploitation of a very specific demand on a very specialized kind of market by a group of entrepreneurs who apparently had no previous experience of international trading. Its success is therefore testimony to the remarkable creativity and inventiveness of this group of merchants. What is also remarkable is how suddenly a large section of the Hindu male youth of Hyderabad, a provincial town of British India, could be drafted into travelling abroad for long periods, contrary to both religious injunctions and social habit. Some social and cultural developments during the second half of the nineteenth century may however have contributed to facilitating the creation of a significant pool of manpower ready to go abroad.

After the annexation, Hyderabad, in spite of having lost its position as the political capital of Sind, expanded considerably. Its population, which was reckoned to be around 20,000 in 1843, was estimated to number over 40,000 at the 1872 Census. Table 4.4 charts the growth in the population of the town during the period of the censuses. From 1891 onwards, Hindus always accounted for over 60 per cent of the town population. The regular increase in population, which accelerated considerably after 1921, was due partly to a constant influx of immigrants from the neighbouring countryside, as well as from the rest of the Bombay Presidency and from Rajasthan. The town's function was mostly that of a market for the produce of the rich countryside irrigated by the Indus river and the Fuleli canal.

The opening of railway connections with the Punjab, Karachi and Rajasthan gave a considerable boost to regional trade. On the other hand, there was very little modern industry,[45] while traditional crafts declined precipitously after 1900. The Sindwork trade obviously accounted for part of the town's wealth from the 1880s onwards, but the exact role played by rich Sindworkies in the development of the town is not clear, beyond the fact that they endowed a certain number of charities, such as hospitals.

Population growth was accompanied by a considerable physical expansion, which started in the 1850s, the decade when the Hyderabad Municipality was constituted (in 1853). Burton, revisiting the place in 1876 after an absence of twenty-five years, was struck by the rise of an entirely new area, known as New Hyderabad.[46] It had many schools, as well as a post-office, a civil hospital and modern barracks. An account of the town at the beginning of the twentieth century also underlines the extent of physical transformation in a fifty-year period.[47] In the first half of the twentieth century, the town continued to expand, as newly built areas kept springing up, in particular Hirabad, north of the old town, which became the residence of many families engaged in Sindwork. The old town, however, remained the privileged location of merchant firms, and its narrow lanes did not change much, in spite of improved drainage facilities and of the arrival of electricity in the twentieth century.

Hyderabad boasted of being a 'progressive' town and the number of its schools made it the intellectual capital of Sind. Burton even quipped: 'I should not wonder . . . if the new Revelation, the Endowment of Research, should first be proclaimed in Sind'.[48] Educational development started in the 1850s: Langley, a Britisher who visited the town in 1858, had already reported on the existence of twelve private schools and one supported by the municipality, with a total attendance of nearly 900 pupils.[49] Educational institutions multiplied in the following fifty-year period. The *Gazetteer of Sind* of 1920 reported that there were in the town three high schools for boys and one for girls, with a total

---

[45] Statistics of large industrial establishments in 1937 show that, apart from one bone mill, the only significant factories in Hyderabad were cotton ginneries. See *Large Industrial Establishments in India 1937*, Delhi, 1939.
[46] *Sind Revisited*, vol. I, p. 261.
[47] Dayaram Gidumal, *Hiranand, the Soul of Sindh*, Karachi, 1932, 2nd edn (1st edn, 1903), pp. 22–3. This biography of a prominent social reformer, founder of the Brahmo Samaj in Sind, offers an interesting description of Hyderabad at the beginning of the century.
[48] Burton, *Sind Revisited*, vol. I, p. 262.
[49] E. A. Langley, *Narrative of a Residence at the Court of Meer Ali Moorad with Wild Sports in the Valley of the Indus*, London, 1860, pp. 148–9.

enrolment of 1,351 boys and 198 girls in 1915–16.[50] There were also two teacher training colleges and one medical school. At the same time, primary schools in Hyderabad *taluka* had a total enrolment of some 12,000, including 2,000 girls, most of whom lived in the town, the vast majority being Hindus.[51] This spectacular development of educational facilities in what was after all but a *mofussil* town of some 70,000, was almost exclusively due to the endeavours of the local Amil community, probably the community with the highest literacy rate of all non-Brahmin groups in the subcontinent. Bhaibands do not appear to have been directly involved in founding schools, but they took advantage of them. Their male literacy rate, although lower than that of the Amils, was fairly high by the 1920s. On the other hand, female literacy was very low in the Bhaiband community, while it was relatively high among Amils. By the 1920s, as a result of these developments, a large proportion of Hyderabad's Hindu male youth was educated to a fairly advanced standard and often had a knowledge of English, which may have partly explained their readiness to take employment abroad. Yet few among the Bhaiband community at large were really fluent in English, and Sindhi always remained the vehicular as well as the vernacular language of the network.

Over time, however, Sindwork merchants showed a fairly remarkable ability to learn languages. One of them, testifying before an Australian Parliamentary Commission,[52] stated that, when he was posted in Massawa in Eritrea, he had succeeded in mastering Italian, Arabic and Amharic. The merchant who became the chairman of the Hindustan Merchants' Association in Panama in the late 1930s was described by the local British consul (perhaps not the most reliable of sources in this field) as a 'good Spanish scholar'.[53] There are many indications that the Sindwork merchants and their staff generally managed to acquire the basic linguistic skills which were necessary for the success of their

---

[50] *Gazetteer of the Province of Sind "B"* vol. II, *Hyderabad District*, J. W. Smyth (comp.), Bombay, 1920, pp. 28–30.

[51] *Ibid.*, Table XXIX-B, pp. 94–6.

[52] Testimony of Odermull Tharamull, 31 August 1898, before Select Committee of the Legislative Council of the Colony of Victoria. The witness, a partner in the firm of Wassiamall Assomull, having stated that he could not write English, added: 'I was about four years in Massowah (Italian Protectorate) and I learnt Italian, Arabic and Shoan (Abyssinian) very well . . .'. Report of the Select Committee of the Legislative Council on the Immigration Restriction Bill, p. 27, in *Victoria, Minutes of the Proceedings of the Legislative Council, Series 1898*, copy in PRO, Colonial Office Records, Victoria Sessional Papers, CO 311/210.

[53] British vice-consul, Colon, to British Consulate, Panama, 17 October 1938, enclosed in British Legation, Panama, to Viscount Halifax, Secret, 1 November 1938, copy in IOR, Public & Judicial Department Records, Departmental Papers: Collections *c*. 1930–47, Collection 108/28 A, 'Indians in Panama' File P&J 5623/38, L/P&J/8/278.

operations, although some instances are also known of cases when insufficient proficiency in English cost them access to crucial information. Nothing is known, unfortunately, of the way in which knowledge about faraway markets was disseminated, stored and transmitted among the merchants of this inland town. It has not been possible to discover whether 'manuals' were written specifically for the use of the Sindwork merchants and one has therefore to fall back on the hypothesis of a purely 'oral' transmission.

Hindu *banias* have often been perceived and described as a profoundly conservative, inward-looking group, not well adapted to operating in a social and economic environment different from that of India. The case of the Shikarpuris appears really not to go against the grain as they managed to somehow recreate a 'Shikarpuri' environment in Central Asia in the *sarais* and to insulate themselves to a large extent from local life, avoiding, in particular, sexual entanglements. The case of the Sindworkies was different: they could not maintain the same degree of insulation from local life in the ports and colonial cities where they resided for periods which were generally shorter than for some of the Shikarpuris in Central Asia. Somehow, they had to interact, if not with the local population, at least with the other merchant communities which toiled and lived in the great cosmopolitan centres where they often operated. Nor did they entirely avoid sexual entanglements. The absence of texts such as diaries makes it difficult to reconstruct perceptions, and in particular the way in which they rationalized the necessity to spend long periods abroad, especially in totally unfamiliar places like North or West Africa, or Central and South America where they were the only Indians around. But the fact is that not only did they manage, but were generally successful in their operations. After the First World War, the network went through a new phase of expansion.

Expansion, retraction and recovery: the Sindworkies c. 1918–1947

The First World War had a surpisingly limited impact on the fate of the Sindwork merchants, considering the amount of overall disruption it brought to world travel and trade. There is no doubt that business went down considerably, and that branches had to be closed in many localities, either for political reasons (being situated in enemy country) or because of a drastic fall in the volume of sales. But, on the whole, the firms survived, certainly thanks to the very large profits accumulated during the immediate pre-war years. There was also a tendency to increase operations in neutral countries, such as the Dutch East Indies,

Table 4.5. *Major Sindwork firms in the 1930s according to date of foundation*

Name of firm	Date of foundation	Number of branches c. 1932–39
Pohoomull Bros. (Europe)	1858 (1932)	17
Pohoomull Bros. (India)	1858 (1932)	11
D. Chellaram	1860	19
J. T. Chanrai	1860	21
W. Assomull	1866	13
M. Dialdas & Sons	1870	21
K. A. J. Chotirmall	1875	5
B. K. Choithram	1880	5
Jhamatmal Gurbhamal	1883	2
K. Hassaram	1885	11
K. Hoondomall & Sons	1888	9
G. Ramchand	1894	8
A. Neechamall Bros.	1896	2
Tikamdas Bros.	1897	6
Watanmal Boolchand	1908	4
Watumull Bros.	1910	4
K. Chellaram & Sons	1915	15
Dalamal & Sons	1916	5
Dayaram Bros. (Japan Bazar)	1918	8
T. Jhamandas	1920	6
Kewalram & Bulchand	1921	3
Verkomal Shewakram	1924	3
OK Gidumal & Watumull	1926	4
Utoomal & Assudamal	1928	3

Sources: The Japan Times Yearbook 1933, s.l., 1933; S. A. Waiz (comp.), *Indians Abroad Directory*, Bombay, 1934; *Business Directory of Hong Kong, Canton, Macao*, Hong Kong, 1938.

the Philippines (prior to the entry of the USA into the war), the Canary Islands and Spanish Morocco. This led to suspicions on the part of the British authorities that some Sindhi firms were using neutral territory for trading with the enemy. The firm of K. A. J. Chotirmall in particular, which was very active in the Dutch East Indies, was the object of an enquiry from the military authorities, even though they were eventually cleared of suspicion.[54]

The return of peace brought in its wake a new spurt of growth in the

[54] The 'China Command Suspect List' compiled at Hong Kong in March 1917, which recorded the names of firms and individuals suspected of having dealings with the enemy had, under the caption 'Chotermall, silk merchant', the following comment: 'Chotermall firm gravely suspect and known to be means of transmitting and receiving enemy money (12.12.15).' A supplementary note was appended, which read: 'Letter from General Staff, Singapore, dated 28 December 1915, states that firm of Chotermall no longer suspicious although their correspondence is still examined.' Unfortunately it

tourism and travel industry, from which the Sindworkies very directly benefited. In the 1920s, new branches were opened in many localities by Sindwork firms, and new territories were added to the map of the network. New firms also came into prominence, the most important of which was K. (Kishinchand) Chellaram & Sons, founded in 1915 in Madras by Kishinchand Chellaram Daryanani, who separated from his father Gianchand, a prominent Sindhi merchant of Madras with a large stake in the textile trade.[55] The new firm developed on a significant scale the trade between South India, the Far East and West Africa, which had been pioneered at an earlier stage by Pondicherry firms in French West Africa. The growth of a West African branch of the network, which in the long term became of crucial importance, coincided with the beginning of a diversification away from the exclusive emphasis on 'silk and curios', a hallmark of the network in the pre-1914 phase. Most of the firms created in the 1920s were exporting firms with branches in Japan and China, who took advantage of the growth in trade between Japan and the rest of Asia, particularly China, the Dutch East Indies and the Straits Settlements. Table 4.5 gives a list of the major Sindwork firms in the 1930s according to their date of foundation and the number of their branches outside Hyderabad.

This table allows us to distinguish broadly between three generations of firms: those which were created between 1858 and 1883 (eight), those founded between 1885 and 1910 (seven), and the post-1914 creations (eight). Firms of the first generation had a total of 114 branches in the 1930s (many branches were closed during the depression years and never reopened), i.e. an average of 14 branches by firm. Those of the second generation had a total of 44 branches, i.e. an average of 6 branches by firm, and the latest wave had a total of 47 branches, i.e. also an average of 6 per firm. Taking the number of branches as an indication of the total turnover of the firm, the superiority of the firms of the first generation is clear. Date of entry was a crucial factor in the overall success of the firms, strongly suggesting the existence of an oligopolistic structure. The only new firm which managed to join the camp of the really big ones was K. Chellaram & Sons. Other firms which did well, like Watanmal Boolchand or Utoomal & Assudamal, continued to specialize in exports and did not therefore compete very directly with the big seven.

The expansion of the network in the Caribbean region, with the opening of shops in Jamaica, Barbados and Curaçao was in response to

has been impossible to trace the document. Enclosed in PRO, Foreign Office General Correspondence (Political), United States 1917, File 1220, FO 371/3065, no. 153 479.
[55] Interview with Mr Lal and Mr Lokumal Chellaram, London, August 1996.

the increase in tourist traffic in the region. Its growth in the Dutch East Indies, spurred on at first by the war, reflected an increasing tie-up between Sindhi firms and Japanese business houses, especially as the Chinese merchants in the East Indies were, for patriotic reasons, reluctant to further Japanese trade. A deposition by a merchant of Hyderabad, found in the archives of the British consulate in Yokohama[56] concerning a dispute with his partners in a firm which operated in Japan and Java, throws some light on the expansion of Sindwork firms in the Indies in the immediate post-war phase. According to the statement, the firm towards the end of 1919 had only a shop each at Bandoeng and Soekabomi in Java, with an export office at Yokohama; its total capital was 331,000 guilders, and it had no credit in the bank. In the next two years, during which it made huge profits of 300,000 guilders in 1920 and 400,000 guilders in 1921, export offices were established at Kobe, Hong Kong and Canton, and several new shops were opened in Java. They included a wholesale and retail business at Batavia, a shop at Semarang, a shop at Buitenzorg, and a grand wholesale and retail business shop at Pasar-Baroe, Bandoeng, which was bought and constructed at a cost of about 250,000 guilders from the profits of the firm; besides, the firm, on the strength of its prosperity, acquired a credit of as much as 300,000 yen in the Bank of Taiwan alone. This phenomenal expansion undoubtedly reflected boom conditions in Java in the immediate post-war period as well as the growth of trading connections between Japan and the Indies, and it is not known how far it was replicated by other Sindwork firms. In the Dutch East Indies, and, more generally in South East Asia, Sindwork firms tended increasingly to specialize in the marketing of Japanese goods. A recent author writes that, in Southeast Asia, 'the Sindhi network was the most important of the Indian networks for the Japanese'.[57] According to R. Brown, across the region, 'Japanese agents maintained stocks for immediate delivery to the main Sindhi importers',[58] who in their turn distributed the goods to the local markets through their regional network of branches. The Sindwork firms also increasingly tended to buy directly from the mills in Japan through their branches in Kobe and Yokohama. In Southeast Asia in the 1920s the regional network of Sindwork firms was becoming increasingly integrated into inter-Asian trade, acting basically in a middleman role between Japan and the European colonial territories. There was, therefore, a tendency for the network to diversify and

[56] Affidavit by Naraindas Tirthdas of Hyderabad-Sind, 22 October 1923, PRO, Foreign Office Records, Embassy and Consular Archives: Japan, Yokohama, 'Earthquake reconstruction 1923–1927', FO 908/8.
[57] Brown, *Capital and Entrepreneurship*, p. 207.   [58] *Ibid.*

become less homogeneous. Some of the firms, like D. Chellaram, Pohoomull Bros., J. T. Chanrai and M. Dialdas, remained specialized in the traditional line of silk and curios on a worldwide basis. Although they expanded even further the network of their branches, they do not seem to have been as prosperous as in the pre-war years. The most successful firms tended to be those, like K. Chellaram, Wassiamall Assomull, K. A. J. Chotirmall, or the more recent Watanmall Bulchand (founded in 1908), which specialized more in regional trade in a wider range of products. Both types of firms were however equally affected by the worldwide depression of the early 1930s.

Between 1930 and 1933, trade in silk and curios practically came to a halt as the tourist and travel industry went through a massive recession worldwide. In spite of that, few firms went under, the most prominent of the casualties being Udhavdas & Co., a firm which traced its foundation to the year 1857, and which had been one of the most active in the Mediterranean trade. Most firms managed to survive the depression by cutting costs drastically through the closure of branches, but few employees appear to have been fired. Some probably had to accept a fall in wages, but little evidence has come to light on that aspect. The very high profits earned in the 1920s added to the oligopolistic structure of the network helped to cushion the blow, as the major firms concluded agreements to divide the market between themselves in many localities. Some of the old firms went through difficult times: for instance, Pohoomull Bros. was partitioned in 1932 between Pohoomull Bros. (India) which took over most of the branches in India and the Far East, and Pohoomull Bros. (Europe) which operated in the rest of the world. The overall resilience of the network in the face of a massive fall in turnover and profits reflected flexibility but also the strength of non-market factors such as solidarity between townsmen, and kinship ties.

In the long run the effect of the depression was to produce a shift in the orientation of the Sindwork merchants from an almost exclusive emphasis on goods which could be called 'semi-luxury', such as fairly fine silks and relatively expensive curios, to a wider range including cheaper textiles and tourist goods. Combined with the effects of the devaluation of the yen in 1931, this led to a growing specialization in the sale of Japanese goods. Sindhi firms often became agents in the commercial offensive of Japan on external markets, particularly those of the British colonial empire. Both in Malaya and in West Africa, Sindhi merchants were thus actively involved in the promotion of Japanese exports to countries which had been largely the preserve of British exporters. Sometimes this brought them into direct confrontation with British custom authorities seeking, from 1934 onwards, to impose strict quotas on sales of Japanese textiles into the British Empire markets so as to preserve the share of British exporters. The increasing tie-up with the Japanese led a growing number of Sindwork firms to open branches in Kobe and Yokohama to buy directly from the Japanese mills. Specialization in Japanese goods never became exclusive, however, and in Southeast Asia, after 1937, when the Sino-Japanese conflict led to a fall in sales of Japanese goods, the Sindwork merchants shifted to British and Indian goods on a significant scale.[59] Expansion in trading operations was facilitated by the good relationship established with the banks by the largest firms. Thus the firm of K. A. J. Chotirmall in Bangkok was able to finance its trade with Japan with the help of important overdraft facilities granted by the Siam Commercial Bank both in Bangkok and Kobe. In French Indochina, a large overdraft facility from the local branches of the Hong Kong Bank played a similar role in regard to the trade between Saigon and the rest of Southeast Asia.[60]

From the mid-1930s, growing international tensions adversely affected the operations of the Sindwork merchants. The Spanish Civil War thus very directly affected the interests of the several firms which had branches in Spanish Morocco and the Canary Islands, leading to financial difficulties for some of them. The Sino-Japanese War brought an end to some of the operations of Sindwork firms in China. All these difficulties were considerably amplified with the onset of the Second World War which brought traditional lines of trade almost to a standstill. Many Sindwork merchants found themselves stranded in Japanese-occupied territory after 1941, while a few were also in German or Italian-occupied zones. They seem to have survived largely by turning to the black market, which did not endear them to the local population, particularly in places like the Philippines or the Dutch East Indies. It is probably in part to protect these economic interests that many Sindhi merchants in Southeast Asia gave their support to Subhas Bose and the Indian National Army. This will be taken up in a later chapter. Overall, the Sindworkies managed to survive the second world conflict with relatively little damage. The decisive trial came for them two years after 1945 with the Partition of India, which led to their dispersal from Hyderabad. But, before looking at this, a broad survey of the worldwide diaspora of the Sindwork merchants will be presented.

Space and function in the Sindworkie network

While the Shikarpuri network had the shape of a more or less regular grid characterized by territorial continuity, the spatial structure of the

[59] *Ibid.*, p. 206.   [60] *Ibid.*, pp. 208–9.

Sindworkie network was much looser and more irregular. Its shape was largely determined by the lay-out of shipping routes. The map of the network largely replicated the map of the routes followed by the P&O steamers and other British steamship companies which linked India and the Far East with the rest of the world. Along these routes however the network was not of a uniform density. It tended to be denser to the east of India than to the west. The main axis consisted of the major sea-route linking the Far East with Britain, from the Japanese and Chinese ports via Singapore, Colombo, Aden, the Suez canal, Malta and Gibraltar. Secondary axes followed the Cape route around West Africa and via the Canary Islands, the southern transoceanic route between the Atlantic and the Pacific via the Straits of Magellan prior to 1914 and the route through the Panama Canal after that date. Along these routes, colonies of Hyderabadi merchants were found in all the major ports and also in a certain number of inland localities, although the network rarely extended far away from the ports. The largest colonies were in localities which constituted the nodes of the network, because they functioned as entrepôts. The importance of the other localities varied in relation to the size of their resident European population and of the tourist traffic and passenger movements which passed through them. The relative importance of places tended to change over time, as global economic trends had a very direct impact on the network. Functionally, three different categories of localities could be distinguished: purchasing and exporting centres, entrepôts, and retailing centres. The distinction between these categories was not always clearcut, and a certain amount of overlapping between them was inevitable.

Purchasing and attendant exporting operations were largely concentrated in a few localities in India, China and Japan. While little is known about the modus operandi of the Sindwork merchants in India, there were colonies of them in all the major ports and cities in the subcontinent, the largest being in Bombay, Calcutta and Madras. The former two were not purchasing centres. Bombay was mostly where the finance for the international trading operations of the Sindwork merchants was arranged with the exchange banks, and it served also, at least prior the First World War, as a redispatching centre for goods imported from the Far East and destined for the markets west of India. Calcutta was mostly a place where Sindwork merchants had retailing establishments for the large resident European population and it was also a transit point on the route to the Far East, with a *dharamsala* specifically maintained for the purpose of accommodating Sindworkies departing for that region. Madras was an important purchasing centre for different kinds of textile goods and curios produced by craftsmen all over South India. It seems however that most of the purchasing by Sindwork merchants in India was done in northern India, particularly in the Punjab, in Kashmir and in some localities in the United Provinces (Agra, Moradabad, Lucknow, Benares), all important centres of craft production of various kinds. On the other hand, in the twentieth century, very little purchasing was done in Sind itself. Sindwork firms appear to have purchased mostly from dealers, who in their turn financed the craftsmen. Direct financing of craft production by Sindwork merchants is mentioned only for Kashmir.

In the Far East, which increasingly emerged during the first four decades of the twentieth century as the major source of supply for the Sindwork merchants, their purchasing operations were concentrated in a few port cities where most foreign traders congregated. No very precise indication as to the beginnings of the Sindworkie presence in Japan has come to light,[61] but commercial directories of the 1890s mention a few Sindwork firms as having branches in Kobe and Yokohama. The network expanded rapidly during the first two decades of the twentieth century and a survey of British firms in Japan around 1920 in a British consular document[62] revealed the presence of almost thirty Sindwork firms, most of which were described as trading with India only. Yokohama was the major location of Sindwork firms in Japan. Actually in Yokohama the Sindworkies represented the bulk of the Indian merchant community, while in Kobe they were only one of the communities (other communities represented were Parsis, Gujarati Hindus, Bohras, Khojas and Marwaris). The reason for this specific choice of location probably has to do with the fact that Yokohama, except for part of the 1920s, was the main centre of the silk trade in Japan. Even when Kobe, after the 1923 earthquake in Yokohama, became for a few years the most important silk exporting port in Japan, it exported mostly the finer qualities of silk, while Yokohama specialized in the slightly coarser varities, in which the Sindworkies tended to deal.[63] Yokohama was also better placed for the purchase of the various goods known as 'curios'. In Japan, the Sindwork firms generally had to

[61] A Sindhi author claims that the first firms were established in 1872, but this is not corroborated by the evidence of commercial directories. See G. A. Chandra, 'The History of Indians in Japan', in J. K. Motwani *et al.* (eds.), *Global Indian Diaspora, Yesterday, Today and Tomorrow,* New York, 1993, pp. 322–5.
[62] 'List (undated) of names and addresses of firms and independent business and professional men', in PRO Foreign Office Records, Embassy and Consular Archives: Japan, Japan Consulates Miscellaneous, FO345/55.
[63] In a memorandum, 22 April 1926, the British consul-general in Yokohama noted: 'The Indian merchant . . . relieves the silk piecegoods market of certain goods which are not suitable for the American and European market, and of rejects and other inferior

employ Japanese staff, and the Hyderabad staff was generally limited to the manager and one employee. Which explains why the demographic size of the Sindworkie community in Japan, probably less than 200 in the late 1930s, did not reflect the actual importance of Japan to the network in terms of contribution to its global turnover. This small group of merchants was however capable of establishing close connections with Japanese suppliers and of nurturing them over time. Allen and Donnithorne, in their study of 'Western' enterprise in Japan (in which they include Indian firms) have stressed the favourable conditions under which foreign merchants operated in Japan after the devaluation of the yen in 1931: goods were bought from Japanese middlemen and as there was keen competition for orders, the exporters could get the supplies they wanted at very low prices.[64] An interesting indication as to the importance of Japan to the Sindwork merchants was given by the governor of Sind in 1941. In a letter to the Viceroy dated 8 August 1941, Dow, reporting on reactions in Sind to the possibility of Japan's entry into the war, wrote: 'The only class really perturbed about Japan are the Sind workies [sic], who claim to have assets worth over a crore and a half of rupees locked up in Japan, and are getting anxious about their employees who are still there'.[65] These assets (which may have been deliberately overestimated) consisted almost exclusively of the stock-in-trade in Japanese goods of the various Sindwork firms, and to a much lesser extent of Indian goods for sale in Japan. Although this figure cannot be taken as an equivalent of the turnover of Sindwork firms, it is nevertheless an indication of the size of their business.

In China, the operations of the Sindwork merchants, who appear to have arrived in the 1880s, were exclusively confined to the treaty ports where, as British subjects, they benefited from the legal and judicial privileges linked to extraterritoriality. Canton, and especially Shameen and the French concession, seem to have been the main locations of Sindwork firms in the Chinese treaty ports prior to the First World War. There were also Sindwork firms in neighbouring Hong Kong from at least the late 1880s.[66] The presence of the firm of K. A. J. Chotirmall in Tsingtao and Port Arthur is attested to from the 1890s onwards. There

---

goods.' PRO, Foreign Office Records, Embassy and Consular Archives: Japan, General, 'British subjects in Japan, 1931', FO 262/1795.
[64] G. C. Allen and A. D. Donnithorne, *Western Enterprise in Far Eastern Economic Development: China and Japan*, London, 1962 (2nd edn), p. 207.
[65] Letter from governor of Sind to viceroy, 8 August 1941, Oriental and India Office Collections of the British Library, European Manuscripts, Dow Papers, MSS Eur E 372, File 5, letters to viceroy.
[66] Three were listed in the *Hong Kong Directory and Hong List for the Far East for 1889*, Hong Kong, pp. 512-28.

were also Sindwork merchants in Hankow prior to the First World War. After the war, the network seems to have expanded mostly in Shanghai, and to a lesser extent in Tientsin.[67] In Shanghai, seven Sindwork firms were listed in 1934 as silk exporters[68] out of a total of forty to fifty foreign firms in the silk export business,[69] mostly French and British. This suggested that they had a significant share of the export of silk and silk goods through Shanghai, which handled the bulk of China's exports in this field.[70] In China as in Japan, the Sindwork merchants purchased goods through local agents, and had no direct linkages to production.

A second class of locality consisted of trading emporia which served mostly as entrepôts from where goods were redistributed across vast areas. They were the real nodes of the network. The major entrepôts were Singapore and Surabaya in the Far East, Cairo in the Middle East and Gibraltar in Western Europe.

In Singapore, from very modest beginnings in 1873, with the opening of a branch by the firm of W. Assomull, the community of Sindwork merchants developed into a cluster of some 17 firms and almost 150 men on the eve of the Second World War.[71] Singapore was an entrepôt from where goods from India were redispatched to the entire Far East,

[67] Little is known about the beginnings of the Sindhi presence in Tientsin. A partnership agreement signed in 1917 between a Hyderabad capitalist and his two working partners, including a Muslim, mentions the existence of the branch of a firm in Tientsin. See 'Deed of Partnership dated 12 August 1917 concluded between H. Vishindas on the one part and Naraindas Gehimal and Gul Hassan Shah on the other part', PRO, Foreign Office Records, Embassy and Consular Archives: China, China Consulates, Personal Estates Correspondence, FO 678/2946. Further evidence from the 1930s, including two probate inquiries and various contractual agreements, shows that there were in Tientsin in the 1930s four Sindwork firms, all having their shops in Victoria Street, the main thoroughfare of the international settlement; one firm had a sub-branch in the French concession. Besides, one of these firms had a branch in Peking, and branches in Moukden and Dairen, another one branches in Moukden and Dairen. The presence in Japanese-occupied Manchukuo was testimony to the connection with the Japanese. It seems that the shops were mostly selling Japanese silks to the European population of Tientsin. Two inventories reveal, as usual, a fairly large stock-in-trade and lists of creditors indicate that the shops were almost exclusively supplied by Sindhi firms from Kobe, Yokohama and Shanghai. See 'Probate enquiry in the goods of Lalchand Pinyamall, deceased, 3 March 1932', FO 678/1233B, and 'Estate of Tarachand Metharam Lalwani, 28 January 1931', FO 678/1938. Tientsin appears to have been the northernmost outpost of the Sindworkie network in East Asia. The size of the community must have been not more than some twenty people, which was typical of the small dispersed Sindworkie communities found all over Asia and the world in general.
[68] *The Shanghai Directory 1934*, Shanghai, 1934, pp. 311–30.
[69] Mentioned in L. M. Li, *China's Silk Trade: Traditional Industry in the Modern World 1842–1937*, Cambridge, MA, 1981, p. 91.
[70] Shanghai's percentage of Chinese raw silk exports (in volume) was always superior to 50 per cent in the 1870–1925 period. See *ibid.*, Table 11, p. 78.
[71] Bharadwaj, *Sindhis Through the Ages*, p. 355.

and goods from Japan and China to neighbouring countries (the Dutch East Indies, in particular Sumatra and Western Java, including Batavia). The Sindhi firms there also had sizeable shops which catered to a clientele of Europeans, Indians and Chinese. They strengthened their positions in the 1930s, especially as the boycott of Japanese goods by Chinese merchants led to a transfer of licences for the import of Japanese textiles from Chinese to Indian traders.[72] In Singapore, the Sindhis were only one amongst the various trading communities, originating from the Indian subcontinent, which included Chettiars and Marakkayars from Tamilnad, Bohras, Khojas and Gujarati Hindus, as well as Punjabi Sikhs and Marwaris. But, as early as in 1921, they formed a Sindhi Merchants Association,[73] which, by 1939, had twenty-one member firms and a building which could be used by Sindhi merchants passing through Singapore.[74] The Sindhi merchants' privileged connections with the big Japanese firms allowed them to steal a march on their competitors in the 1930s and to start emerging as a community of particular importance. A look at successive editions of the Singapore directory between 1900 and 1939 reveals the increasing weight of the Sindhi firms amongst the Indian firms listed. In the 1950s and 1960s the Sindhi community in Singapore was to expand dramatically.

Surabaya was another important entrepôt, closely linked with Singapore, which supplied the very dense network of the Sindwork firms in Eastern Java and in the eastern part of the Indonesian archipelago (Borneo and Celebes). In the mid-1930s, there were eighteen branches of Sindwork firms there, and they did a thriving business. 'Surabaya, as the entrepôt centre for the entire eastern Indonesian archipelago, attracted most of the enterprising Sindhi firms.'[75] The role played by the Sindhis in Surabaya was recognised early by the Dutch authorities which conferred the title of 'Hoofd der Indiers' on a prominent Sindhi merchant. Successful Sindhi merchants often started their careers as managers of a branch of one of the big firms in Surabaya and then set up their own establishment in one of the neighbouring towns of Eastern Java, using the connections they had forged during their time in Java's main port. Although the textile trade, which included the import of Indian as well as Japanese textiles, was the mainstay of the activities of

[72] Brown, *Capital and Entrepreneurship*, p. 211.
[73] Mentioned in message by T. R. Mulani, president, Sindhi Merchants Association Singapore, in *Sindhi Merchants Association, Singapore, Trade and Telephone Directory 1994/95*, Singapore, s.d., p. 11. I am grateful to Mrs Medha Malik Kudaisyia for having provided me with a copy of this directory.
[74] Bhardwaj, *Sindhis*, p. 353.
[75] Mani, 'Indians in Jakarta', p. 101.

the Sindwork firms, they also engaged in importing from India various handicrafts such as brassware, embroidery and wooden and ivory carvings, for a Dutch clientele.

Cairo was the major entrepôt for Sindwork firms in Egypt and the eastern Mediterranean. Its role was particularly important prior the the First World War, when Egypt still accounted for a large share of the global turnover of the Sindwork firms. Its importance diminished after 1918. From Cairo, goods imported from India and the Far East were distributed across the whole of Egypt, in neighbouring Sudan and Lybia, as well as in Lebanon. Cairo was also the seat of very large retailing establishments, because of its role as the main tourist centre in Egypt and also because of the size of its European civilian population and its British garrison. Its function in the network was therefore clearly dual.

Gibraltar[76] was a major entrepot for the entire western leg of the network. From their depots there, Sindwork firms supplied their retailing establishments in the whole of North Africa,[77] in the Canary

[76] One firm of Sindwork merchants, J. T. Chanrai & Co., claimed to have started trading in Gibraltar in 1860, the year it was founded in Hyderabad, but it is difficult to verify this claim. The first mentions of the presence of Indian dealers in Gibraltar occur in the 1890s. In 1899 the governor of Gibraltar complained of the presence of Indian employees of trading firms who, having quarrelled with their employer, found themselves destitute and had to be repatriated to India at the cost of the Exchequer. See governor of Gibraltar to secretary of state for the colonies, dated 8 September 1899, letter enclosed in Despatch no. 141, Public (Emigration) from secretary of state for India to Government of India, 22 November 1900. Copy in Bombay General (Miscellaneous) Proceedings Emigration, February 1901, Serial no. A 2. However a contemporary trade directory mentioned only one firm of Sindwork merchants as having a shop in Gibraltar, which tends to suggest that the Sindwork merchants were not yet accepted as a permanent element of the local trading community. See *Gibraltar Directory and Guide Book 1899*, Gibraltar, 1899. Some twenty years later an official document gave a complete list of Indian firms in Gibraltar, with the number of their shops and employees. It listed sixteen Indian shops in Gibraltar, belonging to seven different Sindwork firms, including the four big firms of J. T. Chanrai, D. Chellaram, M. Dialdas and Pohoomull Bros. They employed a total of seventy-six, including two cooks, the rest being managers and shop assistants. See 'List of Indian Firms in Gibraltar, showing number of shops and Indian employees', enclosed in Gibraltar secret despatch of 1 June 1920, to secretary of state for the colonies, PRO, Colonial Office Records, Gibraltar Original Correspondence, CO 91/474.

[77] A document compiled by the Sindwork Merchants' Association stated that each Gibraltar-based firm generally had eight or ten branches in Morocco, and that the number of staff employed in those branches was therefore eight or ten times the staff employed in Gibraltar. Sindwork firms and independent merchants were thus active in the major towns of the French protectorate in Morocco, primarily in Casablanca, but also in Fes, Rabat, Marrakech, Meknès, Pt Lyautey (Kenitra) and Oujda. There they took advantage of a liberal custom regime to import goods from the Far East which they sold in their shops to a mainly European clientele. They benefited until 1936 from the advantages of the capitulatory regime, consisting, apart from low custom duties, in the jurisdiction of the British consular courts, which were lenient and easy to manipulate.

Islands and West Africa, and even, prior to the First World War, in Central and South America. It had also many retailing establishments[78] which catered to the passengers of the steamers bound for Britain.

Tenerife[79] also played the role of an entrepôt, closely linked to Gibraltar, in relation to West Africa and Central and South America. The presence of a British colony and of a regular stream of visitors from Britain attracted by the mild climate of the islands provided a ready-made market for the Oriental curios sold by the Sindworkies. Prior to the Spanish Civil War, there was a colony of around 100 Sindhi merchants in the Canary Islands, of whom 60 were in Tenerife, 35 in Las Palmas, and 5 in an unnamed island of the archipelago (Palma?).[80] Their business appears to have been thriving prior to the Civil War, and

Their ability to survive after the abolition of the capitulatory regime shows, however, that they did not depend entirely on these favourable political circumstances, but were able to carve for themselves a specific niche in Moroccan trade. There is still a Sindhi community in Morocco.

Sindhis were also present in the other North African countries, Algeria, Tunisia and Libya. In Algeria, a directory of 1901 lists three Sindhi establishments in Algiers. See *Annuaire commercial, industriel, administratif, agricole et viticole de l'Algérie et de la Tunisie, 1902*, Paris, s.d., 'Professions d'Alger', pp. 279 ff. On Sindwork merchants in Lybia, some detailed information is found in PRO, Foreign Office Records, Embassy and Consular Archives: Tripoli (Lybia), 'Properties of Indian Merchants in Tripoli, 1940', FO 161/6. The presence of large European populations was the main attraction of the North African countries for the Sindwork merchants.

[78] In spite of the adoption in the 1920s and 1930s of various legal measures meant to restrict the activities of alien traders, who were not allowed to have more than one shop per firm, and had to obtain special licences to be allowed to trade, the Sindwork merchants continued to expand, and a list of shops and employees as of 1939, compiled by the Sindwork Merchants' Association in 1946, indicated the presence of 21 firms with 25 shops, employing a total of 129, which meant a global expansion, but at the same time revealed the closure of at least 7 of the shops which had been in existence in 1920. See copy of statement furnished by the Sindwork Merchants Association, Hyderabad Sind, showing numbers of Indians in all Indian firms in Gibraltar in 1939, enclosed in letter no. F 123/45 O.S., 16 May 1946, from Government of India, Department of Commonwealth Relations, to secretary, Political Department, India Office, IOR, Public & Judicial Department Collections, Collection 108/12 B, 'Indian Merchants in Gibraltar', File POL 8546 1946, L/P&J/8/236. In 1938, the governor of Gibraltar remarked on the fact that Main Street, the main thoroughfare, had gained the sobriquet of 'Bombay Street'. See governor of Gibraltar to secretary of state for the colonies, 20 April 1938, copy in *ibid*.

[79] The origins of their presence seem to go back to the 1890s when the firm of J. T. Chanrai pioneered trade routes west of Gibraltar, and established a branch in Tenerife. Tenerife and Las Palmas were ports of call for the steamers of the Union Steamship Line which plied the New Zealand–Britain route via the Cape, and Chanrai is known to have had a branch at Cape Town at the time.

[80] See British Consulate, Tenerife, 15 March 1938, to under-secretary to the Foreign Office, enclosed in under-secretary to the Foreign Office to under-secretary to the India Office, dated *ibid*., P.Z. 2402 1938, copy in IOR, L/P&S/12/210. The same document lists twelve branches of Sindwork firms in the islands, of which eight in Tenerife and four in Las Palmas. Four of the big seven firms (D. Chellaram, J. T. Chanrai, M. Dialdas and Pohoomull Bros.) were represented, and altogether these firms

they generally were paid in sterling, which was of course advantageous in more ways than one. The presence of those Sindwork firms laid the basis for the development of a Sindhi colony which is now several thousand strong and is the largest in western Europe and one of the largest in the world, mostly concentrated in Tenerife.

The third tier of localities consisted of those where only retailing operations took place. There were many such localities, widely spread out between Kobe and Panama. Some were large colonial port cities such as Rangoon in Burma,[81] Colombo in Ceylon,[82] Saigon in French Indochina,[83] Algiers and Casablanca in French North Africa, Alexan-

contributed annually a total of approximately 250,000 pesetas to the economy of the islands in the form of taxes, rents and contributions to social services.

[81] The Sindhi presence in Burma seems to have been an offshoot of their move into Calcutta, which happened in the 1870s. The Burma Census of 1891 revealed the presence of 863 natives of Sind, of whom 749 were males, in the province. See *Census of India 1891*, vol. X, *Burma*, part III, *Tables*, Rangoon, 1892, Table XI, pp. 174–83. No detailed information is available as to who they were, but it is probable that at least some of them were Sindworkies. A clearer indication as to the presence of a Hyderabadi community is provided by the 1921 Census which enumerates the surprisingly large number of 2,720 males and 687 females born in the district of Hyderabad. See *Census of India 1921*, vol. X, *Burma*, part II, *Tables*, Rangoon, 1923, p. 163. This figure is to be taken with caution, however, as the number of Sindhi-speakers in Burma was put at only 152 males and 15 females. There remains therefore a lot of uncertainty regarding the actual size of the Hyderabadi diaspora in Burma. However, information gathered from trade directories shows several Sindwork firms in Rangoon to have been active in the silk and curio trade, mostly for a European clientele.

[82] Regarding Sindhis in Ceylon, the evidence available is mostly demographic. The earliest data, from the 1921 Census, indicate the presence on the island of 107 Sindhis, a figure which the census authorities themselves recognized to be 'subject to considerable errors'. See *Census of Ceylon, 1921*, vol. I, part I, Colombo, 1923, p. 229. The story of the presence of Sindwork merchants in Ceylon seems rather specific. Trade directories reveal that none of the well-known Sindwork firms had branches in the island. See the list of firms in *The Ceylon Mercantile Directory 1933*, Colombo, 1933. Seventeen Sindhi firms are listed in Colombo, all in the silk and curio business. This suggests strongly that the first arrivals were pedlars who broke their journey on the way to Singapore and the Far East, and, having found that there was good business in Colombo, an important port of call for steamers plying the Europe–Far East routes, prolonged their stay, and, after a while, set up shop in Colombo, and, later, in other localities of the island with a European population. Apart from the usual silk and curios, they also seem to have been engaged in the export trade in semi-precious stones. Although of less economic weight than other Indian communities like the Nattukottai Chettiars, they were sufficiently distinct to have their own association, the Sindhi Merchants Association of Ceylon. In the 1920s and 1930s the Sindhi population seems to have increased steadily, as the 1946 Census reported the presence of 371 Sindhis. See *Census of Ceylon, 1946*, vol. I, part I, Colombo, 1950, p. 162. The Sindhi community included a few Shikarpuris, who had developed financial interests, but the bulk of it consisted of Sindworkies, who seem to have generally migrated individually and without contracts. They prospered, and one of these merchants, Hirdaramani, became one of the largest industrialists in post-independence Ceylon and owner of a large textile mill.

[83] The pioneering firm there was K. A. J. Chotirmall, whose presence in the colony is known from the 1890s. In the early 1900s, both Pohoomull Bros. and W. Assomull established branches, and smaller firms followed suit. The Sindwork firms came to

dria in Egypt, Batavia in the Dutch East Indies or Manila in the Philippines,[84] where the presence of a large resident population of Europeans or Americans provided a ready-made clientele for the kind of goods the Sindworkies sold in their shops; ship passengers accounting only for a variable share of the overall business. Other ports, like Tangier[85] in North Africa, Valletta in Malta, Suez, Ismailia and Port Said in Egypt or Colon[86] at the Atlantic entrance to the Panama Canal, owed their importance entirely to the large number of ships' passengers who disembarked there and had time to engage in purchases while their ship was in harbour.

largely dominate the trade in Asian silks (while French traders dominated the trade in French silks), and their shops in the Rue Catinat, Saigon's most exclusive shopping location, catered to a mixed clientele of Europeans, rich Chinese and affluent Vietnamese.

[84] The presence of the Sindwork merchants seems to go back to the early 1890s, curiously a time when the Spanish authorities took protectionist measures in an attempt to restore Spain's commercial supremacy in its colony. An incidental insight into the entry of Sindwork firms into the Philippines is provided by the records of claims for compensation filed by foreign merchants with the US authorities following the bombardment and quasi-destruction by the US navy, during the course of the Spanish-American War, of the important commercial town of Iloilo, in the island of Panay, in the Visayas. Three Sindhi firms were included amongst those who claimed damages to their godowns, and one of them was Pohoomull Bros. which seems to have played a pioneering role in the expansion of the network into the Philippines. See letter from British consulate-general, to Sir Edward Grey, secretary of state for foreign affairs, 7 May 1912, PRO, Foreign Office Records, General Correspondence (Political), United States File 259, 1912, no. 25188, FO 371/1542. For the first twenty years of the American regime, the network expanded quietly, until the introduction of immigration restrictions in 1917 created problems. In spite of the difficulties in getting shop assistants from India past US immigration authorities, the Sindworkie community continued to grow up to the Second World War, and was approximately 400 strong in 1939, making it the second largest community outside India after that in the Dutch East Indies. See letter from British consul-general, Manila, to Foreign Office, 20 March 1940, copy in IOR, Public & Judicial Department Collections, Collection 108/29, 'Indian immigration into the Philippines 1938-1941', L/P&J/8/281. Originally, the Sindworkies specialized in the sale of Indian artefacts to a clientele which included a large percentage of Americans. Progressively they enlarged their operations to the sale of Japanese textile goods, which they procured from Singapore. Sindhis are nowadays an active community in business in the Philippines, controlling part of the local garment industry, which is a large exporter to Europe and the USA.

[85] A 'List of commercial establishments belonging to Indians', enclosed in PRO, Foreign Office Records, Embassy and Consular Archives: Morocco, Tangier, FO 174/354, 'British interests and properties in Tangier', 1947, shows that there were eighteen branches of Sindwork firms there.

[86] It would seem that the firm of J. T. Chanrai was the first to establish itself, in the Atlantic port of Colon, around 1905, i.e. before the opening of the Panama canal, but at a time when the Panama route between the two oceans was already in widespread use. Other firms followed with the opening of the canal, and a document of 1927 gave a list of eleven houses of Sindwork merchants in the city of Colon, who had a staff of 100-125. Letter, 17 May 1927 from Pessumal Moolchand, Jairamdas Daulatram to the collector of Hyderabad, copy in IOR, Public & Judicial Department Collections, L/P&J/8/278.

Of inland localities where Sindwork merchants ran successful operations, some were large tourist centres, like Aswan and Luxor in Egypt, or Marrakesh in Morocco, others, like Johannesburg, Salisbury, Nairobi or Bandoeng had a fairly large European resident population.

In a few areas, Sindwork merchants had become sufficiently entrenched locally to avoid being too dependent on the presence of European settlers or soldiers. This was the case in particular in Eastern Java, where they operated in all the sizeable towns, even those without a significant European population,[87] and in West Africa where their network of branches covered by the 1940s most of the important localities in the interior of Nigeria and the Gold Coast.[88] There is also the special case of Spanish Morocco, where, as came to light at the time of the Spanish Civil War in 1936, there were 200 Sindhi merchants who had property worth Rs 50 lakhs[89] and were present in the four main towns, Ceuta,[90] Melilla, Tetuan and Larache. Given the poverty of

[87] Data from the 1930 Census of the Netherlands Indies shows that the number of foreign-born adult male 'Vor-Indiers' in Java and Madura, was 1,884, and it is known that Sindhis represented by far the largest community of Indian-born immigrants in Java (other groups represented were Karachi Memons, specializing in the sugar trade, and some Punjabi Sikhs and Gujarati Hindus). Therefore, an estimate of around 1,000 Sindworkies in Java in 1930 seems plausible. See *Census of the Netherlands Indies 1930*, vol. VII, *Chinese and other Non-indigenous Orientals in the Netherlands Indies*, Batavia, 1935, Table 12. A supplementary indication as to the continuing strength of the network even in the post-depression era is provided in a directory of Indian merchants abroad dated 1934, which lists a total of fifty-eight branches of Sindwork firms operating in twenty-three localities in Java outside Batavia (where there were branches of several firms). See *Indians Abroad Directory*, pp. 84–7. Apart from Surabaya, Bandoeng had the greatest number of branches (five), but even lesser localities such as Probolingo, Pasoeroean or Tjilatjap had two or three branches of Sindwork firms operating.

[88] Regarding the Gold Coast, a detailed picture of the Sindhi trading network in 1948 has come to light, in relation to a spate of riots which affected that colony in February 1948 and targeted, amongst others, the Sindhi traders. A memorandum submitted to the Indian Ministry of Foreign Affairs by the Indian Merchants Association of the Gold Coast on 8 March 1948 claimed that Indians had come to the Gold Coast fifty years earlier, i.e. in the late 1890s, and that they had about 26 firms employing more than 200. See PRO, Colonial Office Records, Gold Coast Original Correspondence, CO 96/796/1, File 31312/2 C 'Disturbances: Payment of compensation'. The Association estimated the losses suffered by the Indian traders in the riots to be in the neighbourhood of £1.5 million sterling. A list of commercial establishments belonging to Indians was appended, which showed that there was a total of ninety of them, including wholesale depots and warehouses, spread over some ten localities in the Colony and Protectorate. As in Sierra Leone, the Sindhi merchants on the Gold Coast were almost exclusively importers, specializing in the sale of textiles and sundry articles, to a clientele which must have been mostly African.

[89] See telegram, 3 August 1936, from Government of India, Foreign and Political Department, to secretary of state for India, P.Z. 5730.1936, IOR, Political External Files and Collections, 'Spanish Civil War', L/P&S/12/210.

[90] The 1935 Census of Ceuta mentioned the presence of fifteen Indians from Hyderabad. M. Gordillo Osuna, *Geografia Urbana de Ceuta*, Madrid, 1972, pp. 138–9.

Spanish Morocco, the absence at the time of a significant tourist trade, and the lack of commercial opportunities generally, the only plausible explanation for such a massive presence of Sindhi traders is the existence of an active contraband trade with Spain across the Straits of Gibraltar, due to the low customs duties on imported goods in Spanish Morocco. Operating through Spanish Morocco was for the Sindworkies a roundabout way to penetrate the Spanish market, which they could not do from Gibraltar, because of the *de facto* closing of the border between the British territory and Spain.

The spatial expansion of the network resulted in a certain amount of functional complexity, as localities which had been chosen as the seat of retailing operations also sometimes became purchasing centres. For instance, Sindwork firms in places like Malta and Tenerife started at some point to purchase lace locally, and this found a market in Egypt, North Africa and West Africa. The Sindwork merchants in Egypt went in for the export of Egyptian textile goods, such as the so-called 'Assiut shawls' to the markets of Europe, etc.

The range of operations of the Sindworkies was increased by their widespread use of pedlars. Some localities served as bases for peddling forays into neighbouring countries. Thus Sindhi merchants from Sierra Leone also used to trade in neighbouring Liberia.[91] The presence of Sindhi pedlars arriving from Gibraltar is occasionally mentioned in the USA.[92] Such pedlars, operating from Panama and Chile in particular, also frequented the Pacific coast of South America, Colombia and probably Venezuela.

Between these widely scattered locations, and the network centre at Hyderabad, a constant flow of men kept circulating. It is to the pattern of circulation in the Sindworkie as well as in the Shikarpuri network that I shall now turn.

---

[91] In October 1912, the governor of Sierra Leone informed the Colonial Office that two 'Hindu' traders, Rettinji and Goodoomal, had sustained losses in a robbery which occurred inside Liberia in November 1911. It turned out that they were employed by the Hyderabadi firm of Pahloomal Bhojraj in Freetown to peddle goods in Liberia. See enclosure 1, sworn statement by Rettinji, Freetown, 13 December 1911, and enclosure 3, statement by Parasram Bhojraj, Freetown, 2 January 1912, in Sierra Leone despatch no. 464, 23 October 1912, PRO, Colonial Office Records, Sierra Leone Original Correspondence, File 34 718, 1912, CO 267/543.

[92] The superintendent of Lascar Transfers at the Liverpool Mercantile Marine Office wrote to the India Office on 17 November 1898: 'Two natives of India, Tolaram Juramall and Reejhumal Bolchand, both of Hyderabad, Scinde, have applied to me for an assisted passage to India . . . They produced passports issued at Gibraltar, in which one is described as a Hawker and the other as a Trader, and stated that they had been to America but got into financial difficulties and the Consul at New Orleans assisted them in getting a passage to this country . . .'. IOR, Public and Judicial Department Annual Files, File J&P 2250/98.

5 Patterns of circulation and business organization in two merchant networks

The Shikarpuri and Hyderabadi networks displayed largely similar spatial configurations, in which the network centres were separated from the actual places of business by vast distances. This spatial configuration in its turn largely shaped the way business was organized. Although such a physical separation between the network centres and the actual places of business was not unique to those two networks, the solutions elaborated by the merchants of Sind to deal with the problem were fairly specific. The major device used by the Shikarpuri merchants, who were the first in the field, was a system of partnership known as the *shah–gumastha*; the Hyderabadi merchants adopted it at first, but gradually modified it. Distance, with the attendant problems of communication it posed, dictated a pattern of functional specialization, by which only a limited number of financial operations, such as accounting, took place in the network centres, while all the commercial operations and some types of financial operations were performed in the actual place of business. This dissociation implied a pattern of regular circulation between the two poles. This was a multiform and multilayered circulation, in which financial and manpower flows did not move along the same lines. While capital flowed unidirectionally from the centres to the actual places of business (to return only in the form of remitted profits), manpower constantly moved to and fro between the two poles. However, this human circulation was socially stratified: the owners of capital as a rule did not circulate much, being content with providing capital and supervising operations from their residence in the network centre. The actual circulating was mostly done by their agents and employees. Other flows of circulation concerned short-term credit (in contrast to long-term capital) as well as information and knowledge. In this chapter, we shall look in detail at this varied pattern of circulation, which was the lifeblood of the two networks, and at the way in which it influenced the forms of business organization. In Shikarpur and in Hyderabad, a small group of capitalists residing in the network centre were able to maintain control over financial and commercial operations which took place in widely dispersed locations. In a manner which may appear paradoxical, it was as much the existence of 'traditional' institutional mechanisms as the advent of 'modern' technological developments which made it possible. The focus of the analysis in this chapter will therefore be the various types of institutional mechanisms through which strong links were forged and maintained over time between the merchant capitalists in the network centres and their partners and employees in the dispersion.

Circulating capital and resident capitalists: the role of the *shah–gumastha* system

The development of long-distance financial and trading networks in which capitalists remained based in Sind was made possible by the existence of a specific system of partnership known in Shikarpur as the *shah–gumastha*. Variants of the system existed in other South Asian merchant networks. Thus, among Nattukottai Chettiars, 'proprietors left the daily operations of their overseas business firms to hired agents (*melals*) and field staff (*kattu kanakkupillai*) while they stayed in India'.[1] However, the Nattukottai agents were not partners in the same sense as the Shikarpuri *gumasthas*. The Shikarpuri system developed in a much earlier period, although the exact temporal and causal sequence is not known: did the system exist prior to the development of long-distance networks or was it invented, so to speak, by the merchants in the course of their ventures? It seems to have been ultimately derived from the system known in Arabic as *mudaraba*, but reached Sind most probably through Persia. The vocabulary definitely points towards a Persian origin. The term 'gumastha' was in widespread use in the Indian subcontinent from at least the seventeenth century onwards to designate an agent; on the other hand, the use of the term 'shah' for 'principal' seems idiosyncratic, and it has not been possible to trace its origins. It is interesting that Hindu merchants in Sind used a partnership system which came from the Islamic world, and had been specifically devised to be in conformity with the *sharia*.[2] In Europe, this form of partnership was adopted very early and evolved into the *commenda* of medieval Italy, and ultimately into the joint-stock company,[3] but in Sind no such evolution is noticeable. Admittedly, the *mudaraba* system of partnership

---
[1] See Rudner, *Caste and Capitalism*, p. 114.
[2] On *mudaraba*, see A. L. Udovich, *Partnership and Profit in Medieval Islam*, Princeton, NJ, 1970.
[3] On the different offshoots of *mudaraba* in Europe and Asia, see M. Cizakca, *A Comparative Evolution of Business Partnerships: the Islamic World and Europe, with Special Reference to the Ottoman Archives*, Leiden, 1996, pp. 20ff.

lent itself particularly well to being used by merchant networks, in which there was a clear-cut demarcation between organizing merchants who stayed in the network centre, and travelling merchants. Armenians, in particular, are known to have used it to organize their worldwide trading operations from their centre of New Julfa.[4]

The system was firmly established in Shikarpur by the time different travellers reported on the Shikarpuri merchants in the first decades of the nineteenth century. It allowed a small group of *sarrafs* and *sahukars* located in Shikarpur itself, a group which, according to the census taken in 1840, did not consist of more than a hundred men, to control financial and commercial transactions over a vast area encompassing Khorrassan as well as Turkestan. Each of these men had a number of agents spread over various localities. One could wonder why it was so necessary to dissociate the fiducial circulation of capital from the physical circulation of capitalists. Several answers can be provided. Firstly, one would have to take into account the sheer physical obstacles to circulation prior to the advent of modern transport in the second half of the nineteenth century. At the time when the system was set up in Shikarpur, it was difficult and dangerous to travel to Central Asia. The existence of a sophisticated *hundi* system made it possible to avoid transporting specie in large quantities along the danger-ridden routes linking Sind with Central Asia and thus limited the necessity for bankers themselves to travel frequently to the area. Capitalists, however, needed trustworthy agents on the spot to conduct transactions, and that was basically the function of *gumasthas*. The availability of such men, ready to bear the physical risks of dangerous travel for a reward which was necessarily unpredictable, could be explained probably by the demographic situation. The influx of displaced *banias* of various origins into Shikarpur during the second half of the eighteenth century must have created a pool of relatively cheap mercantile manpower ready to try the adventure of Central Asian travel.

The *sarraf* or *sahukar* was the merchant capitalist or *shah*: he advanced the funds to his *gumasthas*, who were remunerated in the form of a share in the profits of the financial and commercial operations they undertook for him. From the limited amount of evidence available, it is not possible to say definitely whether, prior to the advent of British rule, contractual arrangements between *shahs* and *gumasthas* in Shikarpur were oral or written. But in the British period written contracts became the rule and were often used as evidence in court cases. As to the exact pattern of sharing of profits, it does not seem to have been fixed by custom, but to

[4] See E. Herzig, 'The Armenian Merchants of New Julfa (Isfahan)', unpublished D. Phil thesis, Oxford, 1991.

have varied considerably. It was a characteristic of *mudaraba* contracts that the division of profits between the parties had to be calculated not in absolute amounts but in proportions. This requirement was apparently always respected in Shikarpur.

Over time no particular trend of evolution is noticeable in the system as it operated in Shikarpur. Most partnerships in Shikarpur seem to have been concluded for a limited duration. One intriguing feature of the Shikarpuri network, especially in contrast to the Hyderabadi network, is that few firms appear to have survived for long periods. In Russian Central Asia, for instance, only two firms appear to have really consolidated: one was a large banking firm in Khokand and the other a trading firm in Jizak specializing in grain and cotton trading. Both firms were located in the guberniia of Turkestan, where Russian commercial law was in operation. But, as far as the emirate of Bokhara is concerned, no large firm is known. Shikarpuri merchants did not apparently create multi-branch firms of the kind the Sindwork merchants did. The difficulty of communications between Shikarpur and Central Asia probably tended to discourage the adoption of a pattern of business organization which relied to a large extent on a rapid and continuous exchange of information between headquarters and branches. Therefore Shikarpuri principals continued to rely on *gumasthas* who were largely on their own once they had reached Central Asia, and were always tempted to start their own businesses. In Central Asia, the system replicated itself, as men who had started their career as *gumasthas* tended to become in their turn *shahs* to other Shikarpuris, given that there was no limit, legal or otherwise, to the number of partnerships a man could enter into. The system worked in the following way: a Shikarpuri banker resident in a big town, who himself might be the *gumastha* of a banker in Shikarpur, was a *shah* in relation to a smaller banker in a small town; the latter in his turn was *shah* to a rural moneylender in a village. The relationship between *shah* and *gumastha* was not however completely symmetrical: one could be the *shah* of an indefinite number of *gumasthas*, but one was rarely the *gumastha* of several *shahs* at the same time.

The basic function of the *shah–gumastha* system was less that of organizing the circulation of men than of ensuring a regular supply of capital for long-distance financial and commercial ventures. In the case of Shikarpur, capital circulated almost exclusively in the form of *hundis*. *Gumasthas* going to Central Asia in the service of a Shikarpuri *shah* would be provided with a *hundi* either for one of his *gumasthas* already on the spot or, in case he did not already have *gumasthas*, with another Shikarpuri banker in Central Asia. Within the Shikarpuri network, *hundis* were honoured on sight and no questions were ever asked; there was apparently no charge incurred either. Frauds were made practically impossible by the use of a special form of the *bania* Sindhi script as well as of specific marks which were very difficult to imitate.[5] Defaulting on a *hundi* would have been such a breach of merchant etiquette that it was not a risk worth taking into consideration.

In Hyderabad there developed over time a kind of dual system which combined features of the traditional *shah–gumastha* with traits borrowed from European commercial practice. From partnerships, which were by definition temporary, there emerged gradually a number of firms which perpetuated themselves across several generations. For purposes of clarification, it is necessary to distinguish between two meanings of the term 'partnership'. On the one hand, in India 'partnership' was a legal term, used for a specific form of business organization, which was different from both the proprietory firm and the joint-stock company. Practically all businesses in Shikarpur and Hyderabad adopted this specific legal form, which had many advantages in terms of taxation and avoided public scrutiny. But here partnership is used, not in a strictly legal sense, but in a more technical sense, as meaning the association of one or several *shahs* or capitalist partners with one or several *gumasthas* or working partners. By 'firm', on the other hand, is meant a form of business organization in which there was a head office and branches, whatever legal status it had. In Sind most 'firms' were legally 'partnerships', but technically these 'firms' represented a modification of the original *shah–gumastha* system of partnership. The reasons why firms were able to consolidate in Hyderabad, in apparent contrast to the case of Shikarpur, have probably much to do with some of the specificities of the trade carried out by the Sindwork merchants. While the Shikarpuri network was basically self-financing (even if, from the late nineteenth century onwards, Shikarpuri bankers in Russian Central Asia tended

[5] For an account of Shikarpuri *hundis* in the 1870s, see Burton, *Sind Revisited*, pp. 252–3: 'The Hundi, that rude instrument with which the Shikarpuri Rothschild works is a short document, in the usual execrable stenography, laboriously scribbled upon a square scrap of flimsy bank-note paper, and couched in the following form:

11/4 True is the deity Shri!
  1 To the worthy in every respect. May you ever be in good health! May you always be fortunate! Our brother Jesumal.
  2 From Shikarpur, written by Kisordas; read his compliments!
  3 And further, sir, this Hundi of one thousand rupees I have written on you in numerals and in letters, Rs 1000, and the half, which is five hundred, of which the double is one thousand complete: dated this . . . of the month . . . in the Era of Vikramditya, to be paid after a term of . . . days to the bearer at Kabul; the money to be of the currency of the place.
In the year of Vikramaditya, etc., etc., etc.

The document contains marks which effectually prevent forgery; they are known only to the writer and his correspondents . . .'.

increasingly to operate as intermediaries for the Russian banks), the Sindworkies, once they started operating in the world of international maritime trade, which was European dominated, had to obtain at least part of their credit from the exchange banks. The latter would open the indispensable letters of credit only to reputable firms with a history of creditworthiness, and this was of course a strong incentive to consolidate.

In spite of this, temporary partnerships remained an essential component of the Sindworkie network well into the 1920s. They allowed new operators to constantly emerge, and in that way contributed decisively to the overall dynamics of the Sindwork trade, which would have been stifled, had the big and medium-sized firms been the only form. Partnerships allowed small capitalists in Hyderabad to invest in trade without necessarily having to leave the town. These partnerships were generally concluded in the form of written contracts, which were legally binding on the signatories. This tends to show that the existence of a bond of trust between the different parties could not be taken for granted, a point which will be taken up later. Partnerships displayed a variety which is quite astonishing, given the fact that the merchant milieu of Hyderabad was after all limited and closely knit. This variety is testimony to the remarkable pragmatism of the merchants, and to their capacity for adapting to different kinds of environments and to changing circumstances.

The following discussion is based on a sample of four partnerships. Table 5.1 presents in a synoptic form the basic data about those partnerships.

It is a perfectly random sample, constructed on the basis of limited material, but it has the advantage of showing the extraordinary diversity of arrangements concluded between the merchants. Of these partnerships, one was concluded in Hyderabad, one in Tientsin, one in Colon and one by correspondence. The locations of the business operations embody the range of travel of the Sindworkies: Cairo, China, Java and Japan and Panama. The common feature of all these agreements is that they distinguish clearly between two categories: the capitalist partners and the working partners. In only one of the agreements was the old *shah–gumastha* distinction used, but the old Persian and new English terminologies appear to have been totally coterminous. The capitalist partners were the ones who supplied the funds (except in one case, when one of the working partners also supplied some funds),[6] while the working partners contributed their labour, which was actually a form of highly skilled labour, implying commercial experience and knowledge of markets (although this was not specified in the contracts). The duration

[6] This was characteristic of the other major Islamic system of partnership, known as *musharaka*. See Udovich, *Partnership and Profit*.

Table 5.1. *Characteristics of partnerships in Hyderabad*

Date	1 1906	2 1917	3 1920	4 1925
Name of firm	Khanchand & Co.	H. Vishindas	K. N. Dhanamall	Primal & Sons
Place of business	Cairo	Tientsin, Shanghai	Java, Japan	Colon, Panama
Capitalist	K. Menghraj	H. Vishindas	D. & N. Kewalran	J. T. Khemrani
Working partners	K. Ramchand N. Kishinchand	N. Gehimal Gul Hassan Shah	N. Tirthdas	H. Primal G. Jhangimal H. Primal H. Jhangimal
Capital	Rs 15,000	$ 20,000	n.a.	Rs 37,000–47,000
Duration	5 years	5 years	5 years	n.a.
Capitalist's share of profits	7 annas out of Rp 1 3 pies	50 per cent	75–80 per cent	8 annas out of Rp 1 3 pies
Share of working partners	4 annas-6 4 annas-6	25 per cent 25 per cent	10–30 per cent	3 annas 2 annas-6 1 anna-6 1 anna

Sources: (1) Copy of partnership deed concluded in Hyderabad on 1st October 1906 between Bhai Khanchand Menghraj, Kodumal son of Ramchand and Naraindas son of Kishinchand, presented as evidence in 'K. Khanchand and Kodumal, plaintiffs, *vs*. Naraindas, Kishindas, defendant,' civil case no. 134 of 1908, PRO, Foreign Office Records, Cairo Consular Court Records, FO 841/101.

(2) Deed of partnership concluded on 12 August 1917 between H. Vishindas, Naraindas Gehimal and Gul Hassan Shah, PRO, Foreign Office Records, China Consulates, Personal Estates Correspondence, FO 678/ 2946.

(3) Affidavit by Naraindas Tirthdas, 22 October 1923, PRO, Foreign Office Records, Japan Embassy and Consular Archives: Japan, Yokohama, 'Earthquake reconstruction 1923–1927', FO 908/8.

(4) Petition of Tejumal Jhangimal Khemrani to the collector of Hyderabad, September 1927, enclosed in collector of Hyderabad to commissioner in Sind, 8 November 1927, copy in IOR, Public & Judicial Department Collections, L/P&J/ 8/ 278.

of the contracts could vary, but a five-year period seemed to be the standard case. Working partners were required to do a two-year stint abroad, followed by a six-month or one-year period of leave in Hyderabad. Capitalists, for their part were not required to go abroad,[7] but

[7] Thus partnership no. 1 has the following clause: 'That the working partners alone shall be bound to work personally and the capitalist shall remain at Hyderabad (Sind), and give such instructions and advice to the working partners as he may deem fit and proper

were in charge of the general supervision of the business from Hyderabad, including, in particular, the keeping of the books of the partnership which was done in Hyderabad where the accounts were settled every six months or once a year.

The greatest diversity is found in the pattern of division of the profits. The rule of a half–half division between capitalists and working partners was observed only in two cases out of four. In the third case, there was the unusual feature of one man being at the same time a capitalist and a working partner, and being remunerated doubly, on the basis of a share of the profits proportional to his investment, and in his capacity as the main working partner. In the fourth case, the exact share of the capitalists and the working partner was not specified in the contract, which gave rise to a dispute, and the working partner actually ended up getting only an 8 per cent share of the profits, which seems extraordinarily low. In two cases out of four, the traditional system of accounting was used, based on the fiction that the entire profit represented 16 annas (i.e. Rp 1), and that 3 pies were set aside for charity. This common Hindu merchant practice was apparently not observed in the other two cases. One important point to note is that in only one out of four agreements was the capitalist partner and the working partners kin-related (in this particular case, the working partners were the brother of the capitalist, his brother-in-law and two of his sons).

This system of partnership allowed a lot of flexibility. In particular, given the extremely cyclical nature of the Sindwork business, it avoided long-term commitments in terms of investment. The question of sharing of risks appears to have been solved in different ways. In classical *mudaraba* contracts, the capitalist had to bear any losses alone, and there was no limited liability. This seems to have been the case also in some Hyderabadi contracts. On the other hand, in one contract (no. 1), it was specified that risks were shared equally between the capitalist and the working partners. As to the gains of the capitalist, it should be noted that they were of a dual nature: financial, as interest on the capital advanced to the working partners,[8] and commercial, as a share of the profits earned on trading operations. For the capitalist to recuperate his initial investment over such a short period of time implied a fairly high rate of profit, given the fact that the capital advanced generally carried an interest of only 6 per cent annually. Most partnerships were,

and shall not be bound to work personally,' while partnership no. 2 includes the following: 'The working partners shall be bound to work personally at the place of business, and the capitalist shall have to do no work on the above firms, but simply to provide the above fixed capital in merchandise.'

[8] This was a clear difference with *mudaraba* contracts, in which there could be no mention of interest, to conform with the *sharia*.

however, renewed, and profit calculations could therefore be made over a longer period. Taking a fairly general view, three of the contracts appear rather skewed in favour of the working partners, while the fourth one is clearly biased in favour of the capitalists. The reason why working partners were able to obtain such relatively advantageous conditions has probably to do with the state of the labour market in Hyderabad: competent and trustworthy *gumasthas* were in great demand and short supply, and could therefore impose their conditions. This seems also to indicate the existence of a surplus of capital in Hyderabad, keen to invest itself in Sindwork because of the hope of good remuneration. In Hyderabad, it would seem, capital was relatively abundant, and managerial talent ready to expatriate itself relatively scarce, including through the kin network. Hence the need to attract it with interesting conditions.

In Hyderabad, 'permanent' firms developed at first from within the system of partnership, but were increasingly able to dispense with it. These firms were created by families which had large financial resources and probably a sizeable extended kin as well (two things which generally went hand-in-hand) which allowed them to recruit their working partners from their kin network and thus exercise a close degree of supervision over them. As the firms expanded, however, the kin network became insufficient, and, to minimize the risks involved in employing non-kin recruits as *gumasthas*, there was a growing tendency to use salaried managers. The Hyderabadi firms adopted the technical system of organization by branches, which was in use in European international trading firms, as well as other South Asian firms operating in the international marketplace. In the spirit of pragmatism which characterizes the entire history of the network, managing partners and salaried managers seem to have been employed rather indifferently by them. Some branches were entrusted to one or several managing partners who were remunerated by a share of the profits, and other branches were put in charge of a salaried manager. Sometimes the latter was under the authority of the former, sometimes he was directly answerable to headquarters in Hyderabad.

The exceptional longevity of many Hyderabad firms is to be explained, on the one hand, in relation to the capacity of extended families to reproduce themselves across generations, and on the other hand, as a function of the specific oligopolistic structure of the trading network. Sindwork firms, like most Indian business firms, were family affairs, and successful intergenerational transmission of assets (which was facilitated by the Hindu succession law in operation in Sind, based on *Mitaksara*), as well as of expertise, was the key to continuity. The major firms remained under the control of the same family over several generations, although a partition of assets at some point was a common occurrence.

But the pattern of control could vary, be either centralized, or decentralized (as in the case of Wassiamall Assomull, which was a kind of federation of sub-firms loosely controlled from Hyderabad); most firms, however, seem to have been able to combine a measure of centralized control with a large amount of initiative left locally to branch managers. Note has already been taken of the increasing tendency of the big firms to use salaried managers, who were generally interested in the business through some kind of profit-sharing scheme. This was also practised among Nattukottai Chettiars: the agents received a salary, and, at the expiration of their contract, a bonus in the form of a share of the profits.[9]

'Resident' capitalists, whether in Shikarpur or in Hyderabad, were far from being a homogeneous social and professional group. Apart from the somehow mysterious distinction between *sahukars* and *sarrafs* in Shikarpur, they differed in terms of their wealth and the nature of their assets, etc. We are fortunate in possessing a detailed survey of the wealth of two big Shikarpuri merchants who entered into an agreement with the Government of India at the beginning of the twentieth century to conduct trade in southeastern Persia. Their assets, as described in detail in an indenture appended to the agreement,[10] consisted of three different categories of properties: urban properties, a total of fourteen buildings in Shikarpur and its immediate surroundings valued over Rs 50,000, agricultural land, nine different plots worth some Rs 56,000, and a share in different mills worth a total of Rs 18,000. The survey excluded liquid assets, which must also have been of sizeable value. Those two capitalists employed *gumasthas* to develop their business in Persia, and they always remained residents of Shikarpur. How far their portfolio was typical of big Shikarpuri capitalists is of course difficult to say. The assets of a Shikarpuri *shah* who died while on a business trip to Central Asia, on the other hand, consisted mostly of monies remitted from Central Asia, apart from the share of an ancestral house.[11]

Most capitalists in the Sindwork business were content to reside in Hyderabad and spend at most part of the year in the actual place of business. Some capitalists, however, established their residence in their main place of business, but often the headquarters of the firm remained in Hyderabad. One Bhai Khanchand who died in 1909 near Karachi, the owner and principal of a firm called K. Khanchand, with headquarters in Hyderabad, and branches in Bombay, Cairo, Luxor, Assouan and

---

[9] Rudner, *Caste and Capitalism*, p. 116.
[10] 'Indenture made on 23 September 1901 between Collector of Shikarpur . . . and Seths Chimansing and Gulabsing', Appendix to Serial no. A 58, BPP, July 1904.
[11] Serial no. A 17, BPP, March 1902, 'Relative to recovery of property of Notandas alias Naro walad Jhamandas who died in Bukhara on 16 June 1900', Appendix A.

Alexandria[12] was described in the probate inquiry held after his death at the Cairo consular court as 'having his fixed place of abode in Cairo'. This seems to indicate that he had moved his residence from Hyderabad to Cairo so as to be able to supervise more closely his business in the Egyptian capital. Jhamatmall Gurbhamal Melwani, the founder and principal of the important firm of Jhamatmall Gurbhamal, was listed in the Singapore directory of 1911[13] as resident of Medan Deli, on the OostKuist of Sumatra, where his firm had its largest establishment. Most owners of firms in South Africa also appear to have established their residence in their places of business after 1920,[14] probably to conform with stringent immigration laws, which made travel from India to South Africa difficult. There were even a few cases where the headquarters of the firm moved to the place of business; thus, according to the Singapore directory of 1911,[15] the firm of Reloomall Baloomall & Co had its head office in Surabaya. While residing in Hyderabad during most of the year and keeping their families permanently there, the principals of the biggest firms were in the habit of conducting worldwide tours of their branches on a somewhat regular basis. Most of the circulating however was done by their agents and salaried employees.

Circulating men: pedlars, *gumasthas* and salaried employees

In a petition addressed to the district magistrate of Hyderabad in 1927,[16] a Sindwork merchant by the name of Jhangimal Tejumal Khemrani gave an account of his career and his voyages between 1914 and 1925. He appeared to have left India for the first time in 1914, as a partner in the firm of M. Dialdas & Sons, and gone first to Gibraltar, then to Tenerife, from there to Borneo, to end up in Colon at the end of the year. Having spent a few months there, he returned to India in April 1915. He does not say anything more of his travels in the service of

[12] See copy of letter, Cairo, 7 January 1908, from K. Khanchand & Co., enclosed in 'K. Khanchand & Co vs. Dettaram Gopomall', PRO, Foreign Office Records, Cairo Consular Court Records, Suit no. 3 of 1908, FO 841/96.
[13] *The Singapore and Straits Directory 1911*, s.d., s.l., 'Merchants, Professions', pp. 128–215.
[14] According to the biodata of several merchants enclosed in *The South African Indian Who's Who and Commercial Directory*, p. 59 (Kundanmal Rijhoomal Dewan, owner of the Eastern Bazaar, resident of Durban), p. 68 (Gurdasmal Gopaldas, of Tikamdas Bros., resident of Johannesburg), p. 132 (Gurdasmal Ramchand, of Tikamdas Bros., resident of Port-Elizabeth).
[15] *Singapore and Straits Directory*, p. 191.
[16] Petition of Tejumal Jhangimal Khemrani to the collector of Hyderabad, September 1927, enclosed in collector of Hyderabad to commissioner in Sind, 8 November 1927, copy in IOR, Public & Judicial Department Collections, Collection 108/28 A, L/P&J/8/278.

M. Dialdas & Sons, with whom he stayed until 1920. We then find him in April 1925 in Malaga in Spain, in the service of the firm of Virumal Lilaram, from whom he separated in June of the same year in Melilla (Spanish Morocco), before moving to Colon in Panama where he established his own firm in partnership with some relatives of his. This kind of wide-ranging travel was fairly typical of the average Sindworkie. In this particular case, spatial mobility seems to have coincided partly with social mobility as the *gumastha* eventually transformed himself into a *shah*.

Shikarpuris as well as Sindworkies did, on the whole, an enormous amount of travelling, either in the service of their *shahs* or firms, or, more rarely, on their own account. This circulation was not haphazard, but on the contrary, was a highly regulated process, in which contractual agreements, either oral or written, played a crucial role. This circulation of managers and skilled manpower was not basically different from other forms of circulation of labour, which occurred on a very large scale in the same period between the Indian subcontinent and the rest of the world, particular with Burma, Ceylon and Malaya. An important difference, however, is that, prior to the passing of the Indian Emigration Act of 1922, the colonial state was not involved in any way in this circulation, either as an organizing or even as a regulating agency. It represented a very specific form of circulation of labour organized entirely by private commercial enterprise. Similar movements existed from Gujarat and Bombay to East Africa, and from Tamilnadu to Southeast Asia. Altogether, this circulation of commercial manpower represented an annual outflow of a few thousand, which was largely offset by a similar number of returns. While it accounted only for a small percentage of the overall annual outflow of labour from India, it deserves notice because of its specific mode of organization by private firms, and of the skills of the departing men.

Since no agreement between *shah* and *gumastha* dating from this period has survived, little is known of the exact modalities of the circulation of men between Shikarpur and Central Asia. Most Shikarpuris who went to Central Asia appear to have gone there in the first place as *gumasthas* of a Shikarpuri merchant. Whether their travelling expenses were covered by their principal or were in the form of an advance on future profits is open to question. It is certain that, for reasons of security, Shikarpuris travelling between their native town and Central Asia, especially through Afghanistan and Iran, travelled either in small batches of a few men or in larger caravans. Thus, in the late nineteenth century we are told of a caravan of Shikarpuris, approximately fifty strong, being stopped by the Russian authorities at the border between Afghanistan and the Russian Empire.[17]

A common practice for a Shikarpuri merchant was to travel to Central Asia, establish a business there and leave it in charge of one or several *gumasthas*. Once they were in Central Asia, *gumasthas* did not always go back to Shikarpur; instead, they often travelled widely in the region, and a growing pattern, in the late nineteenth and early twentieth centuries, was for them to shift from the guberniia of Turkestan to the emirate of Bukhara. Shikarpuris in Central Asia often became 'long-term sojourners'. Very few, however, settled for good in the region, unless they converted to Islam and married a local woman, a rare occurrence. Unmarried Shikarpuri men had to contemplate going back to Shikarpur to get married, and married ones to look after their family. The 'sexual economy' of the Shikarpuri diaspora in Central Asia (which will be analysed in greater detail elsewhere) thus contributed decisively to maintaining a pattern of circulation between Shikarpur and Central Asia.

In Hyderabad the pattern was much more fluid. Men kept leaving and coming back before going out again, and rarely did they remain in the same place for very long. Family relationships were much more easily maintained with this pattern of frequent travel than in Shikarpur. The reason for the difference between the two networks was the ease with which one travelled by sea between Bombay and practically any port of the world, as contrasted with the difficulty of travel by land to Central Asia. The obligations of a working partner in the matter of circulation between Hyderabad and the place of actual business were very precisely spelt out in the contracts. For a standard five-year contract, he was supposed to spend four effective years at the place of business, and one year on leave in Hyderabad. Travelling expenses were taken care of by the partnership.

One particular form of circulation about which little is known is that of the pedlars. In the early phase of the Sindwork trade, which has left very few archival traces, pedlars must have constituted the vast majority of men going abroad from Hyderabad. Some of them were employed by

---

[17] In memorandum no. P-0/1, 16 November 1900, addressed to the secretary to the Government of Bombay in the Political Department, the commissioner in Sind, transmitting a petition, 7 March 1900, signed by fifteen Shikarpuri merchants, stated: 'six months ago about 53 men left Shikarpur via Afghanistan with the object of crossing the boundary into Bukhara but were prevented from doing so and have been obliged to stay at Akcho in Afghanistan . . . these persons had started from Khulum for Bukhara but were detained at the River Amu near Khatif by a Russian officer . . . The men had been about six months and a half on their journey from Shikarpur to the Amu River via Kabul.' BPP, December 1900, Serial no. A 72.

the firms, and some left on their own, with goods they had bought. In some places like Colombo, the whole local Sindworkie community developed from peddling. Elsewhere, pedlars represented only one category, which seems to have gradually faded away during the twentieth century. As evidence from Cairo shows, there was a category of salaried hawkers. We catch a glimpse of a superior class of pedlars through the official correspondence regarding the case of a Hyderabadi who was stranded in London in 1911, and had to borrow a sum of £8 from the secretary of state for India.[18] This man stated that he had left India for Italy with a quantity of goods belonging to his firm (N. Shamdas & Co., which was based in Bombay but was controlled by Hyderabadis), for exhibition and sale in Italy. He claimed that he could speak Italian, but could not write it. Having visited Milan, Turin and other places and found Italian exhibitions' authorities charged too much for space, he decided to move on to Las Palmas, where his firm had a branch. He asserted that he was paid a monthly salary of Rs 110, of which Rs 60 was being paid to his family residing in Bombay. It is not know how large this category of pedlars was.

However, the vast majority of the salaried personnel of Sindwork firms outside India consisted of managers and staff employed in the depots and shops. Although there are also instances of salaried managers of branches of Shikarpuri firms in Persia, salariat remained a marginal factor in Shikarpur till at least the time of the Russian Revolution. In Hyderabad it was becoming common practice to employ salaried personnel: as recruitment gradually overstepped the boundaries of the kin network, salaried employees were perceived as easier to control, especially since the contracts were at least formally a variant of indenture, in which part of the wages were paid in Hyderabad to the family of the employee. Having fixed salaries also facilitated calculations of cost. The establishment of permanent shops, which gradually supplanted (without completely suppressing) the original hawkers, also acted as an incentive towards the use of wage labour. These shops often employed a fairly large number of assistants (twelve was apparently an average number in Egypt in the early years of the twentieth century),[19] and represented a quasi-industrial form of organization, which could not be managed on the basis of family labour only, as were most small shops in India. Two questions arise: why were the shop assistants exclusively imported from

---

[18] Memorandum from India Office, 30 November 1911, IOR, Public and Judicial Department Annual Files, File J&P 4230/1911, L/P&J/6/1121.

[19] Mentioned in the letter, 10 May 1907, from the British consul in Cairo to the secretary to the government in the Foreign Department, Copy in Bombay General (Miscellaneous) Proceedings Emigration, 1907, Serial no. A 112. See Chapter 4, note 19.

Hyderabad, while they could also have been recruited on the spot or elsewhere in India (particularly in Bombay), and, were the recruits men who already had experience as shop assistants in Hyderabad? The first question was to be a recurring one, which would be asked of the merchants at different junctures when obstacles were put in the way of the circulation of commercial employees. To this question, the same answer would invariably be given, i.e. that only young Hyderabadis had the specific skills needed for the job, and that only they could be trusted. As we shall see later, neither of these answers is totally convincing, and another hypothesis has to be considered, namely, the role of patronage exercised by big Sindwork merchants among the Bhaiband community in Hyderabad, which created for them a kind of obligation to provide work to young male members of the community. To the second question, no satisactory answer can be given, for lack of sufficient data, but it seems difficult to believe that a middle-sized town like Hyderabad, which was not a very big commercial centre, having mostly a function as a purely regional emporium, could have generated such a pool of 'skilled' commercial manpower. It is probable that many of the young men who were hired by Hyderabad firms to work abroad for the first time had no previous experience of working as shop assistants in the semi-luxury trade; belonging to Bhaiband families, they had nevertheless some basic training in accounting and commerce, which meant that they were not wholly unskilled. Once again, the exact time sequence escapes us, and it is not possible to say when salaried employees became a standard feature in Sindwork firms.[20]

From the evidence of contractual agreements and other materials, it is possible to conclude that a three-tier labour market existed in Hyderabad for the purpose of Sindwork outside India. The first tier was represented by the *gumasthas* and salaried managers, the second by the shop assistants, and the third one by a category loosely called 'servants'. The principle of segmentation was not caste, since Lohanas, and, more specifically, Bhaibands, represented the bulk of the three categories. Economic and social status must have been the key factor, as Bhaibands had discreet ways of ranking themselves. For them, status was largely based on wealth. Little information is available as to the background and specific skills of *gumasthas*, but it can be assumed that they were generally men with some commercial experience and some knowledge of the specific market for silk and curios, which increasingly constituted the real meaning of the term 'Sindwork'. How they had acquired them in the first place is not always clear, and there must have been some

[20] The oldest contract found in the archives of the Cairo consular court is dated 1901.

mobility between the categories of *gumasthas* and shop assistants. Gradually, the former tended to be replaced by salaried managers, although they never completely disappeared as a category. Unfortunately, no contract of a salaried manager has been found in the archives, and only stray information has come my way. It seems that the salaries of these managers varied widely between Rs 150 and Rs 400 per month; most of them appear to also have had a share in the profits, although little is known about detailed arrangements. Commercial directories reveal the existence of two contrasting types of profile: some managers tended to pursue the whole or most of their career within one firm, being frequently transferred from one branch to another. Thus, one manager listed in a business directory of Hong Kong of 1938,[21] had been with the firm of Wassiamall Assomull for all his working life, from the age of sixteen, being posted first at Penang and Ipoh for ten years, then at Bangkok for one year, Saigon for three years, Surabaya for five years, and Singapore for four years, before becoming at the age of 43 the manager of the firm in Hong Kong. Others tended to remain for long periods in the same place, shifting from firm to firm. Another manager listed in the same directory[22] spent all his working life in Hong Kong, firstly as manager with D. Chellaram for five years, then as managing partner with M. Dialdas & Sons for six years, followed by a five-year stint with Pohoomull Bros, after which he started his own business. This shows that firms did not necessarily follow policies meant to ensure the long-term loyalty of their managers. The ease with which a manager shifted from one Sindwork firm to another (while remaining always in the employment of Hyderabadi firms) tends to indicate that 'poaching' was not considered out of bounds, and that firms did not really have secrets *vis-à-vis* other firms. This reinforces the impression of a fairly closely knit network, in which competition between firms was very much kept within the boundaries of oligopoly.

The second tier in the labour market was represented by the category of 'shop assistants'. In the twentieth century, these shop assistants represented by far the bulk of the dispersed Sindworkie communities across the world. Detailed data show for instance that in Gibraltar in 1939 there were ninety-nine of these shop assistants employed by Sindwork firms as against a total of twenty-five managers,[23] i.e. a ratio of four assistants to one manager. In previous years, the ratio appears to

---

[21] *The Business Directory of Hong Kong, Canton, Macao*, Hong Kong, 1938, Who's Who in Hong Kong section, entry for Harumai (?) Tarachand, p. H 59.
[22] *Ibid.*, entry for Melwani, Fatehchand Thawardas, p. M 90.
[23] Copy of statement furnished by the Sindwork Merchants Association, Hyderabad, IOR, L/P&J/8/236. See Chapter 4, note 78.

have been higher, but restrictions on entry permits obliged Sindwork firms to curtail staff. Looking at the typical establishment of a branch of a Sindwork firm in a foreign locality, as it is described in commercial directories, one notices the existence of a fair degree of specialization amongst the staff. Thus, according to the Singapore directory of 1911, the local establishment of the firm of K. A. J. Chotirmall consisted of one resident managing partner, one assistant, one salesman, one shipping clerk and bill-collector, one Sindhi clerk, one store-keeper and one 'hawkerman' [sic], a total of seven. One Sindwork firm in Singapore had, besides a Sindhi clerk, an English clerk. Another firm had a specialized export clerk. The commercial directories enable us to perceive the existence of a kind of intermediate layer of employees between the managers and the ordinary shop assistants, but it has not been possible to find more detailed information about their wages or their conditions of employment. It is not known whether they were recruited already in Hyderabad with a specialized profile, or had been allotted these specific jobs once they reached the place of business. Athough, at later dates, one finds a few instances of men with Muslim names, as well as some Chinese employees, these cases remained fairly exceptional. Practically all shop assistants were recruited in Hyderabad and its immediate neighbourhood, with contracts which spelt out in great detail their rights and duties, as well as the financial conditions of their employment. Prior to 1922, these contracts were signed in Hyderabad and registered with a local magistrate; they had legal value, but were purely private contracts. After the passing of a new Indian Emigration Act in 1922 (following the abolition of indentured emigration in 1917), which purported to apply to all forms of labour emigration from India, including the emigration of skilled labour, of which commercial staff represented one specific category, these contracts were signed in Karachi before the Protector of Emigrants.

Comparison of a contract dated 1901 concluded at Hyderabad[24] with one dated 1929 concluded at Karachi[25] shows little change in the major clauses and conditions. These clauses concerned the duration of employment, which was, in both contracts, of two and a half years; the

[24] Contract between Fatumal Keumal and Messrs Pohoomull Brothers, 2 November 1901, copy enclosed in 'Pohoomull Brothers, plaintiff and Fatehchand Kayoomull, defendant', PRO, Foreign Office Records, Cairo Consular Court Records, Dossier no. 25 of 1902, FO 841/72.
[25] Memorandum of agreement made on 20 November 1929 at Karachi between Messrs Dialdas & Sons and Mr Sitaldas Naunmal, copy enclosed in 'Sitaldas Naunmal, applicant and Dialdas & Sons, respondent', PRO, Foreign Office Records, Embassy and Consular Archives: Egypt, Port Said Consular Court Records, civil case no. 6 of 1930, FO 846/90.

salary which in 1901 was fixed at Rs 45 to be increased to Rs 50, and in 1929 was fixed at Rs 50 from the beginning of the contract (which was in effect lower than Rs 45 in 1901); the exact nature of the duties to be performed by the employee; the manner of his conveyance to the place of business at the cost of the employer; the matter of his dismissal in case of breach of contract, etc. Supplementary clauses in the 1929 agreement covered the exact nature of the personal expenses of the employee to be defrayed to the employer (while the 1901 contract included only food, in 1929 'boarding, shaving, washing and smoking expenses' were added), the provision of medical attendance, the possibility of anticipated return to India before the expiration of the contract, and precise clauses as to the settlement of any disputes arising (which were to be referred outside India to the British consul and in India to the arbitration of Sindwork merchants). On the whole, the employee was better protected in 1929 than in 1901, but economically his situation had not significantly improved, rather the opposite in fact, which probably reflected some slackness in the demand for labour. A question arises as to whether these contracts could be considered forms of indenture, as was claimed, for instance, by Sindwork merchants in South Africa in a petition to the Cape authorities in 1907.[26] Compared to the standard indenture contracts as they were shaped after 1862,[27] the shop assistants' contracts were distinguished by their shorter duration (two and a half years instead of five), and by the fact that the return passage was provided unconditionally after the expiry of the contract. Besides, the wages were much higher than those provided for agricultural labour in Mauritius for instance (Rs 6 on average).[28] Rs 45 to 50 per month in Sind in 1901 was a decent salary (the average wage of an agricultural labourer was Rs 10).[29] There are indications however, as mentioned above, that the situation of shop assistants tended to deteriorate in relative terms after the First World War. In 1929 the wages paid to a shop assistant in Egypt had not increased in comparison with 1901, and information on the level of wages in Singapore in the 1930s gathered from an enquiry conducted by local journalists[30] indicate that

[26] Memorial addressed to the Cape governor in 1907 by six Sindwork firms to protest a new Hawkers Act, reproduced in S. Bhan and B. Pachai, *A Documentary History of Indian South Africans*, Cape Town and Johannesburg, 1984, pp. 50–2. I am grateful to Dr W. G. Clarence-Smith for attracting my attention to this document.
[27] On indenture contracts, see H. Tinker, *A New System of Slavery: The Export of Indian Labour Overseas 1830–1920*, London, 1993, 2nd edn (1st edn, London, 1974), p. 85.
[28] *Ibid.*, p. 185.
[29] According to *Prices and Wages in India, 19th issue*, Calcutta, 1902, p. 283, the average monthly wage of an able-bodied agricultural labourer in Sind in 1901 was Rs 9 to 12, while that of a skilled artisan was between Rs 5–5 and 32–5.
[30] According to an investigation by *Straits Times*' reporters in 1938, Sindhi merchants in

they were only Rs 30 per month. An elderly Sindwork merchant recalls that he started his career as a shop assistant in Rangoon in 1934 with a monthly salary of Rs 25.[31] Shop assistants remained a relatively well-paid category of workers, especially given the fact that most of their ordinary expenses were paid for by the employer. But they lived in cramped and unhygienic quarters, being generally accommodated in the commercial premises themselves. It appears that they were able to save most of their wages; in any case part of their salary was generally paid to their family in Hyderabad,[32] and most of the rest remitted there on a regular basis.[33] The wages paid to shop assistants as well as the profits made by small merchants allowed many relatively poor Bhaiband families of Hyderabad to survive.[34] These transfers were an important part of the remittance economy which grew in the town around Sindworkies.

There was a third tier in the labour market, represented by a category

Singapore paid their employees a minimum salary of Rs 30 monthly, with annual increments ranging from Rs 5 to 10. Quoted in V. Thompson, *Labor Problems in Southeast Asia*, New Haven, 1947, pp. 89–90.

[31] Interview with P. Lachman, Bombay, 22 December 1992.

[32] In the above-mentioned contract of 1901 between Fatumal Keumal and the firm of Pohoomull Bros., there was a clause which read: 'The sum of Rs 25 the above mentioned masters will give here to my parents for the maintain [sic] of family members'. There was no indication as to whether it was conceived as an advance on future wages, but this interpretation appears the most plausible. In the contract of 1929 between Sitaldas Naunmal and the firm of Dialdas & Sons, the following clause was inserted: 'One half of the said salary may at the option of the employee be paid at Hyderabad during the continuance of this agreement to such dependent of the employee as he may nominate from time to time.' Although such an arrangement was formally optional, it must have been only in rare cases that employees did not exercise that option. In Singapore in the 1930s, according to the above-mentioned investigation, half of the salary was paid to the employee's family in India.

[33] The importance of this question of remittances comes out clearly from documentary evidence regarding the Sindworkies at the time of the Spanish Civil War. The British Consulate in Tenerife wrote to the under-secretary at the Foreign Office on 29 March 1937 that on the 10 December 1936, following a meeting in the Consulate of the managers of the major firms, he asked the military governor to authorize the purchase of sterling by British Indians for the benefit of Indian families in Hyderabad, a request which was rejected. Copy of letter in IOR, Political and External Files and Collections, L/P&S/12/210. On 12 April 1937, the consul at Las Palmas, in a letter to the Foreign Office, mentioned that the principals of the firms tried to obtain permission 'for members of their staffs to be allowed to make regular reasonable remittances for the maintenance of their families in India'. Copy of letter in *ibid*.

[34] Four men working in a shop in Naples who had been interned by the Italian authorities after the outbreak of the war stated, in a memorandum which the Swiss Legation sent to the Foreign Office in 1942, that before the outbreak of hostilities they were able to provide for their families out of the profits of their business (a shop) which they were running in Naples. Copy of letter sent to India on 2 June 1942. Enclosed in Defence Department letter no. B/78918/P.WZ, 19 October 1942. Copy in IOR, Public & Judicial Department Records, Departmental Papers: Annual Files 1931–1950, File 5301, 'British Indian Subjects in enemy territory during World War II', L/P&J/7/3002.

Patterns of circulation 175

of employees generally called 'servants'. A contract signed in 1905 in Hyderabad and found in the archives of the Cairo consular court[35] shows a certain number of similarities with shop assistants' contracts, but also important differences. The most important ones were that the level of wages was much lower (Rs 10 for the first year, rising to Rs 12 in the second year and Rs 15 in the third year), and that the amount which was not paid to the family in Hyderabad was retained by the master till the completion of the period of service. This was undoubtedly a clause which smacked of indenture. But nothing in the contract, which was written in very general terms, clearly differentiated the tasks entrusted to a servant from the duties of a shop assistant. In practice however, and judging from the evidence of a certain number of court cases, the former tasks appear to have been more wide-ranging than the latter. A servant could be asked to perform domestic tasks in the household of the manager, including cooking, and he was also expected to perform the most menial and demanding tasks in the shop, such as cleaning the premises or shelling pearls, etc.

There seems to have been an interesting evolution over time on the question of cooks. During the 1890s, it was customary, according to evidence from Australia,[36] to have high-caste cooks from Hyderabad in a ratio of one to six members of staff, and cooks are still specifically mentioned in a list of employees in Gibraltar in 1920.[37] Gradually the function of cook seems to have been performed by general-purpose 'servants' who were certainly not high-caste people. The progressive disappearance of a specific group of cooks could be seen as reflecting a weakening of religious norms regarding purity and pollution amongst expatriate Hindu merchants, a form of 'acculturation'. It was most probably the result of more mundane considerations, in particular of increasing restrictions on the number of staff permitted to emigrate,

[35] 'Agreement made on 27 September 1905 at Hyderabad between Chellaram Vasanmal (hereinafter called the said servant) and Mr Kissoomal Sobhraj (hereinafter called the said master)', in 'Kissumal Sobhraj, plaintiff, vs. Chellaram Vasanmal, defendant', PRO, Foreign Office Records, Cairo Consular Court Records, civil case no. 7 of 1907, FO 841/91.
[36] In a memorandum dated February 1899 addressed to the secretary to the Government of India in the Foreign Department to protest restrictions on immigration in the Colony of Victoria, Tejumull Gaganmull, the manager of the Melbourne branch of the firm of Wassiamall Assomull stressed that the employees of his firm were 'men of high caste and social status' and added: 'As their religion does not permit them to partake of food cooked by a person other than of their particular caste, so one servant for every six men is necessary.' Copy of letter in India Proceedings (Revenue and Agriculture), Emigration, June 1899, Serial no. A 1.
[37] According to the list of Indian firms in Gibraltar enclosed in Gibraltar secret despatch, 1 June 1920, PRO, Colonial Office Records, Gibraltar Original Correspondence, CO 91/474, two of the seven firms listed employed a cook amongst their employees.

forcing the owners to cut on non-essential staff, as cooks were obviously thought to be.

Evidence from Sinkiang reveals the existence, among Shikarpuris, of a different category of 'servants', who were specifically entrusted with the task of collecting debts from the local peasants,[38] including by force. Some of them appear to have been recruited among local 'bad characters' (*badmashes*), including men who had criminal records. They do not however appear to have been salaried employees. They were apparently remunerated on a kind of commission system, and constituted a specific category of *gumasthas*.

To account for the segmentation of the labour market between the two categories of 'shop assistants' and 'servants', a plausible hypothesis is that of a different level of skills, particularly in the matter of literacy. Shop assistants, it seems, were literate in Sindhi and even often had a smattering of English, including written English, which could be of use when dealing with an international clientele in the shops. Servants, on the other hand, were likely to be illiterate and certainly had no knowledge of English. It is also probable that 'shop assistants' were more likely to have some sort of family connection to the owners,[39] whether as kin or affines, while servants were recruited completely outside the kin and affinal network. This raises the important question of the exact role of the kin network in the development of these long-distance merchant networks.

The role of the kin network

That the kin network was central to the rise and growth of merchant diasporas is somewhat axiomatic, but it is probable that its role has

---

[38] In the Kashgar diary for the period from 16 October to 31 October 1908, Captain Shuttleworth reported from Camp Abad: 'There are a few Shikarpuris here who are endeavouring to collect the debts of their masters who are at Posgam and Tagarchi . . . I had a long story from one of them. He told me it was only a few Shikarpuris who had made any money in this country; most of those who were now in the country had been induced to come under false pretences. The few who had made any money had held out inducements to them when revisiting Shikarpur and told them that if they started money-lending in Turkestan they would soon become as rich as they were. They even offered to advance a little money to enable them to commence operations. Many had come here on those inducements only to find when they had arrived that they were little better than servants and that their sole duty was to endeavour to collect the bad debts of their masters.' IOR, Political & Secret Correspondence with India 1875–1911, Political and Secret Letters from India 1908.

[39] This was clearly stated by the manager of the Melbourne branch of Wassiamall Assomull in the above quoted letter in which he wrote: 'our assistants are men of high caste and social status, and can advance to becoming partners in the firm, being mostly relatives of existing partners'. See above note 36.

tended to get exaggerated. A major difficulty confronting the historian trying to grapple with this problem is the lack of reliable data. The kind of documents more widely available, such as business papers or commercial directories are rarely explicit on this point. More detailed evidence comes from court cases and successional documents, but great caution has to be exercised when making use of them. On the basis of this limited evidence, I can only state that there was no perfect congruence between merchant network and kin network. For instance, most contractual agreements found in the archives were concluded between men who were not kin-related. Of course it could be argued that they were unrepresentative, and that it was precisely when the kin network did not operate that legal contracts had to be signed. But kindred also entered into legally binding written contracts. In the case of Shikarpur, the materials available do not permit an evaluation of the precise role played by kinship in the network, beyond the fact that *shahs* and *gumasthas* were frequently kin-related. However, in the case of Hyderabad, it is possible to arrive at firmer conclusions by looking at the information provided in the certificates of identity delivered in 1915–16 by the district magistrate to men going abroad on Sindwork. Out of a total of 572 men, 212 are described as being sons, brothers, nephews or cousins of Sindwork merchants. So less than 40 per cent of the men were recruited through the close kin network of the merchants. A certain number of men are also described as relatives of Sindwork employees, but the majority belonged to merchant families which were not engaged directly in Sindwork. Some of these may of course have been distant kin of Sindwork merchants, or linked to them by affinal relationships. However, from the fairly detailed data provided by the certificates, it is possible to see the existence of only a limited congruence between kin network and trading network.

There are two ways of interpreting this fact. It could be claimed that preference for employing kin was not as culturally determined among merchants as is often construed, but more a matter of opportunity. In a situation in which a merchant network was not yet well established, merchants employed their own kin because they had no choice; once the labour market opened up more, the possibility arose of choosing between employing kin and non-kin, and other criteria, such as skills, became essential parameters of choice, resulting in a fairly even field. Or one could take the opposite view, that preference for kin was too entrenched 'culturally' to weaken, but that the expansion of the network forced principals to recruit agents and personnel outside the kin network, in spite of their preference for the latter. The question of preference for kin is ultimately bound up with the question of 'trust', since preference for employing kin is generally ascribed to the fact that kinsmen were deemed more trustworthy than non-kin elements. This will be taken up again.

Circulation between the network centre and the actual places of business was therefore not primarily organized through the kin network. As far as Hyderabad was concerned, we have seen that all but 80 of the 572 men who departed for Sindwork in 1915–16 were in the possession of a contract with a firm, which paid their travelling expenses. Most of these employees travelled in groups. It is only in the case of the smaller firms that a high level of congruence between the firm and the kin network existed, but larger firms did not always, in spite of claims to the contrary on the part of the manager of one of the largest firms,[40] give a clear preference to the kin of the principals in their recruitment. It is probably among those who circulated outside a firm structure that kinship played a more crucial role in organizing circulation. One can well imagine that most of these men who left without a contract with a firm were financed by their kinsmen and often acted as a vanguard, in the process typical of 'chain migration'.

The pattern of circulation of personnel in the Hyderabadi network can be seen as a hybrid, mixing traits common to South Asian merchant networks with characteristics of European trading firms. Firms, especially the larger ones, increasingly moved personnel according to considerations which did not have much to do with kinship. At the level of the recruitment and circulation of personnel in the mature network in Hyderabad, kinship operated as a largely residual category, and was certainly not at the core of the logic of the system.

Financial flows

The circulation of men in the network was closely bound up with various forms of financial circulation. The *shah–gumastha* system was devised specifically to link these two forms of circulation. It could not however encompass all the financial flows which animated the networks. Through the *shah–gumastha*, what circulated was basically long-term or medium-term capital, and it circulated only from the network centres to the places of business. For short-term credit the merchants were dependent on other circuits, which were more local. Shikarpuri successional documents show that, amongst the outstandings which were an essential part of most successions, there was a category of 'loans to *banias*' which was different from the category of 'loans to *gumasthas*'.

[40] See above, note 39.

This 'horizontal' pattern of lending coexisted with the 'vertical' pattern characteristic of the *shah–gumastha*. In Central Asia, not all money-lending among Shikarpuris was for the purpose of loans to the local peasantry, although this was increasingly the mainstay of their activities. This parallel credit network, geared to members of the community, probably served the short-term needs of the Shikarpuris engaged in trading and other activities outside their main moneylending business, but lack of data does not allow one to say more. Among Hyderabadi merchants also, this kind of short-term lending was very common, especially in the form of advances from suppliers to their customers on the purchase of goods. Cash advances from big firms to smaller merchants were also fairly common. Most small and medium-sized Hyderabadi merchants purchased goods from the large firms on credit, and the existence of this web of credit relationships was an important element structuring the network. This credit was advanced at a rate which was fixed by custom at 6 per cent per year[41] independently of the rate of the money market at the time of the transaction. In the period prior to 1914, this was a fairly high rate, but in the inter-war years it was rather low.

Another very important form of financial business which seems to have been carried out largely outside the *shah–gumastha* was the business of remittances. A few banking firms in Shikarpur seem to have specialized in that kind of business, and their services were very widely used. It must be noted that they increasingly used the services of the Russian banks, in particular the Russo-Asiatic Bank, to transfer money to India. Among Sindworkies, most remittance business was also done through the agency of the European banks, although a witness to the Bombay Provincial Banking Inquiry of 1930 stated that the firm of Pohoomull Bros was also engaged in it.[42]

Under the overarching term of remittances were actually included different kinds of transfers. There were the remittances sent regularly to their families by the managers and employees of the firms, which were a very important resource for many lower-middle-class families in both

---

[41] In a statement filed in 1918 with the Cairo consular court by the manager of the Gibraltar branch of the firm of J. T. Chanrai, one could read the following sentence: 'It is the custom of the trade of Dealers in Oriental goods to charge interest from the date of the invoice to date of payment at the rate of six per cent per annum'. J. T. Chanrai & Co., plaintiffs, *v.* Pribhdas Rupchand, defendant', PRO, Foreign Office Records, Cairo Consular Court Records, civil case no. 38 of 1918, FO 841/170.

[42] When he was asked why Sindwork merchants had not gone into exchange bank business, K. Bulchand, the chairman of the Khudabadi Bhaiband Cooperative Credit Bank, said that Messrs Pohumal [*sic*] Brothers 'do remittance business while doing their work as merchants'. Oral evidence of Mr K. Bulchand, *Report of the Bombay Banking Enquiry Committee*, vol. IV, p. 272.

Shikarpur and Hyderabad. These served mainly to cover daily expenses, although they could be used also to pay for the dowry of a daughter, or to repair a house. Some of this money was also probably used to purchase land in the immediate vicinity of the towns. But on the whole these remittances circulated outside any circuit of capital accumulation. There was another kind of remittance, which consisted of the trading profits earned abroad and regularly remitted to the principals of the trading firms in Hyderabad. The amounts transferred were much larger than those ino the first category, but cannot be quantified. Some of this money was reinvested in the trade, the rest was retained as profit by the capitalists. These were often considerable, but little is known about the way in which they were employed. A lot of money undoubtedly went into building palatial mansions in Hirabad, where the principals of the Sindwork trade had their residences. Some also went into the purchase of land, but beyond that little is known of the way in which the money earned abroad was recycled into the local economy. What can be said with a degree of certainty is that no process of capital accumulation took place in the long term, by which the profits earned would have been invested in productive activities energizing the local economy. In Hyderabad itself most productive investment in the late nineteenth and early twentieth centuries went into the erection of cotton ginneries and the capital for it does not appear to have come mostly from the gains of Sindwork. In Shikarpur, there was even less productive investment. Whatever had been transferred to Shikarpur before the Russian Revolution must have been used partly to finance the expansion of the Shikarpuri financial network into India and Burma after 1920. The profits gained in Sindwork fed a consumer boom in Hyderabad, where rich merchants were known for maintaining a fairly lavish style of living,[43] dressing their women in expensive clothes and spending heavily on drink. In a medium-sized town like Hyderabad, there were thus ten importers of wines and spirits in the early 1930s,[44] who seem to have all done a thriving business. No wonder that Hyderabad was known as the 'little Paris' of Sind and gave travellers and officials an impression of wealth. Sindworkies do not appear to have conformed to the 'ascetic' model which is supposed to have been characteristic of Hindu *banias*, while Shikarpuris on the whole did. The difference in behaviour

---

[43] A witness to this period mentions that returning Sindworkies 'distributed exotic gifts of silks, perfumes and curios, far beyond the reach of the modest pocket-money of Amil lads', that 'they sported huge diamonds on their fingers and rode in very splashy landaus', but he added that 'they continued to live in ancestral houses in narrow lanes and congested mohallas on the north side of the bazaar in Hyderabad'. S. K. Kirpalani, *Fifty Years with the British*, Bombay, 1993, p. 45.

[44] See *Jagtiani's Handbook and Directory of Sind for 1934*, Karachi, 1934, p. 22-B.

between the merchants of these two towns is intriguing. Were the Hyderabadis influenced by the long periods they spent abroad in the great emporia of the world, where status was often equated with an open display of wealth? It is a plausible hypothesis, but its confirmation would need more evidence from within the world of the Sindworkies. Such change in mentalities presupposes the existence of a fairly 'open' society, where information flows rather freely.

The circulation of information and knowledge

Information was and is probably the most valuable input in trade, much more valuable than any given commodity.

The ways in which it circulated varied. Shikarpuri merchants were heirs to a long tradition of commercial contacts between Northern India and Central Asia and they did not have to build from scratch. When the British came to Sind, they were not slow in recognizing the potential source of information about Central Asia at hand,[45] and they did everything in their power to tap that source. In the late nineteenth and early twentieth centuries, evidence from the successoral documents shows that the *mazhars* regularly exchanged between the Shikarpuri *panchayats* in Central Asia and the corresponding *panchayats* in Shikarpur itself were the principal means of communication between the dispersed communities and the network centre. No detailed information is provided as to the exact mode of circulation of these *mazhars* or to their frequency. They were probably still carried by courier, which means that they took months to travel from a locality in the Emirate of Bokhara to Shikarpur. The telegraph was used only exceptionally, because of its high price, and its limited reach in the region. The difficulty of communication between Central Asia and Shikarpur meant that the Shikarpuri *gumasthas* in Central Asia constantly had to take business decisions without being able to refer them to their principals in Shikarpur. It would thus appear that the kind of information which circulated regularly between Shikarpur and the various localities in Central Asia where Shikarpuris resided was more 'social' information than commercial information. The *mazhars* concerned mostly matters internal to the Shikarpuri community, such as news of deaths or litigations, rather than

[45] Sir Charles Napier himself wrote to Lord Ellenborough on 25 October 1842, from Sukkur, about the advantages to be gained from the annexation of Shikarpur: 'Shikarpore contains many rich banking houses, which is a sure evidence of its being a central point of communication between the surrounding countries, and, consequently, one where the British Government would learn what was going on in Asia. The money market is, generally speaking, the best political barometer.' Correspondence relative to Sinde 1838–1843, London, 1843, no. 379, pp. 362–6.

information relating to prices and markets. The flow of information between the network centre and the places of business in the case of Shikarpur was limited. Shikarpuri speculations regarding the area seem to have been based more upon the wisdom accumulated by successive generations than on a constant flow of new data. Thus wisdom about the fact that 'the Turks repay their debts even after fifty years', which was obviously born of a long experience of contact with the region, still inspired Shikarpuris on the eve of the Russian Revolution.

In contrast, the development of the Sindworkie network was based on a constant flow of information circulating between the network centre and the widely scattered places of business. The telegraph was crucial to the emergence and the consolidation of such a trading network linking Hyderabad with the principal ports of the world. It is no pure coincidence that the network developed mostly after 1880 when almost the entire world was criss-crossed by telegraph lines. Hyderabadi merchants, like other South Asian merchants, were quick to see the advantages of the new technology for the circulation of information about prices and markets. The drawback of telegrams is that they were generally in English, therefore unreliable as a way to transmit information of a confidential nature, and it was only gradually that the merchants got into the habit of using codes. Apart from telegrams, there was therefore an intense circulation of business letters written in Sindhi, either in Arabic or in '*bania*' Sindhi, which were undecipherable by all but Sindhi merchants. It is amusing to note that during the First World War the chief postal censor in Sierra Leone complained to the War Office about the number of letters in Sindhi and Gujarati (by which he probably meant Sindhi letters in the *devanagari* script) received by the local branches of the two Sindwork firms in Freetown, M. Dialdas & Sons and J. T. Chanrai & Co.[46] He lamented the fact that nobody in the office could read them and that the only way he had found to enforce censorship rules was by detaining them until the following mail! Through their worldwide network of branches linked via the telegraph, the principals of the big Sindwork firms had easy access to a lot of information. An anecdote gathered from files in the Colonial Office Records will put it across very clearly. In 1934 the comptroller of customs in Lagos suspected that some Syrian traders in Nigeria were involved in illegal imports of Japanese textile goods into Nigeria in

---

[46] See letter from Postal Censor Office, Sierra Leone to chief postal censor, War Office, London, 11 April 1916, enclosed in File J& P (S) 552/16, 23 May 1916, from Public Department, India Office, to director of special intelligence, War Office, copy in PRO, Colonial Office Records, Sierra Leone Original Correspondence, File 25 930, CO 267/573.

breach of quota regulations tending to restrict the entry of Japanese goods into British West Africa. To check on the source of these illegal imports, he asked the local manager of the Sindwork firm of K. Chellaram & Sons to contact the manager of his firm in Kobe and in that way the source was traced.[47] What is interesting is that the comptroller of customs, a British colonial official, relied on the informal information network of a worldwide Sindhi firm rather than on official channels, which would have taken much longer to activate.

One question, of course, is whether information circulated widely within the network, or was jealously guarded by firms, which were after all in competition with each other. It appears rather implausible that in small communities such as those formed by Sindwork merchants in any given locality, secrecy of any kind could have been maintained. It must be remembered that in no place in the world was the Sindwork community numerically large: Sindwork merchants often had clubs or associations where they met regularly in a rather informal manner and must have exchanged all kinds of information and gossip. These men generally lived without women and socialization with other males of their community was their only outlet. Even though there was a constant flow of information circulating through the network, it rarely leaked to outsiders. Sindwork merchants largely kept to themselves, and do not appear to have socialized much with members of other South Asian merchant communities, and even less of other communities, although they are known to have maintained amicable relations with members of other trading groups.

On the other hand, information circulated very rapidly within the network from one end of the world to the other. An episode which took place in Port-Said around 1930 offers an interesting instance of it. A small Sindhi merchant sued before the Port Said consular court the owners of a local Sindwork firm for defamation,[48] on the grounds that a series of letters they had written to other Sindhi firms in Kobe and Hong Kong had resulted in his suffering heavy loss and damage to his trade

---

[47] See minute of Mr Bust, from the Colonial Office, July 1939, reporting a conversation with Mr Bird, comptroller of customs in Nigeria, who said that the firm of K. Chellaram & Sons 'had been instrumental in helping him to detect smuggling which was being carried on extensively by Syrian traders in respect of Japanese goods which were subject to additional duties . . . he was able to enlist the services of Messrs Chellaram in tracking these offenders, as Messrs Chellaram have an office in Kobe in Japan and they were then able to trace the sources of supply of these Syrian traders.' PRO, Colonial Office Records, Colonies (General) Economic Original Correspondence, 'Textile Import Quotas, West Africa, Gold Coast and Nigeria 1939', CO 852/223/2.

[48] 'S. Baloomal, plaintiff, vs. Ratoomal & Sons, defendants', PRO, Foreign Office Records, Port Said Consular Court Records, civil case no. 13 of 1931, FO 846/97.

and his reputation as a businessman. They had denounced some shady practices on the part of this businessman and publicly questioned his trustworthiness, grave accusations indeed in such a small merchant world. He claimed (Egyptian) £2,000 damages and was finally awarded £400. Although the evidence in the case is not very clear, it throws an interesting light on the way in which business reputations could be made and unmade through the constant flow of correspondence maintained between Sindwork firms across the seas.

Writings on Indian merchants generally stress the importance of the pattern of socialization of the young males within the merchant family and the merchant community to the successful transmission of techniques and practices across generations. The merchant communities of Sind do not appear to have been different in this respect, except that, in comparison with the Marwaris for instance, actual apprenticeship in the firm seems to have started at a slightly later age, with formal schooling lasting a little longer. In Hyderabad at least, more emphasis seems to have been put on the acquisition of some basic literary skills, which explains that the principals and managers of Sindwork firms were often men of some sophistication, capable of putting forward their views in an articulate fashion. Wide-ranging foreign travel also broadened their horizons. However they appear to have remained rather conservative in matters of religion, and gave only limited support to reformist causes, even if some of them, particularly in Southern Africa, were active Arya Samajists. Although men, money and goods circulated widely throughout the network, ideas did not necessarily follow and the quietude of provincial life was not at any point seriously disturbed by returning Sindworkies, who seem to have moved with considerable ease between their home town and the four corners of the world.

6 The business of the Sind merchants

Shikarpuri and Hyderabadi merchants exemplify in two different ways the tie-up which existed between local capital markets in India and markets for financial services and goods situated outside the subcontinent. The extent of capital resources and expertise vested in *bania* communities can easily explain how even small towns in South Asia could exercise a measure of economic control over vast areas outside the subcontinent. In this chapter we shall look in some detail at the precise forms of this tie-up so as to arrive at a better understanding of the business of the merchants. The lack of documents from firms is a severe limiting factor in this exercise and we shall be able to offer only a glimpse of the complex operations performed by the merchants of these two towns. They fell into two broad categories: finance and trade. Shikarpuris combined the two in varying proportions but were primarily financiers, while Sindworkies, although not eschewing finance, were specialized traders. The divergence in the trajectories of these two sets of merchants owes nothing to the existence of different predispositions, but is entirely due to a disjunction in the time sequence and to the specific nature of the economic environment in which each group had to operate.

The Shikarpuri *shroffs* as financiers

There is some broad similarity between the role performed by the Shikarpuri *shroffs* in relation to Central Asia between 1800 and 1920 and that fulfilled by the Nattukottai Chettiars in South East Asia between 1870 and 1940. Both groups specialized in banking and moneylending, but the major difference is that the Shikarpuris started as totally independent operators before becoming intermediaries, while the Chettiars from the outset were intermediaries for the British banks in Burma, Ceylon and Malaya. The Shikarpuris gained their prominent position in regional finance during the brief period of Durrani predominance in the second half of the eighteenth century. Their rise in this period was directly related to their privileged links with the ruling class of the Afghan state. According to Gankovsky,[1] Shikarpuris were prominent among the tax-farmers of the Durranis and conducted themselves as true rulers in their dealings with the people. Apart from their role as tax-farmers, they were also in charge of deliveries for the army and purchased, sold and resold military booty. Their role in financing Ahmad Shah's campaigns into India has already been mentioned. They were also in the business of supplying goods, mostly luxury items, to the royal court and the nobility, and lent to Afghan grandees at high rates of interest. They also lent, not always voluntarily, to the government and the provincial governors, tax revenue often being used as security on these loans. Gradually they came to occupy important posts in the state financial apparatus at the central as well as at the provincial level. Under Timur Shah, Ahmad Shah's successor, they appear to have been largely in control of state finances, as well as participants, through finance, in agricultural and artisanal production. In the process some accumulated large fortunes, reaching up to Rs 10 million.

After the collapse of the Durrani regime, they were able to redeploy in the financing of the caravan trade, between northern India and Central Asia, a niche previously occupied by the so-called Multanis, but vacant at the end of the eighteenth century. They financed this trade through their *hundis*, which, as attested to by contemporary travellers, circulated widely in the entire area between Nijni-Novgorod and Calcutta. The Shikarpuri *hundi*, that 'rude instrument with which the Shikarpuri Rothschild works',[2] more or less fulfilled the role of the letter of credit or bill of exchange nowadays given by banks to traders, basically allowing the latter to tide over the period between the conclusion of the transaction and the delivery of the goods. This, in spite of the fact, emphasized by L. C. Jain in his study of indigenous banking in India,[3] that there was nothing in the *hundi* to show that it was drawn against commercial goods. The reason why, although it was such an imperfect instrument, the Shikarpuri *hundi* played such a role, is simply that there was no alternative instrument of credit to finance the caravan trade. As mentioned earlier, *hundis* circulated mostly within the Shikarpuri community; they were the device through which, without transferring bullion along the dangerous routes followed by the caravans, the Shikarpuri *shroffs*, through the agency of their *gumasthas* in Central Asia, could finance both the purchase of goods in Central Asia by Indian merchants,

---

[1] Gankovsky, 'The Durrani Empire' in USSR Academy of Sciences, *Afghanistan Past and Present*, pp. 76–98.
[2] Burton, *Sind Revisited*, quoted in Chapter 5, note 5.
[3] Jain, *Indigenous Banking in India*, p. 71.

and the purchase of Indian goods by Central Asian merchants. Compensation would take place regularly in Shikarpur itself, where there was a kind of informal clearing house. The profits of the trade, in the form of bullion, were regularly (allowing for the hazards of the road) remitted to Shikarpur, where there was a thriving market for Central Asian gold coins. The *shroffs* also engaged in the business of foreign exchange, where good profits could be earned prior to the 1870s when the fall in the value of the rupee made this kind of transaction much less profitable. Shikarpuri agents in Central Asia seem also to have been involved in the taking of deposits and in advancing money to rulers and members of the elite. It is not clear how deeply they were engaged at this stage in wider moneylending to cultivators.

In the post-1870 phase the latter business became the mainstay of Shikarpuri activities in what had become Russian Central Asia, a process which I call 'Chettiarisation'. This was not a voluntary shift, but the result of new constraints. The decline in the caravan trade between India and Central Asia, which started in the 1880s and accelerated in the 1890s, dried up the major *hundi* business, forcing the Shikarpuris to look to other fields of activity. They also had to contend with growing competition from the Russian banks, fully supported by the czarist authorities. What saved them from extinction was the development of commercial agriculture, in the Ferghana valley in particular and in some areas of the Emirate of Bukhara, which created new financial needs, which the Russian banks could not entirely satisfy because of their lack of knowledge of the area. In spite of the hostility of the Russian authorities, the Shikarpuris managed to retain a role as financiers in Russian Central Asia; and even increased their business in other areas such as Sinkiang, Afghanistan or Iran.

Shikarpuri lending practices are known to us mainly through the accounts of Western travellers. The best description, although cursory, is found in Schuyler's account of his visit to Tashkent in the early 1870s. According to this well-informed witness, 'the Hindoos usually lend sums for twenty-four weeks, to be paid in weekly instalments of one tenga to every tilla, that is one nineteenth, making a gain as interest in the course of the transaction of five tengas, or about twenty-six per cent, which would be fully fifty-six per cent per annum'.[4] He added that, 'as the money is thus paid back in instalments, it is evident that a moneylender with a very small capital can make a very large yearly profit'. This repayment schedule, which differed from the monthly system used in India, ensured repayment of the principal in the first nineteen weeks,

[4] Schuyler, *Turkistan*, p. 186.

and of the interest during the last five weeks. Schuyler's account was of moneylending in an urban milieu where the Shikarpuris were far from enjoying a monopoly.[5] Most loans appear to have been small scale, for purposes of day-to-day expenses rather than of investment, but more substantial loans were also occasionally extended. Schuyler mentions a big army contractor who was heavily indebted to the Hindu bankers of the town.[6]

As regards rural loans, the perusal of successional documents yields some findings about their size. A survey of twenty-nine estates in Russian Central Asia shows a total of outstanding debts of 120,000 roubles (equivalent to £12,000), neither a small nor a very large sum. To put things in perspective, an official report put the debts of the inhabitants registered with the *kazi* in one month, in one village of Namangan district around 1910, in the neighbourhood of 800,000 roubles.[7] Rural indebtedness in Russian Central Asia was of considerable magnitude, and it seems that Shikarpuris held only a small part of it. In some areas of the Emirate of Bukhara however, the situation was different and Shikarpuris occupied a very strong position on the rural credit market, which might have been the legacy of an earlier period.

The data available are not sufficient to allow an estimate in quantitative terms of the impact of the Shikarpuris on the regional economy. It is however possible to form an idea of the variety of the operations of the Shikarpuri moneylenders. Different kinds of documents figure in the inventories of estates: bills of exchange (*hundis*), promissory notes, writs, etc. The fundamental duality of Shikarpuri activities is well captured in the following extract of an application submitted to the collector of Sukkur by the heirs of one Hasomal walad Khemchand, who died in Bukhara in 1912: 'The profession of the deceased during his lifetime in Bokhara was of money dealing with the Bhaibands and of lending money to the inhabitants of Bokhara and the Turks of other surrounding villages'.[8] Money dealings with the Bhaibands, meaning the other Shikarpuris, was thus an activity clearly differentiated from lending money to the local inhabitants. Separate accounts were kept of

---

[5] According to Schuyler, *ibid.*, there were in Tashkent a total of 1,000 moneylenders, mostly local Muslims; only 140 were Hindus (Shikarpuris). The Shikarpuris seem, however, to have been the most active in the business.

[6] Schuyler in *ibid.*, p. 98, has this to say about one Said Azim, one of the leading merchants of Tashkent: 'He has also engaged in the business of army contracts and has fulfilled them with great accuracy, though to do so he has been obliged to borrow much money of Hindoos and others, to whom he is still largely indebted.'

[7] Mentioned in Pierce, *Mission to Turkestan*, pp. 101–2.

[8] Application, 27 July 1912 from Chellaram walad Teunmal, merchant, shopkeeper, and heir of his maternal uncle Haso, alias Hasan walad Khemchand to the collector of Sukkur, BPP, November 1912, Serial no. A 7.

Table 6.1. *The debt portfolio of Totomal wd Jeumal, Shikarpuri banker of Namangan*

Type of document	Amount outstanding (in roubles)
Bills of exchange (hundis)	2,191
Outstandings according to local custom	3,868
Writs	493
Receipts on bills of exchange	1,062
Total	7,624

Source: 'Note verbale' no. 3529, 31 May/13 June 1912, from Russian Ministry of Foreign Affairs to British Embassy at St Petersburg, enclosed in despatch no. 182, from O'Beirne, Embassy counsellor, St Petersburg, to secretary of state for foreign affairs, copy in BPP, July 1912, Serial no A 54.

the two kinds of transactions, the former written in the *bania* Sindhi script, the latter in the local language (Tajik rather than Uzbek). It is easy to infer from it that different rates of interest also applied to these different types of transactions. Within the Shikarpuri community transactions were conducted mostly through the medium of *hundis*, thanks to the compensation mechanisms which existed in Shikarpur, although cash transactions also existed. Transactions with non-Shikarpuris were also sometimes conducted through '*hundis* in the native tongue', but more often through other kinds of documents such as promissory notes or 'créances d'après la coutume du pays', in the French of Russian official documents ('outstandings according to local custom'). There were also writs issued in application of judicial decisions. An idea of the respective importance of these different types of documents is given in Table 6.1, which reproduces the composition of the debt portfolio of a Shikarpuri banker of Namangan (Ferghana valley) at the time of his death in 1907. This table suggests a more or less balanced ratio between transactions 'internal' to the Shikarpuri network, represented by bills of exchange and receipts on bills, and transactions with 'outsiders' ('outstandings according to local custom' and writs). Examination of other debt porfolios however yields different results, and it seems that the situation varied considerably from one area to another. In Bukhara, where Shikarpuris were thicker on the ground than in the guberniia of Turkistan, they often had larger transactions with their own coreligionaries than with the local inhabitants.[9]

Only an examination of the books of some of these moneylenders could tell us exactly to whom they lent and for what purposes. Stray

[9] Thus the Mohandas Janjimal estate, the largest in my sample, was characterized by the predominance of outstandings due from '*gumasthas* and *banias*' over those due by 'Turks and Pathans'. See Chapter 3.

indications in successional documents point towards the predominance of relatively small loans, rarely higher in value than 20 roubles or a few hundred tengas.[10] There is also evidence of larger loans granted to Russian or indigenous Muslim merchants.

The substantial estates left by the Shikarpuris in Russian Central Asia tend to suggest that the profitability of their moneylending operations was fairly high. European observers as well as the Russian authorities were even of the opinion that the Shikarpuris lent at extortionate rates and gained extravagant profits. Shikarpuris in the Katakurgan area of Samarkand district agreed to lower their rates from 60 per cent to 30 per cent to comply with demands from the new Russian administration,[11] but it seems that the move was mostly tactical, to ward off a threat of expulsion. Rates of interest in Central Asia remained extremely high up to the Russian Revolution, and besides, the rate of recovery was also high on outstanding debts, judging from the evidence of successional documents, particularly so in the Emirate of Bukhara where the local *kazis* were good at squeezing the peasantry. The overall level of risk in moneylending operations in Central Asia was therefore relatively limited, especially in comparison with the situation as it stood in Sind at the time. No fortune could be gained in advancing money to the Uzbek and Tajik peasantry of Turkestan, but a regular and substantial income could be earned without too much difficulty, although not totally without danger. Murders of moneylenders were as common an occurrence in Central Asia as in Sind, but Shikarpuris were not deterred.

In neighbouring Sinkiang, according to the evidence in the Kashgar diaries, Shikarpuris lent at even higher rates, although the official level of interest fixed by the Chinese authorities was 33 per cent per annum.[12] During a tour of southern Sinkiang in 1908, the British consular agent heard from the local inhabitants a string of complaints against the Shikarpuris, who were accused of charging exorbitant rates, of not

[10] Two bankers who died suspiciously at the same time in the town of Marghellan in Ferghana left, among other things, one '96 lettres de change pour la somme de 1803 roubles 60 kopecks', and the other '37 lettres de change pour la somme de 523 roubles 60 kopecks'. Notes from the Russian Embassy in London to the Foreign Office enclosed in Foreign Office to India Office, 26 October 1892, IOR, Public & Judicial Department Annual Files, File J&P 1772/92.

[11] Mentioned in E. C. Ringler-Thomson, HBM's consul at Meshed to the secretary to the Government of India in the Foreign Department, 24 June 1893, IOR, Political & Secret Correspondence with India 1875–1911, L/P&S/7/71.

[12] Kashgar diary entry for 18 July 1903, IOR, Political & Secret Correspondence with India 1875–1911, L/P&S/7/157. It was however reported in the entry for 20 October 1908, L/P&S/7/223, that a man called Soba Singh who lent a sum of 5,151 tengas in 1902 asked for repayment of 84,221 tengas six years later! And it was reported in the entry for 2 February 1921, in Political & Secret Subject Files 1902–1931, L/P&S/10/976 that Shikarpuris in Sinkiang charged an average 12 per cent per month on loans.

returning bonds even after debts had been repaid, of falsifying bonds, and of seizing debtors and keeping them in confinement pending repayment of their debts,[13] the sort of complaints currently voiced against Pathans in India.

Moneylenders always get a bad name, but, in view of the literature and of some of the evidence of archival sources, it is difficult to completely avoid the question of the morality of Shikarpuris' activity. Rather than see them as particularly greedy, I tend to perceive their motivation as being relentlessly opportunistic: these were people who were out to get as much as they could, without too many qualms about the ethics of their trade. In many ways, they recall the Gujarati *banias* of early eighteenth-century Yemen about whom Ashin Das Gupta wrote: 'by their tenacious hard work, their thrift and their expertise, they made whatever profit there was to be made (at Mocha). They were, of course, not ideal men . . .'[14] In their native Sind, they were after all used to dealing with a Muslim peasantry which was not that different from the one they met in Central Asia, but the power of *pirs* and *waderos* as well as the hostility of some British administrators restrained their activities, and this rarely happened in Central Asia.

Apart from moneylending, Shikarpuris were also engaged in other kinds of banking activities, such as money changing, deposit taking and remittance business, although little evidence has come to light regarding these aspects of their activity. Moreover, they remained active in trade. Outside observers generally saw their trading as a 'front' activity, only meant to circumscribe the stringent anti-usury regulations that were in operation in the guberniia of Turkestan, but in the emirate of Bukhara, where there were no such laws, and where a record of usurers' profits, on which a tax was levied, was kept by a state official,[15] they were even more active in trade. Their main stake was in the cotton trade in the Ferghana valley and in the grain trade in the Emirate of Bukhara, as shown by the fact that stocks of grain formed part of the assets of many Shikarpuri estates. They also had a stake in the silk trade, traditionally an important branch of the trade between India and Central Asia, even if it was on the decline after 1890, and more generally in the textile and cloth trade. They were also involved in tea trading, although on a much lesser scale than the Peshawari merchants. Their participation in the foreign trade of the region was not limited to exchanges between India

---

[13] Entry for 5 November 1908, L/P&S/7/225.
[14] A. Das Gupta, 'Gujarati Merchants and the Red Sea Trade', in B. B. Kling and M. N. Pearson (eds.), *The Age of Partnership. Europeans in Asia before Dominion*, Honolulu, 1979, pp. 123–58.
[15] Mentioned in Nedvetsky, *Bukhara*, p. 59.

and Turkestan, but they had a stake in the trade of Russian Turkestan with Iran, Afghanistan, Sinkiang and Russia proper.

On the eve of the Russian Revolution, they were still important players in the regional economy, even if they had clearly lost their financial hegemony of the 1800–70 period. Following the disaster of the Russian Revolution, they redeployed largely in India, although they also extended their operations to Burma, Ceylon and even Malaya. A lot of evidence on their Indian operations came to light at the time of the Banking Enquiry Committee reports of 1930. By that time, the number of so-called 'Multani' firms was estimated to be around 100, and their own capital valued at Rs 5 million,[16] which appears low in comparison with the Rs 250 million of capital held by the Chettiar banking firms at that time.[17] But this capital circulated rapidly: at any time, the Shikarpuris had Rs 50 million in current bills, four-fifths of which were rediscounted with banks, the rest being sold at Shikarpur, where there was a market for bills. This circulating capital was used mostly for loans to agricultural producers, merchants, artisans and small industrialists. In southern India, an area where they were particularly active, they were described as 'intermediaries between the merchants and the joint-stock banks, giving advances to merchants on the personal credit of the latter to be used for advances to agricultural and other producers and also on transactions covering goods in transit'.[18] In Bombay, which was the main centre of their activities, the Shikarpuris financed mostly traders and small industrialists (pressmen, thread-makers, bottle-makers, etc.).[19]

The Shikarpuri bankers advanced either their own money or money borrowed at Shikarpur at low rates of interest (4–6 per cent). The loans were made either on account or on *hundis*, sometimes through a personal security ensuring the safe return of the money, but rarely on mortgage. The loans were generally short term, for a period of two to three months, sometimes extended to seven months. Shikarpuris did little deposit business, and less and less remittance business, because of competition from the Imperial Bank of India. One of their main activities was the rediscounting of *hundis* with the banks to take advantage of differences in rates: they discounted *hundis* in Rangoon which were sent to Bombay for rediscount to take advantage of the fact that the

[16] *Report of the Burma Provincial Banking Enquiry Committee 1929–30*, vol. I, *Banking and Credit in Burma*, Rangoon, 1930, pp. 187–8.
[17] Rudner, *Caste and Capitalism*, pp. 70–3.
[18] *The Madras Provincial Banking Enquiry Committee*, vol. I, *Report*, Madras, 1930, pp. 190–2.
[19] 'Special note concerning the activities of the Shikarpuri shroffs', enclosed in *Report of the Bombay Provincial Banking Enquiry Committee 1929–30*, Bombay, 1930, vol. IV, *Evidence*, 'Evidence from the Shikarpuri Shroffs' Association', pp. 336–44.

bank rate at Bombay was generally 2 per cent below the rate at Rangoon.[20]

The rates of interest charged ranged from a low of 9–13 per cent at which rate most business was done to a maximum of 24 per cent on small loans with little security. These figures are much lower than those quoted for Central Asia, confirming that the rates in that region had been particularly high. As to the net income of the bankers on their capital, estimates varied between a low of 7–8 per cent according to the Shikarpuris themselves[21] and a high of 9–12 per cent according to the *Report of the Madras Provincial Banking Enquiry Committee*, a discrepancy which is fairly small and easy to explain.

All reports noted a marked shift in the operations of the Shikarpuri *shroffs* from deposits, which had been an important area of activity prior to 1914 (as is seen clearly in the Central Asian successional documents), to *hundis* which were considered a simpler and more efficient way of making money. In Shikarpur in the inter-war period, even ordinary lower-middle-class people were in the habit of purchasing *hundis*, because they got interest in advance, and after sixty-one days could renew them and receive interest again. There was thus in Shikarpur a thriving business in *hundis* originally underwritten by Deccan agriculturists or Bombay traders and industrialists which, after having been sold and resold in Shikarpur, were reexported to the Deccan and Bombay by the *shroffs*, thus depriving local agriculture and trade of much needed capital.

In the long term, it appears that the role played by Shikarpur as a centre of international and interregional finance resulted in a certain amount of decapitalisation, as funds borrowed locally were systematically transferred to other places. On the other hand there were regular remittances, but after 1920 their amount seems to have diminished, as the Shikarpuri bankers increasingly used Bombay as the main base and treated Shikarpur only as a place of residence and a secondary financial market. The decentred position of Shikarpur in relation to the new areas of activity of its bankers favoured a gradual shift of the centre of gravity of the network towards Bombay. Shikarpur had thrived as the gate of Khorrassan, but the partial end of the Central Asian connection dealt it a blow from which it never really recovered, in spite of the talent of its bankers and of their attachment to their native town. The record of the Shikarpuris remains nevertheless impressive: in spite of the losses suffered in the Russian debacle, they were able to reinvent themselves as the foremost community of 'indigenous bankers' in India, challenging

---

[20] *Report of the Burma Provincial Banking Enquiry Committee*, p. 188.
[21] 'Evidence from the Shikarpuri Shroffs Association'.

Gujaratis and Marwaris on their own ground. Their major assets were their reputation for scrupulous honesty (no Shikarpuri banker ever defaulted on a *hundi*), which ensured wide acceptance for their bills, including from European banks, and their flexibility, their readiness to move *hundis* quickly from one place to another to take advantage of differences in interest rates. It explains largely how, in spite of their limited capital resources due to the relative poverty of their native town, they could play an important financial role in a very extended area over a long period of time: the rapidity of circulation of their *hundis* had a multiplier effect, allowing them to cover many transactions without mobilizing too much of their own capital. It is obvious that accounting skills were an important component of their expertise, although little is known in detail of the specifics of their accounting system. They combined, to an astonishing degree, a strong conservatism with a remarkable capacity for adaptation to changing contexts and conjunctures. Their Hyderabadi colleagues were less conservative, but did not show a similar capacity for sudden shifts; their story is rather one of gradual change.

From niche traders to global players: the evolving nature of the Sindwork trade

If Shikarpuris remained basically a community of bankers, the Hyderabadi merchants known as Sindwork merchants or Sindworkies, who came from the same background, developed over time a specialization in certain branches of trade which were highly specific. Their trade, known as the 'Sindwork trade' represented a rather unique mix, combining international import–export trade with wholesaling and retailing, dealing in luxury as well as in ordinary goods, bringing together a highly specialized line, the silk trade, and a much more undifferentiated one which went under the generic appellation of curio trade. Gradually the Sindwork merchants emerged as global players on the world textile markets.

Originally the term 'Sindwork trade' covered all kinds of craft productions of Sind, particularly Lower Sind, which found an outlet on the Bombay market, mostly with a European clientele, following the annexation of Sind to the Bombay Presidency. It was basically an itinerant bazaar trade in which unbranded goods produced in small quantities by Muslim craftsmen working at home or in very small workshops were sold by hawkers, who received them from merchants who advanced money to the craftsmen. No material dating from these early days of the trade has come to light, and nothing is known of the exact way in which the merchants organized the trade.

At a later stage, silk and silk goods entered the repertoire of the Sindwork merchants. Originally they seem to have procured the silk and silk goods from India, particularly from the Punjab and from Benares, but from the 1890s onwards, Chinese and Japanese silks and silk goods figured with increasing prominence in inventories of shops and lists of goods traded. This specialization in the silk trade is somewhat puzzling. Silk is a highly specific line of trading, which necessitates knowledge and skills acquired over long periods in tightly knit merchant communities, as was the case in China, Japan, France or Italy. There is moreover no indication of a prior specialization by Hyderabadi merchants in that line, even if different kinds of silk goods figured among currently traded items in Sind in the nineteenth century. One possible explanation for this pattern of late specialization may lie in the specific state of the silk market in India in the second half of the nineteenth century, where no hereditary group of silk traders with a clearly dominant position emerged. This relatively 'open' situation may have facilitated the entry of newcomers into the trade. Having gained a foothold in the silk trade in India (they appear as silk traders in Calcutta from the 1870s onwards), the Sindworkies managed to acquire the basic knowledge and skills which allowed them to extend their silk-purchasing operations to the Far East. At the time when they made this move, around the late 1880s, other groups of Indian merchants, mostly Gujaratis, were in the habit of purchasing silks in the Far East to supply the Bombay market. It is possible that, finding the Bombay market too crowded, the Sindworkies looked for outlets outside India in the countries where they had established a foothold as curio merchants. Statistics on the reexport of silk manufactures from India, mostly from Bombay, to certain destinations, where Sindwork merchants were active, can give some idea of the size of their trade. Table 6.2 presents the data.

It is worth noting that between 1893–94 and 1913–14 reexport of silk products to Malta and Egypt declined considerably, an indication that the Sindwork merchants increasingly tended to consign silk goods directly from Japan and China to these destinations, by-passing India altogether. The opening of branches in China and Japan by some of the largest Sindwork firms facilitated the trend.

In China, the Sindwork merchants were attracted first to Canton, which was less active than Shanghai in the silk export trade, but had a large trade in piecegoods for foreign markets.[22] After 1920, they shifted the focus of their activities to Shanghai, where *Pongees*, made of *tussah* silk, a relatively cheap variety, were a popular item for export.[23] One of

[22] Li, *China's Silk Trade*, p. 73.
[23] *Ibid.*, p. 79.

Table 6.2. *Reexport of silk manufactures from India to selected destinations in 1893–1894 and 1913–1914 (in rupees)*

Destination	1893–94	1913–14
Gibraltar	65,349	55,185
Ceylon	86,015	87,240
Natal	16,729	98,100
Zanzibar and Pemba	63,861	102,255
East African Protectorate	n.a.	60,210
Malta	36,297	5,010
Portuguese East Africa	18,883	25,560
Egypt	97,830	9,585
German East Africa	n.a.	21,315
Tunis and Tripoli	n.a.	10,305

Source: *Report on an Inquiry into the Silk Industry in India*, H. Maxwell-Lefroy and E. C. Ansorge, Calcutta, 1917, vol. II, p. 88.

the attractions of the silk trade to the Sindwork merchants, apart from the existence of a steady demand from tourists and travellers, was probably its highly speculative character. Speculation was rife in the silk trade in China, first because of sudden shifts in both demand and supply which created great uncertainties, and second, because of the wild fluctuations in exchange rates due to the fact that, unlike most of the world, China was on a silver standard.[24] Speculation, and the high profits it brought to skilful operators, probably explains why niche traders like the Sindworkies, who had no stake in either of the two big markets for Chinese silk, France and the USA, were able to prosper and entrench themselves in a fairly competitive market, in which they had no particular advantage. In Japan, where, as S. Sugiyama noted, the opening of regular shipping services and the establishment of branches of Western banks made it possible for merchants with little capital to join the trade and compete with the established Western firms,[25] the Sindworkies at first purchased mostly silk handkerchiefs, for which there was a large demand from tourists, and then gradually enlarged their range.

They also developed an interest in other highly specialized lines of trade, such as the shawl trade and the lace trade. Specialization in the former is easily explained by the existence of an early trading connection between Hyderabad and Kashmir. However, shawls from Kashmir were not the only ones sold in the shops of the Sindworkies: in Egypt, for

[24] *Ibid.*, pp. 88–90.
[25] S. Sugiyama, *Japan's Industrialization in the World Economy 1859–1899: Export Trade and Overseas Competition*, London, 1988, pp. 38–9.

instance, they sold locally produced shawls known as Assiut shawls. Their venture into the lace trade seems to have developed originally as an offshoot of the establishment of trading connections with regions where there was a tradition of lace production, such as Malta or Tenerife. Some Sindhi merchants in Egypt did a thriving trade in Maltese lace, which was in great demand there, particularly from the Jewish population.

Together with these fairly specialized lines of trading went a more undifferentiated one, known as the curio trade. The exact origin of the term 'curio' and its use to cover a whole range of so-called 'exotic' goods would by itself be worthy of further research. The definition of the term could actually vary. In some cases, it included the trade in antiques and art objects, but definitely not for the Sindwork merchants, who always tended to avoid becoming involved in this highly specialized trade which necessitated a kind of knowledge which they did not possess. In Egypt they left that line entirely to the Armenians, the Levantines, the Greeks and the Jews, and concentrated instead on the lower segment of the market represented by 'tourist' goods, which did not appeal to the same extent to connoisseur taste. These goods had various provenances, and were meant to satisfly a clientele of tourists and travellers.

Ultimately it is the specific nature of the demand on the part of European and North American tourists and travellers which shaped the particular mix of goods on offer in the Sindhi shops. This type of customer was not interested in buying in large quantities, and was not too demanding as regards quality either. Travel purchase is a very specific branch of the trade, where a lot of the usual constraints on the seller are attenuated. The customer is more ready to buy than in the course of 'normal' shopping, and, since the purchases are generally part of a separate budget earmarked for travel, he or she is not inclined to look too closely at the price. In any case they have only limited time, generally while the ship is at anchor. International long-distance ship passengers were generally taken to the shops by touts, and represented a kind of captive market. Compulsion to buy was strong, as returning home empty handed from a long voyage to the Orient would have been seen at home as unworthy. On the other hand, they rarely had a very precise idea of what they wanted to buy. Hence the importance of developing persuasion techniques to cater to that kind of clientele. Before the era of mass advertising, it could be done only through personal contact. It was therefore necessary to have managers and shop assistants capable of talking cutomers into buying the most expensive items, which put linguistic skills at a high premium among Sindworkies. Since demand was not highly focused on specific items, actual purchases were easily influenced by the availability of supplies. It was advisable to always have a wide range of goods available in large quantities during the high season. That is why a large stock-in-trade is characteristic of all shop inventories found in the archives. Shops did a particularly brisk trade at the height of the tourist season (winter in Egypt), a period during which turnover had to be very high to generate good profits. Besides, such a trade was very sensitive to even small fluctuations in the number of tourists and travellers, and also highly dependent on largely unpredictable changes in fashion and taste. It was characterized altogether by a high degree of uncertainty and risk.

To mitigate the risks, Sindwork merchants tried to escape an exclusive reliance on the tourist trade and sought to develop more regular lines of trade with more permanent custom. Given the kind of goods they traded in, they found that clientele mostly among the resident European population of colonial and semi-colonial countries, like the British in Egypt, Dutch settlers in the East Indies or French colons in North Africa. British troops were also an important market, as officers and soldiers liked to bring back souvenirs from their years of service in the East. All these uprooted Europeans were good customers because they combined an often high purchasing power with a taste for the 'exotic'. In places like Singapore, customers were also found among wealthy non-Europeans, mostly Chinese. At a later stage, as the range of goods sold in the shops broadened to include different kinds of textiles besides silk, more 'native' customers were attracted to the Sindhi shops.

Pricing policies followed by Sindwork merchants did not conform to the usual bazaar practice of not having fixed prices and of underselling to dispose of limited stocks as quickly as possible to ensure a rapid turnover. On the contrary, in their shops, there were prices which were fixed and quite high, and bargaining was not an accepted practice. These shops were actually modelled on the 'oriental' shops which were mushrooming at the same time all over Europe and North America, and there was a deliberate attempt on the part of the Sindwork merchants to appear different from the stereotypical 'oriental' trader, so as to gain respectability and inspire confidence in a mostly European clientele full of racial prejudice. They made it a point to behave in as European a fashion as possible. For instance, they avoided selling on credit as much as possible, which was wise in any case when customers were often ship passengers ready to depart.

Location and presentation were two very important factors in ensuring a steady volume of sales. Generally Sindwork merchants had their shops in prestigious locations, either in some of the main commercial thoroughfares, or in big hotels and in the main tourist areas. In

Cairo, their shops were spread between the major hotels and the principal tourist bazaar, the Khan-i-Khalil. In Singapore, they were mostly on High Street, in Saigon on the rue Catinat. The shops were generally rented, and rents represented a large part of the overhead costs of the Sindwork firms. They were reluctant to buy because real estate prices were generally very high in exclusive shopping areas and they liked to keep their assets as liquid as possible, to facilitate mobility.

If a wealthy clientele was easily drawn into well-located shops, the quality of internal arrangements was essential to further captivate their attention. Sindhi merchants, influenced by the example of the new 'oriental shops' in the great capitals of the world, appear to have paid a lot of attention to that aspect, with results which could be impressive. One of Rangoon's main Sindhi shops, that of T. K. Tejoomal, so much impressed visitors and resident Europeans that it was even the subject of a poem published in the *Rangoon Gazette* in July 1922.[26]

If the specific nature of demand largely dictated the assortment of goods which were on offer in the shops or which were hawked by the pedlars, supply was an equally important factor in shaping the trade. The originality of the Sindwork merchants in this matter is that they systematically attempted to control the entire supply chain. In an early phase, big Sindwork firms had their own workshops in Hyderabad for the production of certain kinds of goods. Thus in 1899 both Pohoomull Bros and Wassiamall Assomull advertised themselves as manufacturers of silver embroidery, a traditional craft of Sind. This direct link to craft production snapped as the productions of Sind were replaced by those of other areas. It is worth noting however that in 1930 Hyderabadi merchants were mentioned as financing craft production in Kashmir on a significant scale.[27] At various moments, Sindwork firms purchased small factories in different locations,[28] but such direct forays into

---

[26] The poem read:
Mr Tejoomal stands and smiles
On the steps of his fairy store
Luring you into the silken piles
And the glitter of gems galore.
It is reproduced in A. Macmillan (comp. and ed.), *Seaports of the Far East. Historical and Descriptive, Commercial and Industrial: Facts, Figures and Resources*, London, 1923, p. 103.

[27] A witness before the Bombay Provincial Banking Enquiry Committee, Seth Dharamsey testified that he had seen 'many of the Hyderabadis financing the small trader in Kashmere', 'Evidence of Karachi Indian Merchants Association', *Report of Bombay Provincial Banking Enquiry Committee*, vol. IV, p. 15.

[28] The firm of D. Kundanmal & Co. was listed in the *Trade Directory of Japan*, Calcutta, 1940 under 'silk and rayon goods manufacturers'. The firm of J. Kimatrai & Co., according to the entry on Seth Sobhraj Jhamatmal, proprietor of the firm in the *Who's Who in Sind*, Karachi, 1944, owned a silk mill in Ahmedabad.

production were rarely successful. Apart from these failed attempts, the main thrust of the Sindwork merchants was towards controlling the entire supply chain, from the workshop or the factory floor to the ultimate customer, and to cut out the middlemen as much as possible. Only firms of a certain size however attempted to perform all the operations in the chain, from wholesale purchasing at the factory floor to retail selling in shops via exporting, importing and wholesale distributing. In this respect, Sindwork firms could be divided into two broad categories: truly 'global' firms which were exporters as well as importers, wholesalers and retailers, and smaller firms which operated only at the importing end of the chain.

Out of a total of Sindwork firms which, in the 1930s, was much more than 100, only about 50 were listed as exporters from Japan and China, which were by then clearly the major sources of goods for the network. There were also a few firms which exported only from India, but Indian goods accounted for a diminishing share of the total supply. In the big exporting firms, different branches handled different types of operations: the Yokohama branch would do the wholesale purchasing and exporting, the Gibraltar branch the importing and wholesale distributing for the Western Mediterranean and the Atlantic, while retail selling could be done in many locations, either in shops or by hawkers.

A survey of some twenty firms listed as exporters from Japan in 1940[29] shows that they operated mostly in the textile trade. A broadening of the range of goods they exported is however noticeable, as most firms added cotton and rayon piece-goods to their traditional trade in silk piecegoods. On the other hand, only two firms are listed as curio exporters, which may be due to underreporting. Sundry goods, such as handbags, hosiery goods or parasols are also listed among goods exported by these firms, which confirms the trend towards a broadening of their range.

Evidence from Southeast Asia reinforces this impression. In the 1920s and 1930s the big Sindwork firms, such as K. A. J. Chotirmall, K. Chellaram and Pohoomull Bros. began to engage in the multilateral trade between Japan and the Netherlands Indies, exchanging Indian raw cotton for Japanese textiles which they sold in the Indies.[30] The firm of K. A. J. Chotirmall was particularly active in this process of 'globalisation'. In the 1920s it broke into the German and Swiss textile markets, and played an important role in the textile trade between French Indochina and the rest of Southeast Asia. Allied firms Lalchand and Rewac-

---

[29] Based on 'Classified list of exporters, importers and manufacturers', *Trade Directory of Japan*, Calcutta, 1940, pp. 49–212.
[30] Brown, *Capital and Entrepreneurship*, p. 207.

hand exported textiles from Indochina, France, French India and Hong Kong to Malaya and the Dutch East Indies.[31] Eschewing narrow specialization in the silk trade, the major firms were able to respond to short-time fluctuations in demand, as well as to broaden their sources of supply. They drew sustenance from the network, which gave them access to a considerable pool of knowledge about markets that even Japanese firms were interested in tapping.

The 'global' exporting multi-branch firm was the crucial force in the network, because it largely controlled the sources of supply. Although no quantitative data are available about the level of purchases of different firms from Japan and China, it is highly probable that the big seven firms cornered a large share of it, even if two or three other firms also appear to have purchased on a fairly significant scale. As to the smaller firms, some seem to have specialized in supplying the Indian market rather than foreign markets. Small firms which were not in the exporting business, which were the majority, depended on the big exporting firms for the supply of their goods.[32] Small dealers got goods from the big firms either on credit, or by payment on delivery. It would, however, be a mistake to view the network as totally self-sufficient.

The transactions of the Sindwork merchants could be divided into three broad categories: intra-firm transactions, intra-network transactions, transactions with outsiders. Intra-firm transactions were transactions between different branches of the same firm and, given the importance of the big firms, these transactions probably accounted for the bulk of all transactions. Intra-network transactions were conducted between different Sindwork firms. They were mostly vertical, bringing together big firms as suppliers and small firms as purchasers. Big firms appear to have done little business with each other. The third category included all transactions concluded by Sindwork firms with outsiders, whether as buyers or as suppliers. Actually, most of these transactions were with suppliers, mostly producers of goods. Sindwork merchants did not sell much to other merchant firms, since they controlled the

---

[31] *Ibid.*, pp. 208–9.
[32] As evidenced from a case in the Cairo consular court. In 1918, the large Sindwork firm of J. T. Chanrai & Co., through the manager of their Gibraltar branch, sued Pribhdas Rupchand, a Sindhi dealer of Cairo, for non-repayment of a debt incurred on purchases he had made from Chanrai in Gibraltar. Evidence presented in court showed that during a three-year period Chanrai had sent to Rupchand from Gibraltar goods amounting to the total value of £426 in twelve different purchases, suggesting the existence of a regular relationship. These were goods imported from European countries by Chanrai's Gibraltar branch which were then reexported to Cairo where Rupchand sold them in his shops. 'J. T. Chanrai & Co. vs. Pribhdas Rupchand', PRO, Foreign Office Records, Cairo Consular Court Records, Dossier no. 38 of 1918, FO 841/170.

retailing end of the chain. Altogether, intra-network transactions seem to have been more important than transactions with outsiders but the latter were nevertheless crucial to ensure a regular supply of goods to the entire network.

Why did the big firms try to control the entire supply chain? One of their motivations may have been the desire to keep transaction costs low, but other possible motives may have been the will to exclude outsiders, and the desire to give employment to townspeople. Controlling the entire supply chain had its costs: it meant fulfilling different specialized functions, such as exporting, importing and wholesaling which demanded specialized skills and stretched to the limit the human resources of firms which were, after all, by the standards of world capitalism, medium-scale operators. Such lack of specialization did not facilitate calculations of cost and of margins, and may have been a drag on profitability. On the other hand, it probably brought in side benefits which were not negligible, such as the possibility of playing on currency fluctuations between different trade zones. It seems that in the 1930s, in particular, foreign currency operations accounted for a growing share of the profits of the big firms.[33] Controlling the supply chain also gave a lot of flexibility and allowed them to respond quickly to shifts in demand from one type of goods to another. But the ultimate explanation for this desire is probably to be found in the precarious internal balance of the network. Only by controlling the supply chain could the big firms maintain their overall dominance, which was constantly threatened by the emergence of new players. Control of the supply chain was thus clearly linked to the oligopolistic nature of the network. Oligopoly had to be constantly reasserted, for it could have been eroded by the natural dynamics of the trade. Since the dominant players could not use a hierarchical caste structure to their advantage, they had to manipulate market factors to reach their aims.

Lack of quantitative data hampers any attempt at evaluating the overall importance of the Sindwork trade. An estimate of 1936, already quoted, mentioned a total turnover of Rs 20 crores.[34] The big seven firms must have accounted for a large share of it, which means that, with a turnover of more than Rs 1 crore each, these firms were among the largest Indian commercial firms at the time.

As regards profits, no overall estimate is available. Stray indications in archival sources suggest wide variations in rates of profit, depending on

---

[33] From evidence in the archives of the Siam Commercial Bank in Bangkok, it is clear that the firm of K. A. J. Chotirmall had large monthly earnings from bullion and foreign exchange transactions. See Brown, *Capital and Entrepreneurship*, pp. 206, 280, note 52.
[34] See Chapter 4.

time and place. A firm in Java in 1920 recorded an annual profit of almost 100 per cent,[35] while a firm in Panama had a profit of 50 per cent in 1924–25,[36] and another in Cairo a profit of 20–25 per cent in 1906–07.[37] On the other hand, another document from Cairo in the early twentieth century suggests that a rate of 10 per cent was considered 'normal'.[38] One way of looking at this question is to use remittances as a substitute for profits, on the supposition that most profits were remitted to Hyderabad. One estimate of total remittances into Sind in the late 1930s puts their value at some Rs 5 to 10 crores annually.[39] Taking the lower figure of 5 crores, and assuming that half of this amount was remitted by Sindworkies (Amils and Shikarpuris also remitted large sums annually), one would reach a figure of Rs 25 million, which, measured against a turnover of Rs 200 million, gives a gross profit rate of about 12.5 per cent, an estimate which probably errs on the side of caution.

Another way of estimating profitability is to look at the wealth of the Sindwork merchants. The paucity of data on successions originating from Hyderabad, in contrast to Shikarpur, makes this a difficult task. It is worth noting, however, that in the 1930s the banks estimated the fortune of the Chotirmall family, the principals of the firm of K. A. J. Chotirmall, to be US$17 million.[40] Indirect evidence points to the wealth acquired by Seth Pratap Dialdas, the principal of the firm of M. Dialdas & Sons[41] and a major financier of the Congress Party in

---

[35] The profits of Messrs. K. Dhanamall & Co. were put at 300,000 Dutch guilder on a capital of 331,000 guilders in 1920. Affidavit by Naraindas Tirthdas, 22 October 1923, PRO, Foreign Office Records, Embassy and Consular Archives: Japan, Yokohama, FO 908/8.

[36] Calculated from information contained in the petition of Jhangimal Tejumal Khemrani to the collector of Hyderabad, September 1927, IOR, L/P&J/8/278.

[37] From deposition of Naraindas Kishinchand, one of the partners of the firm of K. Khanchand & Co. in 'K. Khanchand and Kodoomal vs. Naraindas Kishinchand', PRO, Foreign Office Records, Cairo Consular Court Records, suit no. 134 of 1908, FO 841/101.

[38] An award given by an arbitrator in a dispute between a hawker and his supplier included the following rubric: 'Loss of profit on missing goods at the rate of 10 per cent on their cost price'. Award enclosed in 'Udhandas Signanmal vs. Tarachand Mulchand', PRO, Foreign Office Records, Cairo Consular Court Records, suit no. 18 of 1907, FO 841/92.

[39] Mentioned in 'Gandhidham: its History and Implications', by Bhai Pratap Dialdas, in Sindhu Resettlement Corporation Ltd., *Gandhidham*, Bombay, 1951, pp. 8–12: 'A large part of our people were not dependent for their livelihood on the soil of Sind. In fact they fed Sind with an annual stream of wealth calculated to be at least five to ten crores of rupees.' Bhai Pratap Dialdas was the principal of the firm of M. Dialdas & Sons.

[40] Mentioned in Brown, *Capital and Entrepreneurship*, p. 208.

[41] In his memoirs, *Fifty Years with the British*, p. 45, S. K. Kirpalani, a prominent Hyderabadi Amil recalls his meeting with Seth Pratap's son Narain during a ship voyage

Sind. Recent estimates of the wealth of Indian expatriate business families in the United Kingdom place the Chanrai and Chellaram families, with respective fortunes of £60 million and £30 million among the richest.[42] Both made their fortune in Sindwork with the firms of J. T. Chanrai & Co. and K. Chellaram & Sons. This gives an idea of the kind of fortune which could be made in Sindwork. Sight must not be lost of the fact that a lot of money which had been invested by returning Sindworkies in land and real estate in and around Hyderabad was wiped out at the time of Partition in 1947–48. Smaller merchants could also build up wealth on a significant scale.[43] Hyderabad was known, prior to 1947, as a prosperous city, and a significant part of its wealth had its origins in the gains of the Sindwork trade. But, if the profits of the trade were fairly high, they were far from equally distributed. The owners of the big firms accounted for a big share of them, but there were also marginal operators who never made much profit. In the Japanese silk trade, some of the smaller traders made their actual profit not on the sale of the silk but on the resale of the wooden cases in which the silk was shipped.[44]

To illustrate the highly diverse and changing nature of the Sindwork trade, two case studies will be presented of Egypt and West Africa.

The Sindwork trade in Egypt c. 1900–1930

In Egypt, during the first three decades of the twentieth century, Sindwork merchants were typical niche traders, who specialized in some lines of trade, but do not appear to have had a global impact, despite the large-scale operations of some firms. It is significant that the literature on trade in Egypt makes no mention of this group of specialized Indian traders. Compared to Greek, Levantine, Jewish and Armenian merchants, they must have been fairly inconspicuous. Court cases before the Cairo consular court give some idea of their business, and are particularly informative on the smaller traders. Many of the cases concerned disputes between hawkers and the merchants who supplied them with goods. They often include detailed descriptions of hawkers'

between India and England in the 1930s. While the ship was passing through Port Said, Narain invited all the first class passengers, 300 in all, to dinner at the Casino and paid a bill of $15,000, an enormous sum in those days, 'without so much as batting an eyelid'.

[42] Cragg, *The New Maharajahs*, p. 92.
[43] Kirpalani, in *Fifty Years with the British*, p. 365, tells the story of a school friend of his, Punwani, who, after a career of three decades in Sindwork in Trinidad, came back with some US $200,000 which he invested in a piece of landed property. He lost his fortune when he had to leave Hyderabad in 1948.
[44] Mentioned in Chandra, 'The History of Indians in Japan'.

bundles presented as evidence in court. In this way it is possible to know what kind of goods the Sindhi pedlars sold in Egypt in the early twentieth century.

An analysis of four bundles belonging to three different hawkers[45] shows that all silks and silk goods, including painted silk, crepe silk, plain silk, striped silk, silk handkerchiefs, silk kimonos and silk blouses, were of Chinese or Japanese origin, while the bulk of non-silk goods were of Indian origin, including Madras brass and mantelpieces, Ludhiana curtains, Agra cushions, Delhi tables, etc. There were also 'Turkish', Maltese, Egyptian and Sudanese goods, as well as many objects of unknown provenance, indicating that Sindhi merchants in Egypt sourced very widely. The hawkers, most of whom were on contract with a merchant, appear to have travelled all across Egypt and even in the Sudan. It is probable that most of their customers were Egyptian, Europeans in Egypt being few outside Cairo, Alexandria and the Suez Canal towns. The existence of these hawkers and the range of their travels testifies to an attempt on the part of the Sindwork merchants to avoid being too dependent on the tourist trade with its high seasonal fluctuations. It is clear that they succeeded in capturing some market share in a country where there were already many active trading communities. Their major asset appears to have been their trading connections with India and the Far East, which no other community in Egypt had at the time. But they also sold local goods, which reveals the existence of trading connections in the region.

Some cases in the Cairo consular court records throw a vivid light on the activities of small traders. Thus the story of a firm called K. Khanchand & Co can be largely reconstructed from the evidence contained in several cases which came before the court between 1906 and 1913. The firm had been constituted in 1904 apparently as a partnership between four merchants for a period of four years, but after two years three of the original partners withdrew, and the remaining one concluded a new partnership agreement with a Hyderabadi capitalist.[46] The founder remained as a working partner and a second partner was brought in from Hyderabad. According to the terms of the partnership, a sum of Rs

---

[45] 'List of goods entrusted to Tarachand Mulchand', in 'Dhanamall Chellaram vs. Tarachand Mulchand', PRO, Foreign Office Records, Cairo Consular Court Records, suit no. 10 of 1904, FO 841/80; 'list of goods entrusted to same', in 'Udhandas Signanmal vs. Tarachand Mulchand', *ibid.*, suit no. 18 of 1907, FO 841/92; 'list of goods missing from the bundle of Dettaram Gopomall', in 'K. Khanchand & Co vs. Dettaram Gopomall', suit no. 3 of 1908, *ibid.*, FO 841/96; 'amount sent by plaintiff in partnership with defendant', in 'Koshiram Daulatram vs. Dettaram Wattamull', suit no. 47 of 1908, *ibid.*, FO 841/97.
[46] Partnership agreement reproduced in Appendix III.

15,000 was invested in the purchase of goods. The firm had two shops in Cairo 'for the purpose of trading in Indian goods and curios', one of which was on the premises of the Bristol Hotel, and the other one in the Khan-i-Khalil, the main tourist bazaar in Cairo. One of the partners was in charge of the main shop in the bazaar, the second one in charge of the other shop. The former left for India in April at the end of the busy season and took the books with him to show them to the principal in Hyderabad. The latter, who was eighty years old, came to Cairo on an inspection tour, but, having fallen ill, had to go back to India and died on the ship before reaching Karachi.

The probate enquiry into the goods of the deceased[47] included a list of the creditors of the firm at the time of the principal's death. Interestingly, of the fifteen names on the list, only two are those of Sindhi firms. The largest creditor was a Muslim merchant, and there were also European creditors (including a firm in Vienna, Austria). Money had been borrowed from non-Sindhis. A small Sindhi firm in Cairo had a wide range of suppliers and creditors, indicating a good insertion into the local trading milieu. But the partners and employees were Hyderabadis.

Some indications are also given of the profits of the firm: during the first winter season, they were high (Rs 6,000–7,000 on an investment of Rs 15,000), but in the following summer season, as debts had to be repaid to merchants, there was a loss of Rs 1,000. This illustrates the highly seasonal nature of the Sindwork trade.

An interesting aside is the mention in one document of a reverse flow of goods from Egypt to Calcutta and Singapore for an amount of Rs 1,000. No details are given, but this piece of information confirms the opportunism of the Sindwork merchants, who never neglected a possibility of making profits even outside their usual lines of business.

Another court case[48] gives interesting information on the way in which a small Sindwork merchant was supplied with goods. He arrived in Egypt in October for the beginning of the tourist season, bringing with him £35 worth of goods from India, consisting of jewellery and other goods. He also got £80 worth of goods from Yokohama, £20 worth of goods from China and £12 worth of lace from Malta, all payable on delivery, not on credit. He also bought some goods locally on credit, apparently from a big Sindwork merchant who later sued him for non-payment. Such operators who came to Egypt just for the tourist

---

[47] 'Probate enquiry into the goods of Bhai Khanchand, deceased, PRO, Foreign Office Records, Cairo Consular Court Records, dossier no. 103 of 1909, FO 841/107.
[48] 'Dialdas Kalachand vs. Kodoomal Ramchand', PRO, Foreign Office Records, Cairo Consular Court Records, Dossier no. 14 of 1911, FO 841/118.

Table 6.3. *The sales account of a Sindhi merchant of Port Said in 1930–31*

Period	Sales (in £ Egyptian)
March 1930	536
April	584
May	302
June	266
July	372
August	500
September	412
October	515
November	628
December	566
January 1931	392
February	232
March	499 (partly due to credit collecting)
April	244
May	330
June	222
July	312
August	301
September	133

Source: 'S. Baloomal vs. Ratoomal & Sons', PRO, Foreign Office Records, Port Said Consular Court Records, civil case no. 13 of 1931, FO 846/97.

season were an important component of the Sindworkie community. It is significant that the same merchant acknowledged that he did not keep books. He must have hawked the goods, but he was no salaried hawker, rather an independent operator who had some capital since he could pay for goods on delivery.

More detailed information on the operations of a small merchant comes from the minutes of a case before the Port Said court.[49] This merchant was suing his ex-employers, a Sindwork firm of Port Said, for defamation and he produced books showing the amount of sales in his shop between March 1930 and September 1931. The figures are reproduced in Table 6.3.

The wide fluctuations in the volume of sales reflect on the one hand the precariousness of the position of marginal operators, highly dependent on the volume of passenger traffic passing though the Suez canal and on the purchasing capacity of the passengers, and on the other hand the growing impact of the world depression on the volume of sales. A more detailed look at the monthly flucuations reveals two peaks of

[49] 'S. Baloomal vs. Ratoomal & Sons', PRO, Foreign Office Records, Port Said Consular Court Records, civil case no. 13 of 1931, FO 846/97.

activity, one in April 1930, which coincided with the end of the busy season and probably some liquidation of stocks, and one in November–December 1930, which corresponded to the height of the tourist season.

It is interesting to note that even small operators of this kind, whose annual turnover was around £1,500, managed to get credit from the banks. The local manager of Barclays Bank in Port Said, testifying before the court, stated that S. Baloomal, the small merchant, had a bank balance which varied between £100 credit and £40 debit. He was given an overdraft of £39, and the bank occasionally discounted drafts for him. The manager had no complaint about the behaviour of the merchant during the six-month period when he kept an account with the bank.

A list of suppliers supplied by him included only names of Sindhi firms in Shanghai, Hong Kong and Yokohama, suggesting that the merchant specialized in the sale of 'Oriental' goods to ship passengers passing through Port Said.

In Egypt the Sindwork trade was an umbrella term for a variety of trading operations performed by different types of merchants. The overall rate of profit on these activities seems to have been fairly high prior to the First World War, and still satisfactory in the 1920s. The world depression dealt a severe blow to the Sindwork trade in Egypt, from which it really never recovered.

In contrast to the case of Egypt stands West Africa, where the Sindwork trade became much more diversified at an earlier date.

Sindwork merchants as global operators: the big firms in the West African trade

West Africa offers a completely different story. In that part of the British colonial empire, the Sindworkies had very little scope to develop their traditional lines of trade. They never became niche traders, but operated as general traders. Three of the big seven firms, J. T. Chanrai, K. Chellaram and M. Dialdas were active in the region and for the first two, West Africa emerged clearly in the 1920s and 1930s as their main area of operation. Of the three territories, Nigeria, with its large population and vast resources, became the most important for both Chanrai and Chellaram. In the Gold Coast, the depression brought about the closure of the local branches of Dialdas and Chanrai, but in 1935 Chellaram entered the fray and by 1948 it had clearly ensured a dominant position for itself. In that territory, however, there were many small operators, most of whom seem to have been ex-employees of the big firms who then tried their luck on their own.

West Africa offers a good vantage point from where to chart the rise of some Sindwork firms to the status of global traders. Nowhere else did Sindhi merchants deal in such a variety of goods of such diverse provenances. If goods from India, in particular the famous Madras kerchiefs, figured at first prominently in the trade of the Sind merchants, they were quickly supplemented by various kinds of British and continental goods which the Sindwork firms procured from their depots in Gibraltar and in the Canary Islands. In the 1930s the Sindhi firms became the main suppliers of Japanese textiles to West Africa, a move which testified to the global nature of their operations. It was in connection with their West African operations that Messrs K. Chellaram & Sons became the first Sindwork firm to open a branch in London in the 1930s. This led to a new stage in globalization, as the firm started procuring textiles in the UK for sale abroad.[50]

On the West African coast, the Sindwork merchants played the role of general traders, largely modelling themselves on the big European firms such as the United Africa Company, although they operated on a much smaller scale. A detailed look at an advertisement for the firm of M. Dialdas & Sons in the *Sierra Leone Handbook* published in 1925[51] shows the diversity of the goods they traded in. On the one hand, one finds listed the kind of goods which were typical of the Sindwork trade: 'Silk, linen, cotton, embroideries and drawn-thread work made by hand; also Maltese, Spanish and Madeira laces of all descriptions. Ornaments of the newest designs in great variety. Curios, arts and objects made of ivory, mother-of-pearl, tortoise-shell, satsuna, demsen work, ebony, sandalwood, brass, copper, gold and silver jewelleries.' The only original feature was the addition of Spanish and Madeira laces to the usual Maltese ones. Besides the firm also stocked 'English fancy goods for ladies and gentlemen', undoubtedly for the local European population. These were the goods sold in their main store in Freetown. But they also had a wholesale and retail provision store in town, where they sold groceries, which were not part of the usual repertoire of Sindwork merchants.

In the 1930s, the Sindwork firms on the West African coast, particularly Chanrai and Chellaram, became active in the import of Japanese goods, mostly textiles which the devaluation of the yen made highly competitive on external markets. From 1934 onwards, with the passing by the British colonial authorities of an ordinance imposing quotas on

---

[50] In January 1946 the London branch of K. Chellaram & Sons applied for a licence to export a large quantity of woollen goods to Afghanistan, IOR, Political & Secret Department Records, Political External Files and Collections, L/P&S/12/1116.
[51] *The Handbook of Sierra Leone*, T. N. Goddard (comp.), Luton, 1925.

imports of Japanese textiles into West Africa, this made them an object of attention on the part of the colonial authorities, and some documents found in the Colonial Office records throw light on their activities. Thus, in October 1934, K. Chellaram & Sons complained to the secretary of state for the colonies of having been harshly treated by the customs authorities at Lagos.[52] They had placed large orders in Japan between February and May 1934 for goods which were 'of Nigerian design and . . . absolutely unsuitable for any markets in the world except Nigeria and the near territory'. As the goods had been manufactured specifically on order, a considerable time had elapsed before they were actually delivered. In the meantime two ordinances had been passed to regulate imports of textiles into Nigeria and on 13 September 1934 it had been officially notified that the quota in respect of cotton and rayon textiles imported from Japan had attained the figure prescribed. On 12 September two very large consignments arrived by ship in Lagos, totalling 269,000 yards of cotton and rayon goods, of which 169,000 were cleared out, leaving a balance of some 100,000 lying in the godowns awaiting reshipment to another destination. The firm asked to be allowed to release them, and to send part to Zinder in the French colony of Niger. In December further consignments arrived at Lagos, which could not be released. Eventually a compromise was reached by which the firm was allowed to bond the amount of its quota for 1935 plus some other amount. A total of 500,000 square yards of bonded goods in the name of K. Chellaram & Sons was thus lying in the Lagos warehouses at the end of 1934; these were gradually released in 1935, the firm deciding not to import any further consignment that year.[53]

The episode shows the scale of the operations of some Sindhi firms in West Africa. Total imports of cotton piecegoods and artificial silk goods into Nigeria in 1933 reached 100 million yards, and the 700,000 yards imported by Chellaram represented almost 1 per cent of the market. The Sindhi firms also controlled the bulk of textile imports from India, which were the main beneficiaries of the anti-Japanese quotas.[54] The strong position they occupied on the Nigerian textile market was due to

[52] G. F. Hunt & Shersin, solicitors (on behalf of Messrs K. Chellaram & Sons) to the secretary of state for the colonies, 22 October 1934, same to the under-secretary of state for the colonies, 5 December 1934; same to same, 10 December 1934, PRO, Colonial Office Records, Colonies (General) Economic Original Correspondence, 'Textile Import Quotas West Africa 1934', CO 323/1305/4.

[53] Officer administering government, Nigeria, to Sir Philip Cunliffe-Lister, secretary of state for the colonies, 20 December 1934, *ibid.*, CO 852/17/14.

[54] Imports of cotton piecegoods from India into Nigeria, which were insignificant in 1929 represented 5.8 per cent of the total value of imports in 1933 and 20.8 per cent in 1938. M. Perham (ed.), *Mining, Commerce and Finance in Nigeria*, London, 1948, Table XV, p. 99.

their good knowledge of the specific needs of that market (they had goods manufactured specially in Japan) and to their good connections with Japanese mills. They were thus able to take advantage of opportunities created by shifts in demand and prices.

In West Africa, the Sindwork traders departed at a relatively early date from the classical pattern of the Sindwork trade centred on silk and curios. They dealt in a much broader range of goods, and this worked to their advantage in the long term. In West Africa, particularly in Nigeria, Sindhis have become an entrenched business community and play an important role in various sectors of the economy. Their achievements were obtained at the expense of both the Europeans and the Lebanese. It was in the 1960s that they really emerged on the scene in a big way, but the foundations for their success had been laid down by the endeavours of a few firms in the 1920s and 1930s.

This West African success story, in a region situated so far away from their base home, shows that by the 1940s the Sindwork merchants had become a group of truly global operators, capable of dealing in a great variety of goods across the entire world. Although textiles were still their major field, they had a breadth of vision which would keep them in good stead when, in the aftermath of Partition, they would face the task of reorganizing their network to adapt to a new phase in the history of world trade.

This survey of the business activities of two groups of Sind merchants has tended to emphasize the differences between them; these should not however be exaggerated. The *banias* of Shikarpur and Hyderabad basically belonged to the same mercantile culture, used the same accounting techniques and had largely similar forms of business organization. Both groups combined trade and finance in varying proportions. If the Shikarpuris were mostly financiers, they did not eschew trading altogether. On the other hand, financial skills were crucial to the success of the Sindworkies as traders; the ability to arrange finance for their trade and to speculate on commodities as well as on currencies contributed greatly to their success. The differences between the two groups ultimately had a lot to do with differences in the political environment in which they operated. The political dimension of the history of these two networks cannot be ignored.

7 The politics of merchant networks

Sind merchants often liked to present themselves as apolitical, and, as a rule, they did not take much interest in politics, either at home or abroad. But running international trading and financial networks entailed political costs which could be high and, to face that problem, even 'apolitical' merchants had to organize themselves so as to become relatively efficient political operators. One of the major dilemmas Sind merchants confronted was the nature of their relationship to the British Empire. After 1843, they became *de facto* British subjects, and, in 1858, following the queen's proclamation, they were legally recognized as such, and therefore entitled to the protection of the British crown wherever they travelled. Being British subjects was however not necessarily the undiluted blessing it was often thought to be. For Shikarpuris in particular, there was a price to pay in Central Asia, especially after the region fell under the dominance of Britain's imperial arch-rival, Russia. Managing the British connection in widely contrasting contexts so as to maximize its advantages and minimize its costs became an essential survival skill for the Sind merchants. On the whole, the Sindworkies were more successful at it than the Shikarpuris. In the process, they evolved political skills which allowed them to gradually emancipate themselves from too exclusive a dependence on the British connection.

The British connection: instrumentalizing Empire?

The merchants of pre-colonial Sind had close links to various groups of indigenous rulers. The Shikarpuris had a very strong connection with the Afghan rulers during the period of Durrani dominance, but their relationship to the Talpurs was cool, even after Shikarpur returned to Sindhian control in 1824. They also forged connections with the rulers of the Uzbek khanates in Central Asia, in Khokand as well as in Bukhara. In spite of an episode of 'persecution' in the early 1830s, their position in Bukhara appears to have been well entrenched.[1] Their attitude to the British, who occupied Shikarpur in 1839 and annexed it in 1843, was not devoid of ambiguity. While they welcomed their advent, which allowed them to get rid of the Talpur regime for which they had no love, they were wary of being perceived as agents of British expansion in Afghanistan and Central Asia. They seem to have adopted a fairly neutral position towards the British expeditionary force which used Shikarpur as an advanced base for the march into Afghanistan in 1839. Once British rule was established however, they showed themselves loyal, as during the Mutiny when the bazaar was lit for three days to celebrate the fall of Delhi.[2] Being loyal British subjects did not however bring any advantages to the Shikarpuris when they travelled in Afghanistan and in the Uzbek khanates; on the contrary, they were widely suspected of being spies for the British, a stigma which became even harder to bear after most of Central Asia fell to the Russians. From the 1880s onwards, the Shikarpuris were in the uncomfortable position of being caught in the middle of the Great Game, as the main group of Indian subjects of the British crown engaged in regular travel between British and Russian territory.

The attitude of the Sindwork merchants to British rule was quite different. Unlike the Shikarpuris, they had enjoyed a close relationship with the Talpur rulers in pre-annexation Sind, and did not therefore particularly welcome the British, especially since they did not gain anything from the new regime. But they were quick to perceive the benefits they could derive from the forging of closer connections with Bombay, once Sind was made part of the Bombay Presidency in 1847. And after they embarked on their long-distance maritime travels, from 1860 onwards, they did not hesitate to demand protection from the British authorities, whenever required.

At this stage, it is necessary to pay some attention to the legal situation of Indians travelling abroad. After 1858, all residents of British India (and to a large extent, the residents of the Indian states) were entitled to

[1] It was reported in a 'Supplementary notice on the states of Toorkistan', enclosed in *Reports and Papers, Political, etc.*, pp. 46–50, that at some point the emir of Bukhara had forbidden the cremation of dead bodies in his dominions, leading to a partial exodus of Hindus. The disruption caused in trade and the protests of neighbouring states led the emir to remove quickly the restrictions so injudiciously imposed. The episode demonstrated that the Shikarpuris had some clout in Bukhara.

[2] See letter no. 379, 14 October 1857, from H. Bartle Frere, commissioner in Sind, to secretary to Government of Bombay reporting, on the authority of the lieutenant of police in Shikarpur, that 'on the news of the fall of Delhi being received at Shikarpur the Hindoo inhabitants of that town illuminated the bazaars in the City for three nights'. In letter no. 2510, 26 October 1857, the secretary to the Government of Bombay informed Bartle Frere that 'His Lordship in Council has derived great gratification from this intelligence', IOR, Political & Secret Department Records, Secret Correspondence with India 1792–1874, L/P&S/5/517.

crown protection. For them, the world divided itself into four groups of countries. In the territories under crown rule, they had, at least on paper, a right to travel and reside at will, without carrying any documents. In the territories of foreign countries which had normal diplomatic relations with Britain, they were also free to move without documents, but had to register themselves with the local British consulate if they wanted to benefit from the protection of the crown. One of the few exceptions to this situation was the Russian Empire, where foreigners had to have passports, and where no consular protection was available in Central Asian territories. However, in Central Asia the Russian authorities, before 1909, accepted as passports the certificates of identity which collectors in Sind were empowered to grant under a notification of 1863. These certificates had to be endorsed at the Russian consulate in Calcutta, but this was a mere formality. After 1909, Indians travelling to Russian territory had to provide themselves with proper passports. In some foreign countries, being a British subject carried with it extraterritorial privileges, such as the right to trade freely and the right to be tried by British consular courts in cases involving British subjects or by mixed courts in cases involving natives of the country. This was the case in the Ottoman Empire (including Egypt) prior to 1914 and in Morocco under a capitulatory regime which was abolished only in 1936, in Persia until 1928, in China between 1842 and 1943, and more briefly in Japan (until 1899) and in Siam (until 1909). On the whole, prior to the late 1890s, Indian merchants could travel quite freely across the world without documents (except in Russia).

Difficulties occurred in the 1890s when, following the example set by California, the Australian colonies as well as the Boer Republics and the colony of Natal started adopting anti-Asiatic legislation, which made the entry of Indians increasingly difficult. Other European colonies soon followed suit, and it became necessary for merchants and employees of merchant firms travelling abroad to provide themselves with certificates of identity proving their status as British subjects. The era of free travel was coming to a close. The First World War dealt it the final blow, and after 1917 all Indians travelling abroad had to be provided with passports. Even then, access to some countries, including the British dominions of Australia and South Africa, became increasingly difficult. After the First World War, the number of countries imposing restrictions on the entry of Indians continued to increase. This became a major constraint for the Sindwork firms, which needed men to constantly circulate between the network centre and the widely dispersed places of business. Being a British subject did not entail any more automatic freedom to travel; it became necessary to obtain practical help from the

British government to lift or limit restrictions on freedom of movement. Hence the need to organize to lobby the authorities.

The existence of these constraints led the Sind merchants to adopt a pragmatic attitude to British rule and to the British Empire. It left little place either for sentiment or for ideological considerations, and could be called 'instrumentalist'. It was summed up somewhat cynically by a governor of Sind, who wrote in 1938, *à propos* the Sindworkies: 'These Sindhi merchants . . . take no interest whatever in politics and all they care about is that the British Empire should be strong enough to afford protection when the foreign countries in which they have locked up their money are politically disturbed'.[3]

The British, for their part, were much less pragmatic. Their attitudes was strongly influenced by ideological considerations and racial prejudice. While, at first, they posed as liberators of the Hindus of Sind from the yoke of Muslim oppression, their attitude to the *banias* underwent profound changes at the end of the nineteenth century. Little attention has been paid to the ideological aspect of British attitudes to Indian *banias*. British official discourse on the plight greedy *banias* represented for the peasantry has often been accepted uncritically.[4] A closer look at it would, however, reveal how much it reflected the anti-Semitic prejudices of the squirearchy adapted to a slightly different context. It led British officials to entertain a dual view of the role of the *banias*. As moneylenders, they were considered a parasitical class, even if there were some dissenting voices in officialdom regarding this view. As traders, they could be acceptable, provided they conformed to certain 'ethical' rules, and therefore attitudes to them oscillated widely. But there was also an element of political expediency in the way British officials appraised Indian merchants outside India. If they were useful to the advancement of British economic and political interests, they had to be encouraged, whatever moral qualms one could have regarding the way they exploited the peasants. The attitude of the British authorities towards the Chettiar moneylenders in Burma is typical of this trend. Although the Chettiars were considered particularly greedy usurers, their settlement in the rice-growing areas of Lower Burma was encouraged and they got full protection from the law.

In the case of the Sind merchants, there was very little advantage to be derived from their activities. Once the British had abandoned their

[3] Graham, governor of Sind, to Linlithgow, letter no. 52, 26 May 1938, Oriental and India Office Collections of the British Library, European Manuscripts, Linlithgow Papers, MSS Eur. F 125, vol. 93.
[4] Even an author like D. Hardiman, in his otherwise interesting *Feeding the Banya: Peasants and Usurers in Western India*, Delhi, 1996, tends to accept rather uncritically British officials' strictures on the *banias*.

dreams of the Central Asian market, the activities of the Shikarpuris in the region were not very important to them. The major way in which they could be used was as informants and spies. Only in Southeastern Iran could the Shikarpuri merchants be used to advance British economic interests, but the relationship was not always a happy one, as illustrated by the failure of official efforts to develop trade between India and Seistan. As far as the Sindworkies were concerned, they were of even less consequence. The goods they sold were Indian and other Asian craft products, and no British interest was at stake. They also tended to operate partly in non-British colonial territories. British attitudes to the Sind merchants, prior to the First World War, were marked by a mixture of ignorance and indifference, while officials expressed some measure of puzzlement at the legal complications created by the problem of Shikarpuri successions in Russian Central Asia. It is significant that in 1917, when the question of the position of British subjects in Russia came up for review, a high official at the India Office acknowledged that he was not aware of the existence of a large Shikarpuri community in Central Asia.[5] And yet there were hundreds of files on Shikarpuri successions lying in the office. Apparently, nobody had ever bothered to go through them in a systematic way. They had been treated on a purely *ad hoc* basis.

This remarkable pattern of official ignorance deserves to be noticed, in view of current discourses about 'colonial knowledge'. It shows that the colonial bureaucracy was particularly good at retaining information at the lower echelons and not passing it along the chain of command. Information about merchant networks was collected by the district collectors of Sukkur and Hyderabad, because they had to deal on a regular basis with practical problems arising out of the operations of the merchants. A good example is the enquiry conducted by the collector of Sukkur, Rieu, in Shikarpur about the question of merchant successions in Bukhara. Some of this information reached the level of the commissioner in Sind, but a lot of it was lost in transmission from the commissioner to the Bombay government. To the authorities in Bombay, Sind was a peripheral and slightly marginal province which evoked only occasional interest, and the Bombay bureaucracy wanted to know as little as possible about it. The Government of India was even less interested. While a lot of information was collected about the

---

[5] See Minute Paper from Secret Department dated 6 June 1917 by an unidentified official: 'We really know very little of these people . . . They all seem to be from Shikarpur. I had no idea that there were thousands of them'. IOR, Political & Secret Department Separate (or Subject) Files, 'British consular representation in Central Asia', L/P& S/10/ 247.

merchants, it was never systematically processed into knowledge, and the upper echelons of government in Bombay, Calcutta (or Delhi) and London remained largely unaware of the existence of these wide-ranging networks, as long as they did not create political problems. The merchants themselves kept as low a profile as possible and did everything to avoid attracting too much attention from the authorities.

Being caught in the Great Game was a difficult situation for the Shikarpuris, but they nevertheless managed to survive relatively unscathed. They even derived some indirect benefits from the Anglo-Russian rivalry, as the desire of the Russians not to antagonize the British led them to devote particular attention to the legal problems created by Shikarpuri successions. It is doubtful whether so much time would have been devoted to the question by the Russian bureaucracy, had there not been such a tension between the two empires. It was largely British insistence that led the Russians into pressurising the Bukharan authorities to lengthen the legal delay within which claims could be presented. Why did the British take an interest in the question, given the fact that no British interest was directly at stake? Considerations of prestige, of *izzat*, seem to have been uppermost in dictating British responses. It was unacceptable that in the dominions of the czar, British subjects, even if they were scoundrels (and that is clearly what most British officials thought of the Shikarpuri moneylenders) should not be treated fairly. Hence the decision to entrust the Consulate General in St Petersburg with the task of overseeing the question, in the absence of a British consulate in Central Asia. British intervention on the whole ensured fair treatment to the families of Shikarpuris who died in Central Asia, at least those who chose to operate through the official channels. British protection was not as effective however in regard to the activities of the Shikarpuris during their lifetime. When Shikarpuris were arrested by the Russian authorities for breach of the anti-usury laws, and, in some cases, condemned to transportation to Siberia, the British authorities did not intervene on their behalf.

The improvement in Anglo-Russian relations after 1907 following the conclusion of the Triple Entente did not apparently benefit the Shikarpuris. Russian suspicions appear even to have been heightened, and measures against Shikarpuris became more common. During his meeting with his Russian counterpart Sazonov in 1912, Lord Grey, the secretary of state for foreign affairs, presented a long list of grievances on behalf of British Indians,[6] but little seems to have been done by the Russian authorities to address them.

[6] See Chapter 3, note 48.

The level of protection Shikarpuris (and other Indian merchants) received from the British authorities in the course of their Central Asian venture was less than that given to most British Indians living in territories under non-British sovereignty, but it was nevertheless useful. Without any British protection, it is doubtful that Shikarpuris could have avoided a mass expulsion in the guberniia of Turkistan, the situation in the Emirate of Bukhara being altogether different.

In return for this protection, Shikarpuris were expected to act at least as informants and to report on happenings inside Russian territory. It seems that British officials were in the habit of interviewing returning merchants to gather information, though on occasion things went further. The evidence of a civil suit against the secretary of state for India before the Sukkur-Larkana district court throws an interesting light on a little known episode of the Great Game. Suit no. 15 of 1907, dated 9 August 1907, was brought by two prominent Shikarpuri merchants, Seth Chimansing Ramsing and Seth Gulabsing Ramsing (who are familiar to us for their role in the failed trading venture in Seistan) against the secretary of state.[7] The plaintiffs claimed 40,000 rupees as damages for breach of contract. Their claim was that in August 1903 Seth Chimansing, who had gone to Simla to discuss with the finance member of the government the terms of a loan, was contacted by the commander-in-chief, Lord Kitchener. They contended that on 8 August 1903 Seth Chimansing had signed a contract with the commander-in-chief on the following conditions:

(1) that the plaintiff would send his agent Chuharsing to Central Asia for intelligence purposes on payment of 10,000 rupees by Government; (2) that for the above-mentioned concerns the plaintiff would employ his men in different places for which he would be given 10,000 rupees by the Government at Shikarpur; (3) that the plaintiff would send one man from Shikarpur to Kabul to carry on the same business for which he would get sufficient compensation from the Government; (4) that the plaintiff would send his men as tea merchants who would outwardly carry on tea business; (5) that after the lapse of the above-mentioned period the Government would give at Shikarpur a fair compensation to the plaintiffs for their own and their Agent Chuharsing's labour, trouble, capital and risk.

They went on to contend that 'on 30 July 1904 the defendant (Kitchener), without assigning any reason, wrote to the plaintiffs, enjoining that they should stop their business as the Government needed no help from them'. This, they commented, 'was contrary to the conditions of

---

[7] Enclosed in letter no. 6314, 23 September 1907, from E. L. Sale, collector of Sukkur, to the commissioner in Sind. BPP, October 1907, Serial no. A 56.

the contract'. They complained of substantial losses and claimed 40,000 rupees as compensation.

It is difficult to assess this extraodinary document,[8] a rare instance of a suit filed for 'breach of spying contract'. The fact that it was published in the Bombay Political Proceedings is in itself quite astonishing. In an accompanying letter, the collector of Sukkur explained that he had not treated the matter confidentially since it was in any case public. Is the claim by the Shikarpuri merchant that he had entered into a proper contract with the commander-in-chief credible? It seems highly unlikely that such an august official as Lord Kitchener himself would have directly dealt with a Shikarpuri merchant. What is plausible is that the merchant had some kind of informal conversation with the commander-in-chief or, more plausibly, with one of his aides, in the course of which they might have toyed with the idea of using trading as a cover for spying activities. This seems an indirect confirmation that this was not an unknown practice. It is also highly plausible that Kitchener might have promised a pecuniary compensation; Shikarpuris did not spy on the Russians out of any patriotic sentiment, but must have treated the matter as an ordinary business transaction, the sale of information, which, for merchants, is the most precious commodity of all.

The document, apart from confirming that Shikarpuri merchants did spy on the Russians in Central Asia, is interesting in what it reveals of the mentality of a big Shikarpuri trader. The merchant did not hesitate to sue the most powerful man in the land, a kind of demi-god, the nemesis of Lord Curzon himself, before a district court in British India. This shows either unusual courage or complete unawareness of the realities of power (in November, however, it was announced that the suit had been withdrawn). Basically it betrays a level of political naivety, which is rather unexpected coming from a prominent merchant in a town like Shikarpur whose traders had always known how to exploit political connections to their advantage.

Political naivety seems to have been an enduring characteristic of Shikarpuri merchants. Evidence from southern Iran in 1912 is further confirmation of it. Shikarpuri merchants had suffered losses due to widespread insecurity on the Bandar Abbas–Kirman road, and they were seeking compensation. One group of merchants sent a telegram addressed 'to the Private Secretary to His Imperial Majesty King-Emperor George, Calcutta [sic]', in which they asked the king to direct the Foreign Office to take immediate steps to ensure their safety and

---

[8] It escaped the attention of an historian of British intelligence activities in Central Asia. See L. P. Morris, 'British Secret Service Activity in Khorrassan, 1887–1908', *Historical Journal*, vol. 27, no. 3, 1984, pp. 657–5.

suitable compensation!⁹ In 1918, a Shikarpuri merchant, filing a claim for compensation with the government for losses sustained during the Russian Civil War, blamed the Russian authorities for not having given him advance notice of their intention to bomb the town of Kermine in the Emirate of Bukhara!¹⁰ Shikarpuris continued, well into the 1930s, to file claims for compensation from Soviet authorities for properties confiscated in Central Asia in the apparent hope that they would actually get something. They seem to have been taken completely by surprise when the Russian Revolution came to Central Asia, and therefore lost practically everything which had not been transferred prior to 1917. In the 1930s they were similarly unprepared when an anti-Chinese rising in Sinkiang turned into an anti-Shikarpuri pogrom in some localities.

It thus appears that Shikarpuris were not very good at evaluating political risk. In spite of the dangers lurking, they did not start disinvesting from Central Asia after 1914, and had to bear huge losses when the collapse came. Such lack of political skills on the part of a community which had for long thrived on political connections is somewhat puzzling, as if political change had been too quick and had left the merchants behind. They paid a high price for their lack of political acumen.

Shikarpuris never managed to organize themselves in an efficient manner to defend their interests with the British authorities. The merchant *panchayat* of Shikarpur did not play the role of a pressure group, and as a result the British could easily ignore the Shikarpuri merchants. In 1912–13, an association called Hindu Jamiat manifested itself in connection with the troubles in southern Iran, but it seems to have had an ephemerous existence.

On occasion, however, Shikarpuris benefited from a direct intervention on their behalf on the part of British consular representatives. This was the case in particular in Sinkiang in 1907, when, following widespread anti-Shikarpuri agitation by local Uighurs in some localities of southern Sinkiang, George Macartney, the British representative at

---

[9] Telegram from Lilaram, Isardas and others, Shikarpur, to Private Secretary His Imperial Majesty King-Emperor George, Calcutta, 3 January 1912, enclosed in no. 114 of 1912 from the Government of India in the Foreign Department Secret External to the secretary of state for India, 7 November 1912, IOR, Political & Secret Department Separate (or Subject) Files, L/P&S/10/214.

[10] In a petition, 14 August 1918, addressed to the under-secretary to the Government of Bombay in the Political Department, Doolamal and Radhomal, two Shikarpuri traders complained that they had suffered 'an exorbitant loss . . . owing to such treatment of the Russian Government by suddenly bombarding the City of Karimina without giving (them) any knowledge, where (their) goods, cash and chattels were stored . . .'. BPP, October 1918, Serial no. A 385. See above, Chapter 3.

Kashgar, convinced the *taotai*, the local Chinese official at Kashgar, to issue a proclamation enjoining Chinese subjects to live in good understanding with the Hindus.[11] On the other hand, when Macartney tried to intervene with the Chinese provincial authorities to obtain the recall of measures aimed at prohibiting Chinese subjects from borrowing from Hindus, he was rebuked by his superior, Younghusband.[12] Shikarpuris did not succeed in exercising any direct influence on British policies, even when they were of direct concern to them.

The Sindworkies did, however, fare better for themselves, although they were relative latecomers to politics. No evidence has come to light of any involvement of these merchants in any kind of political activity at home or abroad prior to the First World War. They pursued their trading activities almost everywhere in the world without attracting the attention of the British authorities. When individual merchants or firms got into difficulties, they resorted to petitioning. Thus in 1898, when the parliament of the Colony of Victoria in Australia seemed bent on passing an Immigration Restriction Bill which threatened to jeopardize the interests of the large Sindwork firm of Wassiamall Assomull, the manager of the Melbourne branch petitioned both the secretary of state for India and the secretary of state for the Colonies to ask them to intervene.[13] Although he got a sympathetic response from Lord George Hamilton,[14] nothing was done by the British government to dissuade the Australian colonies from adopting measures which would limit the freedom of movement of the Indian subjects of the crown within the empire. Following the passing of the Immigration Restriction Act by the new Commonwealth of Australia in 1901, imposing a dictation test on would-be entrants, the intervention of the Government of India resulted in a small concession to Indian sentiments in the form of an exemption of certain kinds of travellers, including merchants, from the infamous

---

[11] See copy of letter no. 109–G, 9 July 1907, from Sir Francis Younghusband, resident in Kashmir, to Sir Louis Dane, secretary to the Government of India in the Foreign Department, in which Macartney's intervention is mentioned, and which encloses a translation of the *taotai*'s proclamation. IOR, Political & Secret Correspondence with India 1875–1911, L/P&S/7/205.

[12] See Younghusband to Dane, 23 September 1907, IOR, L/P&S/7/207.

[13] See above, Chapter 4.

[14] The under-secretary of state for India wrote to the under-secretary of state for the colonies in a letter dated 18 July 1899: 'Lord George Hamilton thinks it possible that if the very reasonable representations of the memorialist are supported by Her Majesty's Government, the legislation of Victoria may consent to further extend the concession proposed to be made in favour of such perfectly unobjectionable immigrants as are employed by the memorialist and his class, and to modify the provisions of the stringency of which he complains.' IOR, File J & P 797/1899, copy in India, Revenue and Agriculture (Emigration) Proceedings, December 1899, Serial no. A 4.

test.[15] But the term 'merchant' was interpreted in a restrictive sense, to cover only independent merchants with their own capital, excluding from the purview of the Act salaried employees and managers. When in 1908 the firm of Wassiamall Assomull tried to send a new manager to Australia, he was refused a visa on the ground that he was not a 'merchant' and the Government of India refused to intervene on behalf of the firm.[16] Sindwork merchants in the Cape Colony were more successful in their protests against the Hawkers Licences Act of 1906. Their petition to the governor resulted in their being *de facto* exempted from the law.[17] But this was an isolated victory. After 1917, similarly restrictive measures were taken in many colonial territories and independent countries, and a new kind of organization was needed to defend the interests of the merchants.

The First World War was an important turning point in the relationship between the Sind merchants and the British authorities. The existence of a group of Indian merchants so widely dispersed across the world came apparently as a surprise to the British. They became worried that trading connections could be used for subversive purposes. At the time of the San Francisco conspiracy case, when Indian revolutionaries in the USA belonging to a group calling itself the Ghadr Party were accused of conniving with Germany at instigating an anti-British rising in India, and Indian communities abroad fell under suspicion of being hotbeds of subversion, a fantastic idea seems to have entered the minds of a certain number of British officials, that is, that the Sindworkies served as a conduit for funds and propaganda for the Ghadr Party. The

---

[15] In a letter to the viceroy of India, 18 August 1904, the governor-general of Australia, Lord Northcote, informed him that 'the Minister of State for External Affairs in the Commonwealth Government has had under consideration the question of so administering the Immigration Restriction Act as to afford an opportunity for Indian merchants, students and tourist travellers to enter the Commonwealth temporarily without being subjected to any restrictions, with the result that it has now been decided that any persons bona fide of the classes mentioned desirous of visiting Australia will be admitted to the Commonwealth, provided they are in possession of Passports from the Indian Government . . .'. India Revenue and Agriculture (Emigration) Proceedings, October 1904, Serial no. A 1.

[16] An application for a passport to Australia was submitted in November 1908 by one Hemandas Rupchand, who had been hired as assistant manager by the firm of Wassiamall Assomull & Co. Although he was not identified as a 'merchant', the commissioner in Sind requested that he be treated as one. BPP, November 1908, Serial no. B 231. In a letter, 20 January 1909, from the assistant secretary to the Government of India in the Foreign Department to the secretary to the Government of Bombay in the Political Department, the Government of India stated that they were unable to approach the Australian government on the lines suggested, and that it would be unadvisable to ask for further concessions from Australia. BPP, February 1909, Serial no. A 7.

[17] Bhan and Pachai (eds.), *Documentary History of Indian South Africans*, p. 50.

British consul in Panama, Sir Claude Mallet, became convinced at the beginning of 1917 that some employees and managers of the Sindwork firms at Colon were members of the Ghadr Party and were planning to go to Singapore to instigate a rising there.[18] These men travelled through Tenerife, from where the British consul reported that they were engaged in normal trading activities.[19] This did not calm Mallet's fears. Although reports received from British consular officials and intelligence agents in different places did not confirm the theory of a widespread conspiracy and Sir David Petrie, an Indian police official sent on a tour of the Indian communities in the Far East, reported in December 1916 that in Canton, 'the considerable number of Sindhi merchants are described as mostly engrossed in business, respectable and reputedly loyal',[20] Mallet continued to monitor closely the movements of Sindhi employees leaving Panama. About one of them, a pedlar working for the firm of D. Chellaram, he wrote: 'Nathirmal's influence is nil, but he is a contributor to the revolutionary fund, as are all the employees working for this firm and the sum total collected from them is remitted to San Francisco from time to time'.[21] In a memorandum dated March 1917, he gave a list of firms in Hong Kong alleged to have contributed to a fund for the purchase of munitions for an armed rising in the Far East.[22] The list included, among others, the well-known firms of Pohoomull Bros., D. Chellaram, M. Dialdas and J. T. Chanrai. The total contribution was said to be some (Hong Kong) $45,000. There was nothing substantial to support these allegations, except for reports from informers. In a letter

[18] See 'Memorandum no. 3 on East Indian sedition and Japanese espionage on the Isthmus of Panama', enclosed in Sir C. Mallet's despatch no. 2, 10 January 1917, PRO, Foreign Office Records, Foreign Office General Correspondence (Political), United States File 1220, 1917, FO 371/3064: 'Choturmall Asudamall of Hyderabad has applied for a passport to go to India via Gibraltar . . . With him is associated Wadhoomal . . . These two men are dangerous and belong to the Gadar [sic] Party. The journey is said to have for its object the raising of a revolt in Singapore. Choturmall is to go to Hong Kong, where arms and ammunition are concealed with three firms (one of them J. T. Chanrai or the Agents of this firm), which Choturmall, with accomplices, will endeavour to remove to Singapore.'
[19] The British consul in Tenerife reported to the Foreign Office on 15 February 1917 about the arrival of three Sindhi merchants, including Choturmall and Wadhumal, who stayed at a house belonging to the firm of J. T. Chanrai & Co. The manager of the Tenerife branch of the firm, interviewed by the consul, stated that they worked for the firm and were loyal subjects of the crown. The consul added that British Indian commercial employees regularly passed through the island on their way to Spain or elsewhere. Letter enclosed in United States File 1220, FO 371/3065.
[20] 'Note on a recent tour of the Far East' by Sir David Petrie, 4 December 1916, enclosed in File J & P (S) 1319, from India Office, 23 March 1917, copy in *ibid*.
[21] 'List of East Indians who left Panama for India via Hong Kong on Kiyo Maru', enclosed in Sir C. Mallet's despatch no. 85, 6 November 1917, *ibid*.
[22] See 'Memorandum dated 7 March 1917 on East Indian sedition in Panama', enclosed in Sir C. Mallet's despatch no. 11, 7 March 1917, *ibid*.

to the India Office, an official of the Home Department in the Government of India wrote, about the role of the Panama Sindhis:

The Government of India are aware that the partners and employees of such firms abroad are in many cases seditiously inclined and probably find it lucrative to keep in with the revolutionary party. We also know that they subscribe money, help to circulate seditious papers and accommodate plotters in distress; but we have no evidence that any firm is constantly using its business organisation to further the ends of revolution.[23]

This was a relatively moderate assessment (although it was difficult to understand how helping the Ghadr Party could be a 'lucrative' activity), but it cut no ice with Mallet and other officials who believed in conspiracy theories. The director of Criminal Intelligence, C. R. Cleveland, in an introduction to a 'Report on Indian Sedition in the Far East in 1917', wrote: 'The amount of disloyalty among the Sind Worki firms ... which are scattered about all over the world, have been found to be extensive beyond reason or comprehension.'[24] Lists were compiled of addresses to which Ghadr literature was sent, and these lists included many Sindhi firms. It was well known however that the Ghadrites sent their literature free to all Indians abroad whose addresses they could get.

All these fantasies culminated in an extraordinary piece of self-deception. In August 1918, the War Office sent the Foreign Office the decoded version of a code telegram sent by the Colon branch of the firm of J. T. Chanrai to the Tenerife branch of the same firm.[25] The telegram was ostentatiously about the quality and price of Panama hats, but the decoded version read: 'Advise me when is the time fixed for the Army to march from Persia. Received letter from Sher Singh; Nabha is ready to help. I still have 4,000 left. Have received offers to blow up the English Legation; considering how to do it. Cannot get dynamite ...', suggesting that these Sindhi merchants were engaged in a deep conspiracy with international ramifications. There was an added comment that J. T. Chanrai of Colon 'were known as supporters of the Indian revolutionists'. In September 1918 50 copies of a secret memorandum about Sindhi merchants[26] were printed and sent to British consular offices

---

[23] Letter from J. H. du Boulay, of the Home Department of the Government of India to Seton, secretary to the Public & Judicial Department of the India Office, 20 February 1917, copy in *ibid*.

[24] Introduction by C. R. Cleveland, Director, Criminal Intelligence, to 'Report on Indian Sedition in the Far East in 1917', File P/2375, IOR, Political & Secret Department Records, Departmental Papers: Political & Secret Annual Files 1912–1930, L/P& S/11/136.

[25] S. Newby, of War Office to R. A. C. Sperling, Foreign Office, 29 August 1918, enclosed in PRO, Foreign Office Records, Foreign Office General Correspondence (Political), United States File 327 of 1918, FO 371/3425.

[26] Enclosed in Newby to Sperling, 7 September 1918. Ibid., FO 371/3426. See Appendix IV.

around the world. It had been compiled by the MI5 at the War Office. It gave a list of suspicious facts about the behaviour of Sindhi merchants abroad, including Chanrai's telegram, but the conclusion was fairly cautious:

As yet there is no evidence that the Sindhi merchant firms, as such, are engaged in any seditious conspiracy . . . It is . . . not surprising to find German inspired propaganda passing along the channels offered by the trade activities of these firms. Whether the Sindhis concerned have deliberately lent their services in this connection in order to assist the enemy, or whether, being Banias by caste and very susceptible to fear, they are more or less the unconscious tools of the Indo-German revolutionary intriguers cannot yet be definitely stated.

Fifty more copies of the memorandum were sent a few days later, but by the end of October the War Office wrote that they did not think that 'the matter is of sufficient importance to justify the expense of printing new copies, especially in view of the result of the enquiry regarding the "Chanrai" message.'[27] It was obvious that the storm had blown over.

The whole episode could be treated as farcical, and as a supplementary proof of the tendency of officials to panic in times of war, but it also revealed real fears among British officials of the subversive potential offered by the existence of worldwide merchant networks from India. Suddenly the British awoke to the reality of a Sindhi dispersion which was almost fifty years old. As far as the attitudes of the Sindwork merchants are concerned, a distinction should be made between individual attitudes and the policies of firms. Sindwork firms had no reason to be pro-German. In economic terms, they could not possibly derive any benefits from a German victory and British defeat. The principals of the firms at that time were still solidly loyalist, reflecting the fact that, prior to 1920, the impact of Indian nationalism was very limited in Sind. On the other hand, individual employees and managers of the branches of Sindwork firms could be influenced by revolutionary ideas. Sindhis are Nanakpanthis, i.e. non-Khalsa Sikhs, but they are very close to the Khalsa Sikhs. Therefore it is quite plausible that some of them might have been influenced by the propaganda of the Ghadr Party, especially in Panama, where there were quite a few Sikhs who were Ghadr sympathizers. What seems to have worried the British most, however, is that they discovered that there were rich Indian merchants with international connections, capable of moving funds from one part of the world to another, and that they knew nothing about them.

The episode does not however appear to have influenced official attitudes in a significant way. It was soon forgotten, and, after the war, when Sindwork merchants applied to the authorities to intervene on

[27] Newby to Sperling, 23 October 1918, *ibid*.

their behalf in different contexts, they were on the whole favourably received. This was not due to a change of heart on the part of the British regarding the *banias*. Anti-*bania* sentiment continued to be widespread among British officialdom, but they did not dictate policies to the same extent as before. From 1919 onwards, the growth of a powerful nationalist movement in India forced the British to pay more attention to the plight of Indians abroad, so as to avoid giving pretexts for the growth of anti-British feeling in India. The attention of the Government of India and of the India Office focused mostly around the situation in South Africa, and, after 1920, in Kenya. Another flashpoint was Zanzibar in the late 1930s. In these three territories, there were Sindhi merchants, but they were a very small component of large Indian communities, and their specific preoccupations did not attract any attention.

In three territories, however, it was the problems met by Sindhi merchants which led to regular interventions on the part of the Government of India and the India Office. These territories were a British colony, Gibraltar, where Sindhi merchants were practically the only Indians; an American colony, the Philippines, where Sindhis represented only one half of the Indian community (Punjabi Sikhs accounting for the rest), but where they attracted the bulk of official attention; and an 'independent' country, the Republic of Panama, where the Sindhis accounted for only a small part of the Indian population (Sikhs were much more numerous there, and there were also Gujaratis and Bengali Muslims), but where the importance of their economic interests also gave them a disproportionate share of official attention. In these three territories, the Indian population was small, and that is why the problems of these Indian communities never attracted much scholarly interest.

The problems the Sindworkies confronted in these territories seem to have been a major incentive to the creation of an organization called the Sindwork Merchants' Association, which became a vehicle for lobbying. Founded around 1920, it later became part of the Federation of Indian Chambers of Commerce and Industry (FICCI), the main all-India business association. It systematically intervened with the authorities in New Delhi to defend the interests of the Sindwork merchants when they were threatened, and often obtained some success. The authorities in New Delhi were, however, powerless to directly influence foreign governments or even British colonial governors. To be successful, pressure had to come from the imperial Government itself. This meant that the India Office had to pressurise the Foreign Office or the Colonial Office into taking an interest in the matter, and that was not always easy. As far as foreign countries were concerned, a lot could depend on the attitude of the local British consul, who was the man on the spot. The attitudes of consuls to the plight of Sind merchants could vary. Official records show that the consuls in Manila and Panama, two of the major trouble spots, took to heart the problems of the Sindwork merchants and even went out of their way to help them.

The Sindworkies were also able to use the close connections that some of them established with the Congress Party to pressurise the colonial government into intervening on their behalf. The authorities in Delhi were increasingly wary of giving pretexts to nationalists to criticise them on the grounds that they did not defend the interests of Indians abroad with sufficient energy. Links between the Congress and the Sindwork merchants appear to have been forged in the early 1920s at the time of the Khilafat and non-cooperation movement,[28] which was the first mass movement in Sind. The Hyderabad District Congress Committee became heavily dependent on financial contributions from Sindwork merchants.[29] Amongst contributors, the most prominent was Seth Pratap Dialdas,[30] the principal of the large firm of M. Dialdas & Sons, who himself had links with Gandhi. Besides, the two Sindhi politicians who became influential figures in all-India politics were from Hyderabad and had close links to the Sindwork merchants. One was Jairamdas Daulatram Alamchandani, a Hyderabadi Amil who was a prominent member of the Congress right wing.[31] In the 1920s he often intervened on behalf of the Sindwork merchants. The other figure was Acharya Kripalani, also a Hyderabadi Amil. He did not have such close links to the Sindwork merchants, but could occasionally take an interest in their problems. At the provincial level, the Congress Party was not much influenced by the Sindwork merchants, the reason being that the latter had few economic interests in the province; Amils and other groups of *banias* had more influence. But they had some clout at the national level, and it helped them pressurise the Government of India into intervening on their behalf. Most of the lobbying was done through the Sindwork Merchants' Association, which was in close touch with various local associations of Sindhi merchants in different countries.

[28] The money collected in Hyderabad for the Tilak Swaraj Fund in 1920 came mostly from 'rich Sindwork merchants'. See B. G. Kunte (ed.), *Source Material for a History of the Freedom Movement*, vol. V, *History of the Non-cooperation Movement in Sind 1919–1924. Collected from Maharashtra State Records*, Bombay, 1977, p. 49.
[29] *Ibid.*, p. 125.
[30] See the entry on Bhai Pratap Dialdas in *Dictionary of National Biography (Supplement)*, vol. I, ed. N. R. Ray, Calcutta, 1986, pp. 361–2.
[31] At the Seventh Sind Provincial Congress Conference at Sukkur in April 1920, he was the most prominent pro-Besantine delegate from Hyderabad. The Besantine party was strong mainly in Hyderabad, while delegates from the rest of Sind were generally Tilakite. See Kunte, *Source Material*, pp. 14–15.

The development of associations in many places where there were colonies of Sindwork merchants, and the umbrella role played by the Sindwork Merchants' Association helped a pattern of collective action to emerge to defend the interests of the merchants. But individualism remained entrenched, and firms still resorted to direct intervention with officials and to petitioning when they felt they had been badly treated. Thus, when in 1939 the firm of K. Chellaram & Sons felt they had been unjustly treated by the comptroller of customs on the Gold Coast about a breach of quota regulations which they claimed had been involuntary, they raised the matter directly with the secretary of state for the colonies in London through interviews and a petition,[32] and they obtained partial redress.

While they did not hesitate to use their connections to the nationalist movement to pressurise the British government, the Sindwork merchants were careful, when they addressed the authorities, to express feelings of loyalty to the crown, sometimes in an even hyperbolic manner. When the Sindwork Merchants' Association requested the authorities to intervene on behalf of Sindwork merchants in the Canary Islands who faced discriminatory measures on the part of the Spanish authorities, they wrote 'We are always told and reminded that as Subjects of the most Powerful Empire we can always claim the full rights of free entry and bona fide trade in any part of the world and that our rights will be jealously safeguarded.'[33] Loyalist sentiments were still widespread among these merchants, but did not preclude pragmatic attitudes when interests were at stake.

This is illustrated by the attitudes of many Sindhi merchants towards Subhas Chandras Bose and the Indian National Army in Japanese-occupied territories during the Second World War. There were important colonies of Sindwork merchants in most territories occupied by the Japanese, i.e. Burma, Malaya, Singapore, the Dutch East Indies, the Philippines, Hong Kong and French Indochina. Many of these merchants had close economic links to Japanese firms, but the Japanese occupation as such did not bring them any particular benefits. Their links to the Japanese nevertheless helped them survive, in particular by engaging in black market activities, but they had no special place in the 'co-prosperity sphere of Greater East Asia'. Some were drawn into the

[32] See 'The Petition of Messrs K. Chellaram & Sons', addressed to the secretary of state for the colonies, 19 June 1939, enclosed in Governor of Gold Coast, to the secretary of state for the colonies, dated 2 August 1939, PRO, Colonial Office Records, Colonies (General) Economic Original Correspondence, CO 852/223/2.
[33] See letter, 12 October 1935 from M. K. Chandanmal, president, Sindwork Merchants Association to the commissioner in Sind (through the collector of Hyderabad). PRO, Foreign Office Records, General Correspondence (Political), Spain, FO 371/20561.

orbit of the India Independence League and the Indian National Army. A list of delegates from East Asia attending a conference of the India Independence League in July 1943[34] contains at least four Sindhi names, those of delegates representing Manila, Java, Sumatra and Bangkok. At a general meeting of businesses and Chettiars for collection of funds held on 25 October 1943 in Singapore, one of the speakers was the manager of the local branch of K. A. J. Chotirmall & Co., a Mr Udharam, who is mentioned elsewhere in connection with funds collected for the Japanese Red Cross.[35] In Singapore too, a Mr Khiamal from the firm of L. Khiamal is said to have been close to Subhas Bose and to have helped collect some $200,000 for the INA.[36] A Sindwork merchant from Indonesia, 'Chacha' Tejumal was a member of the inner circle of Subhas Bose advisers and in Indonesia at least forty Sindhi merchants joined the INA and contributed millions of rupees to the movement in 1943–44.[37] In the Philippines, according to a British consular report of May 1945,[38] Sindhis had massively engaged in collaboration with the Japanese. They were involved in what was known as the 'buy–sell racket', purchasing goods at cheap prices from the Japanese surplus stores which they sold to the Filipino population at a very high profit. They invested these profits mostly in real estate in Manila, and they lost most of their assets in the destruction of the city in 1945. However, even after that disaster, they appeared not to be destitute, which showed that their accumulated wealth must have been fairly considerable.

It should not be forgotten however that, from 1942 onwards, the managers and employees of the Sindwork firms in the Far East were completely cut off from their principals in Hyderabad, from whom they used previously to receive instructions on a daily basis, and now had to make their own decisions. The participation of employees and managers of Sindwork firms in the activities of the India Independence League and the Indian National Army cannot therefore be construed as proof of the complicity of the firms with the brand of nationalism associated with Bose. According to what local Indian leaders told the British consul in

---

[34] From Report by a British agent on the Indian Independence Movement in East Asia, 25 November 1945, File no. 164/H/INA Papers, Ministry of Defence Historical Section, reproduced in T. R. Sareen (comp.), *Select Documents on Indian National Army*, Delhi, 1988, p. 280.
[35] *Ibid.*, pp. 277, 291.
[36] Bhardwaj, *Sindhis through the Ages*, p. 355.
[37] *Ibid.*, p. 317.
[38] Letter from British consulate-general, Manila, to Foreign Office, 25 May 1945, enclosed in PRO, Foreign Office Records, General Correspondence (Consular), File 654 of 1945, FO 369/3161.

Manila,[39] 'the whole community was compelled by the Japanese to join the India Independence League . . . under threat of having to close their businesses and of being treated as enemy subjects'. The consul was not totally convinced by this explanation and, while he conceded that 'the rank and file may . . . have been coerced into collaboration', he underlined that 'many leaders of the community were active propagandists for the Japanese cause and contributed to anti-Allied funds'.

In Europe and North Africa, some Sindwork merchants were caught by the outbreak of the Second World War in German-occupied and Italian territory. Some evacuees from Gibraltar on their way to India were captured by the Germans after their ship had been sunk near the Cape of Good Hope.[40] The Germans treated them as prisoners-of-war and no attempt was made to enrol them. There is no evidence that Sindwork merchants outside the Far East displayed any sympathy for the cause of the Axis powers. One employee of a Sindwork firm who had been interned in a camp in the German-occupied part of Italy was even shot for having aided the Italian underground. This tends to suggest that the alignment of some Sindwork merchants with Subhas Bose in the Far East had more to do with preserving their own life and livelihood than with deep-seated pro-Japanese sympathies, though this does not rule out the possibility that some of them had a strong commitment to Indian independence.

The major incentive to the Sindwork merchants to organize themselves as a lobby and to seek political influence was the spread of restrictive immigration legislation across the world which made it increasingly difficult for the firms to move personnel around. In this struggle they were able to score some successes.

The Sindwork merchants and the fight against immigration restrictions after 1920

Prior to 1917, immigration restrictions in various territories and countries only marginally affected the Sindwork merchants. South Africa and Australia were the two countries in the British Empire which pioneered anti-Indian legislation. They were, however, relatively marginal areas of operation for the Sindworkies. In Australia, there was only one significant firm, Wassiamall Assomull, which employed eighty people in

---

[39] *Ibid.*
[40] See 'General note on evacuation of Indians from within war zone' in IOR, Public & Judicial Department Collections, Collection 110/H1, 'Evacuation of Indians from within War Zones', L/P&J/8/399. A list of eight Sindhi merchants of Gibraltar, passengers of SS *Kemmerdine*, who were captured by the Germans, is appended.

Melbourne in 1898. Following the adoption of the Immigration Restriction Act by the Commonwealth, it had to reorganize itself by using mostly locally recruited staff. In South Africa, where there were many more firms, they seem also to have adapted by turning to locally recruited staff.

Outside those two white Dominions of the empire, problems arose only temporarily in Gibraltar, around 1899, when disputes between firms and their employees forced the authorities to repatriate some destitute men. This led them briefly to contemplate the adoption of restrictive measures on the entry of Indians into the territory,[41] but such projects were shelved following an intervention by the India Office.[42] The problem resurfaced in Gibraltar at the end of the First World War, following an influx of Sindhi traders and the opening of new shops, leading the governor, in 1919, to contemplate restrictive measures.[43] The Government of India, in a correspondence with the India Office, noted that 'employees and merchants belong to classes many of whom are unobjectionable and restriction contemplated is about to arouse outcry and seems unjustifiable'.[44] Apparently sensitive to these arguments, the India Office intervened with the Colonial Office to block the proposed measure. In this episode there is no trace of direct intervention by the Sindwork merchants themselves. It would seem that the Government of India acted on its own, without being subjected to any specific pressure. The volatile political situation in India in 1919 is probably sufficient to explain their attitude: they did not want to give any further cause for agitation to an Indian public which was already sufficiently aroused. If the intervention of the India Office was able to stave off the adoption of restrictive legislation, it did not deter the governor from taking *ad hoc* measures to limit the influx of Sindhis onto the Rock. In June 1920, the governor wrote to the secretary of state for the colonies:

I do not wish to interfere more than is necessary with the trade of firms long established here, but I consider that each of these Indian firms should be limited

[41] In a comment, appended to a letter dated 8 September 1899 to the secretary of state for the colonies, the governor of Gibraltar mooted the idea of an educational test on Indians of the type adopted in Natal. PRO, Colonial Office Records, Gibraltar Original Correspondence, CO 91/422.

[42] On 5 October 1899, the under-secretary of state for India wrote to the under-secretary of state for the colonies that the secretary of state for India 'would most earnestly deprecate the initiation in a Crown Colony of legislation avowedly based upon the Natal Act in question'. File J & P 1787/1899, copy in CO 91/423.

[43] The governor wrote to the secretary of state for the colonies on 9 August 1919 that he might contemplate refusing entry into Gibraltar even to British subjects. Ibid., CO 91/471.

[44] Telegram from viceroy, Home Department, to secretary of state, 25 January 1919, enclosed in J&P (S) 3052/19 from under-secretary of state, India Office to Under-secretary of State, Colonial Office, copy in CO 91/472.

to one shop and a small number of assistants. I therefore propose to refuse fresh permits of residence to Indians until the number resident here is reduced to reasonable proportions.[45]

In Gibraltar, the colonial authorities used the pretext of limited space to impose a limitation on the number of shops by firm, under an Alien Traders Ordinance which was passed in 1924, and raised only limited objections on the part of the Government of India[46] and the India Office. Such legislation regulated the movement of Indian personnel by a system of permits, but it did not on the whole negatively affect the operations of the firms.

A much more serious problem arose in connection with the Philippine Islands, and around that question, the newly founded Sindwork Merchants' Association manifested itself for the first time in the public arena as a lobby defending the interests of the Sindwork merchants. The problem in the Philippines stemmed from the passing of a restrictive immigration law by the US authorities, in February 1917, aimed specifically at hampering the movements of Indian 'subversives' who used Manila as a staging point between the Far East and San Francisco, where the Ghadr Party had its headquarters. Certain categories of people, in particular merchants, were specifically excluded from the purview of the Act, and for a few years it does not appear to have affected the operations of the Sindhi trading firms in the islands. In 1920, however, a more restrictive interpretation of the Act by the immigration authorities in Manila led to difficulties for employees of Sindwork firms when they tried to reenter the Philippines following a period spent in India. Some of them were refused entry, and some who were readmitted were on bond, liable to deportation at any moment. This affected the smooth working of the firms.

In a lengthy 'Memorandum regarding the position of British Indian Merchants in the Philippines under the existing immigration regulations', dated June 1921,[47] the British consul in Manila exposed the situation as it had been explained to him by the merchants. Recalling

[45] Governor of Gibraltar to secretary of state for the colonies, 1 June 1920, CO 91/474.
[46] In a minute, 17 April 1924, in *ibid.*, a Colonial Office official wrote: 'It is difficult to conceive that the Government of India can have any real objection against the proposed legislation from the point of view of the interests of British Indians ... The necessity for the Ordinance arises out of purely practical considerations of Gibraltar's position as a fortress and its limited accommodation, and has, of course, no ulterior political motive.' He added that, because of problems about Kenya one or two years before, 'it was agreed, as a general rule, that we should always let the India Office and the Government of India have their full say on questions arising in Colonies in which the interests of Indians appear to be involved'.
[47] PRO, Foreign Office Records, General Correspondence (Political), United States, 1921, FO 371/5661.

that, prior to 1917, British Indians were admitted freely into the Philippines and that a number of stores and bazaars, staffed practically entirely by Indians, had been established in the islands, it went on to detail the effect of the new legislation on the operations of commercial firms. The difficulty stemmed from the narrow interpretation of the term 'merchant' by the authorities, which excluded pedlars, clerks and salesmen and even managers, as well as those who entered the country with a partnership agreement signed with a merchant, while they were not themselves already engaged in trade, a fairly common situation for young Hyderabadis of the mercantile class. The memorandum put forward an argument which would recur constantly, namely that 'for various reasons . . . which appear sufficiently cogent, businesses of this nature cannot be carried on by Filipino salesmen', and it ended on dire predictions about the impending extinction of the trade unless new legislation was passed.

It was at this stage that the newly created Sindwork Merchants Association entered the fray. In December 1921, the secretary of state for India received a telegram from the Foreign and Political Department of the Government of India which stated that the Sindwork Merchants Association requested that Srinivasa Sastri, who was the representative of the Government of India in a British delegation to the United States, 'be instructed to represent Indian merchants' grievances at Washington, and endeavour to secure the removal of immigration restrictions'.[48] Sastri received permission from the secretary of state to raise the question in Washington,[49] but his intervention had no immediate impact on the situation in the Philippines. Given the continuing difficulty of getting permission to enter the Philippines, authorities in Sind became reluctant to issue passports to Sindhi merchants travelling to the islands.[50] Following an intervention by the managers of the major firms,[51] it seems that the commissioner in Sind started reissuing passports in 1924 and the situation progressively 'eased out'. Sindwork firms

[48] Copy of telegram in IOR, Industries & Overseas Department Papers 1921–1924, File 1375/1921, L/E/7/1227.

[49] Telegram of secretary of state to S. Sastri, British Delegation, Washington, 9 December 1921: 'You are authorized to act as suggested by Viceroy (in telegram) . . .'. Enclosed in Overseas File no. 12, from India Office to governor-general of India, 6 April 1922. *Ibid.*

[50] The consul-general in Manila wrote to the secretary to the Government of India in the Foreign and Political Department, 31 January 1924, that the firms in Manila complained that 'they find considerable reluctance on the part of the Indian authorities to issue passports to mercantile assistants'. Enclosed in *ibid.*, File 1375/1921, L/E/7/1227.

[51] See letter to the secretary to the Government of India in the Foreign and Political Department signed by representatives of six firms, in which they asked the government to instruct the commissioner in Sind to facilitate the delivery of visas to merchants going to the Philippines. Enclosed in under-secretary to Government of India in the

were able to continue their operations more or less unimpeded for a number of years, in spite of having had to close a certain number of branches outside Manila.

This episode is interesting in two ways. First it shows how crucial the question of free movement of personnel was to the Sindwork firms. Free movement meant not only admission into the country, but also, and as importantly, readmission after a period of stay in Hyderabad. If the employees were in danger of not being readmitted after their period of leave, the whole foundations of the system of labour relations would have been undermined, since a six-month leave period after a two-year stint was a clause included in all the contracts. Its breach would have caused considerable dislocation. One wonders why the principals of the Sindwork firms were so adamant about wanting to employ only Hyderabadis in their shops, with a few exceptions. They themselves argued that these were the only ones who had the necessary skills[52] and that they could also be trusted more than locally recruited employees. Both arguments actually look slightly doubtful. The skills involved in working in the shops, leaving aside accounting and Sindhi correspondence, which obviously could not be entrusted to strangers, were not so specialized that local employees could not have been trained to acquire them. The argument about trust is not totally convincing either; disputes often arose between Hyderabadi employers and their Hyderabadi employees, as shown by the evidence of many court cases in the British consular courts in Egypt and Morocco. Besides, in strictly economic terms, Hyderabadi employees cost much more than local ones, given the need to pay for their travel and board. One suspects that there were other motivations at work in this fierce defence of a 'closed shop' system. Patronage is probably the real key to the preference shown for recruiting Hyderabadis. Jobs as shop assistants, which carried with them

Foreign and Political Department to secretary to the Government of Bombay in the Political Department, 15 May 1924. Copy in IOR, L/E/7/1227.

[52] In a letter to the governor-general of the Philippines, 14 October 1920, the British consul-general in Manila quoted their arguments: 'I asked whether local assistants or clerks, Filipino or others, could not be employed and was informed that while some were actually employed in Manila branches it was impossible to employ them throughout the country branches . . . or to dispense with Indian assistants. For one thing the business in Indian goods generally required a certain special knowledge and experience which only Indians would have acquired in India; again, though acquainted sufficiently with English and Spanish for business requirements, they could but feel at home if using their own better known language for phrases of works, instructions, communications with India, calculations of accounts for communication to Head Office in India, etc. which would necessitate Indian members of the staff. The nature of their business (largely curios, art goods, embroideries, etc., of Indian manufacture) requires some expert knowledge and experience in India.' Copy of letter in IOR, L/E/7/1227.

fairly good salaries and the possibility of saving large amounts, were a most sought-after resource amongst lower-middle-class Bhaiband families of Hyderabad, and handing them out allowed the principals of the firm to affirm clearly their dominant status in the Bhaiband community. By employing young Amils, they could even reverse the traditional hierarchical order of the Lohana 'caste'. Let us not forget that, among Bhaibands and more generally Lohanas, status was not so much a matter of ascription as of achievement. Ranking between different Bhaiband segments was largely determined by wealth, as manifested in the standard of dowry, and what better way to display one's wealth and enhance one's prestige in such a mercantile society than to offer jobs to scions of poorer families in the community? This probably explains why the principals of the firms fought so decidedly to keep as unimpeded as possible the movement of personnel between Hyderabad and the places of business.

To achieve that aim in the face of growing obstacles, they had to be able to organize so as to influence the Government of India, in order that, through the agency of the India Office, pressure could be applied on the Foreign Office or the Colonial Office to intervene with foreign governments or colonial authorities. Local pressure exercised through the collector and the commissioner in Sind could influence to a certain extent the government of Bombay, but it was necessary to be able to talk directly to the powers in Delhi. Hence the importance of having an association which could be recognized by the Government of India as the legitimate representative of the merchants. One of its tasks was to keep the members of the Central Legislative Assembly informed of the plight of Sindhi merchants in various places, and, as a result of its intervention, questions were regularly asked in the Assembly. It even managed to have questions asked in the House of Commons in London.[53] At the same time, pressure also had to be applied locally on colonial authorities or on British consuls so that they could feed the Colonial Office or the Foreign Office with accurate and detailed information not easily available in London. Hence a dual policy of having one association in Hyderabad, the Sindwork Merchants' Association, specifically to lobby the Government of India, and several local associations in Manila, Gibraltar or Panama, to wield influence at the place of business. In the case of the Philippines, the Sindwork Merchants'

[53] See Parliamentary Notice, Session 1920, 17 November 1920, House of Commons, question 104 by Mr Bennett: 'to ask the Under Secretary of State for Foreign Affairs whether he is aware that a number of East Indian store clerks formerly resident in the Philippine Islands have, on returning from visits to India, been denied by the American customs officials at Manila permission to land . . .'. Enclosed in *ibid*.

Association in Hyderabad closely coordinated its interventions with an association in Manila, called the Bombay Merchants' Association, which represented the five big Sindwork firms in the islands.

A lot, however, could depend on the kind of relationship established with the local representative of the British government, be he a consul or a colonial governor. The attitudes of these officials varied enormously. Thus it seems that, in the early 1920s, the British consul in Manila went out of his way to help the Sindwork merchants fight the effects of the restrictive immigration legislation adopted by the US authorities. He even risked the wrath of his superiors by writing directly to the Government of India, by-passing the Foreign Office.[54] It is not known how the Sindhi merchants in Manila managed to capture the confidence of this representative of His Majesty's government, but his determined support undoubtedly helped them to get a hearing from Delhi and London. On the other hand, the governor of Gibraltar, who was traditionally a military man, had no sympathy for or interest in the Sindhi merchants and only reluctantly allowed the India Office to interfere in the business of the colony.

In Gibraltar and the Philippines, in the early 1920s, the Sindwork merchants succeeded in preserving the freedom of circulation of their employees, even if they had to accept some limitations on it. After 1925, the major problem for them was the immigration restrictions in Panama, but the case of this independent Republic will be taken up in a separate section.

Apart from Panama, the major trouble spot in the 1930s was Spain, due to the Civil War. In 1936 there were 200 Sindwork merchants in Spanish Morocco and 100 in the Canary Islands. Many Sindwork firms, including four of the big seven (Pohoomull Bros., D. Chellaram, J. T. Chanrai and M. Dialdas) had branches which were doing good business in these two territories. As soon as the conflict started, the Sindwork Merchants Association alerted the Government of India to the plight of the Sindhi merchants in Spanish Morocco, and New Delhi cabled the India Office that they would be 'grateful for any action that may be possible for protection of British Indian interests in Spanish Morocco'.[55] The British consul in Tetuan, who tried to intervene on their behalf with the Nationalist authorities, had to confess in December 1936 that 'the only alleviation (he) could obtain for them (was) a

---

[54] Consul Parke-Smith wrote two letters addressed directly to the secretary to Government of India in the Foreign and Political Department in January and May 1924.

[55] Telegram from Government of India, Foreign & Political Department to secretary of state for India, 7 August 1936, File P.Z. 5730, copy in IOR, Political & External Files and Collections, L/P&S/12/210.

promise to consider their demands favourably'.[56] In February 1937 the Sindwork Merchants Association, in a telegram to the Government of India, harped on the 'terrible hardships' suffered by Sindhi merchants in Morocco and the Canary Islands, due to the Spanish authorities having banned all withdrawal of money and merchandise, and not allowing men to leave Spain. These unheard-of restrictions, the telegram went on, have created panic in business circles. 'Entire Sind work business . . . nearly paralysed. Disastrous consequences. Pray help release money, men, merchandise from Spain.' Faced with these shrill demands, the Government of India could only reiterate that it would be 'grateful for any action that may be possible for protection of British Indian interests in Spain, Morocco and Canary Islands'.[57]

In February 1937, the British consul in Tetuan reported that he had obtained from the Nationalist authorities in Spanish Morocco permission for the merchants in Tetuan and Ceuta to close their shops and transport their goods to Gibraltar.[58] Similar interventions by the British consuls in Tenerife and Las Palmas in favour of the Sindhi merchants in the Canary Islands did not meet with much success. The great problem for the firms was that the income they derived from sales was mostly in sterling, and they were obliged to change sterling at the official rate, which was extremely disadvantageous. As a result, they had no sterling available to send remittances to their families and principals in Hyderabad, or to pay for passages to India.[59] Attempts by the British consul in Tenerife to get a monthly sterling quota for the firms[60] were rejected by the Nationalist government in Burgos.[61] The Sindworkies in the Canary Islands were thus forced to stay, and their principals in Hyderabad had

[56] British consul, Tetuan, to consul-general, Tangier, 30 December 1936, copy in File PZ 8319 (?1936), *ibid*.
[57] Telegram from Government of India, Foreign & Political Department, to secretary of state for India, 15 February 1937. File PZ 1086 1937, *ibid*.
[58] Consul Tetuan to consul-general Tangier, dated 17 February 1937, enclosed in Foreign Office to under-secretary of state for India, dated 3 March 1937, File P.Z. 1491 1937, *ibid*.
[59] See the petition addressed on 15 November by representatives of eight Sindwork firms to the British consul in Santa Cruz de Tenerife, enclosed in British Consul, Tenerife, to Foreign Office, 17 November 1937, enclosed in under-secretary of state for foreign affairs to under-secretary of state for India, File P.Z. 8030 1937, *ibid*.
[60] See British consul, Tenerife, to under-secretary of state, Foreign Office, 15 March 1938, enclosed in under-secretary of state, Foreign Office to under-secretary of state, India Office, File P.Z. 2402 1938, *ibid*.
[61] Hodgson, the British ambassador at Burgos, wrote to Lord Halifax on 10 May 1938 on being informed by the Ministry of Finance that 'the Foreign Exchange Committee cannot grant foreign exchange to cover the expenses in India of British subjects residing in the Canary Islands. Nor can they grant foreign exchange to cover the journey expenses of their return to India.' Enclosed in under-secretary of state, Foreign Office, to under-secretary of state, India Office, File P.Z. 3687 1938, *ibid*.

to transfer money from India to Spain to keep them going, which meant losses for the firms. In spite of the good relations between the Conservative government in Britain and Franco's regime, the British authorities could not do anything to alleviate the plight of the Sindhi merchants in the Canary Islands. This was a clear sign of more hardships to come.

In Gibraltar, following the adoption of a first Alien Traders Ordinance in 1924, which imposed a system of licences and restricted the number of shops to one for each firm, new efforts were made by the authorities to control the activities of Sindhi merchants, resulting in a new Alien Traders Ordinance passed in 1933.[62] In the case of Gibraltar, over and above the conflict between the Sindwork merchants and the colonial authorities, there was superimposed another conflict, internal to the Sindhi community. In 1924, the established firms agreed to limit to one the number of shops they could have, but some of the premises they freed were seized by smaller merchants, generally former employees of the big firms who had set up shop on their own,[63] and these started competing with their former employers, to the latter's utmost displeasure. The big firms started to look with less disfavour at the attempts by the authorities to regulate the trade,[64] provided their own interests were not affected. But it was a fine balance to achieve, and neither the government of the colony nor the big firms could prevent the mushrooming of shops operated by small merchants, some of whom had moved from Spanish Morocco at the time of the Spanish Civil War. In 1939, out of twenty-two firms operating in Gibraltar, only seven were branches of established firms; the others were owned by small-scale operators.[65] As a rule they do not appear to have had problems in bringing personnel from Hyderabad on a regular basis, in spite of occasional disputes with the authorities.

The real trial for the Sindhi merchants of Gibraltar came with the Second World War and the evacuation of the civilian population of the

[62] See the correspondence between the India Office and the Colonial Office about the Ordinance in PRO, Colonial Office Records, Gibraltar Original Correspondence, CO 91/494/8.

[63] According to a memorandum by the attorney-general in Gibraltar, 23 July 1936, these small Indian operators evaded the law by forming companies with a capital of only £100, 61 per cent of the capital being held by Gibraltarians who were actually nominees. PRO, CO 91/500/10.

[64] See letter no. 114 from governor of Gibraltar to secretary of state for colonies, 4 August 1936: 'the larger and old-established Indian firms here have in their own interests welcomed the proposal to introduce legislation . . .'. *Ibid.*

[65] See copy of statement furnished by the Sindwork Merchants Association, enclosed in letter no. F 123/45 O.S., 16 May 1946, from Department of Commonwealth Relations to the secretary, Political Department, India Office, POL 8546/1946, IOR, L/P&J/8/236.

Rock. The Sindhis resisted the evacuation order as much as possible, and refused to follow the Gibraltarian population to Madeira, where it was resettled for the duration of the War.[66] Some went to Morocco, West Africa and the Canary Islands, while a small group embarked for India on a ship which was sunk by U-boats near Cape Town. Those who were not drowned ended up in various Stalags in Germany. Only a few remained in Gibraltar to keep watch on the shops which had been closed. When the war came to an end, and civilian evacuees were gradually repatriated to the Rock, the military authorities showed little willingness to allow the Sindhis to return. Once again the Sindwork Merchants Association had to embark upon a full-scale campaign and to enrol the support of the Government of India and the India Office to make the local authorities relent and allow the firms to resume commercial operations with their pre-war staff, or at least with those who were in the region.[67] To the hostility of the military and political authorities was added that of the local traders belonging to the so-called 'Gibraltarian' trading community, who saw in the Sindworkies dangerous competitors,[68] as they shifted from an exclusive specialization in luxury and 'Oriental' goods to more diversified lines of trading which had been the preserve of these 'Gibraltarian' traders. That the Gibraltar Sindhis were able to overcome these difficulties and to become one of the most prosperous Sindhi communities in Europe is testimony to their

---

[66] The governor of Gibraltar cabled the secretary of state for the colonies on 29 July 1940 about the Indians in Gibraltar (all Sindhis): 'Women and children have left. 12 male adults left for India via the Cape. There remain 65, of whom 17 propose to go to Tangier. Remaining 48 do not wish to be evacuated to the UK and have not applied for Madeira'. Copy of telegram in IOR, Public & Judicial Department Collections, 'Evacuation of Indians from within War zone', L/P&J/8/399.

[67] See Files POL 6568/1945, POL 1355/1945, POL 2870/1945, in IOR, L/P&J/8/236. In August 1945 the Government of India received a delegation from the Sindwork Merchants Association who pleaded their case. It considered their request reasonable and urged that 'all Indian firms which operated in Gibraltar before the War be given trading licences and entry-permits for pre-war number of employees though not necessarily same persons, in order to restore status quo'. See confidential telegram from Department of Commonwealth Relations, Government of India to secretary of state for India, 11 August 1945. File POL 8083/1945, *ibid*. See also secretary, Department of Commonwealth Relations, Government of India to under-secretary of state for India, 14 October 1946: 'I am directed to say that the Government of India are most anxious that Indian traders who were in Gibraltar before the War should be allowed to reestablish fully their business there on the pre-war scale.' File POL 11 561/1946, *ibid*.

[68] A local attorney who took up the cause of the Indian traders wrote to H. Polak, a London-based lawyer long associated with Gandhi, who specialized in defending overseas Indians: 'The Indians trading in Gibraltar are definitely not popular with the trading native community. Their system of bargaining and their methods generally are disliked and it is fashionable to credit them with every commercial immorality that can be imagined.' S. P. Triay to H. Polak, undated letter, copy in File POL 2870/1945, *ibid*.

resilience and dogged determination. But they appear to have remained outsiders to the politics of Gibraltar to this day.

In the Philippines, following the difficulties of the early 1920s, the Sindhi merchant community enjoyed a period of growth and prosperity until the late 1930s. There was a growing diversification in the ranks of the community, as testified by the enlargement of the ranks of the Bombay Merchants Association, which, from a five-member body at the time of its creation in 1920 had grown to a membership of some twenty firms in 1938.[69] Occasional problems cropped up with the immigration authorities. In 1938, a merchant coming as a partner to an existing firm was refused entry, which led the Bombay Merchants Association to protest to the local authorities as well as to the British Consulate. The passing of a new immigration law in 1940 threatened to make things difficult again, but the escalating international tension, followed by Japanese occupation, introduced new preoccupations.

By the time the Second World War ended, it was clear that not much was to be gained any more from the protection of the once mighty British Empire. In the meantime, for the first time, the danger was at home, where the flames of Partition were threatening the fragile communal peace in Sind. But the Sindworkies were too cut off from the realities of their home province to play any role in the drama which was unfolding. After Partition, it became crucial for them to retain their vast assets abroad. They could not place much hope in the actions of the government of independent India, with which, as refugees from Pakistan, they had very little clout. Although it occasionally intervened on their behalf, it had little influence on either independent countries or British colonies, and the Sindhi merchants after 1947 largely had to fend for themselves. They had to find new ways of defending their interests, through local intervention. The story of their political involvement in Panama showed one possible way.

Sindhi merchants as independent political agents: the case of Panama

In the Republic of Panama, Sindwork merchants established their first shops around 1905, i.e. two years after the separation of the country from Colombia, and by 1927 there were ten firms in Colon employing

---

[69] The British consul in Manila wrote to the secretary of labour of the Commonwealth of the Philippines on 12 May 1938: 'The Bombay Merchants' Association . . . comprises the twenty principal Indian firms established in the Philippine Islands, which jointly have several millions of pesos invested in their businesses here.' Copy of letter in P&J 4008/1938, IOR, Public & Judicial Department Collections, Collection 108/29, L/P&J/8/281.

some 100 to 125 men. Their business was mostly the sale of 'Oriental' goods to the passengers of the ships which crossed the Panama canal. They had a complete monopoly over that trade, which was worth several million US dollars,[70] and, in the 1920s, fetched high profits. Sindworkies were the richest of the Indian communities in this Central American Republic (where there were also Sikhs and Gujaratis) and they appear to have forged some political connections from the 1920s onwards. When a new immigration law which threatened to prevent the entry of Indians and other Asiatics came before parliament in 1926, the local Sindhi merchants were not content with alerting the British consul. They took matters directly in hand in the form of a 'memorial submitted to the National Assembly by the members of the Hindu colony',[71] addressed to the president of the National Assembly, actually signed by the managers of two of the largest firms, but probably drafted in Spanish by a local attorney. In the preamble, they admitted to hesitating over the mode of intervention chosen:

We have deeply meditated as to whether we should address ourselves through you to the august body of the National Assembly of Panama, and after making a thorough survey of the situation, of the interests of Panama, and above all, of the duty imposed upon us to make known to you our respectful observations in regard to the erroneous concepts in which we are considered, we have eventually been impelled by a legitimate desire to submit, most respectfully, to the august National Assembly this petition . . .

For traditionally 'apolitical' merchants to intervene in such an open way in the political arena was undoubtedly a bold step to take. There followed some rhetorical flourish about the pain of having to leave a country 'where we had accustomed to admire the respective virtues of its sons; patriotism, nobility, hospitality, justice, altruism, etc., etc'.

They then developed a three-pronged argument. First, regarding the racial aspect, they refuted allegations that they were a 'degenerate' race, stressing, on the contrary, the purity of their blood maintained through strict adherence to the caste system: 'We are proud to belong to a high Caste of East Indians which we can safely call an Aristocracy, and from this point of view, we do not permit foreign blood to be introduced . . .' They then proceeded to differentiate themselves from Indians of the coolie class, conceding that 'against this type of Hindu . . . exclusion (would) be deemed justifiable from an economical standpoint'. They

[70] As indicated by the fact that the firms in 1925 paid more than US $80,000 in customs duties on goods imported into Panama, at a time when duties were very low. Mentioned in 'Memorial submitted to the National Assembly by members of the Hindu colony', enclosure no. 3 in Panama despatch no. 102, 20 July 1927, Economic & Overseas Department Annual Files, File E&O 6008/1927, copy in IOR, L/P&J/8/278.
[71] Ibid.

nevertheless came to their defence on the ground that they were not 'degenerates in the strictest sense of the word, although there may be undesirables among them . . .' In the second part, they defended their contribution to the local economy, by pointing out that they paid large amounts to the Treasury in taxes and customs duties. In the last part, they considered the moral aspect:

> From this point of view, our behaviour as foreigners corresponds exactly to our inborn pride of the Caste System, a Caste which is moderate in living principles, but without vices. We are hard workers, honest and with a veneration for the higher virtues of man. We respectfully ask that the Police Records, Hospital and Asylum be examined, and we feel assured that such institutions cannot produce any record where a single Hindu has caused any trouble to the State, either by violations of the law, or because the State has had to take care of him. Our names have never appeared in the records of the Criminal Courts and we have never caused any trouble whatever to the authorities . . .

They emphasized their contributions to charitable causes and recalled the sacrifices consented by Hindus [sic] for the cause of freedom during the Great War, which made it impossible to classify them as undesirables. They ended with a plea not to be confused, in the new law, with coolies or third-class migrants, stressing that their memorial was not a protest, but a way of bringing notice of a complaint which grieved their hearts.

This document reveals a desire on the part of the merchants to be recognized as legitimate actors in the economic life of the country, but not as political actors. They stressed that they were harmless and useful foreigners, but at the same time, by addressing the Assembly, they overstepped the boundaries of merchants' traditional withdrawal from politics.

When, in spite of their protests, the law was passed, they tried to put pressure on the Panamanian authorities through the British government. In a telegram sent in January 1927 to the private secretary to the viceroy, on behalf of Sindwork merchants, Pessumal Moolchand, himself a prominent merchant, and Jairamdas Daulatram, a lawyer and politician with close links to the Sindwork merchants, wrote: 'Sindwork merchants strongly appeal Viceroy to request British Government to approach Panama Government to amend Panama immigration law recently passed which vitally affects interests of Indian merchants amounting practically to their deportation and abandonment of all trade'.[72] In a letter to the collector of

---

[72] Telegram, 24 January 1927, from Pessumal Moolchand, Jairamdas Daulatram on behalf Sindwork merchants Hyderabad Sind to personal secretary to the viceroy, Economic & Overseas Department Annual Files, File E&O 1485/1927, copy in IOR, Public & Judicial Department Collections, Collection 108/28 A, L/P&J/8/278.

Hyderabad dated May 1927,[73] the same writers elaborated further on the difficulties that the adoption of such a piece of legislation would cause the merchants. It would prevent them from replacing staff and would also make it impossible for the principals of the firms to come on short-term visits of inspection. It developed a fairly sophisticated argument about the necessity of keeping the shops and godowns staffed with personnel from India:

If it is argued that the staff could be replaced by bona fide residents of the Republic in Colon, the answer is that the merchants will not be able to put their faith in strangers nor will they confide the secrets of their trade to men who might oust them out of their business. Nor will it be possible for the Indian Merchants to keep their present staff tied down to Colon for the whole of their lives for apart from the hardship involved in living for all time in a foreign country the members of the staff will dictate terms to their principals and hold them at their mercy, if induced to stay away there for good.

An interesting new line of argument is brought in here, which has little to do with 'trust' and more to do with the advantages of keeping the labour market 'flexible' (an argument which sounds curiously contemporary to the reader of 2000). The letter ended with a plea to the Government of India 'to press to the attention of the Republic of Panama the serious situation which will be created by enforcing the law of immigration against the Indian Merchants'. These protests, probably combined with measures of a more practical character to enlist support from influential Panamanians, eventually won the day. In April 1928, the consul in Panama announced to the Foreign Office[74] that, under a new law, East Indians did not come under the category of persons whose immigration was restricted.

A crucial step towards a more collective pattern of action was the formation, in 1930, of a Hindustani Merchants Association, which represented the major Indian merchants in Panama and Colon, Sindhis as well as Punjabi Sikhs and Gujaratis, but which, because of the economic preponderance of the Sindwork merchants, was always *de facto* dominated by them.

In 1931 it was confronted with a new attempt on the part of the Panamanian authorities to restrict the entry of Indians. By then, the context in Panama had changed. The world depression had set in, resulting in increased poverty and massive unemployment for the

---

[73] Letter, 17 May 1927, from Pessumal Moolchand, Jairamdas Daulatram to collector of Hyderabad, enclosed in letter no. 1543/8383, 15 July 1927, from secretary to the Government of Bombay in the General Department, to the secretary to the Government of India in the Foreign Department. Copy in L/P&J/8/278.
[74] 'Memorandum on immigration laws, Panama', enclosure no. 3 in Panama despatch no. 3, 25 April 1928, copy in IOR, L/P&J/8/278.

Panamanian population. There was intense resentment against foreigners, and the Indians, whose ranks had been swelled in the late 1920s by an influx of Sikhs and Bengali Muslims, were a target alongside other foreign communities. In May 1931, a decree[75] reestablished restrictions on the entry of Indians into the country. The text of the decree emphasized that there were a large number of East Indians in the country, which was 'sufficient to take care of the needs of the East Indian commercial establishments existing in the cities of Panama and Colon, under whose guarantee the immigration into the country of the majority of those elements has been permitted'. The sole article of the decree was that 'the immigration into the country of elements belonging to the Hindu race [sic] is prohibited, with the exception of those who prove to the satisfaction of the Ministry of Foreign Relations that they come to establish themselves with capital able to be drawn upon'.

As pointed out in a report of the British Legation,[76] the argument of the Panamanian authorities was that the Sind merchants could recruit their staff from the surplus Hindu population. 'This', the report added, 'is not possible owing to differences of education, language, caste, etc.' It went on to state that Panamanian employees were 'useless owing to their ignorance of bazaar goods, and their unwillingness to keep long hours'. However, the authorities tried to impose a quota of 75 per cent of Panamanian employees on all foreign commercial firms.

In March 1932, following a campaign of protests, the firms were given some facilities for the replacement of employees who had died or absented themselves definitively,[77] a concession which was minor but indicated that the authorities were prepared to relent.

In 1933, the Hindustani Merchants Association intervened actively in the crisis about the new Panamanian legislation, seeking to impose a quota of 75 per cent of Panamanian employees in foreign firms. Its intervention was of a dual nature: on the one hand, it used the mediation of the British consul to make its hostility to the measure known to the Panamanian authorities,[78] and on the other hand it organized a shop-

---

[75] Decree no. 43, 27 May 1931, enclosed in British Legation, Panama, to Arthur Henderson, Foreign Office, 2 July 1931, copy in IOR, L/P&J/8/278.

[76] British Legation to Henderson, 27 July 1931, copy in IOR, L/P&J/8/278.

[77] Decree no. 16 of 1932, enclosed in Panama despatch no. 84, 21 March 1932, copy in IOR, L/P&J/8/278.

[78] In a letter to the British ambassador in Panama, 20 January 1933, the president of the Hindustani Merchants Association, Colon, Manghanmal Detaram, extended 'sincere thanks and appreciation of the courtesy you extended to our delegates who called on you in [sic] behalf of the recent . . . Law 47 of 1932 and your representation to the Panamian Government in having the same amended in our favour from 75 to 50 per cent'. Enclosure in Panama despatch no. 27, 20 January 1933, copy in IOR, L/P&J/8/278.

keepers' strike which lasted for two or three days.[79] The result of this combined pressure was that the Panama government agreed to lower the quota of Panamanian employees to 50 per cent.

When a new crisis erupted in 1935, following the adoption by the National Assembly in December 1934 of a new immigration law prohibiting the entry of Hindus into the country, the Association addressed a memorial directly to the president of the Republic,[80] in which they stressed the problems they would face if they had to replace their Indian staff with locally recruited staff.

A stalemate seems to have ensued, during which period the law was not actually implemented, but remained on the statute book. A compromise was found, by which Indian firms could retain some of their staff by labelling them 'experts'.[81] In 1937, however, new attempts were made by the merchants to obtain the revocation of the law. In September the Hindustani Merchants' Association approached the minister for foreign affairs directly with its demand, without going through the office of the British consul, who complained about it.[82] This newly found confidence in direct political connections apparently had its source in the fact, as told to the British consul by the minister himself, that 'President Arosemena was undoubtedly well disposed towards these merchants, who had lent him considerable sums, which he had since repaid, for his electoral campaign when he was a candidate for the Presidency'.[83] It thus seems that Sindhi money played a role in deciding the outcome of the 1936 presidential election in Panama.[84] Arosemena's links with the Sindhi merchants seem to have been of fairly long standing, since the British consul mentioned in 1935 that 'Arosemena is himself interested in a prominent Indian enterprise'.[85]

Having one of the country's most prominent politicians as a partner in a firm proved a shrewd move when the same politician was elected president of the country. Sindhi merchants did not have to wait for too

---

[79] See British Legation, Panama, to Sir John Simon, Foreign Office, 20 January 1933, copy in IOR, L/P&J/8/278.
[80] Petition of Indian merchants to the president of the Republic, 22 March 1935, enclosure no. 2 in Panama despatch no. 90, 8 April 1935, copy in *ibid*.
[81] Mentioned in British Legation, Panama, to Sir John Simon, 8 April 1935. Copy in *ibid*.
[82] In a letter to Eden, 27 September 1937, the British ambassador in Panama mentioned that the merchants had presented their memorial to the minister for foreign affairs before coming to the Legation. They declared themselves nevertheless anxious to enlist his support with the minister and the president of the Republic. Copy in P&J 4864/37, *ibid*.
[83] Mentioned in *ibid*.
[84] This election was marked by 'high levels of fraud and violence'. See M. L. Conniff, 'Panama since 1903', in *The Cambridge History of Latin America*, vol. VII, *Latin America since 1930: Mexico, Central America and the Caribbean*, Cambridge, 1990, p. 621.
[85] British Legation, Panama, to Simon, 8 April 1935.

long to collect their dividends, and by the end of 1938, things appeared to be shaping up for them. In October, in a report to the consulate in Panama,[86] the vice-consul in Colon commented on the election of a man called Choithram Hemraj as the new president of the Hindustan Merchants Association. Stressing that he had been a resident of Colon for a considerable time, having been employed in big firms before setting up his own shop, he added:

I have not previously regarded him as outstanding enough in the Hindu colony to be elected President of their Association, and this appointment in fact appears to be due to exceptional circumstances. I learn that the Hindu colony has lately approached the President of Panama with a view to obtaining some relaxation of the legislation prohibiting or at least hampering the immigration of new employees from India. His Excellency apparently promised to take steps on their behalf and suggested that if, as a preliminary step, possible opposition from the deputies of the National Assembly could be avoided by the means usual in such cases, he would introduce a measure relaxing the requirements for the immigration of Hindus. The Hindu colony has already taken the necessary steps to win over the deputies, and hopes to engage in discussions with the President in the near future. For the purpose of these negotiations it is felt that the Hindu Association [sic] should have a suitable spokesman in their president, and as Mr Hemraj not only is held to possess the necessary flair for such delicate conversations, but is also a good Spanish scholar, he has been preferred this year above elder and more prosperous men.

This carefully coordinated campaign, in which corruption (the 'usual means' alluded to) combined with public relations work, seems to have met with success, and for a two or three-year period no more complaints about restrictions on the entry of Indians into Panama came to the knowledge of the British consular authorities. Such an episode reveals the political maturation of the Sindhi community, and its gradual emancipation from British tutelage. There appears to have been a logical sequence of action: at first, Sindhi merchants coopted a prominent politician as a business associate, then they financed his electoral campaign, and, once he was elected, they collected their reward in the form of a change in legislation. It is not suggested here that Sindhi merchants acquired a 'hegemonic' position in the politics of Panama, which were largely shaped in any case by American strategic and economic interests, but, as one of the richest and most compact foreign business communities, they were capable of gaining some political clout, which helped them limit attacks on their business interests. Their conception of politics was of a purely 'defensive' kind, but what is worthy of note is their ability

---

[86] British vice-consul, Colon, to British Legation, Panama, 17 October 1938, enclosed in British Legation, Panama, to Halifax, 1 November 1938. File P& J 5623/38, L/P&J/8/278.

to emancipate themselves to a certain extent from an exclusive dependence on British diplomatic interventions. Acquisition of linguistic skills was an important element in this emancipation, as mastery of Spanish was necessary to penetrate the world of Panamanian politics.

For Sindhis in Panama, however, the end of their troubles was not in sight. In 1941 a nationalization law, passed under a new president, created new problems. In February 1942, Indian merchants petitioned the minister of commerce, industry and agriculture, asking to be allowed to liquidate slowly their business in the Republic,[87] but in March 1942 all the shops in Colon were closed. Regarding the situation, the British consul commented: 'These Indians seem very well able to take care of themselves. We have already been told that they are "realists" and no doubt they have made some suitable financial arrangements with the Minister concerned'.[88] By the end of 1942, as shown by censored mail, the Sindhis were doing well again, in spite of the closure of many shops. The boom continued till 1946, when deteriorating economic conditions brought about a new hardening of official attitudes to Indian merchants. In 1949, they were voicing their concerns to the authorities of independent India,[89] concerns which appeared to be more or less the same as those of fifteen years earlier. Sindhi merchants were however so deeply entrenched in Panama that no amount of restrictive legislation could put an end to their activities, which continue to this day. In the case of Panama, the acquisition of political clout proved crucial in protecting business interests.

When their interests were at stake, and when the political system was relatively 'open', as in a country like Panama, which did not have a well-entrenched oligarchy, but was mainly a land of recent immigrants attracted by the Canal,[90] Sindhi merchants were capable of shedding their image of meek *banias* and of actively intervening in political life, with a measure of success.

The 'apolitical' nature of Indian traders is largely a myth. Political skills were crucial assets in the long term in the development of international financial and trading networks. The partial eclipse of the Shikarpuris after 1917 has much to do with political miscalculations in

---

[87] Petition, 2 February 1942, enclosed in Panama despatch no. 34, 23 February 1942, copy in POL 2631/1942, L/P&J/8/279.
[88] See Panama Legation to Foreign Office, 16 February 1942, copy in *ibid*.
[89] See letter to under-secretary, Ministry of External Affairs, India, 8 August 1949, enclosed in British Legation, Panama, consular section to Chancery, British Embassy, Washington, copy in L/P&J/8/280. The consulate was asked by the Department of External Affairs of the Government of India to send an appreciation of the situation of Indian merchants in Panama.
[90] On Panamanian society and its history, see A. Castillero Calvo, *La sociedad panamena: historia de su formacion e integracion*, Panama, 1970.

Central Asia. At a later stage, however, it is their close links with the shah of Iran which allowed the Hinduja family to gain ascendancy in business. On the other hand, the ability of the Sindworkies to extend the range of their operations in an increasingly unfavourable international context owed much to their acquisition of some political skills, both in lobbying the authorities in New Delhi and in forging connections locally with different kinds of influential political actors.

8 Community and gender in two merchant networks

The literature on trading diasporas lays great emphasis on the notion of community, which is generally defined on the basis of a common ethnicity and a common religion, sometimes also of a caste. It will be argued here that, in the case of the Sind merchants, this definition did not really apply. For Shikarpuris and Sindworkies, community meant above all locality, and the bonds which defined it were those of co-residence and kinship rather than of ethnicity, religion and caste. In the dispersion, these bonds became somewhat loosened and though great store was set on the fictive kinship ties of 'brotherhood', they were more an idealized fiction than an actual factor of solidarity. As a result, trust was not easy to establish, opportunistic and violent behaviour of different kinds was widespread. One of the contributing factors was the absence of women, and that is why it is not possible to overlook the problem of gender and of the specific sexual economy of these merchant networks.

The meaning of community among Sind merchants

The first point to note is that there did not develop an overarching sense of 'ethnic' solidarity between Sind merchants belonging to different towns even when they met abroad. Shikarpuris and Sindworkies in particular do not appear to have interacted even when both groups were represented in a locality. Thus in the 1920s and 1930s Shikarpuri financiers were present in Colombo and Rangoon, where there were large colonies of Sindwork merchants, but the two groups remained separate. Similarly, in the Persian Gulf region, the Bhatias of Thatta, who were the oldest merchant community from Sind, did not mix with either the Shikarpuris or the Sindworkies,[1] neither of whom were

---

[1] The evidence from a case in the Bahrain court in which two Thatta merchants sued a Hyderabadi pearl dealer is significant. The defendant's son, a Bombay lawyer, wrote to the political agent of the Government of India in Bahrain on 21 April 1939 that his father had 'excited the jealousy of some British Indian merchants' and he added: 'He

represented in a big way. Nor do they appear to have interacted with the Hyderabadi Khojas, the only significant Muslim diasporic community from Sind, mainly represented in Masqat. The absence of a feeling of ethnic solidarity between merchants of different towns in Sind was partly due to the fact that both Shikarpur and Hyderabad were multi-ethnic merchant cities.

Shikarpur, as already mentioned, was a kind of *bania* 'melting pot', where merchants from diverse regional and ethnic backgrounds congregated in the second half of the eighteenth century to take advantage of opportunities offered by the rise of Durrani power. The Punjabi ethnic element was an important component of the Shikarpuri mosaic, but, by the late nineteenth century, most merchants of Punjabi origin had adopted the Sindhi language and had, through intermarriage, become part of the so-called Bhaiband 'caste'. The only recognizable Punjabi elements were the Khatris, who accounted for only a small part of the Shikarpuri merchant population. They interacted and intermarried with members of the other two merchant castes of the town, the Bhaibands and the Bhatias. The same appears to have been true of Marwari merchants, whose origins are identifiable through onomastics, but who did not survive as a separate caste group in Shikarpur at the end of the nineteenth century. The situation in Hyderabad was slightly different. There was less ethnic diversity in the local merchant community, Sindhis being clearly the dominant element. There were, however, Punjabi merchants in Hyderabad and one of them was drafted as a working partner in an agreement concluded in 1906 for the operation of a shop in Cairo.[2]

Most Sind merchants defined themselves as Hindus, at least from the 1891 Census onwards,[3] but they were actually Nanakpanthis. While there is practically no evidence of any participation by Muslim merchants in trading activities outside India (though a Muslim merchant, probably a Khoja, was drafted as a partner of a Sindwork

---

had gone to Bahrain for the purpose of doing all business on cash basis . . . But there were Indian merchants like Messrs Dhamanmal Issardas, who are also hailing from the same province of India, Sind, as my father. But, my father belongs to the town of Hyderabad in Sind, and the said Messrs Dhamanmal Issardas hail from the town of Tatta in Sind. There is not a single merchant there from the town of Hyderabad, Sind.' 'Dhamanmal Isardas and Rattanchand Dipchand, plaintiffs, vs. Bheroomal T. Relvani, defendant', IOR, Persian Gulf Residencies Records, Bahrain Court Records, R/15/3/69.

[2] One of the signatories to a partnership deed concluded for doing business at Cairo in 1906 was one 'Kodumal son of Ramchand Hindu Punjabi resident of Hyderabad Sind', PRO, Foreign Office Records, Cairo Consular Court Records, 'K. Khanchand and Kodoomal vs. Naraindas Kishinchand', FO 841/101. See above, Chapter 5.

[3] See above, Chapter 2.

firm operating in China in 1917),[4] and none of the 572 applicants for certificates of identity in 1915–16 was a Muslim, the existence of a common religion did not by itself create strong links and a sense of community. Hinduism in Sind was a fluid reality, in which the influences of Sikhism and sufism were strongly felt. There were some differences in the way merchants in Shikarpur and Hyderabad related to Hinduism. Shikarpuris were real 'frontier' Hindus of beyond the Indus, who had lived under direct Afghan rule for a long period while the participation of Hyderabadis in 'mainstream' Hindu culture seems to have been greater, as exemplified by the fact that most of the great merchant families of the town had a pandit in Benares who kept a record of births and deaths.[5] Among these merchants, piety was often a very personal affair, and religion did not structure community to the same extent as among other Hindu merchant groups.

If religion was not a structuring factor, neither was caste. A major question mark hangs around the meaning of caste in the mercantile milieu of these two towns. The vast majority of Shikarpuri merchants belonged to the Lohana or Bhaiband caste, but, interestingly, in official documents, when asked to fill in the entry under caste, they generally gave the name of their lineage. This is an interesting indication of the difference between 'official' and 'indigenous' perceptions of caste. The term 'Lohana' which was the one used in the official nomenclature in the censuses, does not nowadays generate a response among Sindhi merchants when interviewed; the term 'Bhaiband' does, but it was not used in the censuses and other official documents. If caste was meant to convey ranking, 'Lohana' was of little use, as all merchants in Sind, except for Khatris and Bhatias, belonged to that 'caste'; only the mention of the specific lineage gave an indication of ranking to members of this mercantile society (but not to the contemporary observer). Data on Shikarpuri successions in Russian Central Asia, bearing on a total of seventy successions, yield the names of thirty-seven 'castes', of which only one, Khatri, is the name of a known 'caste'. All the other names are names of Lohana *nukhs* or sections[6] or names of lineages, most of which

---

[4] In a deed of partnership concluded in 1917 for doing business in China, one of the two working partners was one Gul Hassan Shah. He was a Muslim resident of Hyderabad, but nothing more is known about him. PRO, Foreign Office Records, Embassy and Consular Archives: China, Personal Estates Correspondence, 'Partnership between Vishindas H., Gehimal N. and Gul Hassan Shah, Tientsin 1917', FO 678/2946. See above, Chapter 5.

[5] Oral interview with Mr Lal and Mr Lokumal Chellaram, London, August 1996.

[6] Many of them are listed in Appendix F 'Caste Indexes in the Presidency', part IV, 'Remarks on special tribe names in Sind', in *Census of India, 1931*, vol. VIII, part I, *Bombay Presidency. General Report*, A. H. Dracup and H. T. Sorley, Bombay, 1933, p. 574.

are Lohana lineages. The most widespread lineage name is Chugh, represented nine times in the sample. On the other hand, in Hyderabad, merchants used 'Lohana' when filling in questionnaires for certificates of identity. The reason for the difference in usage between the two towns is a matter for speculation. As compared with the mercantile milieu in the rest of India, what is striking is the absence in both towns of a strong Bhaiband caste *panchayat* capable of intervening in disputes between merchants and of backing its decisions with effective sanctions. The merchant *panchayat* of Shikarpur, which included members of the three merchant castes, did not for, instance, intervene when conflicts between Shikarpuri merchants erupted around successions in Central Asia.

Whatever sense of community existed among merchants was strongly rooted in the locality, which increasingly meant the town rather than a specific bazaar. After Partition, it was noticed that Sindhi Hindu refugees in India tended to interact and socialize mostly with townsmen.[7] Solidarity between merchants belonging to the same town had its source in the bonds created by co-residence, kinship and matrimonial alliances, which cut across ethnic, caste and religious boundaries. Detailed mapping of the residential patterns of merchants in the two towns is not available, but most *banias* appear to have had their places of residence very close to the bazaars, where the firms had their seats. In Hyderabad, the Shahi bazaar was the seat of most mercantile activity in the city, and most traders seem to have lived in the many narrow lanes which branched out of the bazaar. In the 1920s and 1930s, there developed a new residential area in Hirabad, north of the bazaar, where rich Sindworkies, in particular, built their often palatial residences. In Shikarpur, the pattern was looser, as there were several bazaars at some distance from each other, and the *bania* population was therefore less concentrated than in Hyderabad, but this dispersal does not appear to have resulted in a fragmented pattern of identity. In medium-sized towns such as Shikarpur and Hyderabad, the webs of kinship must have been dense and extended. If one adds the widespread town endogamy which seems to have prevailed among members of the *bania* castes, one will stress the extreme density of criss-crossing networks in which most merchant families were enmeshed.

However, it would be bold to conclude, from these scattered observations, that a specific mercantile culture emerged in these two towns. While conceptions of mercantile honour, which were largely equated with credit, stressed the importance of not defaulting on repayment of

[7] See Thakur, *Sindhi Culture*.

Community and gender 253

debts and were central values for the merchants of Shikarpur and Hyderabad, as they were for the merchants of other regions of the subcontinent, different attitudes to wealth and its display can be identified. Shikarpuri merchants undoubtedly tended to conform more to traditional values of austerity and thrift and to avoid ostentatious displays of wealth, while they were generous in endowing charities and in contributing to the building of temples. In Hyderabad, however, among Sindworkies, there was a growing tendency to ostentatious displays of wealth through conspicuous consumption of alcohol and luxury goods, which would have been looked upon as unsuitable in most Indian mercantile milieux, except probably among the Bombay Parsis. This did not preclude engaging in more traditional charities and temple building, but it certainly set the Sindworkies apart from what is at least the most widespread ideal typical image of the Hindu merchants.

Were these differences in merchant ethos the outcome of diverging experiences in the dispersion? The question arises in particular of the means merchants had at their disposal to fulfil their religious obligations and satisfy their spiritual needs.

On this aspect, some fairly detailed material has come to light concerning the Shikarpuris. In Central Asia, Shikarpuri merchants found various ways of satisfying their religious needs. The Shikarpuri diaspora there included a small number of religious specialists. Among Shikarpuris who got passports for Central Asia in the early 1890s, were several Brahmins, both Saraswat and Puskharna,[8] who pursued a double career as traders and religious specialists. One of them, who died in 1889 in Tashkent, shared quarters with six other men, for whom he probably cooked, and served as a priest to a small temple.[9] At the same time, he was engaged in a business partnership as a *gumastha*. From such scattered evidence, it is not possible to conclude that there was a ratio of one Brahmin to six *banias* in the entire Shikarpuri population of Central Asia. It is clear that many Shikarpuri colonies, probably even

[8] See 'Statement of Indian British Subjects proceeding to Central Asia to whom passports were granted during year 1890, 1891 and 1892', Accompaniment to Despatch no. 7 from Bombay to the secretary of state for India, 17 February 1894, IOR, Political & Secret Correspondence with India 1875–1911, L/P&S/7/305. In 1890, out of a total of 124 passports given to Shikarpuri Hindus, 3 were given to Brahmins, including 2 to 'Sarsud' (Saraswat) Brahmins.

[9] See letter, 21 July/2 August 1895, from Chichkine, of the Asiatic Department of the Russian Ministry of Foreign Affairs to the British Embassy in St Petersburg, enclosed in St Petersburg despatch no. 198, 9 August 1895, enclosed in Foreign Office to India Office, 21 August 1895, copy in Public & Judicial Department Annual Files 1880–1930, File J&P 1424/1895. According to the information available to the Russian authorities, a Brahmin called Amanomal, who had died in Tashkent in 1889, shared quarters in a *sarai* with six other Indians who declared that 'celui-ci, desservant de leur Mosquée [*sic*], vivait des ressources que lui fournissaient ses ouailles'.

the majority of them, did not have Brahmins in residence. Another type of religious specialist, more common in Sind than the Brahmin, was the *bawa*, or Nanakapanthi priest, who looked after the *tikhanas* which were found in most localities of the province. A man, who died in 1895 in Russian Central Asia, was described in official documents as a *bava* (or *bawa*), by caste an *Udasi fakir*; he had a *dharamsala* in Samarkand and was the disciple of another *bava* who claimed his inheritance (a claim which was rejected by the Russian authorities).[10] Interestingly, the man who died was at the same time the *chela* and the *gumastha* of the other Bava, who was both his guru and his principal. Business and religion went hand-in-hand among Shikarpuris in Russian Central Asia. In some documents, there are also references to a third group of men endowed with some form of religious authority who are called *pirzadeh*, i.e. descendants of *pirs*, but who happened to be Hindus. Whether they were *murids*, who claimed spiritual ancestry from a *pir*, or whether the term had a more precise meaning is not known. The fact is that such men were obviously endowed with great prestige[11] and were often considered leaders in the Shikarpuri diaspora in Central Asia. Some of these *pirzadehs* came from the Punjab, but their following appears to have been mostly among the Shikarpuris (although there were also Punjabi Hindus and Muslims in Central Asia). It is worth noting that the Hindu places of worship in Central Asia mentioned in archival documents or travellers' accounts were all in the guberniia of Turkestan, where Russian rule ensured a certain amount of religious freedom. On the other hand, there is no evidence of the existence of such places of worship in the emirate of Bukhara,[12] in spite of the presence of a large Shikarpuri colony.

The difficulties created by distance and by the shortage of Brahmins and other religious specialists meant that often Shikarpuri merchants had to improvise to cope with situations such as death, which imperatively required the presence of Brahmins. The almost pathetic aspect of such situations comes out well in the dry language of official documents, as in this narrative of the funeral ceremony held in 1914 in the town of

[10] See despatch no. 25, 31 August 1897, from Bombay to the secretary of state for India, IOR, Political & Secret Correspondence from India 1875–1911, L/P&S/7/308.
[11] In an application dated 6 February 1909 addressed to the collector of Sukkur, Musamat Bhajibai, the widow of a Shikarpuri deceased in Bahadin near Bukhara complained of the fraudulent manoeuvres of one Chimandas, her late husband's partner and a *pirzadeh*, stressing that the latter 'carries great influence among the Hindus being a Pirzada', BPP, April 1909, Serial no. A 21.
[12] An English visitor to Bukhara in the early 1870s wrote, about the Hindus in the emirate: 'They are not suffered to build temples or set up idols, or indulge in religious processions.' J. Hutton, *Central Asia: from the Aryan to the Cossack*, London, 1875, pp. 288–9.

Andijan, in the Ferghana valley, for one Gidalmal Ramalmal, who had just died. The narrator is the 'Indian Bazaar-Aksakal' of Andijan, i.e. the representative of the local Shikarpuri community *vis-à-vis* the Russian authorities, and this is the story told in his own words:

> I . . . hereby certify that deceased British Indian subject Gidalmal Ramalmalov [sic] died after a prolonged illness on 13/26 May 1914 in the quarter Ishi Kapa and that on the following day in my presence at a general meeting of Indian friends of the deceased [he] was cremated in accordance with Brahmin rites without the services of a priest owing to there being none. The burial [sic] rites were performed by us in the outskirts of the town of Andijan . . .[13]

This sober narration well captures the isolation of a small colony of Hindus devoid of Brahmins who had to perform rituals without proper guidance. They nevertheless managed to maintain some semblance of religious life, which must have helped them bear the weight of long periods of expatriation. It is also probable that they took part in the worship of Muslim saints, which was an important feature of Central Asian Islam. The existence of longstanding links between Central Asia and Sind through some *sufi* orders must have facilitated their participation. But the vast majority of the Shikarpuris, in spite of being *murids* of various *sufi pirs* in Sind and in Central Asia, remained nevertheless faithful to their specific brand of Hinduism mixed with Sikhism.

The situation for the more widely dispersed Sindwork merchants was much more varied. Some of the places they went to, like Colombo or Rangoon, had long-established Hindu communities and many temples where they could worship. In other localities, the Sindworkies shared places of worship with Khalsa Sikhs. This was the case, for instance, in Singapore, Hong Kong or Manila in the Philippines. In Singapore, the first *gurdwara* was built with funds donated by the great Sindwork firm of Wassiamall Assomull. In Manila, the *gurdwara* built in 1933 was largely financed by contributions from the local Sindhis, while the local Punjabi Sikh community managed its affairs.[14] This symbiotic relationship with Khalsa Sikhs and this sharing of places of worship was a feature of Sindhi communities in many places. It came to an end only in 1984 when, following Mrs Gandhi's assassination by her Sikh bodyguards and a spate of anti-Sikh rioting in India, Sindhi Hindus suddenly stopped going *en masse* to the *gurdwaras* to worship.[15] But Sindworkies

---

[13] See *note verbale*, 27 August/9 September 1914, from Asiatic Department in Russian Ministry of Foreign Affairs to British Embassy, St Petersburg, enclosed in St Petersburg despatch no. 262, enclosed in Foreign Office to India Office, 29 September 1914, copy in IOR, Public & Judicial Department Annual Files, File J&P 4231/1914.

[14] See Ajit Singh Rye, 'The Indian Community in the Philippines', in Mani and Sandhu (eds.), *Indian communities in South East Asia*, p. 734.

[15] Tensions between Sindhis and Punjabi Khalsa Sikhs surfaced in Manila in the 1960s,

also travelled to places where there were neither other Hindus nor Khalsa Sikhs. In these places, they do not appear to have built their own temples or *tikhanas*. Sometimes a rudimentary place of worship was installed on the premises of a firm, like in Gibraltar in the 1930s,[16] but generally worship was conducted only in the homes of the merchants. One of the reasons why Sindwork merchants did not build temples was that they had no priests to attend to them. Bringing in religious specialists would have forced them to draw on their already limited quota of employees, and they were not ready to do that. In many places, merchants and employees had to manage wihout proper places of worship and without specialists. On the whole, religious practice did not play the role of a structuring element in the organization of the dispersed communities, and places of worship were not loci of socialization, in contrast to what happened in the Sikh diaspora. In some places, conversions to Christianity are known to have occurred among Sindworkies,[17] in the same way as conversions to Islam took place in Shikarpuri communities in Central Asia. Most Sindhis however remained faithful to their Nanakpanthi faith, and found ways of maintaining their religious identity intact through many tribulations. Some participated actively in different reformist organizations, such as the Arya Samaj or the Radhaswami Satsang, but a lot depended on individual inclinations and choices.

Caste associations did not exist in the diaspora, but there were Shikarpuri *panchayats* in many localities of Central Asia, and they corresponded regularly with *panchayats* in Shikarpur itself. The *mazhars* exchanged between these two kinds of *panchayats* were the principal means of communication between the merchants in Shikarpur and those in the diaspora in Central Asia. *Panchayats* were a form of collective organization which ensured some basic form of solidarity. Thus, when a Shikarpuri died in Central Asia, the *panchayat* generally advanced the money needed for the funeral expenses so that the corpse could be cremated immediately. Shikarpuri *panchayats*, which often included members of the three merchant castes, differed from caste *panchayats* in that they had no very effective way of implementing their

leading to the establishment of a separate Hindu temple in 1962, but the definite break between the two groups occurred only in 1984, *ibid.*, pp. 737 ff. On the desertion of the *gurdwaras* by the Sindhis in North America after 1984, see R. Brady Williams, *Religions of Immigrants from India and Pakistan: New Threads in the American Tapestry*, Cambridge, 1988, pp. 77, 82.

[16] Mentioned in *Indians Abroad Directory*.

[17] Singh Rye, 'Indian Community in the Philippines', p. 756, mentions that more than 100 Sindhi Hindus converted to catholicism in the Philippines, although he says nothing about the dates of those conversions. Similar conversions occurred in the Canary Islands.

decisions, as shown in numerous instances of disputes between the *panchayat* and one merchant or group of merchants. These councils testified, however, to the existence of a corporate identity among Shikarpuri merchants. The basis of this corporate identity was the solidarity between townsmen reinforced by the fictive ties of the brotherhood or *bhaiband*. All Shikarpuris in the dispersion thought of each other as brothers, and the ties of brotherhood were strong, even if not devoid of ambiguity.

Among Sindworkies, there were no corporate institutions equivalent to the Shikarpuri *panchayats*. Only in the Dutch East Indies, in Surabaya, is there mention of a *Hoofd der Indiers*, the head of the local Indian community who was a Sindhi.[18] Elsewhere, Sindworkie communities do not appear to have had any form of legal existence or to have benefited from recognition by the authorities. There too the fictive kinship ties of brotherhood were important in linking men. Even if the vast majority of Sindworkies left their home town with a contract with a firm and if the principals of the firms do not appear to have particularly encouraged their employees to mix with those of other firms, contacts were inevitably made, as is normal with small isolated communities. Since there were generally no specific places of worship or other 'communal' meeting places, most of this socializing between employees of the various firms seems to have taken place informally in bars and other public places. The managers of the firms tended, however, to socialize in a different context and Sindhi clubs were created, like the one founded in Hong Kong in the 1930s. Increasingly, however, the need was felt to have associations representing the Sindwork merchants *vis-à-vis* local authorities and British consuls. They differed from *panchayats* in as much as they were voluntary associations charging membership fees. Table 8.1 gives a list of the major associations which have been identified. Not all these associations advertised themselves as specifically representing 'Sindhi' interests, but all of them, whatever their name, were dominated by Sindwork merchants. Of the eleven associations listed, only two, in Batavia and Colon, also had non-Sindhi members, who were nevertheless in a minority and did not influence policy. Interestingly, in Manila there were for a while two different associations claiming to represent the interests of the local Sindhi merchants. One, the Bombay Merchants Association, represented the big firms, while the other, called the Indian Association, claimed to speak on behalf of smaller operators.[19]

[18] Mani, 'Indians in Jakarta', in Mani and Sandhu (eds.), *Indian Communities in Southeast Asia*.
[19] See letter, 2 December 1920, from Indian Association, Manila, to British consul,

Table 8.1. *Associations representing Sindhi merchants*

Locality	Name of association
Colombo	Sindhi Merchants Association of Ceylon
Batavia	Indian Merchants Association
Surabaya	Sindhi Association
Yokohama	Yokohama Silk Merchants Association
Manila	Bombay Merchants Association
Saigon	Sindhi Silk Merchants Association
Singapore	Sindhi Merchants Association
Colon	Hindustani Merchants Association
Gibraltar	Indian Merchants Association
Hong Kong	Sind Hindu Merchants Club
Accra	Indian Merchants Association

The latter, however, had a short-lived existence, as it was suspected by the local British consul of harbouring anti-British elements.[20] The Bombay Merchants Association emerged clearly as the most representative of the two and progressively attracted even the smaller merchants to its fold.

These associations, besides cooperating with the Sindwork Merchants Association in Hyderabad to fight restrictive immigration policies and more generally to defend the interests of the Sindwork merchants when they appeared threatened, also facilitated ententes between firms to divide markets and regulate profits, especially in periods of depression.

In many areas where there were active communities of Sindwork merchants, there did not emerge formal associations, but this did not preclude forms of collective action. Thus, during the Spanish Civil War, all the firms represented in Tenerife and Las Palmas engaged in a joint effort to wrest concessions from the nationalist authorities with the help of the British consulates.[21]

In spite of the fierce individualism often displayed by Sindwork merchants, they were capable of joint action when their interests were threatened. This solidarity was, however, 'class' rather than 'communal' solidarity. The principals and managers of the firms acted in unison to maintain the labour market in a state of relative fluidity by keeping open the channels of circulation between Hyderabad and the places of business. But this solidarity was largely aimed at preventing the em-

---

Manila, copy in IOR, Industries & Overseas Department Annual Files, File 7 of 1921, L/E/7/1173.
[20] See British consulate-general, Manila, to Lord Curzon, secretary of state for foreign affairs, 18 February 1921, copy in *ibid*.
[21] See above, Chapter 7.

ployees from taking advantage of the situation to demand higher wages and better working conditions.[22] It is significant that the firms were generally able to maintain a united front, and that there was no attempt at overbidding and enticing employees away from other firms by offering them a better deal. Solidarity in the Sindworkie community was above all 'horizontal' solidarity between capitalists rather than 'vertical' solidarity between capitalists and employees.

Even among 'capitalists', there was a frequent divide between principals or capitalist partners on the one hand, and working partners on the other. It could at times erupt into open conflict about the sharing of profits. Some of the court cases in the records of the consular courts are centred on disputes of that nature, and they clearly show the limits of solidarity between big merchant capitalists and their less wealthy partners. Some of the aggrieved parties amongst the working partners tried to present that type of conflict as a form of class struggle. In an affidavit found in the records of the British consulate in Yokohama,[23] one merchant who was a working partner gave an account of his dispute with his principals about the division of profits between the two parties. As no agreement could be reached, the working partner drew a sum from the firm, claiming that he had a 'moral and legal right to draw that much money', and he added the following comment: 'This step was neither unusual nor astounding, many of my oppressed brethren in the near past having adopted the same course in order to safeguard their rights, which most of the Capital Partner [sic], terming themselves as "Sethias", always try to trespass.' This attempt at enlarging an ordinary conflict between partners into a more general antagonism rested on the deployment of a rhetoric of oppression which sounds a bit hollow. But it is significant of the tensions which existed in that mercantile society between the owners of capital and those who were only aspiring capitalists.

We clearly have to move away from an 'irenic' reading of the nature of relationships within a particular merchant community. Solidarity between merchants did not preclude conflicts and recourse to arbitration did not necessarily ensure a satisfactory resolution of conflict. In the above-mentioned case, the dispute was submitted to the arbitration of three Sindhi merchants, who produced an award, which was signed by only two of them, and was not accepted by either party, so that the matter was eventually taken to court. Similar instances of arbitration awards rejected by one of the parties are to be found in the records of the consular courts, leading to the conclusion that there was no fool-

[22] See Chapter 7.
[23] PRO, FO 908/8. See above, Chapter 5.

proof 'internal' mechanism for solving disputes between Sindwork merchants, and that aggrieved parties did not hesitate to go to court.

The existing literature on merchant communities has been inclined to an 'irenic' reading for two reasons: firstly because it has been influenced by the image that merchants themselves tried to project of harmony, and secondly, because little attention has been paid to court records, which are in any case difficult to find and to use. Nevertheless it would be dangerous to put too much stress on the elements of conflict within merchant communities. Economic interests constantly pit merchant against merchant even when they are partners, and there is nothing surprising in the occurrence of regular conflicts. It is rather a question of balance. Was 'communal' solidarity between merchants of the same town sufficiently developed to contain the inevitable conflicts between private parties and prevent them from spilling over into the public arena, thus compromising both actual business and the image of the community? A positive answer to this question involves implicit assumptions about the existence of a bond of trust between merchants of the same town. It is however highly problematic.

The problem of trust

There is no accepted definition of what constitutes trust in business relationships, but it is acknowledged to be a necessary ingredient to the successful conduct of transactions. Markets could not actually function without the existence of a modicum of trust between agents engaged in transactions. However, there is no way of measuring trust, except negatively, in the form of the costs incurred from breaches of it. Trust can be generated in many ways, but it is often construed that the prior existence of affective links between agents is one of the surest ways. Hence the idea that, within a group of merchants having a common religion, ethnicity and/or caste or geographical origin, generally manifested in a dense network of kinship relations, trust flourishes so to speak 'naturally', and does not need to be generated by systematic trust-building measures. This 'organicist' or 'primordialist' view of trust as embedded in a given set of affective relationships has been challenged by authors inspired by the new institutional economics, who, on the contrary, stress the element of rational calculation involved in trust.[24] They show how trust is related to expectations about behaviour and has to do ultimately with reputation. In their view, an agent will trust another party in a transaction only if, on the basis of the latter's

[24] See in particular, P. Das Gupta, 'Trust as a Commodity', in D. Gambetta (ed.), *Trust: Making and Breaking Cooperative Relations*, New York and Oxford, 1988, pp. 49–72.

reputation, he can reasonably expect the other party to behave in a certain way, conducive to the successful implementation of the transaction.

Seen in this light, trust is not necessarily in greater supply among participants in a network than among others. Firstly, it is necessary to dispel the widely held fallacy that family and kinship are privileged breeding grounds for trust. The history of Indian business enterprise is full of stories about disputes between members of the same family leading to the demise of once successful firms. Between brothers, in particular, sibling rivalry is a powerful inducement to quarrel and an antidote to trust. Between non-kin-related participants of a given trading network, trust is subject to the same limitations as between 'ordinary' traders. However, reputations are more credibly established in the context of a particular network than in other contexts, because of the speed and ease with which information circulates and can be checked. Between Sind merchants, a reputation for honesty was not simply established on the basis of bazaar gossip, but rested on a dense flow of accumulated information about past behaviour in transactions, of which there was often even a written record which was easily accessible. To sum up, a Sindwork merchant did not trust another Sindwork merchant simply because he was from Hyderabad; he trusted him if he had a clean record which could easily be checked. On the other hand, a reputation could easily be ruined by the disclosure of information about dishonest behaviour, and such damage, once inflicted, was difficult to repair.[25] Trust within the community of Shikarpuri or Sindwork merchants was not an automatic outcome of kinship ties or solidarity between townsmen, but the result of a process in which information about past behaviour played a crucial role.

A frequent corollary of the 'primordialist' view of trust is the idea that between merchants belonging to the same 'community', oral contracts are more frequent than written ones; a handshake or some other form of physical contact between agents is deemed to carry more weight than a written agreement. If this were the case, then why would merchants bother to conclude written agreements, which involve hiring a lawyer and paying stamp duties? As far as the Sind merchants are concerned, it is clear that, from a certain point in time at least, they tended to have written agreements, in the matter of partnerships in particular. This could be seen as a direct effect of the introduction in Sind of the British Indian court system, with the primacy it gave written documents over

---

[25] See the case of the small Port-Said merchant who sued another Sindhi firm because they had written to other Sindhi firms to warn them against him. 'S. Baloomal vs. Ratoomal & Sons', FO 846/97. See above, Chapter 6.

oral testimonies. The argument is certainly valid, but only up to a point. The embracing of the written form of contract may have been in the first place a response to the introduction of a new juridico-legal system, but over time it became internalized and could not but influence the mental universe of the merchants who embraced it.

This opens up the whole question of litigiousness and its relation to the court system in British India. Was litigiousness a function of a court system which encouraged it, or was it the other way round, the 'natural' litigiousness of Indians having found an outlet thanks to the courts? I shall not enter into this chicken-and-egg kind of debate here, but it should be noted that the consular court system itself was an even greater incentive to litigation than the British-Indian court system. The reason was that in that system the judges were the consular officials themselves, men who often had only a limited knowledge of the law[26] and could be easily manipulated by wily operators. Some cases in the consular court records of Morocco show an astonishing level of naivety among British consular officials there,[27] and unscrupulous merchants often had a field day. When taking into account the evidence of cases in the consular courts, the existence of such a bias should not be overlooked, and one should beware of deriving too definite conclusions from such material. But a look at some of these cases is nevertheless revealing of some aspects of the moral economy of diasporic networks.

Most court cases involving Sindhi merchants in Cairo in the late nineteenth and early twentieth centuries revolved around one kind of 'breach of trust' or another. One common characteristic of most of these 'breaches of trust' is that they did not occur between 'equals' but between contracting parties which were in a position of subordination and superordination in relation to one other. The three most common forms of breach of trust occurred between capitalist partner and working partner, between employer and employee, and between merchant and hawker under contract to the merchant.

This shows clearly that the question of trust cannot be completely divorced from an examination of power relationships within the com-

---

[26] See D. C. M. Platt, *The Cinderella Service: British Consuls since 1825*, London, 1971, p. 214: 'The British consular courts were always an imperfect instrument of justice . . . The consuls themselves were often ignorant of the law, and sometimes eccentric in applying it.'

[27] A case in the Fez consular court is typical of the carelessness of British consular officials in judging matters relating to Indian traders. A young Sindhi pedlar was killed in a bus accident near Oujda in December 1929. A local Sindhi merchant came forward with a claim to the goods and money left by the deceased, on the basis of some vague paper, and the court awarded him the goods. See 'Probate jurisdiction in the case of Tolaram Tarachand', PRO, Foreign Office Records, Embassy and Consular Archives: Morocco, Fez Consular Court, FO 909/228.

munity itself. Between unequals, a relationship of trust was clearly more difficult to sustain over time than one between equals. Inferiors as well as superiors had the possibility of engaging in opportunistic behaviour, and rarely resisted it. Working partners were constantly exposed to the temptation of 'cooking the books', taking advantage of the fact that the principal was sitting thousands of miles away in Hyderabad and had no way of checking daily on them. Employees, who were overworked, but not subjected to very close supervision, were inclined to steal or to shirk work. Hawkers tended to retain part of the goods entrusted to them to sell them on the side. On the other hand, principals often tried to deprive working partners of a share of the profits due to them, attempted to cheat on payment of salaries to employees, and did not always supply hawkers with the quantity and quality of goods prescribed in the contracts.

In these cases, the guilty party seems to have assumed often that, because of solidarity between townsmen, he would be able to escape punishment. In other words, implicit assumptions about solidarity could be powerful inducements to breach of trust. The guilty party would seem to have calculated that the aggrieved party would prefer to accept losses rather than go to court and expose themselves to close public scrutiny. In the particular cases reviewed here, this assumption of course proved wrong, and the aggrieved party did take legal action. But one can legitimately speculate that in many other cases they preferred to settle out of court. Unfortunately we do not know the ratio of out-of-court settlements to suits filed in courts.

An important question is whether litigiousness was enhanced by the dispersion of the merchants and the breach of collective discipline and surveillance it could entail. The same kind of questioning can be applied to the numerous cases of fraud and disputes that were generated around the problem of Shikarpuri successions in Central Asia.

There also, in spite of the closely knit nature of the community, which was much more in evidence than in the more cosmopolitan and relaxed atmosphere of Cairo, opportunistic behaviour was prevalent. Successions in particular were viewed as opportunities for profit, and some Shikarpuris apparently built fortunes on the basis of questionable operations linked to different successions. According to Rieu, this behaviour, which he found morally objectionable, was considered legitimate by Shikarpuris in Central Asia as well as in Shikarpur.[28] The legitimation of opportunistic behaviour seems *a priori* to be incompatible with the existence of a core of values strongly adhered to. This apparent paradox

---

[28] See above, Chapter 3.

should perhaps lead us to a more 'contextual' reading of the meaning of 'opportunistic behaviour'. This contextual reading should take into consideration the fact of dispersion and exile itself. For Hindu merchants of Sind, there was obviously no strong taboo on travelling beyond the Indus and the Bolan Pass, but the strict taboo against women travelling seems to indicate the existence of at least a residual interdict. Might it not be possible that a certain relativisation of norms occurred once one had left one's native land? In other words, what would have passed as unacceptable opportunistic behaviour in Shikarpur itself became acceptable in Bukhara.

The concept of a 'moral economy' which was prevalent among Sind merchants in the dispersion was fairly elastic. An important element which contributed to this plasticity was the role of the fictive kinship links of the brotherhood. The term *bhaiband*, in spite of being increasingly used as a caste name, basically meant a group of brothers, and among Sind merchants fraternalism was elevated to the rank of an ideology. Maintaining the links of the brotherhood was an obligation, and any breach of it could attract moral condemnation. When a Sindhi firm in Port Said publicly disclosed information about the dishonest business practices of a Sindhi trader, the latter had recourse to an arbitrator who gave an award in his favour. Although he recognized that the information disclosed was true, the arbitrator stressed that the statements were made 'without justification' and with 'impure motives', and added that it was also 'most unbusinesslike'. He concluded his award with a call to the parties to 'adopt a magnanimous attitude towards each other and not to give importance to small matters and to bear always a brotherly feeling'.[29]

Trust between network members was the result of a constant compromise between a 'rational-empirical' view in which the record of past behaviour was the crucial element, and a more affective one in which there was a kind of moral obligation to trust one's *bhais*, whatever was their actual behaviour.

It should not be forgotten either that colonies of Sind merchants, whether Shikarpuri colonies in Central Asia or Sindworkie colonies in Egypt or Panama, were almost purely male communities. Although their 'sexual economy' could vary, as will be seen, at the level of affect the absence of women gave an added intensity to the relations between males. The tensions induced by sexual frustration and affective deprivation might have found their translation in certain forms of aggressive behaviour. Evidence from Central Asia shows that violence between

[29] Letter from C. D. Mukhi, Hyderabad, chosen as arbitrator by the two parties in 'S. Baloomal vs. Ratoomal & Sons', FO 846/97. See above, note 25.

Shikarpuris was not uncommon, resulting in some fatalities, and that thefts also occurred. Apart from one theft inside the main Shikarpuri *sarai* in Bukhara which created a particular scandal, instances of fraud and cheating are too numerous to be considered mere accidents. Evidence from the Cairo consular court records also reveals a pattern of violence and widespread stealing within the Sindworkie community of the Egyptian capital.

Small colonies of men without women dispersed across vast distances, separated from their brothers in the closest colony by hundreds of miles of ocean or difficult terrain, obviously found it difficult to stick to very strict norms of conduct; hence the development of various forms of opportunistic and violent behaviour which even *panchayats*, where they existed, were powerless to prevent.

Separation from women for long periods, a general characteristic of Hindu merchant communities outside India, thus decisively affected patterns of behaviour among males. In spite of not being directly involved in the networks, women nevertheless influenced them in many ways.

Three models of sexual economy in the dispersion

Reviewing, at the time of the abolition of indentured emigration, the question of the desirable sex ratio among colonies of Indian labourers overseas, a Sind official commended the Shikarpuris and Sindworkies for being able to do without women.[30] His view of the 'sexual economy' of these two merchant diasporas appears to have been largely idealized. Among dispersed Sind merchants, three models of sexual economy can actually be distinguished, one which could be called 'ascetic', one 'permissive' and one intermediate.

The 'ascetic' model was exemplified by the case of the Shikarpuris in Russian Central Asia. Shikarpuri merchants in this region of Central Asia appear effectively to have lived without women. According to the evidence of archival sources as well as that of travellers' accounts, no Shikarpuri woman ever came to Central Asia. The taboo on their

[30] In a memorandum, 2 November 1916, addressed to the secretary to the Government of Bombay in the General Department, the commissioner in Sind wrote: 'There are sections of the population of Sind whose mode of life illustrates the proposition that the company of women is not indispensable. In the higher social strata, the merchants of Shikarpur visit Central Asia and Russia for periods of several years, and never take their womenkind. The merchants of Hyderabad visit every portion of the globe on contract with their employers, also for periods of several years, and never take their women.' Bombay General Confidential Proceedings (Miscellaneous), January 1917, Serial no. A 2.

travelling seems to have been enforced very strictly, the most likely explanation being that it was a substitute for the taboo on male travelling. Widespread insecurity on the roads was also a strong disincentive to women to travel, as their male companions, who went about unarmed, would have been unable to offer them protection.

Judging from the evidence of successional documents, the majority of Shikarpuri men in Central Asia were unmarried. As for married men, who account for a little less than half the sample of those whose deaths were recorded, all lived in Central Asia, sometimes for fairly long periods, without their wives, who stayed in Shikarpur. Did these lone men, whether married or unmarried, find female company in their place of residence? From the evidence of successional documents, it appears that they did not form lasting relationships with local women. No mention of claims by local heirs ever occurs in any of the documents. If this absence of claims were limited to the documents originating from Shikarpur, it would not be very significant: widows or other heirs of the deceased merchants obviously had no reason to mention rival claims to the authorities. But the lack of mention of such claims even in documents emanating from the Russian and Bukharan authorities seems to suggest that there were no claimants.

The major reason why Shikarpuris in Russian Central Asia could not form durable relationships seems to have been the attitude of the local Muslim population towards the infidel Hindus. If a Shikarpuri wanted to have a relationship with a local woman, even as a concubine, he was expected to convert to Islam.[31] There is no doubt that some Shikarpuris became Muslims, probably largely for matrimonial purposes, but they then dropped out of the community and their cases did not come to the knowledge of British officials. It should also be mentioned that, in strictly Sunni Bukhara, the temporary marriage, a typical Shia practice, seems to have been little used. Shikarpuris in Russian Central Asia lived in all-male households of two to ten men,[32] generally in rooms situated inside *sarais* which they owned or rented. All contemporary observers noticed that these men without women looked 'sad', an appearance which they attributed to exile and the status of barely tolerated minority

[31] The fact was mentioned by Mohan Lal in his account of his visit to Bukhara in the 1830s: 'if a Hindu . . . falls in love with a Muhammadan girl, he communicates it to the king, who makes him a Musulman and tells the parents of the girl to give her in marriage to him'. Mohan Lal, *Travels*, p. 130.
[32] Schuyler wrote in *Turkistan*, pp. 185–6: 'These Hindoos live in little ménages of one or two exclusively in the caravanserai, partly in order to be near the business centre of the town, and partly for safety, as they have thus greater protection against the possibly murderous designs of insolvent debtors, than they would have in remote houses or gardens.'

Community and gender 267

in a predominantly Muslim country. Sexual frustration and the lack of family life are more plausible contributing factors to this 'sadness'.

The situation in Russian Central Asia was in complete contrast to that in neighbouring Sinkiang where Shikarpuris often had local Uighur women as concubines or even common law wives. The difference between the sexual economies of the Shikarpuri diaspora in Russian Central Asia and in Sinkiang is a rather fascinating topic. The two regions had a mostly Muslim population to whom the Shikarpuri Hindus were anathema both as infidels and as greedy moneylenders. But while in the Russian territory the local Muslims were successful in denying the Shikarpuris access to their women (unless they accepted conversion to Islam), in Sinkiang they could not prevent the same Shikarpuris from forming durable relationships. The explanation for the contrast appears to lie in a certain number of correlated factors. In Sinkiang, there was a tradition for Chinese officials to have local Muslim concubines, while in Russian Central Asia it was not the case with Russian officials. There was therefore more tolerance in Sinkiang towards relationships between local Muslim women and infidel men, especially as, in a political context marked by the existence of extra-territorial privileges for British subjects, Shikarpuris used to pose as sort of official agents and did not hesitate to use force to seize women.[33] The second factor is related to the economy, its level of marketization and monetization and the commodification of land. In Russian Central Asia, land tended increasingly to be a marketable commodity, and was commonly used as collateral for guaranteeing loans by moneylenders to peasants. In Sinkiang, on the other hand, the land market was undeveloped and land was not as a rule used as collateral in moneylending transactions. The only collateral most Uighur peasants could pledge in guarantee of repayment of the loans they took from Shikarpuri moneylenders were their women and children. Therefore Shikarpuris often acquired local women as chattel in lieu of collateral to guarantee loans. Since the Uighur peasantry was generally too poor to repay its debts to the Shikarpuris, the latter kept the women after the expiry date of reimbursement of the loan, and set up more or less permanent house-

---

[33] In his diary for ten days ending 20 October 1903, the British agent in Kashgar wrote, under the entry for 17 October: 'The Aksakal of Karghalik reports that a Hindu, Girdhari, has taken the daughter of a man who owed him tengas 150. This caused a complaint from the Muhammadans to the *amban* (local Chinese official) and Girdhari returned the girl to her parents. Tursa (another Hindu) then appears to have complained, saying that Mr Macartney had permitted Hindus to take wives in this country, and they would not obey the *amban*'s orders in that respect.' IOR, Political & Secret Correspondence with India, Political & Secret Letters from India, 1903, L/P&S/7/159.

holds, in which children born of their union with these women were raised. A certain amount of cultural misunderstanding often seems to have existed between Shikarpuris and their Uighur peasant debtors on this question. For the Shikarpuris, the women were collateral, and their possession did not cancel the debt owed to them by the borrower. Uighur peasants seem to have taken the opposite view and this divergence of interpretation explains why, during the anti-Chinese and anti-Shikarpuri rising of 1933, one of the main demands of the rioters, apart from the cancellation of all debts, was that the women kept by the Shikarpuris should be returned to their original owners.[34]

The comparison between the cases of Russian Central Asia and Sinkiang shows that sexual asceticism was not an inbred characteristic of Shikarpuris. In Russian Central Asia, avoiding sexual entanglements with local Muslim women was the only way to ensure the survival of the community and the transmission of inheritances to Shikarpur. Had local Muslim women acquired valid claims to successions, the latter would have been recognized by the Russian and Bukharan authorities and heirs in Shikarpur would have been largely deprived of their inheritance. On the other hand, in Sinkiang the concubines of the Shikarpuris, because of the attitude of the Chinese authorities due to the extra-territorial privileges claimed by the Shikarpuris as British subjects, were not in a position to claim a share of their inheritance. Although some Shikarpuris showed themselves humane and generous towards their mistresses,[35] most of them seem to have treated the local women as chattels devoid of any right.

Avoidance of local sexual entanglements also ensured freedom from affinal relationships, a definite asset for moneylenders who tended to charge high rates of interest on loans. One school in sociological literature has stressed the advantage derived from being a stranger in order to maintain the objectivity best suited to the establishment of market relationships. Others have taken the opposite view, that kinship and affinity could make important contributions to the development of trading networks. However, when it comes to running a moneylending

---

[34] See 'Narrative to Appendix C, Karghalik, 24 March 1933', enclosed in British consul, Kashgar, to secretary to the Government of India in the Foreign and Political Department, 23 January 1936, copy in PRO, Foreign Office Records, General Correspondence (Political), China 1936, FO 371/20 220. The text said: 'At Karghalik, Non-Moslem Chinese and Hindus were killed and their property looted. It was a case of mob violence, the people were in no mood to halt and enquire which of the stories were true: That the Hindus were infidel, That they were sheltering Chinese, That they were firing on the crowd, That they refused to hand over their Turk wives. The Hindus were mostly money-lenders and the mob hoped thus to cancel their debts.'

[35] Like the man who included in his will a clause about the keeping of his concubine by his partner and heir after his death. See above, Chapter 3.

Community and gender 269

business, as opposed to a purely commercial one, affinity and kinship are best left out of the picture. Sexual asceticism could be a highly rational conduct on the part of a small community of moneylenders operating in small colonies dispersed across vast territories. The advantages gained from such conduct come out clearly if one compares the fate of the Shikarpuris in Bukhara, where they never became a target of mob violence, and in Sinkiang, where their sexual acquisitiveness exposed them to popular anger at the time of the 1933–34 rising.

These contrasting models of sexual economy amongst the Shikarpuri diaspora both rested on the complete absence of Shikarpuri women. They also implied that many men remained unmarried for very long periods of their lives, which was totally contrary to canonical Hindu ideas. It is interesting to note that when Richard Burton visited Shikarpur, in the early 1870s, he claimed that young Shikarpuri males left for their voyages only after having got married and begotten a child.[36] Data on successions show otherwise: out of 118 men in the sample of successions, the majority died unmarried, and, amongst the married ones, almost half died either issueless or with only female issue. Either Sir Richard's information was incorrect or the conditions on the marriage market in Shikarpur altered radically between the early 1870s and the 1890s, which seems rather unlikely. How could such a situation be justified in the context of a culture which placed such a premium on the engendering of male heirs? In this particular case, it could be rationalized as deferment rather than dereliction of duty as a householder. Deferment could be very long term indeed, since stays of ten to twenty years in Central Asia were commonplace among Shikarpuris. However cases are known of merchants who, having spent more than twenty years in the region, were able to go back to Shikarpur in middle age to marry.

The Sindworkie network was characterized by a slightly different sexual economy. Although most Sindwork merchants and employees, even when they were married, went abroad as single men, the exclusion of women was never absolute. There was even a growing tendency by managers, in the 1920s and 1930s, to take their wives with them. A survey of the Sindworkie community in Gibraltar[37] in 1939 reveals that, out of a total of 25 managers, 9 lived in Gibraltar with their wives and

[36] He wrote in *Sind Revisited*, vol. II, pp. 253–4: 'The Shikarpuri Hindu, after receiving a sound commercial education and studying the practice of trade at home, marries with much solemnity and ceremony. The birth of the first child is the signal for leaving home; the jeune père takes leave of his family with tears and sobs; and he forthwith sets out alone for some distant land, with the probable intention of spending in exile half his life.'

[37] Statement by Sindwork Merchants Association, Hyderabad, enclosed in Government

children. Still the sex ratio was 9 adult women to some 120 adult men. Ordinary employees, even when they were married, which occurred rarely, were never allowed to bring their wives with them. Lists of Sindworkies stranded in enemy territory during the Second World War nevertheless reveal some degree of variability in the sex ratio. In Japan, the ratio seems to have been approximately 1 woman to 10 men.[38] On the other hand, in Libya the local Sindworkie community was all male.[39]

In the cosmopolitan milieu of the port cities in which most Sindwork merchants resided for quite long periods, opportunities for sexual encounters were many, especially given the relative affluence of these men. Frequenting prostitutes seems to have been common among members of the employee and servant class, according to the evidence of court cases in Egypt and Morocco. Managers and independent merchants, for their part, often had concubines or common law wives. This was the case, for instance, in the Philippines, where most Sindhi merchants who stayed for extended periods formed longstanding relationships with local women.[40] Marriages between Sindhi merchants and local women are known to have taken place in Japan, China and Egypt.[41] Some of those who formed permanent relationships abroad had a wife and children in Hyderabad, and situations of bigamy were therefore not unknown, a fact which was not without consequences in

of India, Department of Commonwealth Relations to secretary, Political Department, India Office, 16 May 1946, POL 8546/1946, IOR, L/P&J/8/236.

[38] A list of 140 Indians, mostly Sindhis, evacuated from Japan in 1941 on S.S. *Anhui* included several women and children. PRO, Foreign Office Records, General Correspondence (Consular), File 810 of 1945, 'Assistance for British subjects in liberated territories', FO 369/3164 to 3170.

[39] A list of fifteen Sindhis stranded in Libya in 1940 included only names of males, IOR, Public & Judicial Department Collections, File 5301 'British Indian subjects in enemy territory during World War II', L/P&J/7/3002.

[40] According to Singh Rye, 'Indian Community in the Philippines', p. 716: 'Most of the early immigrants were young and the married ones left their wives behind. Eventually, whether single or married, Sindhi or Punjabi, they either took in "common law live-in-wives" or formally got married, to escape the boredom of a lonely existence. Even though such live-in marital arrangements were common in Manila, they were discreetly kept a secret from the families in India to avoid social sanction and family embarrassment.' It is however doubtful that such secrecy could be maintained over a long period of time.

[41] A Sindhi merchant of Cairo married a Copt woman. See 'Marriage of P. Khanchand', IOR, Public & Judicial Department Annual File, File P&J 4465/1935, L/P&J/7/957. A Sindhi merchant of Kobe married a Japanese woman in 1925. See 'Bhagwandas Vussamall Uttamchandani', PRO, Foreign Office Records, Embassy and Consular Archives: Japan, Yokohama, FO 908/64. A Sindhi merchant of Tientsin, who was killed in the famous Mukden rail incident in September 1931, had a Chinese wife. See 'B. L. Pinyamall', PRO, Foreign Office Records, Embassy and Consular Archives: China, China Consulates, Personal Estates Correspondence, FO 678/1733.

Hyderabad itself. It is now time to turn to the women who were left behind.

The women left behind

The annual departure of many relatively young men for often very long periods, besides acting to regulate the matrimonial market, had a very direct impact on the life of many of the women who stayed in Shikarpur or Hyderabad. Married women whose husbands departed were not the only ones affected. Often widows saw their entire male offspring leave to seek their fortune abroad. Nor were women involved in the diaspora only as wives and mothers of departed men. Many young girls saw their brother(s) depart so as to earn the money needed for their dowry.

The women had to deal with solitude, as some households were depleted of all their male members; the remittances which were their livelihood did not always come on time and were sometimes insufficient to ensure their maintenance and that of their children. When a male member of the family died on a voyage, there were often problems in collecting his inheritance. The ways in which the women coped with the situation varied however considerably.

Some evidence has come to light concerning the Shikarpuri women through the successional documents. They first permit an assessment of the actual situation in the matter of inheritance, which somewhat departs from the accepted truth regarding the matter.

Sind, as a part of the Bombay presidency, was under the *Mitaksara* system, in which women's rights in matters of succession were extremely limited.[42] Under *Mitaksara* law, the widow, on condition that she remained chaste, could enjoy a limited (lifetime) interest in her husband's property but only in the absence of male heirs up to the fourth generation. Given that context, it comes as something of a surprise that, out of a total of 118 successions in which the name of the legal heir is known, a woman's right to inheritance was recognized by the court in 42 cases, and that she was awarded a certificate of heirship, an indispensable document to get her claims recognized by the Russian courts and the Bukharan judicial authorities. In more than half of these cases, the legal heir recognized was the widow of the deceased, who generally had died issueless or without male issue. In a few cases, the widow was recognized as heir only temporarily, on behalf of minor male children. More surprisingly, in a certain number of cases when the deceased died unmarried, a female member of the family was recognized as legal heir,

[42] See J. Nair, *Women and Law in Colonial India: a Social History*, Bangalore, 1996, pp. 196–7.

generally the widowed mother. This was in fact inheritance by survivorship, but the court does not appear to have made fine distinctions in the matter. Legal evidence, however, does not tell the whole story, and we do not know whether these women who were recognized as legal heirs were not actually controlled and manipulated by male members of their own family. Other documentary evidence on Shikarpuri women, drawn mostly from travellers' accounts, tends however to suggest that in Shikarpur women had a greater say in family affairs than elsewhere in Sind or more generally in India. It has been mentioned already that they themselves often chose the marriage partners of their sons and daughters. Successional documents often include petitions addressed to the district magistrate by widows, which are fairly revealing of the mentality of Shikarpuri women. Although these petitions were written by a local attorney whose main aim was to enrol the sympathy of the collector for the plight of women whose husbands, sons, brothers or fathers had died in Central Asia, they manage to convey something of the frustrations, hopes and fears of the women of Shikarpur, and as such deserve attention.

The Shikarpuri widows, whose voices can be heard, filtered through the medium of a foreign tongue, in the dry language of official documents, do not appear generally as meek victims of a pitiless fate, but as fighting women determined to get their rights recognized and their claims fulfilled. One of these widows, Mussamat Isarbai, in a petition addressed in 1899 to the collector of Shikarpur,[43] displays in full this fighting spirit. She recalls that she applied to him to recover a sum of over 10,000 tengas left by her deceased husband Nandomal, who had died three years earlier in Katerji, a town in the emirate of Bukhara, and forwarded the required documents. After fifteen or sixteen months, she received only the equivalent of some 600 tengas. She writes:

You may well imagine the shock occurred to me by this incident, as instead of Rs 3,550, which I expected to receive, I have hardly got 1/20 part of the property which I had claimed and to which I had every right. The distress and suspense which I have been subject to cannot be described and unless you will be pleased to assist me in recovering the remaining portion of my property, it would break my heart and be a death blow to me as well as to my two fatherless daughters.

In her deposition taken before the city magistrate of Shikarpur,[44] she gives a few more details about her life. Claiming to be a housewife aged

---

[43] Petition from Mussamat Isarbai, 15 May 1899, to the collector and district magistrate, Shikarpur, enclosure no. 1 in despatch no. 4, 31 January 1900, from Government of Bombay to secretary of state for India, BPP, January 1900, Serial no. A 136.

[44] Deposition, 24 November 1899, enclosure no. 2 in *ibid*.

38, she recalls that her husband Nandomal left eleven years earlier to seek his fortune in Central Asia, leaving her with two minor daughters. She says nothing about regular remittances from Central Asia, but they must have been her only source of income, judging from the fact that the value of her husband's property in Shikarpur itself is put at only Rs 800 in the certificate of heirship. Laying hands on the money left by her husband in Bukhara was for her a matter of life and death, and that is why she fought with great determination to get her due. In this particular case, the story ended happily and the widow got the whole of the inheritance she claimed. Others were not so lucky, but they all fought for their claims. Another widow painted a particularly grim picture of her situation: 'By the death of my husband, she wrote, I am left entirely to my own resources, the consequence of which is that I have fallen into great pecuniary difficulties, and am perishing with famine having two daughters, also for whom I am to provide'.[45] She added that she had spent all the little money she had on stamps, fees and the obtaining an heirship certificate.

These documents allow us a glimpse into a world of lower-middle-class *bania* families hard pressed for money but very conscious of dignity and status, and of the importance of the rightful performance of religious rites for those who died far away from home. In 1888, the widowed mother of a Shikarpuri merchant who had died three years earlier in Russian territory wrote to the British consul at St Petersburg: 'I am an old and helpless widow. I have incurred a large debt in performing some of the customary ceremonies incidental to a Hindu's death and some ceremonies have still to be performed, to meet which money is needed', adding: 'I am very anxious to see that the property of my deceased son is remitted to me to enable me to enter into the requisite ceremonies for the benefit of the soul of my deceased son and my own – a fact too dear to a Hindu's heart to admit of any description'.[46] Here the pain of the loss of a son is compounded by the desire to perform the right ceremonies, at whatever financial cost.

Most of the women left behind were still young and the question cannot fail to arise of their own sexual behaviour in Shikarpur in the absence of their husbands. Interestingly, the same level of asceticism was not expected from them as from their husbands. The reputation of Shikarpuri women for sexual freedom and 'lewdness' has remained well

---

[45] Application dated 6 February 1909 from Musamat Bhajibai to the collector of Sukkur.
[46] Petition, 12 January 1888, from Pohaunch, widow of Sobhraj, to the British consul at St Petersburg, enclosed in Political Letter no. 15 from Government of Bombay to secretary of state for India, 7 March 1888, IOR, Public & Judicial Department Annual Files, File J&P 404/1888.

established in Sind to this very day. One of the first European travellers to have echoed it was Ferrier, a Frenchman who travelled in neighbouring Afghanistan in the early 1840s. He met Shikarpuris in Herat and has the following story to tell:

The Indians I saw at Herat had been there for upwards of twenty years, without even leaving it; but their wives, in almost every case, had never joined them. One of them had, however, a son of about fifteen years of age with him; and I was wondering how he came there, considering that his mother had lived at Shikarpoore for a score of years, and his father the same number at Herat; when I received a solution of the enigma from my acquaintance, Syud Elias, an Afghan merchant, who had made a good many journeys to India, and was familiar with the customs of the people of that country. According to his showing, an Indian, when he leaves his home, leaves also a pair of pantaloons for his wife, who puts them on when she is desirous of being in that condition so natural to, and, generally speaking, so much coveted by married women; no husband, it appears, would ever dream of repudiating a child obtained by this simple method; to do so would be a perfect scandal.[47]

Such almost perfect asymmetry in sexual behaviour between 'lewd' women[48] and 'ascetic' men tends to stretch our credulity a little. However, as already mentioned, there are many indications that in Shikarpur women often had a high degree of autonomy in financial matters, which seems to reveal some independence of mind. Besides, producing heirs outside the marital bed did not entail dangers of division of family wealth, especially if the local sexual partner, often described as a 'wandering Afghan' (of whom there were many in Shikarpur) stayed in the background. On the other hand, the acquisition of a second family by the husband in Central Asia could have led to such an outcome. It can, therefore, plausibly be argued that, in this particular case, repression of male sexuality was more instrumental to safeguarding family interests in the long term than repression of female sexuality. The specific 'sexual economy' of the Shikarpuri merchant family appears to have been functional to its survival in a diasporic context in which periodic visits by the husband to his home town were impossible, and dearth of resident male relatives, most of whom were probably also in

---

[47] J. P. Ferrier, *Caravan Journeys and Wanderings in Persia, Afghanistan, Turkistan and Beloochistan*, London, 1856, pp. 453–4. Ferrier, a French officer sometime in the service of Persia, left an unpublished manuscript in French which was published in an English translation.

[48] Richard Burton echoed this view in *Sind Revisited*, vol. II, p. 255: 'The fair sex at Shikarpur, both Moslem and Hindu, has earned for itself an unenviable reputation . . . The women are far-famed for beauty, the result of mixing with higher blood; for freedom of manners amounting to absolute "fastness" . . . By these exploits the fair dames have more than once involved their lords in difficult and dangerous scrapes. Moreover, when the young husband that was, returns home old and gray, to find a ready-made family thronging the house, scandals will ensue . . .'.

Central Asia or elsewhere, made controlling the women a difficult enterprise.

In Hyderabad, where there was much more circulation between the network centre and the actual places of business, wives remained much more controlled by the family, and no stories about illegitimate children are told (although what the actual situation was is of course difficult to know). Frustration by local Bhaiband women is even given central place in the genesis of a particular Hindu sect, called Brahma Kumari, which was created in Hyderabad in the 1930s and has become nowadays a worldwide phenomenon. Lawrence Babb was the first to draw attention to the emergence of the sect in the particular milieu of wives of Sindwork merchants in Hyderabad.[49] Elaborating on that, Prem Chowdhry[50] has emphasized the tensions created amongst women by the concentration of all sexual reproductive activity in the short span of the six months' period during which husbands were in Hyderabad in between their stints abroad. They had to conceive, preferably a son, during this period, or they would remain barren for a three-year period. The same author stresses that 'the pressures and demands upon a woman's productive functions only increased the suspicions regarding her sexuality, the insecurities of migrant males only reinforcing the familiar stereotype of a sexually starved woman out to satiate herself at the first opportunity'. She sees this kind of pressure as one the reasons for the success of a sect which put a high value on female celibacy.

The thesis of a direct correlation between female asceticism and male migration is alluring, but it should not be overlooked that such a situation of females without males was and is extremely common in many localities in the subcontinent. So it remains to be explained why such a sect originated in the specific milieu of the Sindwork merchants, and nowhere else. More contingent factors, such as the personality of the first guru, Dada Lekhraj, and his first female disciple, might have to be taken into account more. What must be noted is that the sect generated fierce hostility in Hyderabad, which led it to transfer its seat to Karachi after a few years, before shifting to India after Partition. The emergence of the sect is not in itself proof that women in Hyderabad suffered more oppression from a patriarchal regime than elsewhere. What may have contributed to the early popularity of the sect in the Sindworkie milieu however is the particular insecurities felt by Bhaiband women about the fidelity of their husbands residing abroad for long

---

[49] L. A. Babb, 'Amnesia and Remembrance among the Brahma Kumaris', in *Redemptive Encounters: Three Modern Styles in the Hindu Tradition*, Berkeley, CA, 1986, pp. 96–8.
[50] P. Chowdhry, 'Marriage, Sexuality and the Female "Ascetic": Understanding a Hindu Sect', *Economic and Political Weekly*, vol. 31, no. 34, 24–31 August 1996, pp. 2307–21.

periods. Knowledge of the sexual exploits of Hyderabadi men outside their home town must have been widespread and led some women to seek comfort in the preachings of a sect which devalued sexuality altogether and put a special premium on the purity of women.

The only petition from a Hyderabadi widow found in the archives[51] is certainly different in tone from the petitions of Shikarpuri widows. It emphasizes the helpless character of the widow, who claims to be in *purdah*, and her inability to manage her financial affairs. It would be hazardous however to generalize on the basis of one case about differences between the position of widows in Shikarpur and Hyderabad.

Regarding Hyderabad on the other hand, scattered evidence has come to light in commercial directories of participation by women in trade in localities outside India, in particular in Hong Kong. In a few instances, widows appear to have managed the business left by their husband. This is in contrast to Shikarpur, where no women appear to have left the town and engaged in business activities and where many married women and widows appear to have eked out a rather precarious existence and benefited only by irregular remittances from Central Asia. In spite of the greater female participation in business life in Hyderabad, and of the fact that the women of the better-off families lived in style, due to the fact that covering one's women in jewels and fine clothing was a preferred mode of displaying wealth among successful Sindwork merchants, women in that town do not seem to have acquired more independence than in Shikarpur in matters of family life and of choice of sexual partners. Shikarpuri women certainly paid a price for remaining in Sind without their men for longer periods than did the women of Hyderabad, but the prolonged absence of the men also offered them greater opportunities to acquire a space of their own, which some women at least appear to have seized on.

[51] Petition, 28 July 1937, from Radhi bai, wife of late Mr Teckchand Dayaram, to British consul, Tetuan, enclosed in British consul, Tetuan, to British consul-general, Tangier, 8 October 1937, copy in IOR, Public and Judicial Department Annual Files 1931–1950, File P&J 4936/1937, 'Estate of late Mr Teckchand Dayaram', L/P&J/7/1362.

9 Epilogue: the Sindhi diaspora after 1947

The partition of British India brought in its wake a large-scale exodus of non-Muslims from Sind to independent India. *Banias* from Shikarpur and Hyderabad left *en masse*. They settled mostly in Bombay, but many did not remain there more than a few years. The existence of a functioning network of firms, mostly Hyderabadi, facilitated relocation abroad. Therefore, from the 1950s onwards, there grew a worldwide Sindhi diaspora around the core formed by the Sindwork merchants. At first this Sindhi diaspora remained a purely merchant community, but in the 1960s Amil professionals started in their turn to migrate in significant numbers, mostly to North America. In the 1990s, the Sindhi diaspora consisted of two kinds of communities: on the one hand, communities which were still largely engaged in trading, i.e. most of the dispersed Sindhi communities across Asia, Africa, Latin America and the Caribbean; on the other hand, communities which were more diversified in their occupations, with a predominance of professionals, especially in the United States, Canada and the United Kingdom.

The exodus of Sindhi Hindus to India, 1947–1948

Sindhi Hindus seem to have been caught largely by surprise and were unprepared when the political situation in India made the partition of the country an inevitable outcome of growing Hindu–Muslim tensions and of the failure of Congress and the Muslim League to reach an agreement. Although most Sindhi Hindus supported Congress, they seem to have taken the birth of Pakistan with some equanimity, being reassured in particular by the nomination as governor of Sind of Sir Ghulam Hidaiyatullah, a Muslim politician who had always enjoyed good relations with the Hindu community.[1] The situation deteriorated seriously only after the Quetta riots of 20 August 1947, which led to the

---

[1] Kirpalani, *Fifty Years with the British*, p. 355.

first exodus of non-Muslims from Sind to India. In September, a Bombay newspaper reported that 'the powerful Bhaibund community have left *en masse*', adding that 'taking advantage of their worldwide connections they had shifted their capital to Indian centres.'[2] According to a report, some 125,000 refugees had left Sind by 11 October.[3] This first exodus was spontaneous, not organized by the two governments, and it brought to India mostly people who had resources and connections. Although details are lacking, it is highly probable that many *banias* of Shikarpur and Hyderabad belonged to this first wave of relatively well-off refugees, whose entry into India did not attract a lot of attention.

The real mass exodus started after the Karachi riots of 6 January 1948, when Muslim refugees from Eastern Punjab started a looting spree of Hindu property in the capital of Sind.[4] This produced a wave of panic, which spread to all urban centres of the province. Already in Hyderabad, a meeting of Hindu leaders on 25 December 1947 had concluded with a call to Hindus to leave Sind altogether.[5] This second wave of departure was organized by the two governments, but it was nevertheless accompanied with widespread chaos and panic. However, attacks against persons were limited in Sind and there were no massacres comparable to the ones which took place in the Punjab at the same time. Most of these refugees of the second wave could bring with them only a few possessions and this massive influx stretched the resources of the provincial government in Bombay to the limit. Refugee camps were established and a certain dispersal of the refugees took place outside the Bombay Presidency. By mid-1948 it was reckoned that a total of 1,200,000 non-Muslim refugees from Sind and Baluchistan had entered India.[6] The Census of India in 1951, however, recorded the number of Sindhi speakers to be less than 800,000,[7] a discrepancy which can be explained partly by the fact that non-Sindhis, mostly Punjabis, Gujaratis and Rajasthanis, accounted for a significant share of the non-Muslim population of pre-Partition Sind. More than half of the Sindhi-speakers were in Bombay and Saurashtra, but significant concentrations also existed in Rajasthan and Ajmer, as well as in Madhya Pradesh and Madhya Bharat. Of some 400,000 displaced persons in Bombay, 40 per cent were described as engaged in trading occupations.[8] Most of these were petty traders. The specific fate of the Shikarpuri and Hyderabadi

[2] *Free Press Journal*, 17 September 1947, quoted in Anand, *National Integration of Sindhis*, p. 29.
[3] Anand, *National Integration of Sindhis*, p. 40.
[4] *Ibid.*, pp. 49–50. [5] *Ibid.*, p. 48. [6] *Ibid.*, p. 56. [7] *Ibid.*, p. 64.
[8] *Census of India 1951*, vol. IV, *Bombay, Saurashtra and Kutch*, Delhi, 1955, Table D.V., pp. 212–13.

banias largely gets lost in this story of mass exodus, but the existence of a network of commercial firms with branches in most big Indian cities helped them to rapidly find their feet.

Sindhi migration from India: the shift from network to diaspora

Among refugees who had family connections abroad, many left India in the 1950s and 1960s to relocate themselves in various countries[9] where Sindwork firms in particular had branches. The specificity of this new migration, as compared to pre-1947 movements, was that it was not any more a purely male migration, and that it often acquired a more or less permanent character. No statistical record of these movements exists, but an influx of Sindhi traders and employees was noted in various places from the late 1940s onwards, and it continued throughout the 1950s and 1960s. The main destinations were the great emporia where Sindhi traders were already a force to be reckoned with, such as Hong Kong and Singapore,[10] but other important destinations included the Canary Islands, Gibraltar, Indonesia, the Philippines, etc. The largest influx undoubtedly was into Hong Kong, where, in the mid-1960s, Sindhis were said to account for some 75 per cent of an Indian population of 20,000, i.e. some 15,000.[11] The spectacular growth of the Hong Kong Sindhi community, from a couple of hundred at the time of its recapture by the British in 1945, to some 15,000 around 1966 is not well documented, but all the evidence points to it being fundamentally a movement of traders, mostly small scale, who took advantage of the many opportunities offered by the economic boom of the British colony. Comparable growth took place in the Sindhi trading communities of Singapore, Indonesia and the Philippines in the Far East. On the other hand, some communities did not expand, or even contracted as a result of political trouble: this was the case in French Indochina, Algeria, Morocco or Egypt. There was some expansion in Latin America and the Caribbean, but the most spectacular growth occurred in West Africa, where Nigeria in particular attracted Sindhi traders in a big way in the 1960s and 1970s, due to an oil boom. Sindhi colonies grew also

---

[9] See P. Hiranandani, *Sindhis: the Scattered Treasure*, Delhi, 1980, pp. 31–45.
[10] *The Straits Times*, 6 December 1948, reported: 'Hundreds of Sindhis have arrived in Singapore in the last few months . . . Singapore Sindhi merchants who are concentrated in High Street set up an organisation early this year to receive and disperse the new arrivals'. Quoted in Sandhu, *Indians in Malaya*, p. 122.
[11] Calculated from K. N. Vaid, *The Overseas Indian Community in Hong Kong*, Hong Kong, 1972, pp. 20–4.

in Sierra Leone,[12] Ghana[13] and Liberia. The oil boom of the 1970s also attracted many Sindhis, traders as well as employees and professionals to the Gulf countries, a region which had longstanding commercial links with Sind. A spectacular expansion also took place in the Canary Islands which was directly related to the advent of mass tourism to the islands.

From the mid-1960s onwards a new kind of Sindhi migration has been going on, which is primarily one of professionals, mostly Amils, who left for the USA, Canada and the UK. Not much is known about the details of that migration, but various surveys of Indian immigrants in the USA revealed the presence of a group of Sindhi-speakers which was not insignificant.[14] Some Sindhi businessmen also emigrated to the countries of the developed West, mostly to Britain, where a small presence of Sindhi traders was noticeable from the late 1930s onwards.

Compared to the pre-Partition Hyderabadi network, the present-day Sindhi trading diaspora presents a very different profile. It can be argued that this diaspora constitutes one of the most important elements of an emerging international bourgeoisie of South Asian origin, which plays a growing, if largely unrecognized, role in the political economy of the contemporary world.

Table 9.1 gives an estimate of the size of Sindhi communities in a certain number of countries. These estimates must be treated as no more than informed guesswork. No estimate is presented of the large Sindhi communities of the Gulf countries, because of the lack of reliable statistical data relative to that area.

As can be seen from Table 9.1, the vast majority of Sindhi communities, outside North America and the UK, are still exclusively or mainly engaged in trading. These dispersed communities are direct heirs to the communities of Sindwork merchants from Hyderabad which spread across the globe from 1860 onwards. The Shikarpuri element is present also, mainly in the USA and the UK, but plays a much less important role. It appears that most Shikarpuri *banias* relocated themselves after 1947 in India, using the dense network of the so-called 'Multani' banking firms to get work. Shikarpuris constitute the last group of

[12] The Indian population of Sierra Leone, almost exclusively Sindhi, grew from 90 in 1948 to 633 in 1974. See Merani and Van der Laan, 'Indian Traders in Sierra Leone', Table 1, p. 242.
[13] The Indian population of Ghana, also mostly Sindhi, grew from 197 at the 1948 Census to 881 at the 1960 Census. See *The Gold Coast. Census of Population 1948. Reports and Tables*, Accra, 1950, Table 16, p. 83, and *1960 Population Census of Ghana*, vol. III, *Demographic Characteristics*, Accra, 1964, Table 11, p. 101.
[14] See the survey of the Indian population of Kalamazoo, Michigan, in 1984, showing a proportion of Sindhi-speakers of 5.1 per cent. A. W. and U. M. Helweg, *An Immigrant Success Story: East Indians in America*, Philadelphia, 1990, Appendix H, p. 263.

Table 9.1. *The Sindhi worldwide diaspora*

Country	Estimate of the size of the Sindhi community	Occupational structure
USA	50,000(?)	Mostly professional
Canada	10,000(?)	Mostly professional
Panama	500	Exclusively trading
Caribbean Islands	1,000–5,000	Exclusively trading
Chile	200–300	Exclusively trading
UK	5,000–15,000	Professional and trading
Spain (mostly Canary Islands)	10,000	Exclusively trading
Gibraltar	500	Exclusively trading
Morocco	500	Exclusively trading
Egypt	500(?)	Exclusively trading
Nigeria	5,000–10,000	Exclusively trading
Rest of West Africa	5,000(?)	Exclusively trading
Singapore	5,000	Mostly trading
Malaysia	1,000	Mostly trading
Hong Kong	7,500	Exclusively trading
Indonesia	3,500	Exclusively trading
Philippines	4,000	Exclusively trading
Thailand	1,000(?)	Exclusively trading
Japan	1,000(?)	Exclusively trading
Taiwan	200(?)	Exclusively trading
South Korea	200(?)	Exclusively trading
Total	120,000–140,000[15]	

Sources: My own estimates, except: for Indonesia, Mani, 'Indians in Jakarta', p. 109; for the Philippines, Singh Rye, 'Indians in the Philippines', p. 719; for Singapore, Bharadwaj, *Sindhis through the Ages*, p. 355; for Hong Kong, B.-Sue White, *Turbans and Traders*, p. 123.

'indigenous' bankers in India, and, although they operate largely on the margins of the formal economy, they are still of some importance. Recently, some diversification has taken place in their activities in India and big firms in the construction industry in Bombay are controlled by men who originally migrated from Shikarpur.[16]

An international bourgeoisie?

Affluent immigrants of Indian origin, often known by the acronym NRI (Non-Resident Indians), located in business, in academia or in the professions, constitute a kind of international bourgeoisie, which is

---

[15] This estimate is considerably lower than the estimate of a 1 million strong diaspora quoted in J. Kotkin, *Tribes: How Race, Religion and Identity Determine Success in the New Global Economy*, New York, 1992, p. 206.
[16] Such as K. Raheja, who owns one of Bombay's largest construction firms.

highy mobile geographically and socially, but has managed to retain close links to its region of origin. It is characterized by a great diversity in terms of regional origins and historical trajectories. Among the various regional groups which constitute this expanding galaxy, Sindhi Hindus are neither the most numerous, nor the most conspicuous. It should be noted, however, that the richest of all South Asian business families in the world, the Hinduja family, is a Shikarpuri family which made its fortune in Iran before emerging on the global scene. Sindhis have recently attracted some attention as forming one of the 'global tribes' which play an increasing role in the globalized world of today.[17] The claim made for them here is more modest, but no serious study of the emerging international South Asian bourgeoisie can overlook this particular segment, which is geographically the most widely dispersed of all South Asian groups, and, financially, a force to be reckoned with, as recognized by the Government of India itself, which has made specific efforts at attracting investment into India from that quarter.

The following concise survey will concentrate exclusively on the business activities of the Sindhis, leaving aside their increasing contribution to academia and to the professions. There has been basically a diversification in these activities from the time of the Sindwork trade. While the textile trade has remained the mainstay of Sindhi business, consumer electronics has emerged as an equally important field. On the other hand, trade in curios and related activities (such as costume jewellery) has declined in importance, while remaining significant in some parts of the world. A survey of member firms of the Sindhi Merchants Association, Singapore, reveals that, out of a total of 307 firms, 216 are engaged in import–export, of which 88 are in general import–export trade, in most cases a combination of textile and electronic goods, while 69 specialize in textiles, and 56 in electronic products.[18]

The main institutional innovation has been a certain amount of managerial and financial decentralization. While Sindwork firms were all directly controlled and managed from Hyderabad, the new Sindhi firms (many of which are direct descendants of Sindwork firms) are controlled from various places and managed in a much more flexible way. The dual structure, resting on the radical separation of the network centre from the actual places of business, has been shattered, as Bombay, while being the 'spiritual' centre of the Sindhi diaspora, has not been a perfect substitute for pre-Partition Hyderabad. Nowadays many Sindhi firms are controlled from one of their places of business,

---

[17] See Kotkin, *Tribes*, p. 206.
[18] Calculated on the basis of the list of member firms *in Sindhi Merchants Association, Singapore, Trade and Telephone Directory 1994–1995*.

i.e. generally Hong Kong or Singapore, through the medium of financial companies which have their base in one of the many fiscal havens of the planet (Bermuda or the Cayman Islands). The principals of the firms rarely reside in India. Sindhi business families are international families, and various members will reside in different countries, and have different passports. There is generally one member or one branch in Bombay, but the rest of the family can be located almost anywhere. This dispersed structure is meant to maximize response to changing business opportunities worldwide as well as to minimize taxation of profits. While the top layer of the community has transformed itself into a kind of transnational group, the lower echelons have on the contrary tended to entrench themselves much more locally while maintaining international linkages which facilitate business.

The economic success of Sindhi traders has been very uneven. In some parts of the world, they have remained mostly small-scale operators, exploiting limited opportunities in relatively small markets. One could give the instance of the Canary Islands, where the 5–6,000 strong local Sindhi community, mostly concentrated in Tenerife, owns hundreds of bazaars, in which they sell different kinds of goods, mostly consumer electronics imported from the Far East. They benefited for many years from the existence of a free zone, which is being gradually abolished to conform with EU regulations, leading to a fall in profits and an increasing exodus towards mainland Spain.

In contrast, Nigeria offers the example of a successful diversification from trading into manufacturing. There, Sindhis represent an important element in the local economy, which is the largest in sub-Saharan Africa (with the exception of South Africa). A recent book[19] has attracted attention to the role of Indian firms in the Nigerian economy. Their total investment is estimated to be close to $4 billion. Sindhi firms probably account for some 75 per cent of this total, i.e. approximately $3 billion. Several Sindhi firms, such as Inlaks (Shivdasani family), Chellarams (Daryanani family), Kewalram Chanrai, Bhojsons (Chanrai family), Polyproducts (Bhojwani family), Texlon (Mirchandani family), Varaman (Hemnani family), Western Textile (Vaswani family), Churchgate (Mahtani family) and Enpee Industries (Kirpalani family) play an important role in various sectors of the economy (textiles, plastics, chemicals, agro-industry, etc.).[20]

Large-scale investment in manufacturing industry by Sindhi capitalists has not occurred much outside Nigeria, although Sindhi firms have

---

[19] T. Forrest, *The Advance of African Capital: the Growth of Nigerian Private Enterprise*, Edinburgh, 1994, pp. 51–2.
[20] *Ibid.*, and commercial directories.

made industrial investments on a significant scale in a certain number of Asian countries, such as Hong Kong, Indonesia or the Philippines (in the latter country they are said to control some 10 per cent of the local garment industry which exports large quantities to the USA).[21] Globally, Sindhi businessmen have remained a community of traders. International trading linkages created by the dispersion of Sindhi families across the world are the key even to the success of Sindhi firms in Nigeria, where they rose largely on the strength of profits realized in the import of goods from the Far East, mostly Hong Kong. Their ability to play the role of international middlemen remains the major asset of Sindhi businessmen worldwide.

The new pattern of migration has produced a complete change in the sexual economy of the diaspora, with the women joining the men and raising their families abroad. Most present-day Sindhis were born outside Sind, either in India or in any number of foreign countries. Sindhis have often become settlers, planting roots in countries where they used to be simple sojourners. They have taken the nationality of the host country, adopted its language, sometimes married local women and in rare cases converted to another religion. Given this diversity of situations, is it still meaningful to talk of a Sindhi diaspora?

From scattered observations (a full study of the present-day Sindhi diaspora was not the focus of this work), it would appear that the decentring of the community in relation to Hyderabad (and also, to a lesser extent, to Shikarpur) has weakened the network but strengthened the sense of community. The network has been weakened because diversification has entailed entering into business relationships across a much wider spectrum. Both intra-firm and intra-network transactions have seen their importance diminish in the overall transactions of Sindhi firms. There remain however important linkages, and Sindhi businessmen in a given country will always prefer doing business with other Sindhis in other countries than with non-Sindhis. New Sindhi or predominantly Sindhi associations have sprung up in a certain number of places, facilitating contacts between Sindhi traders across national borders.[22] But the increasing complexity of international business

---

[21] Singh Rye, 'Indian Community in the Philippines', p. 743.
[22] A list of these Associations in *Sindhi Merchants Association, Singapore, Trade and Telephone Directory 1994–95*, pp. 222–3, includes the names of ten associations, of which two were in Chile (Santiago and Iquique), and one each in South Korea, Dubai, Malaysia, the Philippines, Sri Lanka, the UK, the Virgin Islands and Hong Kong. There are, however, Sindhi associations in many other places. An 'Alliance of Sindhi Associations of Americas' includes a total of eighteen associations, of which one is a religious association, the other seventeen being regional, covering most of the US, British Columbia and Toronto in Canada, as well as the Virgin Islands.

makes it more difficult to find the right partner inside a given community at all times.

However, if Sindhis are less of a network, they are probably more of a community than in pre-Partition days. Firstly, the old divides between Amils and Bhaibands, Shikarpuris and Hyderabadis have largely given way to a more inclusive definition of the community in ethno-religious terms. Similarly, a redefinition of religious boundaries has been at work, towards a clearer affirmation of a Hindu identity. The Hinduism of the Sindhis first underwent a redefinition in India, where pressure to fit within 'mainstream' Hinduism became strong and led to a reshaping of beliefs and practices. The cult of Jhule Lal, *de facto* identified as an avatar of Vishnu, has become the central marker of the new emerging religious identity of the Sindhi Hindus in India. Nanakpanthism and *sufism*, which were such crucial features of Sindhi Hindu beliefs, have been largely relegated to the background, when not openly repudiated. In the diaspora, the main thrust has been towards a clearer demarcation *vis-à-vis* the Khalsa Sikhs, especially since 1984, and an increasing alignment with the Vishwa Hindu Parishad as a symbolic statement of belonging to the 'Hindu' fold. The most spectacular manifestation of this new 'Hindu' identity has been the widespread construction of specific Sindhi Hindu temples in many localities of the world, thus providing a space for communal life which did not exist in pre-Partition days. This new identification with a reformed and homogenized form of Hinduism carries in itself a danger of dissolution of the specific identity of the Sindhi Hindus. Attempts at preserving the Sindhi language in the diaspora seem to be largely unsuccessful as the pressure to adopt English grows stronger by the day. Whether such a small and dispersed community as the Sindhi Hindus, who in India are threatened with a loss of their specific linguistic and religious identity, can durably maintain a separate identity within the NRIs at large is therefore an open question.

Conclusion

This work evolved from a critique of the unitary notion of one South Asian diaspora. I felt that the existing literature, by laying too much emphasis on permanent migration and by concentrating almost exclusively on the study of Indian communities in a few selected countries, tended to ignore more widespread phenomena of circulation between South Asia and the rest of the world. I proposed to shift the focus of inquiry at least partly from the place of arrival or sojourn of the so-called migrants to their place of origin and to the circulation between the two locations. The rationale for this shift was that I felt that most circulating migrants kept close links with their home towns or villages and that their identities were defined much more in relation to these places of origin, to which they regularly returned, than in relation to the places where they happened to be sojourning. I thought it necessary, in order to understand the dynamics of this circulation, to descend to the level of particular regions and even localities within South Asia. More specifically, my focus of interest was the circulation of merchants and commercial employees. The choice of two particular localities in Sind was dictated first, by the exceptionally wideranging travel of their merchants and, second, by the discovery of a wealth of detailed empirical material available in official records, which partly compensated for the unavailability of private records, a major obstacle to the study of merchant communities. But the questions addressed were of a general nature and concerned the patterns of merchant circulation from South Asia as well as the role played by international merchant networks from Asia in the European-dominated world economy of the 1850–1950 period.

I sought in particular to understand how 'indigenous' merchant networks, using traditional business techniques and traditional forms of business organization, could find a niche in the modern world capitalist economy. No single conclusion can be drawn regarding this point, as the two networks studied represented two very different forms of adaptation to that specific context. Shikarpuris sought to preserve the 'spatial niche' they had carved for themselves in Central Asia during the period of Durrani domination, when their control of state finances allowed them to establish an overall financial domination over a vast area. They were able to further entrench themselves in the economies of Central Asia during the first two-thirds of the nineteenth century by exploiting the vacuum created by the unresolved imperial rivalry between Britain and Russia, which allowed indigenous states to maintain a precarious independence. Their main asset was their unrivalled skill in settling payments through the rapid circulation of *hundis* from one end to the other of this immense region. Once the area was carved up between the two empires, leaving only Afghanistan as a fledgling buffer state, Shikarpuris adapted by taking up a new type of middleman function. In Russian Central Asia, they became basically intermediaries for the Russian banks, borrowing funds which they lent to the local peasantries and landed elites. In southeastern Iran and in Sinkiang, they exploited the British connection, serving in Iran as intermediaries for British firms and in Sinkiang using the protection afforded by extra-territoriality to corner part of the credit market. Altogether, they benefited from the fact that their main areas of operation remained extremely peripheral in relation to the world capitalist economy, which protected them from competition. In Russian Central Asia, the Russian Revolution put an end to their role, while in Iran and Sinkiang they continued to play the same part up to the 1930s, when political turmoil forced them to scale down their operations. From 1920 onwards, they redeployed largely by assuming the function of 'indigenous bankers' in India, in the Bombay and Madras Presidencies, as well as in Burma and Ceylon.

The mode of insertion of the Sindworkies into the global economy was very different: instead of a 'spatial niche', they sought to carve for themselves a functional niche in two specialized branches of trade, the silk trade and the curio trade. Their specialization was not the result of particular predispositions, but occurred, one might say, serendipitously, because they found themselves in Egypt at the right moment, that of the birth of modern tourism, and were able to provide tourists with craft products which satisfied their taste for exoticism. They then followed the major maritime routes, establishing shops in the ports where international travellers called, and, in the process, extended their trade almost to the entire world. Financial skills were as essential to their success as marketing skills: they made large profits in currency speculation, and were able to forge a good relationship with the exchange banks to finance their trade. In the course of becoming a group of international middlemen, they transformed themselves: while they remained faithful to traditional accounting techniques, they increasingly adopted forms of business organization which were close to those of large European trading firms. In the inter-war period they started a transition from niche traders to global operators in the world textile markets, and in particular acquired a very strong position in the marketing of Japanese textiles in Southeast Asia as well as in West Africa. This enlargement of their activities in terms of products as well as of markets helped them strengthen their position in international trade, and they have remained to this day a powerful group of middlemen. The Japanese connection was from the 1930s onwards an essential ingredient of their success, and in that sense they became a true Asian trading network. The story of the Shikarpuri and Hyderabadi networks shows that European colonial domination in Asia was never entrenched enough to prevent some indigenous merchants from maintaining and establishing links across borders, and from remaining autonomous actors in the international economy.

Although both groups of merchants managed to establish themselves firmly in the world of international trade and finance, and contributed in no small way to the recent emergence of an international bourgeoisie of South Asian origin on the global scene, their story mixed success and failure in a rather paradoxical way. Neither the two home towns, nor Sind as a whole, benefited significantly in the long run from the existence of such active entrepreneurial communities. Shikarpur increasingly became a backwater, while the neighbouring town of Sukkur emerged as the major regional centre in Upper Sind. Hyderabad, on the other hand, grew consistently throughout the twentieth century but the nature of the town was completely changed by the influx of *muhajirs* from India in the wake of Partition; it is not a Sindhi town any more. The reasons why the two towns did not in the long term gain much from the dynamism of their merchants were both economic and political. In the case of Shikarpur, widespread export of capital from the town, firstly to Central Asia, and then to other regions of India, led to a certain amount of decapitalization of the local economy, in spite of the fact that some of the remitted profits were invested in local purchases of land and real estate. It is probable that an increasing share of the profits was transferred to Bombay, which became in the 1920s and 1930s the main base of operation of the Shikarpuri bankers. As regards Hyderabad, there was apparently less seepage to Bombay, but most of the remitted profits appear to have been on the one hand dissipated in conspicuous consumption, and on the other hand invested in purchases of land and real estate which were a net loss when the *banias* had to leave the town in 1947–48. Eventually there was little to show for one or two centuries of sustained entrepreneurial activities. As to the interpretation of these facts, it is hard to decide between a more structural one, which would emphasize certain traits of capitalism under a colonial regime, as well as the mentality of 'traditional' merchants, and a more conjunctural one, which would stress the role of largely unpredictable political developments. There remains the question of why these merchants were not very good at assessing long-term political trends and their possible impact on their business operations. Although the Sindworkies undoubtedly developed political skills which helped them survive difficult periods in a hostile environment, even they mostly neglected their home base and eventually paid a heavy price for this neglect. Using the home town only as a residence and a place for recruiting manpower without nurturing it through a systematic policy of economic, social and political investment proved a risky strategy in the long run. Charities, however generous, were not enough to ensure continued acceptance, especially since the Muslim population did not derive any real benefit from them. The *banias* of Shikarpur and Hyderabad, in spite of their wealth which gave them a lot of influence on the local branches of the Congress Party, found themselves increasingly alienated from the political mainstream in Sind, especially after the separation of the province from the Bombay Presidency in 1936 reinforced Muslim predominance. As a result of this political isolation, the Partition of 1947 left them no other choice than exodus to India. Such an exodus did not significantly affect their day-to-day business operations, since they were conducted mostly outside Sind, either in India proper (for the Shikarpuri bankers) or in dispersed locations across the world (for the Sindwork merchants). The forced departure from their home towns however destroyed the very mode of functioning of the two networks, which had been based on maintaining a regular flow of circulation of men, goods, capital and information between the network centres and the actual places of business. As a prominent Sindwork merchant told Congress leader Acharya J. B. Kripalani, himself a Hyderabadi Amil, 'if the members of the community were scattered throughout India, commercial concerns would find it difficult to run their business in foreign lands with Sindhi assistants and salesmen'.[1]

The description and analysis of this variegated pattern of circulation, which was largely unknown, forms the core part of this work. Archival research has been especially fruitful in allowing manpower flows from

---

[1] Acharya J. B. Kripalani, 'The Sindhu Resettlement Corporation', in The Sindhu Resettlement Corporation Ltd., *Gandhidham*, Bombay, 1951, pp. 1–4. He was quoting the words of Bhai Pratap Dialdas, who tried to set up a Sindhi colony in Gandhidham, near Kandla, in Kutch, a venture which ended up in failure and in Pratap Dialdas' imprisonment for embezzlement.

Shikarpur and Hyderabad to be reconstructed. Absolute numbers were low, consisting of only a few hundred men every year; however, measured against the Hindu male population of age group 15–45, in the two towns, they acquire a different dimension. Thus it can be said, that, at the time of the First World War, in Hyderabad, one in ten Hindu males aged 15–45 of the Bhaiband 'caste' left each year for one of some fifty destinations worldwide. It has also been possible to uncover the existence of significant annual flows of remittances between the places of business and the network centre.

An important finding is the astonishing spatial extension of these two networks, particularly that of the Sindworkies. Even the area of operation of the Shikarpuri merchants was impressive: at the time of its maximum expansion on the eve of the Russian Revolution it included a large part of Russian Central Asia, with two major concentrations in the Ferghana valley and in the central areas of the Emirate of Bukhara, that part of the Chinese province of Sinkiang known as Altishahr (or sometimes as Kashgaria), as well as most of Afghanistan and southeastern Iran. In this vast area there were widely dispersed colonies of Shikarpuri merchants, often not more than ten or twenty strong, with a big concentration in Bukhara and its immediate surroundings, and other significant concentrations in the major towns of the Ferghana valley, in Kabul, Herat and Kandahar in Afghanistan, in Bandar Abbas and Kirman in Iran. In all these localities, most Shikarpuris in residence were agents of Shikarpur *shroffs*, with whom they kept in fairly close touch in spite of the difficulty in communications, but these agents were themselves a hierarchically ordered group, some of them having in their turn other agents. Although they thought of themselves as sojourners and did not plant roots in the area, some Shikarpuris, as revealed by successional documents which are the main source on this community, stayed in the region for very long periods and died there. The Shikarpuri diaspora was a few thousand strong at the time of the Russian Revolution, and after 1917 most of the Shikarpuris who escaped from Russian territory came back to India to take up employment as agents of banking firms in many localities of western and southern India. After a rising in Sinkiang led to another exodus of Shikarpuris from there in the 1930s, Iran and Afghanistan remained the only two areas outside the subcontinent (except for Burma and Ceylon) where they continued to operate, be it on a somewhat reduced scale. Iran assumes special importance however as the place where the Hinduja family started its meteoric race towards international prominence.

The Sindworkie network was much more extended, but characterized by much less territorial continuity. It was basically a maritime network, and most Sindwork merchants and employees were located in a string of ports extending from Kobe and Yokohama in Japan to Panama and Colon in Central America. In some areas, they penetrated some distance inland. This was the case in particular in Java, where their dense network included almost all the sizeable towns, especially in eastern Java, and in Egypt where they operated in the main tourist centres such as Cairo, Luxor and Aswan. Merchants and employees circulated easily and speedily between these different localities, at least before the era of immigration restrictions made travel more difficult.

In these two merchant networks, circulation was not haphazard, but on the contrary organized and structured. There were two different, though related patterns of circulation. In an early phase of the history of the networks, Shikarpuris and Sindworkies left their native town with a partnership agreement, as *gumasthas*, i.e. agents or 'working partners' of a capitalist who was a resident of the town. Their contracts were ultimately derived from the Islamic contract known in Arabic as *mudaraba* which also inspired the *commenda* contract of medieval European traders. Their expenses were sometimes covered as part of the agreement, but they were not salaried employees, being remunerated in the form of a share in the profits of the partnership, which could vary considerably from one contract to another. From the end of the nineteenth century onwards, most circulating men in Hyderabad were salaried employees of firms, either managers or shop assistants or servants, who left the town with a contract of employment for a certain number of years (two and a half was the most usual case). These contracts had some similarities with indenture contracts, but gave more freedom to the employee and ensured his return home at the expiry of the stipulated period. Their travel was organized and paid for by their employer. Very few men left without any kind of contract or agreement. A very important point to note is that those who did most of the circulating between the network centre and the actual places of business were not the capitalists themselves, but the working partners and the salaried employees. Capitalists generally spent most of the year in the network centre. From Shikarpur, they rarely went to Central Asia, because of the dangers attendant on travel between Sind and that region. From Hyderabad, they tended to leave regularly on tours of inspection of the branches of their firms; a few even established residence in one of their places of business and used to 'commute' between Hyderabad and that locality. Very few, however, prior to 1947, established permanent residence outside Hyderabad. The pattern remained one of circulation, not emigration.

It was, however, a circulation of men only. Shikarpuri women never went to Central Asia, and, among Sindworkies, only a few wives of managers accompanied their men on their voyages. This had important consequences, and this aspect is often overlooked in the literature on merchant diasporas. Not all men dealt in the same way with the absence of their women. In the dispersion, three models of 'sexual economy' can be identified, one which could be called 'ascetic', represented by the case of the Shikarpuris in Russian Central Asia, one which was 'permissive', exemplified by the Shikarpuris in Sinkiang, and one intermediate, in the case of the Sindworkies, who sometimes formed liaisons with local women. As for the women left behind, they also coped with the situation in different ways: in Shikarpur, it was common for women to take lovers and have children with them, while in Hyderabad, family control over females was much more strictly enforced.

What is remarkable also is how little political borders and changes in political domination affected the circulation of merchants. Shikarpuris continued to operate in the same area even after it went through momentous political changes in the second half of the nineteenth century. Only a cataclysmic world event like the Russian Revolution could significantly affect the range of their operations. As for the Sindworkies, they extended their operations to territories under many sovereignties. This relative imperviousness to political change suggests that the logic and temporality of merchant networks must be perceived as *sui generis*, and to a certain extent divorced from the logic and temporality of states and empires. Thus, while the Shikarpuri network emerged in close connection with the rise of the so-called 'Durrani Empire', it was able to survive its collapse for more than a century. Even after Sind had been annexed by the British, its merchants maintained a degree of independence *vis-à-vis* the British connection. Shikarpuris dispensed altogether with British consular protection in Russian Central Asia and nevertheless managed not only to survive but to thrive. The Sindworkies made very few demands on the British prior to 1920, though afterwards they needed British help to overcome growing restrictions on the circulation of employees between India and some countries. The merchants of Sind benefited however in many ways from their status as British subjects, which gave them a competitive edge over other groups of Asian merchants. The British on the other hand derived very little advantage from the existence of such extended networks of British Indian traders. Only in southeastern Iran did Shikarpuri traders act as agents for British firms; elsewhere they were largely independent operators. Shikarpuris did occasionally spy for the British in Russian territory, but their value as a source of intelligence was on the whole limited. The Sindworkies contributed even less to the furtherance of British economic and political aims. Moreover, in the 1930s, some of them became agents for the major commercial rivals of the British, the Japanese, and helped bring about a rise in sales of Japanese goods throughout the British Empire. If there was instrumentalization, it appears that it was the British Empire which was instrumentalized by the Sind merchants rather than the opposite.

Economic independence *vis-à-vis* the British did not however translate into political hostility to British rule. Sind traders tended to be rather loyalist in politics, and, after 1920, when some of them supported the Congress, their support went to the more moderate elements in the nationalist party. Even the support extended to Bose and the INA by some of the Sindwork merchants in Japanese-occupied Southeast Asia during the Second World War had a lot to do with pragmatism and the necessity to survive in a difficult situation. The case of the Sind merchants confirms the existence of a widespread lack of congruence between economic interests and political attitudes amongst Indian merchants. As for the British attitude to the Sind merchants, it alternated between indifference, largely bred of ignorance, and occasional bouts of panic when suddenly the existence of such wideranging networks appeared to pose a political threat to British rule, as during the two world wars. This panic culminated in 1918 at the time of the San Francisco conspiracy case when some British officials became convinced that firms of Sindwork merchants served as conduits for funds for the Ghadr Party, a suspicion which was to all appearances unfounded.

Detailed empirical study of two networks leads us to question a certain number of widely held assumptions about the nature of international trading diasporas. Most studies of diasporas have emphasized the role of factors such as ethnicity, religion and caste in maintaining solidarity and generating trust between merchants. In the case of Shikarpuri and Hyderabadi *banias*, ethnicity was not a crucial factor, since the merchant milieu of the two towns was multiethnic. Although the merchants were practically all Hindus, the specific nature of Hinduism in Sind, its fluidity as well as its very low level of institutionalization, did not make religion a factor for cohesion. As for caste, its role was far from clear. While most Sind merchants belonged to the so-called Bhaiband segment of the Lohana caste, there were also among them Khatris and Bhatias, and in any case there were no strong caste *panchayats* either in Shikarpur or Hyderabad capable of imposing strict rules of behaviour and of enforcing them through effective sanctions. Solidarity between townsmen and kinship ties, whether actual or fictive, appears to have been the glue holding together these small groups of merchants dispersed across immense spaces. Solidarity between townsmen manifested itself in the existence of *panchayats* and voluntary associations. In most localities of Central Asia, prior to the Russian Revolution, there were Shikarpuri *panchayats*, and they kept a constant flow of correspondence through *mazhars* with *panchayats* in Shikarpur which brought together the Shikarpuri merchants trading with particular Central Asian localities. In places where Sindworkies were well represented, they generally had one association, often called the Sindhi Association or Sindhi Chamber of Commerce, where they could meet and organize themselves to defend their interests. Kinship ties were also of great importance, especially in the early phase of development of the networks, when most business partnerships were concluded between members of the same kin group, and the fictive kinship ties of the brotherhood, or *bhaiband*, were equally important in ensuring some minimal solidarity in the place of business. Solidarity between townsmen who were often kinsmen did not however automatically generate trust between them. Opportunistic behaviour was very widespread, sometimes even among members of the same family, and trust depended largely on reputation. Credit was extended to fellow townsmen at a lower rate (fixed by custom at 6 per cent) than to strangers, but Sindhi creditors did not hesitate to sue Sindhi debtors before the courts in case of delay or default in repayment. Individualism was very strong, especially among Sindworkies, and nowhere do we find the spirit of 'collective capitalism' which, according to a recent author, characterized the Nattukottai Chettiar bankers.[2] In Hyderabad, powerful family firms remained active in business across several generations, defying both Marshallian expectations and conventional wisdom about Indian merchant families. In many ways these big firms were undistinguishable from other international trading firms with which they competed in most of the great ports and emporia of the world. They remained, however, very closely controlled by the families of the founders and the headquarters were situated in Hyderabad where the principals resided. This dissociation between network centre and actual place of business was an important characteristic of most South Asian international business networks, particularly those of Hindu merchants.

The picture which emerges from the detailed empirical study of these two networks is therefore contradictory. While Shikarpuris remained mainly a group of 'traditional' indigenous bankers dealing mostly in *hundis*, Sindworkies successfully carved a niche for themselves in the world of international trade and partly adopted European techniques and even European mores. In that way, they strongly recalled another

---

[2] Rudner, *Caste and Capitalism*, pp. 104–30.

trading group from the subcontinent, the Parsis. In spite of the importance of 'networking', the ultimate success or failure of merchants had to do with the capacity for developing specific skills and a good knowledge of countries and markets. The importance of such skills to business success even among so-called 'ethnic' networks is a point which has been made in a recent study of Chinese family firms.[3] The present study largely confirms this insight.

The overall balance-sheet of the external ventures of the Sind merchants remains uncertain. By transferring outside Sind at an early date the bulk of their operations, they limited the risk created by the growing political instability in the region, but on the other hand, the loss of their home base in 1947 forced them to reorganise completely their mode of operation, and cost them dearly in purely financial terms. In the course of their ventures, they developed impressive financial and marketing skills, which smoothed the transition to a new mode of functioning and allowed them to prosper on an unprecedented scale. But after 1947 they were condemned to a diasporic existence which was not of their own choosing, and in which they are in danger of losing for good their cultural identity.

At a more general level, the existence of a regular pattern of circulation of men, capital and information which continued for many decades between two medium-sized towns of a peripheral province of British India and many localities in a number of other countries poses a direct challenge to the dominant historiography of the world system, with its clear-cut division between centre, periphery and semi-periphery. Although both Shikarpur and Hyderabad could be seen as belonging to the semi-periphery, in relation to their own network they undoubtedly occupied a very central position. It could even be argued, although it would perhaps be stretching the point too far, that both these towns were centres of specific 'micro-world economies', which were loosely articulated within the larger world capitalist economy. Being centres of specific 'micro-world economies', they could rightly be considered 'micro-world cities'. The concept of world city is popular with geographers who generally use it to refer to big metropolises, such as New York, London or Tokyo, and to the overall control they have over vast flows of trade and capital investment across large parts of the world. But there is no reason why the notion could not be applied to towns which controlled smaller flows, given a comparable geographical range. From that point of view, Hyderabad in the first half of the twentieth century was undoubtedly a world city, whose merchant firms controlled

---

[3] See Choi Chi-Cheung, 'Kinship and Business: Paternal and Maternal Kin in Chaozhou Chinese Family Firms', *Business History*, vol. 40, no. 1, 1998, pp. 26–49.

operations in the four corners of the world. In the first half of the nineteenth century, Shikarpur, which occupied the position of a financial metropolis for the vast Central Asian region, also answered the definition. The history of these two towns reveals the existence of longstanding connections between the 'local' and the 'global', much antedating the latest developments in the rise of a global capitalist economy. In this respect it appears largely disconnected from the more general trends at work in the economic history of South Asia.

The history of the merchants of Shikarpur and of Hyderabad cannot be written within the framework of the national histories of either India or Pakistan. It cannot even fit within the parameters of a regional history centered on Sind. Although Sind was the province where the two towns were situated, the Sind context impinged only marginally on the history of the networks. The origins of the Shikarpuri network are to be found in developments which are specifically 'Afghan', linked to the rise of the Durrani 'Empire' centred on Kandahar. The following phase was related to historical developments in the Uzbek khanates, culminating in the Russian conquest of the 1860s and 1870s. Even as far as Hyderabad is concerned, the history of the Sindwork merchants got disconnected from developments in Sind at a fairly early stage, in the 1870s, when they started procuring most of their goods from outside the province. From that time onwards, both Shikarpuris and Sindworkies were groups of international middlemen who used Sind only as a recruiting ground for manpower but traded in goods produced elsewhere, and used mostly capital borrowed outside the region. One of the findings of this book is that, contrary to the idea which is widespread among Sindhi Hindus, the departure from Sind of some Hindu merchants was not a response to a deterioration in the situation of the Hindu minority in the province. Over time the connections between the history of the province and that of the networks became increasingly loose.

The history of these two merchant networks from South Asia is thus situated at the intersection of several histories. The local history of two Sind towns became connected in surprising ways with the histories of faraway lands. For Shikarpuris, the most important events in twentieth-century history, apart from the Partition of 1947, were the Russian Revolution of 1917, which led to a massive exodus from Central Asia to Shikarpur, and the Sinkiang rising of 1933 which led to a flight from that 'Chinese' province. Events in Iran and Afghanistan also had direct repercussions on the fate of the Shikarpuri merchants. As for the Sindworkies, given the spread of their network, they could be affected by events happening anywhere: a change in immigration legislation in

Australia, Panama or the Philippines, a Civil War in Spain, riots in the Gold Coast. Writing the history of international merchant networks can only be an exercise in connecting local histories with world history, by-passing the level of 'national' history.

Appendix I: Employment contract of a shop assistant

I the undersigned Fatumal Keumal Hindu aged 33 years of Hyderabad Sindh do hereby agree to enter the service of Messrs Pohoomull Brothers viz Mr Moolchand, Mr Lekhraj, Mr Sahijram sons of Khiamul on the following conditions.

I   That I shall serve the said firm for the period of two and a half years to commence on the 2nd day of the month of November 1901 in any place they may be willing to send me at the salary of Rs 45 per month for first 15 months and Rs 50 per month for last 15 months and to be supplied with my daily food by the same firm during the period of my serving them.

II That all my travelling expenses to and from any place shall be at the charge of the said firm.

III My salary will commence from the date of departure and will be ceased from the date of leaving the destination.

IV That I bind myself to serve the said firm honestly and faithfully and be obedient to my masters, their managers or persons in charge of their business in any place and at any time I shall be serving and I shall do all the works they impose on me.

V   The accounts to be settled at Bombay or Hyderabad Sindh where the said masters wish.

...

XI The sum of Rs 25 the above mentioned masters will give here to my parents for the maintain [sic] of family members.

Dated thus the agreement 10th October 1901

Source: 'Pohoomull Brothers, Plaintiff and Fatehchand Kayomull, Defendant', PRO, Foreign Office Records, Embassy and Consular Archives: Egypt, Cairo Consular Court Records, Dossier no. 25 of 1902, FO 841/72.

Appendix II: Employment contract of a servant

This agreement made this 27th day of September 1905 at Hyderabad Sind between Chellaram Vasanmal resident of Hyderabad Sind (hereinafter called the said servant) and Mr Kissoomal Sobhraj of Hyderabad Sind (hereinafter called the said master).
1 The said servant agrees to serve the said master at Cairo (Egypt) or any other part or place as a general servant wherever the said master may be pleased to send or depute him for the said purpose.
2 The engagement is to hold good for the period of 3 three years commencing from the day 27th September 1905.
3 The salary of the said servant during the said period shall be Rs 10 ten per mensem for the first year, Rs twelve per mensem for the second year and Rs fifteen per mensem for the third year. Out of this salary Rs 6 six shall monthly be paid to his parents at Hyderabad and the remainder shall be kept by the said master and be paid to the said servant on his return after the expiration of the said period . . .
4 The said servant shall be conveyed from Hyderabad to the business place at the expense and cost of the said master and back to Hyderabad after the expiration of the said period . . .
5 The said servant will have free Board and Lodging, Washing and Shaving wherever he be placed on duty. The said master shall also pay to the said servant Rupees 18 eighteen per an [sic] year for clothing at the place of duty.
6 The said servant hereby undertakes to serve and perform all the duties that are assigned to him by the said master . . .
 . . .
8 The said servant further undertakes not to disclose to any body the secrets of his master's trade, not to keep any private communication with any other person or firm, not to desert or leave service or neglect duties and not to join or take service under any other person or firm during the said period.
 . . .

10 The said servant has received Rs 20 twenty in advance which should be deducted from his salary.

Source: 'Kessumal Sobraj, plaintiff, *vs.* Chellaram Vasanmal, defendant', PRO, Foreign Office Records, Embassy and Consular Archives: Egypt, Cairo Consular Court Records, Dossier no. 7 of 1907, FO 841/91.

Appendix III: Partnership deed between three Hyderabad merchants

This indenture made the first day of October one thousand nine hundred and six between Bhai Khanchand Menghraj Hindu Luhano trader residing at Hyderabad Sind Bombay Presidency (India) of the one part herein called the Capitalist

Kodumal Son of Ramchand Hindu Punjabi resident of Hyderabad Sind now at Cairo of the second part hereinafter called the working partner and Naraindas Son of Kishinchand Hindu Luhano resident of Hyderabad Sind of the third part hereinafter called the working partner witnesseth as follows.

1. That the said Khanchand, Kodumal and Naraindas do hereby for themselves, their heirs, their executors and administrators covenant with one another, that they the said Khanchand Kodumal and Naraindas will become and remain partners for the purpose and period and subject to the stipulations and provisions hereinafter expressed and contained and that is to say:

   That the first party Khanchand Menghraj is owner and capitalist of a firm dealing in oriental goods at Cairo (Egypt) called after 'Mr Khanchand'...

3. That the business of the partnership shall consist of importation and sale of Indian, Chinese and Japanese goods and curiosities usually termed 'Sind works' at Cairo.

4. That the said partnership shall... continue for 5 years...and shall commence from the day when the said Naraindas Kishinchand the third party will go to Cairo and will take charge of the business jointly with the said Kodumal Ramchand the second party who is already at Cairo...

5. That the Partnership business should be carried on under the name, style and firm of Mr Khanchand.

6. That the working partners alone shall be bound to work personally and the capitalist shall remain at Hyderabad (Sind) and give such instructions and advice to the working partners as he may deem fit and proper and shall not be bound to work personally.

7 That the capital required for carrying on the business of the partnership shall be supplied by the capitalist to an extent of rupees 15,000 (fifteen thousand) according to the requirements of the business . . .

8 That the shares of the parties in the profits and losses of the business shall be as follows: – out of every sixteen annas and three pies only: – The Capitalist the said Khanchand shall get 7 seven annas. The working partner the said Kodumal shall get 4 annas and six pies.
The working partner the said Naraindas Kishinchand shall get 4 annas 6 pies. Three pies shall be appropriated to Charity.

9 That the capitalist shall pay every month from the partnership income twenty rupees to the family of the said Kodumal Ramchand and Rupees 60 sixty to the family of the said Naraindas Kishinchand and each of the working partners shall be entitled to draw at the business place for his private use every month any sum up to Rs 10 (ten only) a month – all these payments and drawings shall bear interest at 6 p.c. per annum. And the capital supplied by the capitalist shall also bear interest at 6 p.c. per annum. . .

. . .

16 That each partner (working) shall be bound to remain at the business place and after expiry of two years shall be entitled to return home and spend there six months. . .

. . .

18 That a partner committing dishonesty or doing loss to the partnership business shall be entitled to no profit whatever but shall be made liable for all losses and shall be immediately expelled by the capitalist. . .

. . .

22 That the working partners shall not vend goods on credit but may give credit in proper cases provided that the total credit of a year shall not exceed one thousand rupees. All transactions besides shall be made for cash and money realized from time to time shall be regularly remitted to the capitalist at Hyderabad Sind.

. . .

Source: 'K. Khanchand and Kodoomal, Plaintiff vs. Naraindas Kishinchand, Defendant', PRO, Foreign Office Records, Embassy and Consular Archives: Egypt, Cairo Consular Court Records, Dossier no. 134 of 1908, FO 841/101.

Appendix IV: Secret War Office Memorandum 'Sindhi Merchants'

There are a large number of firms of Indian merchants with headquarters in Hyderabad (Sind), which have branches in practically all tropical and subtropical countries. They do general import and export trade in the countries where they are established, and their shops for the sale of fancy goods at places like Gibraltar, Malta and Port Said are familiar to all travellers...

It has generally been accepted that persons belonging to these firms, like the majority of the Bania class are too engrossed in the pursuit of gain to take any interest in politics, and the natural supposition is that they appreciate the peace and security of life and property ensured by British rule in India and the facilities for trade which their status as British subjects gives them, and that they do not wish for any change in the present order of things. The following is a summary of facts tending to show that the contrary is the case.

1. In January 1916, one JETHMULL of the firm of RATHOOMALL & SONS was arrested at Port Said on information received from Hong-Kong that he had been engaged in the Indian revolutionary movement in the Far East. The man had harboured in Canton members of the Ghadr party returning to India from America. His house was searched and some suspicious documents containing references to the Turks and Germans and prophecies of the defeat of the British and their expulsion from India were found. Enquiries in India failed to disclose any evidence of anti-British sentiments among this man's employers in Hyderabad.

2. In July 1916, it was reported from a French source that the firm of POHOOMULL BROS., with branches in Algiers, Ceuta, Melilla and Tenerife, was suspected of assisting in the distribution of German oriental propaganda pamphlets. On the other hand such pamphlets have never, so far as is known, been found among such persons' belongings.

3 In consequence of the visit to Panama of the Ghadr leader BHAGWAN SINGH in August 1916, a wave of seditious excitement passed through the East Indian population of the Isthmus, and this is reported to have affected the employees of the Sindhi firms with the rest, and they are said to have subscribed largely to the revolutionary funds. It should be noted, however, that the managers of the four principal firms sent to the local press a public disclaimer of any connection with or sympathy for BHAGWAN SINGH's propaganda. It was also reported in December 1916 that some of these Sindhis, in common with Indians of other classes, were at the instigation of the German consul at Colon taking out naturalization papers as subjects of Panama. In consequence of all these reports H.M.'s Minister at Panama has since the latter part of 1916 notified the departure from the Isthmus of all East Indians, whether travelling eastwards or westwards. These travellers have included many Sindhis and all opportunities have been taken of interrogating them and searching their belongings, but nothing of an incriminating nature has till quite recently been discovered . . .

4 The Government of India, writing on the 20th February 1917, with reference to the alleged participation of certain Sindhi firms in Sierra Leone with the Ghadr movement in America, stated: 'We are aware that the partners and employees of such firms abroad are in many cases seditiously inclined and probably find it lucrative to keep in with the revolutionary party. We also know that they subscribe money, help to circulate seditious papers and accommodate plotters in distress; but we have no evidence that any firm is consistently using its business organisation to further the ends of revolution.'

5 Writing on the 1st March 1918, the Director of Criminal Intelligence, Simla, stated: – 'The amount of disloyalty among the Sind Worki [sic] firms, which are scattered about all over the world, has been found to be extensive beyond reason or comprehension.'

6 In July 1918, H.M.'s Minister at Panama notified the departure of one PERMANAND SHEWARAM from Colon to Cadiz on a Spanish steamer and described him as 'very anti-British'. It is reported that on arrival at Cadiz the man was seen to hand some documents to the German Consul there.

7 In the same month the United States Postal Censorship authorities operating in the Canal zone intercepted a letter in a simple cypher from the firm of J. T. CHANDRAI & Co., Colon, to the same firm at Tenerife. When decyphered it was found to read as follows: 'I wrote MOHAN LAL; no answer yet. PESUMAL has been arrested in San

Francisco. The work will be kept back much at home. Send news to HARDYAL LALA at once from your place. Advise me when is the time fixed for the Army to march from Persia. Received letter from SHER SINGH; NABHA is ready to help. I still have 4,000 left. Have received offer to blow up the English Legation; considering how to do it. Cannot get dynamite. Send me news quickly. SOIRAJ.'

(Note. – PESSUMAL is one of the men whose departure had been notified by H.M. Minister and who was in consequence examined at San Francisco.)

LALA HARDYAL is the founder of the Ghadr Party, and is now in Germany or Turkey.

NABHA must mean the Maharaja of a Native State of that name in India.

MOHAN LAL and SHER SINGH are unknown.

SOIRAJ (properly SWARAJ) means 'self-government.'

8 Writing on the 15th June 1918, the Director of Criminal Intelligence, Simla, reported that alarmist rumours were rife in Sind that an invasion of India from Persia was imminent, and that many of the Hindu inhabitants were migrating to Native States. Telegraphing on the 23rd August, the Chief of the General Staff, India, reported that several employees of J. T. CHANDRAI & Co [sic] from Tenerife and Panama had been bound over for spreading alarmist pro-enemy rumours.

Conclusion

As yet there is no evidence that the Sindhi merchant firms, as such, are engaged in any seditious conspiracy. Employees of the firms in foreign countries have inevitably come under the influence of the Ghadr propaganda and one can well imagine that in self-defence and to avoid blackmail, if for no other reason, they would almost be bound to subscribe to the funds. Those in Spain and the Canary Islands would be open to the direct influence of German agents, and in Panama also we know that practically no restraint is exercised over the German residents. There is also quite possibly intercommunication between Panama (via Cuba) and Mexico where the leaders of the Indian revolutionary movement are now congregated. It is therefore not surprising to find German inspired propaganda passing along the channels offered by the trade activities of these firms. Whether the Sindhis concerned have deliberately lent their services in this connection in order to assist the enemy, or whether, being Banias by caste and very susceptible to fear, they are more or less the unconscious tools of the Indo-German revolutionary intriguers cannot yet be definitely stated.

WAR OFFICE (M. I.5)
September, 1918.

> *Source:* Enclosed in S. Newby, of the War Office, to R. A. C. Sperling, of the Foreign Office, 7 September 1918, PRO, Foreign Office Records, General Correspondence (Political), United States File 327 of 1918, FO 371/3426.

Bibliography

PRIMARY SOURCES

UNPUBLISHED MANUSCRIPTS AND RECORDS

Nehru Memorial Museum and Library, New Delhi
Indian Merchants Chamber Records

British Library, London, Oriental and India Office Collections

European Manuscripts
Dow Papers, MSS Eur. E 372
Linlithgow Papers, MSS Eur. F 125

India Office Records

Guides to the India Office Records
T. N. Thomas, *Indians Overseas. A Guide to Source Materials in the India Office Records for the Study of Indian Emigration 1830–1950*, 1985
A Select Catalogue of India Office Records relating to Central Asia, Xiao Wei Bond, 1998

Economic Department Records
Departmental Papers: Industries & Overseas Department Papers 1921–1924, L/E/71172–1322

Persian Gulf Residencies Records: Bahrain Court Records
'Dhamanmal Isardas and Rattanchand Dipchand vs. Bheroomal T. Relvani', R 15/3/69

Political & Secret Department Records
Secret Correspondence with India 1792–1874, L/P&S/5
Political & Secret Correspondence with India 1875–1911, L/P&S/7
Departmental Papers: Political & Secret Separate (or Subject) Files 1902–1931, L/P&S/10
Departmental Papers; Political & Secret Annual Files 1912–1930, L/P&S/11
Departmental Papers: Political External Files and Collections *c.* 1931–1950, L/P&S/12

Public and Judicial Department Records
Public Despatches to Bengal and India 1830–1879, L/P&J/3
Departmental Papers: Annual Files 1880–1930, L/P&J/6
Departmental Papers: Annual Files 1931–1950, L/P&J/7
Departmental Papers: Collections *c.* 1930–1947, L/P&J/8

Proceedings of the different governments in India
Bengal Board of Revenue (Miscellaneous) Proceedings, Opium
Bombay General Proceedings
Bombay General Confidential Proceedings (Miscellaneous)
Bombay General (Miscellaneous) Proceedings, Emigration
Bombay Political Proceedings
Bombay Revenue Proceedings
India Commerce and Industry (Emigration) Proceedings
India Foreign Proceedings (External)
India Foreign Proceedings (Political)
India Revenue and Agriculture (Emigration) Proceedings

Public Record Office, Kew

Colonial Office Records
Colonies (General) Economic Original Correspondence, CO 323, CO 852
Gibraltar Original Correspondence, CO 91
Gold Coast Original Correspondence, CO 96
Sierra Leone Original Correspondence, CO 267
Victoria Sessional Papers, CO 311

Foreign Office Records
General Correspondence (Consular), FO 369
General Correspondence (Political), FO 371
Embassy and Consular Archives: China Consulates, Personal Estates Correspondence, etc., FO 678
Embassy and Consular Archives: China, Shanghai Supreme Court Probate Records, FO 917
  'Estate of Dorabjee Nusserwanjee Camajee', 1882
  'Estate of Hormusjee Dorabjee Camajee', 1886
  'Estate of Jwanbai Bomanji Karanjia, widow of Bomanjee Pallonji Karanjia', 1906
Embassy and Consular Archives: Egypt, Alexandria Consular Court Records, FO 847
  'Estate of Gehimall Nanikram Tolleram', 1888
Embassy and Consular Archives: Egypt, Cairo Consular Court Records, FO 841
  'Pohoomull Brothers, plaintiff, and Fatehchand Kayomall, defendant', 1902
  'Kissumal Sobhraj, plaintiff, vs. Chellaram Vasanmal, defendant', 1907
  'Udhavdas Singnamal vs. Tarachand Mulchand', 1907
  'K. Khanchand & Co. vs. Dettaram Gopomall', 1908
  'K. Khanchand and Kodoomal vs. Naraindas Kishinchand', 1908
  'Koshiram Daulatram vs. Dettaram Wattamull', 1908

'Probate jurisdiction. In the goods of Bhai Khanchand of Cairo deceased', 1909
'Dialdas Kalachand vs. Kodoomal Ramchand', 1911
'J. T. Chanrai vs. Pribhdas Rupchand', 1918
Embassy and Consular Archives: Egypt, Port-Said Consular Court Records, FO 846
'Sitaldas Naunmal, applicant, and Dialdas & Sons, respondent', 1930
'S. Baloomal, plaintiff, vs. Ratoomal & Sons, defendants', 1931
Embassy and Consular Archives: Japan, General, FO 262
Embassy and Consular Archives: Japan, Japan Consulates Miscellaneous, FO 345
Embassy and Consular Archives: Japan, Yokohama, FO 908
Embassy and Consular Archives: Morocco, Fez Consular Court Records, FO 909
'Probate jurisdiction in the case of Tolaram Tarachand', 1929
Embassy and Consular Archives: Morocco, Tangier, FO 174
Embassy and Consular Archives: Tripoli (Lybia), FO 161

PUBLISHED RECORDS, GOVERNMENT PUBLICATIONS, ETC.

Published Records and Collections of Documents
Selections from Despatches addressed to the several governments in India by the Secretary of State in Council, London
Correspondence Relative to Sinde 1838–1843, London, 1843
Selections from the Records of the Bombay Government, new series, no. XVII, Bombay, 1855
Selections from the Records of the Bombay Government, new series, no. CXXII, Bombay, 1871
Précis of Papers regarding Affairs in Central Asia, 1867–1872, Simla, 1872
Kunte B. G. (ed.), *Source Material for a History of the Freedom Movement. History of the Non-cooperation Movement in Sind 1919–1924*, vol. V, *Collected from Maharashtra State Records*, Bombay, 1977
Sareen T. R. (comp.), *Select Documents on Indian National Army*, Delhi, 1988
Bhan S. and B. Pachai (eds.), *A Documentary History of Indian South Africans*, Cape Town and Johannesburg, 1984

Gazetteers
Gazetteer of the Province of Sind, E. H. Aitken (comp.), Bombay, 1907
Gazetteer of the Province of Sind 'B' Volume II, Hyderabad District, J. W. Smyth (comp.), Bombay, 1920
Gazetteer of the Province of Sind 'B' Volume III, Sukkur District, Bombay, 1919
Lorrimer's Gazetteer of the Persian Gulf, Oman and Central Arabia, Calcutta, 1908

Census of India Publications
Census of India 1881, Operations and results in the Presidency of Bombay, including Sind, J. A. Baines, vol. II, *Tables*, Bombay, 1882

Census of India 1891, vol. VIII, *Bombay and its Feudatories*, part I, *Report*, W. W. Drew, Bombay, 1892
Census of India 1891, vol. VIII, *Bombay and its Feudatories*, part II, *Report*, W. W. Drew, Bombay, 1892
Census of India 1891, vol. X, *Burma*, part III, *Tables*, Rangoon, 1892
Census of India 1901, vol. IX A, *Bombay*, part II, *Tables, Imperial Tables*, R. E. Enthoven, Bombay, 1902
Census of India 1921, vol. X, *Burma*, part II, *Tables*, Rangoon, 1923
Census of India 1931, vol. I, *India Report*, J. H. Hutton, Delhi, 1933
Census of India 1931, vol. VIII, *Bombay Presidency*, part I, *General Report*, A. H. Dracup and H. T. Sorley, Bombay, 1933
Census of India 1951, vol. IV, *Bombay, Saurashtra and Kutch*, Delhi, 1955

Other government publications in India

Reports and Papers, Political, Geographical and Commercial Submitted to Government by Sir Alexander Burnes, Lieutenant Leech, Dr Lord and Lieutenant Wood Employed on Missions in the years 1835–36–37 in Scinde, Afghanistan and Adjacent Countries, Calcutta, 1839
Note on the Trade Statistics of the Punjab 1870–71, 1875–76 and 1890–91, Lahore
Report on a Mission to Yarkand in 1873, with the Comment of Sir T. D. Forsyth with Historical and Geographical Information Regarding the Possessions of the Ameer of Yarkand, Calcutta, 1875
Prices and Wages in India 1901, Calcutta, 1902
Report on the British Indian Commercial Mission to South-Eastern Persia during 1904–05, A. H. Glendowe-Newcomen, Calcutta, 1906
Report on an Inquiry into the Silk Industry in India, H. Maxwell-Lefroy and E. C. Ansorge, Calcutta, 1917
Report of the Bombay Provincial Banking Enquiry Committee 1929–30, Bombay, 1930
Report of the Burma Provincial Banking Enquiry Committee 1929–30, Rangoon, 1930
The Madras Provincial Banking Enquiry Committee, vol. I, *Report*, Madras 1930
Consolidated Annual Report on the Working of the Indian Emigration Act, New Delhi, 1935, 1936
Annual Report on the Working of the Indian Emigration Act, 1922, in Sind, New Delhi, 1937–41
Large Industrial Establishments in India 1937, Delhi, 1939

UK Parliamentary Papers

Parliamentary Papers, House of Commons, 1831–32, vol. VI
Parliamentary Papers, House of Commons, 1854, East India (Scinde)
Parliamentary Papers, House of Commons, 1864, vol. XLII

UK Official Reports

Royal Commission on Opium 1894–1895, vol. VII, *Final Report*, London, 1895

Publications of other governments
Census of Ceylon, 1921, vol. I, part I, Colombo, 1923
Census of Ceylon, 1946, vol. I, part I, Colombo, 1950
The Gold Coast. Census of Population 1948. Reports and Tables, Accra, 1950
1960 Population Census of Ghana. vol. III, *Demographic Characteristics*, Accra, 1964
Census of the Netherlands Indies 1930, vol. VII, *Chinese and Other Non-indigenous Orientals in the Netherlands Indies*, Batavia, 1935

Directories and Who's Whos
Annuaire commercial, industriel, administratif, agricole et viticole de l'Algérie et de la Tunisie 1902, Paris
The Business Directory of Hong Kong, Macao, Canton, Hong Kong, 1938
The Ceylon Mercantile Directory, 1933, Colombo
The Gibraltar Directory and Guide Book, Gibraltar, 1899
The Handbook of Sierra Leone, T. N. Goddard (comp.), Luton, 1925
The Hong Kong Directory and Hong List for the Far East 1889, Hong Kong,
The Indians Abroad Directory, Bombay, 1934
Jagtiani's Handbook and Directory of Sind, Karachi, 1934
The Japan Times Yearbook 1933, s.l.
Seaports of the Far East. Historical and Descriptive, Commercial and Industrial. Facts, Figures and Resources, London, 1923
The Shanghai Directory 1934, Shanghai, 1934
Sindhi Merchants Association, Singapore, Trade and Telephone Directory 1994–1995, Singapore,
The Singapore and Straits Directory 1911, Singapore, 1911
The South African Indian Who's Who and Commercial Directory 1936–37, Pietermaritzburg, 1935
The Trade Directory of Japan, Calcutta, 1940
Who's Who in Sind, Karachi, 1944

Published books by contemporaries
Adburgham, A., *Liberty's: A Biography of a Shop*, London, 1975
Andrews, C. F., *India and the Pacific*, London, 1937
Baillie, A. F., *Kurrachee (Karachi), Past, Present and Future*, London, 1890
Bharadwaj, P., *Sindhis Through the Ages*, Hong Kong, 1988
Birdwood, G. C. M., *The Industrial Arts of India*, 1880
Burnes, A., *Travels into Bokhara Together with a Narrative of a Voyage on the Indus*, London, 1834, 1st edn (reprint Karachi, 1973)
Burnes, J., *A Narrative of a Visit to the Court of Sinde*, Edinburgh, 1831, 2nd edn (1st edn, Bombay, 1829)
Burton, R. F., *Sind and the Races that Inhabit the Valley of the Indus, with Notices of the Topography and History of the Province*, London, 1851
Sind Revisited, London, 1877
Chotirmall Group of Companies: A Century of Perseverance, 1875–1975, Jakarta, 1975
Curzon, G. N., *Russia in Central Asia in 1889 and the Anglo-Russian Question*, London, 1889

Dresser, C., *Japan, its Architecture, Art and Art Manufactures*, London, 1882
Eastwick, F. B., *A Glance at Sind before Napier or Dry Leaves from Young Egypt*, London, 1849, 1st edn (reprint Karachi, 1973)
Encyclopaedia Britannica, 11th edn, *1910–1911*, vol. IV, Cambridge, 1910, 'Bokhara', pp. 156–7
Feldman, H., *One Hundred Years of Karachi*, Karachi, 1960
Ferrier, J. P., *Caravan Journeys and Wanderings in Persia, Afghanistan, Turkistan and Beloochistan*, London, 1856
Forster, G., *A Journey from Bengal to England*, London, 1808, 3rd edn (reprint Patiala, 1970)
Fraser, D., *The Marches of Hindustan, the Record of a Journey in Thibet, Trans-Himalayan India, Chinese Turkestan, Russian Turkestan and Persia*, Edinburgh and London, 1907
Gidumal, Dayaram, *Hiranand, The Soul of Sindh*, Karachi, 1932, 2nd edn (1st edn, 1903)
Holdich, Sir Thomas, *The Gates of India, Being an Historical Narrative*, London, 1910
Hotchand, Seth Naomal, *A Forgotten Chapter of Indian History as described in the Memoirs of Seth Naomal Hotchand, C. S. I. of Karachi 1804–1878*, Exeter, 1915 (reprint Karachi, 1982)
Hutton, J., *Central Asia: from the Aryan to the Cossack*, London, 1875
Ibn Battuta, *Voyages* (from the Arabic, C. Defremery and B. R. Sanguinetti), Paris, 1854
Jumabhoy, R., *Multiracial Singapore*, Singapore, 1970
Keynes, J. M., *Indian Currency and Finance*, London, 1913
Kirpalani, S. K., *Fifty Years with the British*, Bombay, 1993
Langley, E. A., *Narrative of a Residence at the Court of Meer Ali Moorad with Wild Sports in the Valley of the Indus*, London, 1860
Lansdell, H., *Russian Central Asia, including Kuldja, Bokhara, Khiva and Merv*, London, 1885
Lecarpentier, G., *L'Egypte Moderne*, Paris, 1920
Logofet, D. I., *The Land of Wrong: The Khanate of Bokhara and its Present Condition*, Simla, 1910 (translated from Russian)
Masson, Charles, *Narrative of Various Journeys in Baloochistan, Afghanistan and the Panjab, Including a Residence in these Countries from 1826 to 1838*, London, 1842
Meakin, A. M. B., *In Russian Turkestan: A Garden of Asia and its People*, London, 1903
Mir Izzatullah, *Travels in Central Asia by Meer Izzat Oolah in the years 1812–13* (trans. Captain Henderson), Calcutta, 1872
Mohan Lal, *Travels in the Panjab, Afghanistan and Turkestan to Balk, Bokhara and Herat*, London, 1846, 2nd edn (1st edn, Calcutta, 1834)
Mukherji, T. N., *Art Manufactures of India*, Calcutta, 1888
Pierce, R. A. (ed.), *Mission to Turkestan, Being the Memoirs of Count K. K. Pahlen 1908–1909*, London, 1964
Postans, T., *Personal Observations on Sindh, the Manners and Customs of its Inhabitants and its Productive Capabilities*, London, 1843

Pottinger, H., *Travels in Beloochistan and Sinde, Accompanied by A Geographical and Historical Account of These Countries*, London, 1816
Schuyler, E., *Turkistan, Notes of a Voyage in Russian Turkistan, Khokand, Bukhara and Kuldja*, London, 1876
Scott, A. F. (ed.), *Scinde in the Forties, Being the Journal and Letters of Colonel Keith Young, C. B., Sometime Judge-Advocate-General in India*, London, 1912
Sigma (Dayaram Gidumal), *Something about Sind*, Karachi, 1882
Sindhu Resettlement Corporation Ltd., *Gandhidham*, Bombay, 1951
Sykes, P. M., *Ten Thousand Miles in Persia or Eight Years in Iran*, London, 1902
Vambéry, A., *Travels in Central Asia, Being the Account of a Journey from Teheran across the Turkoman Desert on the Eastern Shore of the Caspian to Khiva, Bokhara and Samarcand*, London, 1864
Vaswani, H. P., *A Saint of Modern India*, Poona, 1975
Watts, Sir George, *Indian Art at Delhi, 1903, Being the Official Catalogue of the Delhi Exhibition 1902–03*, Calcutta, 1903
Woiekof, A., *Le Turkestan Russe*, Paris, 1914
Wolff, J., *A Mission to Bokhara* (ed. G. Wint), London, 1969 (1st edn, London, 1845)
Wu, A. K., *Turkistan Tumult*, London, 1940

Oral interviews
L. Khiani, Gibraltar, 4 September 1992
P. Lachman, Bombay, 22 December 1992
Lal and Lokumal Chellaram, London, August 1996

SECONDARY WORKS

BOOKS AND ARTICLES

Advani, A. B., 'Hyderabad: A Brief Historical Sketch', *Sindhian World*, vol. 1, no. 6, 1940, pp. 356–369
Advani, B. M., *Sindh-je-Hindus-je-Tarikh [History of Sindh Hindus]* (in Sindhi), Hyderabad, s.d.
Allen, C. H., 'The Indian Merchant Community of Masqat', *Bulletin of the School of Oriental and African Studies*, vol. 44, 1981, pp. 39–53
Allen, G. C. and Donnithorne, A. D., *Western Enterprise in Far Eastern Economic Development: China and Japan*, London, 1962 (2nd edn)
Anand, S., *National Integration of Sindhis*, Delhi, 1996
Ansari, S. F. D., *Sufi Saints and State Power: the Pirs of Sind, 1843–1947*, Cambridge, 1992
Askari, N. and Crill, R., *Colours of the Indus: Costume and Textiles of Pakistan*, London, 1997
Babb, L. A., *Redemptive Encounters: Three Modern Styles in the Hindu Tradition*, Berkeley, CA, 1986
Baker, C. J., *An Indian Rural Economy 1880–1955: The Tamilnad Countryside*, Delhi, 1984

Ballard, R. (ed.), *Desh Pardesh: The South Asian Presence in Britain*, London, 1994
Baloch, N. A. (ed.), *The Traditional Arts and Crafts of Hyderabad Region*, Hyderabad, 1966
Banga, I., 'Karachi and its Hinterland under Colonial Rule', in I. Banga (ed.), *Ports and their Hinterlands in India (1700–1950)*, Delhi, 1992, pp. 337–58
Banks, M., 'Jain Ways of Being', in R. Ballard (ed.), *Desh Pardesh: The South Asian Presence in Britain*, London, 1994, pp. 231–50
Barrier, N. G., and Dusenbery, V. A. (eds.), *The Sikh Diaspora: Migration and Experience beyond the Punjab*, Delhi, 1989
Basu, D. K. (ed.), *The Rise and Growth of the Colonial Port Cities in Asia*, Berkeley, CA, 1985
Bayly, C. A., *Rulers, Townsmen and Bazaars: North Indian Society in the Age of British Expansion 1770–1870*, Cambridge, 1983
  Imperial Meridian: the British Empire and the World 1780–1830, London, 1989
  Empire and Information: Intelligence Gathering and Social Communication in India, 1780–1870, Cambridge, 1996
Becker, S., *Russia's Protectorates in Central Asia: Bukhara and Khiva, 1865–1924*, Cambridge, Mass., 1968
Bhattacharya, N., 'Lenders and Debtors: Punjab Countryside, 1880–1940', *Studies in History* (new series), vol. 1, no. 2, 1985, pp. 305–42
Blalock, H. M., Jr, *Toward a Theory of Minority Group Relations*, New York, 1967
Bonacich, E., 'A Theory of Middleman Minorities', *American Sociological Review*, vol. 38 (October), 1973, pp. 583–94
Boreham, N., 'Decolonisation and Provincial Muslim Politics: Sind, 1937–47', *South Asia*, new series, vol. 16, no. 1, 1993, pp. 53–72
Borsa, G. (ed.), *Trade and Politics in the Indian Ocean: Historical and Contemporary Perspectives*, Delhi, 1990
Bose, S., 'The World Economy and Regional Economies in South Asia: Some Comments on Linkages', in S. Bose (ed.), *South Asia and World Capitalism*, Delhi, 1990, pp. 357–62
Brady Williams, R., *Religions of Immigrants from India and Pakistan: New Threads in the American Tapestry*, Cambridge, 1988
Braudel, F., *Civilization and Capitalism 15th–18th century*, vol. 2, *The Wheels of Commerce*, London, 1982
Brown, R., *Capital and Entrepreneurship in South-East Asia*, London, 1994
Burton, A., *The Bukharans*, London, 1997
Castillero Calvo, A., *La sociedad panamena, historia de su formacion e integracion*, Panama, 1970
Chablani, S. P., *Economic Conditions in Sind 1592 to 1843*, Bombay, 1951
Chandra, G. A., 'The History of Indians in Japan', in J. K. Motwani *et al.* (eds.), *Global Indian Diaspora: Yesterday, Today and Tomorrow*, New York, 1993, pp. 322–5
Cheesman, D., *Landlord Power and Peasant Indebtedness in Colonial Sind 1865–1901*, London, 1997
Chen Dasheng and D. Lombard, 'Le rôle des étrangers dans le commerce maritime de Quanzhou (Zaitun) aux 13e et 14e siècles', in D. Lombard and

Bibliography

J. Aubin (eds.), *Marchands et hommes d'affaires asiatiques dans l'Océan Indien et la Mer de Chine 13ᵉ−20ᵉ siècles*, Paris, 1988, pp. 21−9

Chin-Keong, Ng, *Trade and Society: the Amoy Network on the China Coast 1683−1735*, Singapore, 1983

Choi Chi-Cheung, 'Kinship and Business: Paternal and Maternal Kin in Chaozhou Chinese Family Firms', *Business History*, vol. 40, no. 1, 1998, pp. 26−49

Choksey, R. D., *The Story of Sind (An Economic Survey), 1843−1933*, Poona, 1983

Chowdhry, P., 'Marriage, Sexuality and the Female "Ascetic": Understanding a Hindu Sect', *Economic and Political Weekly*, vol. 31, no. 34, August 1996, pp. 2307−21

Cizakca, M., *A Comparative Evolution of Business Partnerships: the Islamic World and Europe, with Special Reference to the Ottoman Archives*, Leiden, 1996

Clarke, C., C. Peach and S. Vertovec (eds.), *South Asians Overseas: Migration and Ethnicity*, Cambridge, 1990

Cohen, A., 'Cultural Strategies in the Organization of Trading Diasporas', in C. Meillassoux (ed.), *The Development of Indigenous Trade and Markets in West Africa*, London, 1971, pp. 266−78

Conniff, M. L., 'Panama since 1903', in *The Cambridge History of Latin America*, vol. VII, *Latin America since 1930: Mexico, Central America and the Caribbean*, Cambridge, 1990, pp. 603−42

Cragg, C., *The New Maharajahs: the Commercial Princes of India, Pakistan and Bangladesh*, London, 1996

Curtin, P. D., *Cross-Cultural Trade in World History*, Cambridge, 1984

Dale, S., *Indian Merchants and Eurasian Trade, 1600−1750*, Cambridge, 1994

Das Gupta, A., 'Gujarati Merchants and the Red Sea Trade', in B. B. Kling and M. N. Pearson (eds.), *The Age of Partnership: Europeans in Asia before Dominion*, Honolulu, 1979, pp. 123−58

Das Gupta, P., 'Trust as a commodity', in D. Gambetta (ed.), *Trust: Making and Breaking Cooperative Relations*, New York and Oxford, 1988, pp. 49−72

Davis, K., *The Population of India and Pakistan*, Princeton, 1951

Dobbin, C., *Urban Leadership in Western India: Politics and Communities in Bombay City, 1840−1885*, Oxford, 1972

  Asian Entrepreneurial Minorities: Conjoint Communities in the Making of the World-Economy 1570−1940, London, 1996

Duarte, A., *A History of British Relations with Sind*, Karachi, 1976

Dusenbery, V. A., 'A Sikh Diaspora? Contested Identities and Constructed Realities', in P. Van der Veer (ed.), *Nation and Migration: the Politics of Space in the South Asian Diaspora*, Philadelphia, 1995, pp. 17−42

Fairbank, J. K., *Trade and Diplomacy on the China Coast: the Opening of the Treaty Ports, 1842−1854*, Cambridge, MA, 1964

Fatimi, S. Q., 'The Twin Ports of Daybul', in H. Khuhro (ed.), *Sind through the Centuries*, Karachi, 1981, pp. 97−105

Forbes, A. D. W., *Warlords and Muslims in Chinese Central Asia: a Political History of Republican Sinkiang, 1911−1949*, Cambridge, 1986

Forrest, T., *The Advance of African Capital: the Growth of Nigerian Private Enterprise*, Edinburgh, 1994

Gambetta, D. (ed.), *Trust: Making and Breaking Cooperative Relations*, New York and Oxford, 1988
Gankovsky, Yu., 'The Durrani Empire', in USSR Academy of Sciences, *Afghanistan Past and Present*, Moscow, 1981, pp. 76-98 (translated from Russian)
Gillion, K. K., *Fiji's Indian Migrants*, Melbourne, 1964
Gommans, J. J. L., *The Rise of the Indo-Afghan Empire, c. 1710-1780*, Leiden, 1995
Gordillo Osuna, M., *Geografia Urbana de Ceuta*, Madrid, 1972
Greenhalgh, P., *Ephemeral Vistas: the Expositions Universelles, Great Exhibitions and World's Fairs, 1851-1939*, Manchester, 1988
Gregorian, V., *The Emergence of Modern Afghanistan: Policies of Reform and Modernisation, 1880-1946*, Stanford, 1969
Gregory, R. G., *India and East Africa: a History of Race Relations in the British Empire*, Oxford, 1971
Gulzad, Z. A., *External Influences and the Development of the Afghan State in the Nineteenth Century*, New York, 1994
Habib, I., 'Merchant Communities in Pre-colonial India', in J. Tracy (ed.), *The Rise of Merchant Empires: Long-distance Trade in the Early Modern World*, Cambridge, 1990, pp. 371-99
Hardiman, D., *Feeding the Banyia: Peasants and Usurers in Western India*, Delhi, 1996
Haynes, D., *Rhetoric and Ritual in Colonial India: the Shaping of a Public Culture in Surat City, 1852-1928*, Berkeley, CA, 1991
Helweg, A. W. and U. M. Helweg, *An Immigrant Success Story: East Indians in America*, Philadelphia, 1990
Hiranandani, P., *Sindhis: The Scattered Treasure*, Delhi, 1980
Jain, L. C., *Indigenous Banking in India*, London, 1928
Jain, R. K., *Indian Communities Abroad: Themes and Literature*, Delhi, 1993
Karaka, D. F., *History of the Parsis, including their Manners, Customs, Religion and Present Position*, London, 1884
Khuhro, H., *The Making of Modern Sind: British Policy and Social Change in the Nineteenth Century*, Karachi, 1978
  'Masjid Manzilgah 1939-40: Test Case for Hindu-Muslim Relations in Sind', *Modern Asian Studies*, vol. 32, 1, 1998, pp. 49-89
Khuhro, H. (ed.), *Sind Through the Centuries*, Karachi, 1981
Kling, B. B. and M. N. Pearson (eds), *The Age of Partnership: Europeans in Asia before Dominion*, Honolulu, 1979
Kotkin, J., *Tribes: How Race, Religion and Identity Determine Success in the New Global Economy*, New York, 1992
Lambrick, H. T., *Sir Charles Napier and Sind*, Oxford, 1952
Lari, S. Z., *A History of Sindh*, Karachi, 1994
Li, L. M., *China's Silk Trade: Traditional Industry in the Modern World 1842-1937*, Cambridge, MA, 1981
Lombard, D. and J. Aubin (eds), *Marchands et hommes d'affaires asiatiques dans l'Océan Indien et la Mer de Chine 13e-20e siècles*, Paris, 1988
Mackenzie, J. M., *Orientalism: History, Theory and the Arts*, Manchester, 1995
McLeod, W. H., 'The First Forty Years of Sikh Migration', in N. G. Barrier and V. A. Dusenbery (eds), *The Sikh Diaspora: Migration and Experience beyond the Punjab*, Delhi, 1989, pp. 29-48

Macpherson, K., 'Chulias and Klings. Indigenous Trade Diasporas and European Penetration of the Indian Ocean Littoral', in G. Borsa (ed.), *Trade and Politics in the Indian Ocean: Historical and Contemporary Perspectives*, Delhi, 1990, pp. 33–46

Malkani, K. R., *The Sindh Story*, Delhi, 1984

Mamdani, M., *Politics and Class Formation in Uganda*, London, 1976

Mani, A. K., 'Indians in Jakarta', in A. K. Mani and K. S. Sandhu (eds.), *Indian Communities in South East Asia*, Singapore, 1993, pp. 98–130

Mani, A. K. and K. S. Sandhu (eds.), *Indian Communities in South East Asia*, Singapore, 1993

Mariwalla, C. L., *History of the Commerce of Sind (From Early Times to 1526 AD)*, Jamshoro, 1981

Meillassoux, C. (ed.), *The Development of Indigenous Trade and Markets in West Africa*, London, 1971

Merani, H. V. and H. L. Van der Laan, 'The Indian Traders in Sierra Leone', *African Affairs*, vol. 78, no. 311, 1979, pp. 240–50

Metcalf, T. R. and S. B. Freitag, 'Karachi's Early Merchant Families: Entrepreneurship and Community', in D. K. Basu (ed.), *The Rise and Growth of the Colonial Port Cities in Asia*, Berkeley, CA, 1985, pp. 55–9

Millward, J. A., *Beyond the Pass: Economy, Ethnicity and Empire in Quing Central Asia 1759–1864*, Stanford, CA, 1998

Mirza, M., 'The Zardozi Art of Embroidery', in N. A. Baloch (ed.), *The Traditional Arts and Crafts of Hyderabad Region*, Hyderabad, 1966, pp. 41–2

Morris, L. P., 'British Secret Service Activity in Khorrassan, 1887–1908', *Historical Journal*, vol. 27, no. 3, 1984, pp. 657–75

Motwani, J. K. et al. (eds.), *Global Indian Diaspora, Yesterday, Today and Tomorrow*, New York, 1993

Mughal, M. Y. (ed.), *Studies in Sind*, Jamshoro, 1989

Nair, J., *Women and Law in Colonial India: A Social History*, Bangalore, 1996

Nedvetsky, A. G. (comp.), *Bukhara: Caught in Time*, Reading, 1993

Nyman, L. E., *Great Britain and Chinese, Russian and Japanese Interests in Sinkiang, 1918–1934*, Lund, 1977

Oberoi, H., *The Construction of Religious Boundaries: Culture, Identity and Diversity in the Sikh Tradition*, Delhi, 1994.

Owen, D. F., *British Opium Policy in China and India*, New Haven, CT, 1934

Pan, L., *Sons of the Yellow Emperor: the Story of the Overseas Chinese*, London, 1990

Pankhurst, R., 'Indian Trade with Ethiopia, the Gulf of Aden and the Horn of Africa in the Nineteenth and Early Twentieth Centuries', *Cahiers d'Etudes Africaines*, vol. 55, 1974, pp. 453–97

Pearson, M., *Merchants and Rulers in Gujarat*, Berkeley, CA, 1976

Perham, M. (ed.), *Mining, Commerce and Finance in Nigeria*, London, 1948

Pinto, C., *Trade and Finance in Portuguese India: a study of the Portuguese Country Trade 1770–1840*, Delhi, 1994

Platt, D. C. M., *The Cinderella Service: British Consuls since 1825*, London, 1971

Rasulzade, P. N., *Is Istorii Sredne-Indiisiskh Svyazei*, Tashkent, 1966

Ray, N. (comp.), *Dictionary of National Biography (Supplement)*, vol. I, Calcutta, 1986
Ray, R. K., 'Asian Capital in the Age of European Domination: the Rise of the Bazaar, 1800–1914', *Modern Asian Studies*, vol. 29, no. 3, 1995, pp. 449–554
Rizvi, J., 'The Trans-Karakoram Trade in the Nineteenth and Twentieth Centuries', *Indian Economic and Social History Review*, vol. 31, no. 1, 1994, pp. 27–64
Rodinson, M., Islam et Capitalisme, Paris, 1966
Rudner, D. W., *Caste and Capitalism in Colonial India: The Nattukottai Chettiars*, Berkeley, CA, 1994
Sandhu, K. S., *Indians in Malaya: Some Aspects of their Immigration and Settlement (1786–1957)*, Cambridge, 1969
Simmel, G., 'The Stranger', in K. H. Wolff (ed.), *The Sociology of Georg Simmel*, New York, 1950, pp. 402–8
Singh Rye, A., 'The Indian Community in the Philippines', in A. K. Mani and K. S. Sandhu (eds.), *Indian Communities in South East Asia*, Singapore, 1993, pp. 708–74
Sipe, K. R., 'The Entrepreneurial Basis of Commodity Exploitation: An Examination of Merchant Group Dominance in Karachi's Cotton Trade', in D. K. Basu, *The Rise and Growth of Colonial Port-Cities in Asia*, Berkeley, CA, 1985, pp. 61–3
Skrine, C. P. and P. Nightingale, *Macartney at Kashgar: New Light on British, Chinese and Russian Activities in Sinkiang, 1890–1918*, London, 1973
Sombart, W., *The Jews and Modern Capitalism*, New Brunswick and London, 1982
Subrahmanyam, S., 'The Portuguese, Thatta and the External Trade of Sind, 1515–1635', *Revista de Cultura*, nos. 13–14, 1991, pp. 48–58
Sue-White, B., *Turbans and Traders: Hong Kong's Indian Communities*, Hong Kong, 1994
Sugiyama, S., *Japan's Industrialization in the World Economy 1859–1899: Export Trade and Overseas Competition*, London, 1988
Szuppé, M., 'En quête de chevaux turkmènes: le journal de voyage de Mir Izzatullah de Delhi à Boukhara en 1812–1813', *Cahiers d'Asie Centrale*, no. 1–2, 1996, pp. 91–111
Thakur, U. T., *Sindhi Culture*, Bombay, 1959
Thakurdas, L. M. M., 'Hindus and Talpurs of Sind', *Modern Review*, vol. 51, 1932, pp. 265–72
Thompson, V., *Labor Problems in Southeast Asia*, New Haven, CT, 1947
Timberg, T. A., *The Marwaris: From Traders to Industrialists*, Delhi, 1978
Tinker, H., *A New System of Slavery: The Export of Indian Labour Overseas 1830–1920*, London, 1993, 2nd edn (1st edn, London, 1974)
T. M. C. Asser Instituut, *The Influence of the Hague Conference on Private International Law*, Dordrecht, 1993
Tracy, J. (ed.), *The Rise of Merchant Empires: Long-distance Trade in the Early Modern World*, Cambridge, 1990
Udovich, A. L., *Partnership and Profit in Medieval Islam*, Princeton, 1970

USSR Academy of Sciences, *Afghanistan Past and Present*, Moscow, 1981 (translated from Russian)
Vaid, K. N., *The Overseas Indian Community in Hong Kong*, Hong Kong, 1972
Van der Veer, P., 'Introduction: The Diasporic Imagination', in P. Van der Veer (ed.), *Nation and Migration: The Politics of Space in the South Asian Diaspora*, Philadelphia, 1995, pp. 1–16.
Van der Veer, P. (ed.), *Nation and Migration: The Politics of Space in the South Asian Diaspora*, Philadephia, 1995
Vertovec, S. (ed.), *Aspects of the South Asian Diaspora*, Delhi, 1991
Wallerstein, I., 'The Incorporation of the Indian Subcontinent into the Capitalist World-Economy', *Economic and Political Weekly*, vol. 21, no. 4, 25 January 1986, pp. PE 28–39
Wang Gugwu, *China and the Chinese Overseas*, Singapore, 1991
Whitteridge, G., *Charles Masson of Afghanistan*, Warminster, 1985
Wink, A., *Al Hind: The Making of the Indo-Islamic World*, vol. I, *Early Medieval India and the Expansion of Islam 7th–11th Centuries*, Leiden, 1990
Wong, J. Y., 'British Annexation of Sind in 1843: An Economic Perspective', *Modern Asian Studies*, vol. 31, no. 2, 1997, pp. 225–44

UNPUBLISHED DISSERTATION

Herzig, E., 'The Armenian Merchants of New Julfa (Isfahan)', D. Phil., Oxford, 1991

Index

Abu Dhabi, 12
Aden, 10, 145
Afghanistan, trade of India with, 16, 93; Indian merchants in, 17; Durrani predominance in, 37–8; political domination of Shikarpur by, 39; role of Shikarpuris in, 61, 99, 186, 212, 213
Agra, as craft centre, 146, 205
Ahmad Shah (Abdali), 61, 186
Ahmedabad merchants in opium trade, 14
Aitken, E. H., 121, 132
Aksu, Shikarpuris in, 96
Alexandria, Sindworkies in, 122–3, 131
Algiers, Sindworkies in, 123, 127, 151 n. 77
Amils, in Sind, 47; in Hyderabad, 111, 138
Amoy, 24
Amritsar, 67, 68
Andijan, 255
Andrews, C. F., 121
Anglo-Russian rivalry, effect of on Shikarpuris, 217
Armenian merchants, 19, 158; in Egypt, 204
Arya Samaj, 184, 256
Astrakhan, 12, 62, 63
Aswan, Sindworkies in, 154
Auranga Bandar, 35
Australia, Sindworkies in, 134, 175; immigration restrictions in, 214, 221–2

Babb, Lawrence, 275
Bahawalpur, 57
Bahrain, 11–12, 35, 36, 249 n. 1
Baku, 63, 81
Balkh, Hindu traders in, 99
Baluchistan, 32, 36, 38
Bandar Abbas, 12, 100, 101, 219
Bandoeng, Sindworkies in, 154 n. 87
Bangkok, Sindworkies in, 127, 131
Bank of Taiwan, 135–6, 142

Barbados, Sindworkies in, 141
Barclays Bank, 136
Barmer, 39
Batavia, Sindworkies in, 134, 153
Batum, 81
Bay Souba Bay Djouba, Shikarpuri moneylender, 92
Bayly, C. A., 28, 32, n. 1
Beira, Sindworkies in, 131
Bela, 63
Benares, as centre of craft production, 117, 146
Berberah, 11
Bhai Khanchand Menghraj, Sindwork merchant of Cairo, 162, 165–66
Bhaibands, in Sind, 47–8; in Hyderabad, 111, 130, 138
Bhatias, of Thatta, 11, 34, 35, 38, 123 n. 26, 249, 250 n. 1; Kutchi Bhatias, 11, 38
Bhatias in Shikarpur, 57, 250
Bhattacharya, Neeladiri, 51–2
Bhojsons, Sindhi firm in Nigeria, 283
Bikaner, 38
Birdwood, Sir George, 118
Birla Bros, 16
Blalock, H., 20
Bogdan Khmelnitsky revolt, 20
Bohras, 23, 26; Kutchi Bohras, 28; in Kobe, 146; in Singapore, 149
Bolan pass, 38, 81
Bombay city, 12, 15, 28, 41, 56, 81; role of, in Sindwork trade, 116–7, 122, 135, 145, 195; Shikarpuri bankers in, 192–3
Bombay Merchants Association, Manila, 240, 252
Bonacich, Edna, 20–1
Bose, Subhas Chandra, 144, 228–9
Brahma Kumari, 275
Brahmins, in Sind, 47; in Hyderabad, 130; in Shikarpuri diaspora in Central Asia, 253

Index

British attitudes to Sind merchants, 215–17, 222–5, 226
British consular courts in Morocco, 262
Broach, 12, 28
Brown, R., 22 n. 27, 142
Budapest, Sindworkies in, 126
Buenos Aires, Sindworkies in, 124
Bukhara city, Shikarpuris in, 57, 64, 65, 66, 68, 71, 80, 83, 104, 105
Bukhara, khanate or emirate of, trade of India with, 70–1, 72; Shikarpuris in, 71, 74, 76–7, 80, 82, 84–5, 93, 94, 104–5, 212–13
Burma, Indian emigration to, 7, 17; Shikarpuris in, 106, 192–3; Sindworkies in, 152, n. 82
Burnes, Alexander, 42, 57, 60, 62, 65, 66, 67
Burnes, James, 43–4
Burton, Sir Richard, 50–1, 137, 160 n. 5, 269, 274 n. 48
Bushire, 12

Cairo, Sindworkies in, 121 n. 19, 129, 131, 148, 150, 199, 205–6
Calcutta, Shikarpuris in, 57; Sindworkies in, 145, 152 n. 81, 195
Campbellpore, 28, 102
Canary Islands, Sindhi merchants in, 1, 124, 127, 128, 129, 140, 144, 151, 152, 256 n. 17, 279, 280, 283
Canton, Sindworkies in, 131, 147, 195, 223
Cantonese migrants, 3
Cape Colony, Hawkers' Licences Act of 1906, petition by Sindwork merchants against, 173, 222
caravan trade, between India and Central Asia, 66–8
Casablanca, Sindworkies in, 150 n. 77, 152
Casbin, 99
caste, role of, in merchant networks, 26; in Shikarpur and Hyderabad, 251–2
Central Asia, trade of India with, 12; trade of Sind with 37; Shikarpuris in trade with, 62–73
Ceuta, Sindworkies in, 123, 127, 154 n. 90, 237
Ceylon, Indian emigration to, 7, 17; Shikarpuris in, 106; Sindworkies in, 152 n. 82
Cheesman, David, 51–2
Chile, Sindworkies in, 124, 127, 131
Chiman Singh, Ram Singh & Co, Shikarpuri firm, 102–3
Chimkent, 81

China, Sindworkies in, 125, 127, 128, 147–8; as source of goods for Sindwork trade, 119, 195–6, 200, 201, 205
China trade, 14, 15
Chinese Central Asia, *see* Sinkiang
Chinese merchants, 19, 120
Chirakchi, 91
Chowdhry, Prem, 275
Christianity, conversion of Sindhi Hindus to, 256
Chulia, merchants, 14
Chuman Dass, Shikarpuri merchant, 65
Churchgate, Sindhi firm in Nigeria, 283
Cleveland, C. R., director of criminal intelligence, 224
Cohen, Abner, 7 n. 10, 21
Colombia, Sindwork pedlars in, 155
Colombo, as transit point for Sindworkies, 124; Sindworkies in, 152
Colon, Sindworkies in, 131, 153 n. 86, 240
Congress Party, links of Sindwork merchants with, 227, 289
cooks, in Sindworkie network, 175–6
Coromandel, 5
craftsmen, Indian itinerant, 120
credit, role of, in merchant networks, 25–6; provision of short-term credit among Shikarpuris and Sindworkies, 178–9
Curaçao, Sindworkies in, 141
Curtin, Philip, 21
Curzon, George Nathaniel, 64

D. Chellaram, firm of Sindwork merchants, 131, 132, 133, 140, 143, 151 n. 80, 171, 223, 236
Dada Lekhraj, founder of Brahma Kumari, 275
Dadu, centre of craft production, 116
Dale, Stephen, 62, 63
Damao, as transit point for Malwa opium, 14, 41, 42
Darband, 66
Das Gupta, Ashin, 191
Daulatram Jairamdas Alamchandani, 227
Davis, Kingsley, 4 n. 7, 18
Debal, 34
Delhi, 60; as craft centre, 205
deposits, role of in financing of Sindwork trade, 135
Dera Ghazi Khan, 57, 65, 66, 67
Diego de Couto, 35
Dipusing walad Jethasing, Shikarpuri moneylender, 91

Index

Diu, as centre of Kapol bania network, 11; as transit point for Malwa opium, 14
Dobbin Christine, 21
Dresser, Christopher, 118
Dubai, 12
Durrani empire, 37–8 , 60–2, 185–6
Dutch East Indies, Sindworkies in, 124, 127, 139, 140, 141, 142, 144, 200, 201, 228–9
Duya Ram Lohana, Shikarpuri merchant, 65
Duzdap (Zahedan), 101
Dwarka Dass, Shikarpuri merchant, 65

East Africa, Sindhis in, 123, n. 26
East African trade, 16
East India Company, 13, 35
Eastwick, 44
Egypt, Sindworkies in, 117, 121, 122–3, 127, 128, 197, 204–8
Enpee Industries, Sindhi firm in Nigeria, 283
Eritrea, Sindworkies in, 127
estates, of Shikarpuris in Russian Central Asia, 73–93
exchange banks, role of in financing Sindwork trade, 135

Faqir Chand, Shikarpuri banker, Kandahar, 99
Ferghana oblast, 80
Ferghana valley, growth of commercial agriculture in, 84, 187
Ferrier, J. P., French traveller, 274
firms, of Sindwork merchants, 132–4, 140, 141; present-day Sindhi firms, 282–3
Forster, George, 63
Freetown, Sindwork firms in, 182, 209
French Indochina, Sindworkies in, 125, 152 n. 83

Gandhi, M. K., 4, 227
Gankovsky, 61, 186
German East Africa, Sindworkies in, 126
Ghadr Party, suspected collusion of Sindwork merchants with, 222–5
Ghana, Sindhi migration to, 280, n. 13
Ghazni, Hindu traders in, 99
Gibraltar, Sindworkies in, 123, 127, 129, 131, 148, 150, 151 n. 78, 231–2, 236, 238–40, 281
Gidalmal Ramalmal, Shikarpuri, 255
Goa, as transit point for Malwa opium, 14
Gold Coast, Sindworkies in, 123, 154 n. 88, 208
Goldsmid, Captain F. G., 62, 65

Goma, Shikarpuris in, 96
Gommans, J., 37
grain prices in Sind, 53 n. 54
Grey, Sir Edward, 76
Gujarat, 5, 11, 15, 27, 28
Gujaratis, 1, 6, 11, 14, 15, 16, 18, 19, 23, 27; Gujarati Hindus, 6; in Kobe, 146; in Singapore, 149
Guzar, 81, 87
Gwalior, native state of, 41

Habsh (Abyssinia), 11
Hadramaut, 11
Hakka migrants, 3
Hala, centre of craft production, 116
Hamilton, Alexander, 35
Hankow, Sindworkies in, 148
Hassomal walad Khemchand, Shikarpuri moneylender, 188
hawkers (pedlars), in Sindwork trade, 155, 168–9, 204–5, 262, 263
Hemraj walad Bhojraj, Shikarpuri moneylender, 91
Herat, 67, 99
Hidayiatullah, Sir Ghulam, Pakistani governor of Sind, 277
Hinduja family, 106–7, 248, 282
Hirabad, locality in Hyderabad, 137
Hokkien migrants, 3; network, 24
Hong Kong and Shanghai Bank, 136
Hong Kong, Sindhi merchants in, 1, 22, 129, 131, 133, 134, 147, 171, 183, 279, 281
Honolulu, Sindworkies in, 125
Hormuz, 35
Hoshiarpur, 28, 95
Hotchand, Seth Naomal, 35, 44–5, 55
hundis, role of, in Malwa opium trade, 42; in Shikarpuri financial operations, 65–6, 159–60, 160 n. 5, 186–7; in financing of Sindwork trade, 135
Hyderabad city, 1–2, 38–9, 42, 43, 47, 110–17, 129–30, 135, 136–8, 161, 163, 164, 165, 180, 184, 204, 250, 252, 275–6, 278, 295–6

Ibn Battuta, 34
Idi Amin, regime in Uganda, 21
Iloilo, Sindworkies in, 153, n. 84
India, 3, 4, 5, 12–13, 16, 17, 18–19, 28, 29; exodus of Sindhi Hindus to in 1947–8, 277–9; migration of Sindhis from 279–81
India Independence League, 229, 230
Indian Merchants Association of the Gold Coast, 154 n. 88, 258

Index

Indian National Army, 144, 228–9
Indonesia, Sindhi migration to, 279; Sindhis in, 281; industrial investment by Sindhis in, 285
Indore, native state of, 41
information, importance of, in merchant networks, 25; circulation of, in Shikarpuri and Sindworkie networks, 181–4
Inlaks, Sindhi firm in Nigeria, 283
Iran or Persia, Indian trade with, 9, 12; Multanis in, 63, 99; Shikarpuris in, 64, 99–103, 106–7
Isfahan, 63
Ismailia, Sindworkies in, 153

Jains, in East Africa, 18
Jaisalmer, 38; merchants of, in Iran, 63
Jamaica, Sindworkies in, 141
Japan, Sindworkies in, 125, 127, 146–7, 270; as source of goods for Sindwork trade, 119, 142, 143–4, 196, 200, 201, 205, 209–10
'japonisme', 118
Jardines, 14
J. T. Chanrai & Co, firm of Sindwork merchants, 131, 132, 133–4, 140, 143, 151 n. 80, 153 n. 86, 182, 204, 208, 209, 223, 224, 236
Java, Sindworkies in, 128, 131, 154 n. 87
Jewish merchants, 19; in Egypt, 204
Jews, in seventeenth-century Ukraine, 20
Jhamatmal Gurbamall, firm of Sindwork merchants, 124, 166
Jhangimal Tejumal Khemrani, Sindwork merchant, 162, 166–7
Jhule Lal, or Uderolal, cult of, 48–9, 285
Jibuti, Indian merchants in, 16; Sindworkies in, 127
Jizak, 94
Jodhpur, 39
Johannesburg, Sindworkies in, 154
Jones, Sir Evan, 51
Jones, Owen, 118
Juyut Sing, Shikarpuri merchant, 64

K. Chellaram & Sons, firm of Sindwork merchants, 140, 141, 143, 183, 200, 204, 208–10, 228
K. Khanchand, firm of Sindwork merchants, 165–6, 205–6
K. A. J. Chotirmall, firm of Sindwork merchants, 131, 132, 134, 140, 143, 144, 147, 152 n. 83, 200, 203, 229
Kabul, 57, 65, 66, 67, 68, 99
Kachan, 99

Kalhora dynasty of Sind, 32, 36, 38
Kandahar, 37–8, 62, 99
Kapol Banias, 11
Karachi, foundation of, 36; rise of as port, 38; role of, in Malwa opium trade, 40–3; role of in economy of colonial Sind, 54–6; Shikarpuris in, 55, 69; role of, in Shikarpuri trade with Iran, 101; riots in 1948, 278
Karachi Chamber of Commerce, 54
Karghalik, Shikarpuris in, 96, 97
Karlsbad, Sindworkies in, 126
Kashgar, Shikarpuris in, 96
Kashmir, craft productions from, 120, 196; financing of craft production in, by Sindwork merchants, 199
Katerji, 91
Kathiawar, 11
Kenya, 226
Keriya, Shikarpuris in, 96
Kermineh, 93
Kewalram Chanrai, Sindhi firm in Nigeria, 283
Khanarik, Shikarpuris in, 96
Kharrakbandar, 35, 36
Khatris, 57, 60, 63, 69, 250
Khelat, Khans of, 36
Khelat town, 63
Khemchand & Sons, firm of Sindwork merchants, 124
Khodjend, 72
Khojas, 15, 23; in Hyderabad, 11, 111; in Kobe, 146; in Singapore, 149
Khokand, Shikarpuris in, 57, 72
Kholum, 66
Khorrassan, 32, 57, 108
Kishinchand Chellaram Daryanani, Sindwork merchant, 141
Kislak Kazan, 91
Kitab, 90
Kitchener, Lord, 218–19
Kobe, Sindworkies in, 142, 146, 183
Krasnovodsk, 81
Kripalani, J. B., 227, 289
Kurakol, 81
Kutch, 28

lace trade, 197
Lagos, Sindworkies in, 127
Lahori Bandar, 34
Langley, 137
Larache, Sindworkies in, 154
Larkana, centre of craft production, 116
Las Palmas, Sindworkies in, 124, 151, 174 n. 33, 237, 258
law, private international, 77 n. 52

Lebanon, Sindwork trade in, 150
  Lebanese merchants, 19
Leech, Lieutenant, 42
Liberia, Sinwork pedlars in, 155 n. 91;
  Sindhi migration to, 280
Liberty's, London shop, 119
Libya, Sindwork trade in, 151 n. 77, 270
Lohanas in Sind, 46–7, 251–2
Lohanis (Powindahs), 66
Lucknow, as craft centre, 146
Ludhiana, as craft centre, 205
Lukman, centre of craft production, 116
Luxor, Sindworkies in, 154

M. Dialdas & Sons, firm of Sindwork merchants, 131, 132, 134, 140, 143, 151 n. 80, 171, 182, 203, 208, 209, 223, 236
Macartney, George, 95
Macassar, Sindworkies in, 124, 129
Mackenzie, John, 118
McLeod, W. H., 6
Madeira, lace, 209
Madras, role of, in Sindwork trade, 141, 145–6
Maimana, Hindu traders in, 99
Malabar, 5
Malacca, 12
Malaya, Indian emigration to, 7, 17; Shikarpuris in, 106
Malaysia, Sindhis in, 281
Mallet, Sir Claude, British consul in Panama, 223–4
Malta, Sindworkies in, 123, 127, 128, 197
Malwa, opium trade, 14–15, 39–43
Manado, Sindworkies in, 124
managers, in Sindworkie network, 170–1
Mandvi, 12
Manila, Sindworkies in, 129, 131, 229
Marakkayars, in Singapore, 149
Maralbashi, Shikarpuris in, 96
Marrakesh, Sindworkies in, 150 n. 77, 154
Marwaris, in opium trade, 14, 41; in India's external trade, 23; as a business community, 27–8; in Karachi, 55; in Shikarpur, 63, 250; in Kobe, 146; in Singapore, 149
Masqat, 11, 17, 34–5, 36
Massawa, 11, 138
Masson, Charles, 61 n. 8, 68
Medan, Sindworkies in, 124
Melbourne, branch of Sindwork firm in, 134, 221
Melilla, Sindworkies in, 123, 127, 154
Memons, 26–7; Kutchi Memons, 28; in Karachi, 55

merchant community, 27–8
merchant women in Shikarpur and Hyderabad, 271–6
Merket, Shikarpuris in, 96
Meshed, 81
MI5, report by, on Sindhi merchants, 225
Miani, battle of, 110
Middle East, trade in, 16
middlemen, as minorities, 20–1
Mir Izatullah, 63–4, 65–6
Mir Muradali, of Hyderabad, 44
Mitaksara system of Hindu law, 75, 271
Mocha, 11 n. 5, 191
Mohan Lal, 66–7
Mohandas walad Janjimal, Shikarpuri moneylender, 90–1
Mohenjo-Daro, 34
Mombasa, Sindworkies in, 127
moneylending by Hindu banias in Sind, 51–7; by Shikarpuris in Russian Central Asia, 82–5, 187–90, in Sinkiang, 96–7, 190–1, in Iran, 103
Moradabad, as craft centre, 146
mudaraba, system of partnership, 157, 159, 163
Mughals in Sind, 35, 37
Muhammad bin Qasim, 34
Multan, 37, 38, 60, 61, 63, 65, 66, 67, 68
  Multani merchants, 12–13, 60, 62, 64
Murshid, 99

N. Shamdas & Co, firm of Sindwork merchants, 169
Nairobi, Sindworkies in, 154
Namangan, 189
Nanikram Gehimall Tolaram, Sindwork merchant, 122–3
Napier, Sir Charles, 32, 44, 110, 181 n. 45
Naples, Sindworkies in, 123, 127, 174 n. 34
Naraindas walad Murjimal, Shikarpuri moneylender, 91–2
Narayan Dass Bhatia, Shikarpuri merchant, 65
Nattukottai Chettiars, 19, 26, 84, 157, 294
New Julfa, 158
Nigeria, Sindhi merchants in, 1, 123, 154, 208, 210–11, 279, 281, 283
Nushki, 101

oil economy, world, role of Indian labour in, 7 n. 9
Oman, 10
Osh, 81
Ottoman Empire, Sindworkies in, 126

Pakistan, 1, 2, 3, 277–8, 296

Index

Pali, 40
Panama, Sindworkies in, 124, 223–5, 240–7
panchayats, Shikarpuri, in Central Asia, 80, 256–7
Parsis, in opium trade, 14, 15, 23
Patidars, in East Africa, 18
Penang, 14, 16; Sindworkies in, 129, 131
Peshawar, 70; Shikarpuri bankers in, 93; Peshawari Muslim merchants in Central Asia, 79, 104, 191
Petrie, Sir David, tour of Far East, 1916, 223
Philippines, Sindhi merchants in, 125, 127, 140, 144, 153 n. 84, 228, 229, 230, 232–4, 235, 236, 240, 255, 256 n. 17, 270, 281, 287–8
Pohoomull Bros, firm of Sindwork merchants, 125, 131, 132, 133, 140, 143, 152 n. 83, 171, 179, 199, 200, 223, 236
Polyproducts, Sindhi firm in Nigeria, 283
pongees, 195
Porbandar, merchants of, 27, 41
Port Arthur, Sindworkies in, 147
Port Said, Sindworkies in, 129, 131, 153, 207–8
Portuguese East Africa, Sindworkies in, 127
Portuguese, in Indian Ocean, 11, 34, 35
Posgam, Shikarpuris in, 96
Pottinger, Henry, 63
profits, in moneylending by *banias* in Sind, 53; in moneylending by Shikarpuris, 193; in Sindwork trade, 202–4
Punjab, 35, 37, 48; connection of Karachi with, 54–5; economic resurgence under Ranjit Singh, 68; craft productions from, 120
Punjabi merchants, in Karachi, 55; in Central Asia, 79; in Shikarpur, 250
Punta Arenas, Sindworkies in, 131

Quanzhou, 10
Quetta, as centre of merchant network, 28, 102; as transit point for Shikarpuri merchants, 81; 1947 riots in, 277
Raheja, K., 281, n. 16
Rajasthan, Sindhi migration to, 1947–8, 278
Rajputana, native states of, 41
Ram Dass, Shikarpuri merchant, 64–5
Rangoon, Sindworkies in, 152, 174; Shikarpuris in, 192–3
Ray, Rajat, 18–19
Relomall Baloomall, firm of Sindwork merchants, 166

remittances, from Central Asia to Shikarpur, 92, 179; to Hyderabad, 174, 179–80, 203
Rieu, Jean-Louis, collector of Sukkur, 86–7, 263
Rio, Sindworkies in, 124
Rodinson, M., 36
routes, used by Shikarpuri merchants between Shikarpur and Central Asia, 81–2
Rudner, David, 26, 294
Russia, Indian trade with, 12; Multani merchants in, 62; conquest of Central Asia by, 72, 74; rivalry with Britain, 74; policy towards Shikarpuris, 74–6
Russian Central Asia, Shikarpuris in, 73–94, 187–90
Russian Revolution, impact of on Shikarpuris, 104
Russo-Asiatic Bank, 179

Sabzawar, Hindu traders in, 99
sahukars (sowcars) in Shikarpur, 64
Saigon, Sindworkies in, 131, 152 n. 83
St Macaire (Nijni-Novgorod), 65
St Petersburg, British consul-general at, 75
Salisbury, Sindworkies in, 131, 154
Samarkand, Shikarpuris in, 57, 71, 72
Sandhu, K.S, 17
sarrafs (shroffs) in Shikarpur, 64, 65
Sastri, Srinivasa, 233
Sayed, G. M., 2
Sazonov, 76
Schuyler, Eugene, 71, 73, 187, 188, 266 n. 32
Sehwan, 35
Seistan, trade in, 101–3
servants, in Sindworkie network, 174–5
Seth Bhojoomal, 35, 36
Seth Dhanamal Chellaram Chulani, Sindwork merchant, 133
Seth Mulchand Dialdas Nandwani, Sindwork merchant, 134
Seth Pratap Dialdas, Sindwork merchant, 203, 227, 289 n. 1
sexual economy, of merchant diasporas, 265–71
Shah Abdul Latif, 49
Shahbandar, 35
shah–gumastha system of partnership, 85, 157–60
Shanghai, Sindworkies in, 148, 195
shawl trade, 197
Shikarpur town, 2, 10, 38, 39, 57, 60, 61–3, 64–5, 67–70, 71–2, 106–8, 158, 187, 193, 213, 250

Index

Shiraz, 36
shop assistants in Sindworkie network, 171–4
Shuttleworth, Captain, 95
Siam Commercial Bank, 144
Sicily, Sindworkies in, 123, 127
Sierra Leone, Sindworkies in, 123 n. 25, 127, 155; Sindhi migration to, 280 n. 12
Sikh diaspora, 6, 256
Sikh traders, in Singapore, 149
Sikhism in Sind, 48 n. 40
Sikhs, relationship of Sindhis to Khalsa Sikhs, 225, 255, 285
silk trade, Shikarpuris, Bukhara and India, 66–7; Sindworkies in Chinese and Japanese silk trade, 195–6
Simmel, Georg, 20
Sind, pre-colonial polity of, 32, 42, 43; trade of, 32–9; role in Malwa opium trade, 39–42; Hindu–Muslim relations in, 44–5; political economy of, in colonial period, 50–5
Sind Encumbered Estates Act, 51
Sindhi Hindus, 3, 43–52, 277–85
Sindhi Merchants Association of Ceylon, 152 n. 82, 258
Sindhi Merchants Association of Singapore, 149, 282
Sindwork Merchants Association, 132, 226, 232, 233, 235, 236–7, 239
Sindwork trade, nature of, 194–204
Singapore, Sindhi merchants in, 1, 124, 129, 131, 133, 134, 147, 171, 183, 279, 281
Sinkiang, trade of India with, 16, 95; Shikarpuris in, 57, 94–8, 190–1, 220–1, 267–9; 1933 rising in, 96, 97, 268
Siraf, 10
Socotra, 10
Sombart Walter, 20
South Africa, Indian merchants in, 18; Sindworkies in, 124, n. 27, 127, 166 n. 14; anti-Indian legislation, 226, 230–1
South Asian merchants, in world economy, 10–19
South Fukienese merchants, 24–5
South Korea, Sindhis in, 281
Soviet Central Asia, Shikarpuris in, 104–5
Spain, Sindhis in, 281
Spanish Civil War, impact of on Sindworkies, 236–8
Spanish Morocco, Sindworkies in, 144, 154–5, 236–7

spying, by Shikarpuris in Russian territory, 218–19
Straits of Magallanes, sea-route through, 145
Sudan, Sindwork trade in, 150
Suez, Sindworkies in, 153
sufi pirs, Hindu merchants in Sind as *murids* of, 49
sufism, in Sind, 49, in Central Asia, 255
Sugiyama, S., 196
Sukkur, 2, 107
Sumatra, Indian merchants in, 12; Sindworkies in, 124, 128
Surabaya, Sindworkies in, 124, 129, 131, 149–50
Surat, 11, 28
Sydney, branch of Sindwork firm in, 125

T. K. Tejoomal, Rangoon shop of, 199 n. 26
Taiwan, Sindhis in, 281
Talpur Amirs, of Sind, 2, 32, 38–9, 40–5, 110
Tangier, Sindworkies in, 123, 153 n. 85
Tashkent, 71, 72, 80, 81, 187–8
Tashkurgan, Hindu traders in, 99
Tenerife, Sindworkies in, 124, 151, 152, 155, 174 n. 33, 237, 258
Tetuan, Sindworkies in, 123, 127, 154, 236, 237
Texlon, Sindhi firm in Nigeria, 283
Thailand, Indian merchants in, 12; Sindhis in, 281
Thakur, U. T., 46
Thatta, 11, 34, 35, 38
Tibet, trade of India with, 16
Tientsin, Sindworkies in, 148, n. 67
Tiflis, British consulate at, 75
Timberg, T. A., 27
Timur Shah (Durrani), 60, 61, 186
Totomal walad Jeumal, Shikarpuri banker, 189
trade diasporas, 21
Trinidad, Sindworkies in, 127, 131, 204 n. 43
Tripoli, Sindworkies in, 127
trust, in merchant networks, 260–5
Tsingtao, Sindworkies in, 147
Tunis, Sindworkies in, 123, 127
turquoise trade, Shikarpuris in, 103
Turshish, 63

Udhavdas & Co, firm of Sindwork merchants, 143
Uganda, tie-up with Bombay capitalists, 16
Umarkot, 39

Index

Umayyads, conquest of Sind by, 34
United Kingdom, Sindhis in, 1, 204, 277, 280, 281
United States, Sindwork pedlars in, 155 n. 92; Sindhis in, 277, 280, 281
Utoomal & Assudamal, firm of Sindwork merchants, 141

Valletta, Sindworkies in, 153
Van der Veer, P., 4
Varaman, Sindhi firm in Nigeria, 283
Venezuela, Sindwork pedlars in, 155
Victoria (Australia), immigration restriction act, 221
Vigo, Sindworkies in, 131
Virumal Lilaram, firm of Sindwork merchants, 167
Vishwa Hindu Parishad, 285

waderos, 2–3, 52
Wassiamall Assomull, firm of Sindwork merchants, 125, 131, 134, 140, 143, 148, 152, n. 83, 164–5, 171, 199, 221–2, 230–1, 255
Wassiamall Assomull Mahtani, Sindwork merchant, 134
Watanmal Boolchand, firm of Sindwork merchants, 141
Weber, Max, 20
Wenzhou, migrants from, 3
West Africa, Sindworkies in, 123, 127, 141, 143, 145, 151, 154, 208–11; Sindhis in, 281
Western Textile, Sindhi firm in Nigeria, 283

Yangi Hissar, Shikarpuris in, 96
Yarkand, Shikarpuris in, 57, 94, 96
Yemen, 11
Yeng Tseng-Hsin, Chinese governor of Sinkiang, 97
Yezd, 63
Yokohama, Sindworkies in, 127, 129, 131, 142, 146
Younghusband, Sir Francis, 221

Zanzibar, 11, 16
Zia Barani, 60

Printed in the United Kingdom
by Lightning Source UK Ltd.
135186UK00001B/172-177/P